European Environmental Law

A Comparative Perspective

Edited by
GERD WINTER
University of Bremen

Dartmouth

Aldershot • Brookfield USA • Singapore • Sydney

Published by
Dartmouth Publishing Company Limited
Gower House
Croft Road
Aldershot
Hants GU11 3HR
England

Dartmouth Publishing Company
Old Post Road
Brookfield
Vermont 05036
USA

British Library Cataloguing in Publication Data
European Environmental Law: A Comparative
Perspective - (TEMPUS Textbook Series on European Law &
European Legal Cultures; Vol.3)
    I. Winter, Gerd II. Series
    341.762

Library of Congress Cataloging-in-Publication Data
European environmental law : A comparative perspective /
    edited by Gerd Winter.
        p.   cm. – (TEMPUS textbook series on European law and
    European legal cultures)
    Includes index.
    ISBN 1-85521-560-8 (hb). – ISBN 1-85521-564-0 (pb)
    1. Environmental law–Europe. 2. Environmental protection-
Europe–Citizen participation. 3. Administrative procedure-
-Europe. I. Winter, Gerd. II. Series.
    KJC6242.E97   1995
    344.4'046–dc20
    [344.0446]   95-44458
                                                                           CIP

ISBN 1 85521 560 8 (hbk)
ISBN 1 85521 564 0 (pbk)

Printed and bound in Great Britain by
Biddles Limited, Guildford and King's Lynn

EUROPEAN ENVIRONMENTAL LAW

TEMPUS Textbook Series
on
European Law and European Legal Cultures

General Editors: Volkmar Gessner and Armin Hoeland

Titles in the Series:

Volume 1
European Legal Cultures
Volkmar Gessner, Armin Hoeland, Csaba Varga

Volume 2
European Economic Law
Hans W. Micklitz, Steve Weatherill

Volume 3
European Environmental Law
Edited by
Gerd Winter

Other volumes in preparation

Contents

v

PART III   INSTRUMENTING SELF-CONTROL

PART IV   THE EUROPEAN COMMUNITY FRAMEWORK

PART V   CENTRAL AND EASTERN EUROPE IN SEARCH OF A FITTING MODEL

Abbreviations

ACP	Africa, Caribbean, Pacific
AöR	*Archiv des öffentlichen Rechts*
BAT	best available technology
BAT (standard)	*Biologische Arbeitstofftoleranzwerte* (biological production materials tolerance values)
BATNEEC	best available technology not entailing excessive cost
BHS	British Herpetological Society
BImSchG	*Bundesimmissionsschutzgesetz* 1974 (Federal Immission Control Act)
BPEO	best practicable environmental option
BUWAL	*Bundesamt für Umwelt, Wald und Landschaft* (Switzerland)
BVerfGE	*Entscheidungssammlung des Bundesverfassungsgerichts*
BVerwGE	*Entscheidungssammlung des Bundesverwaltungsgerichts*
CAP	common agricultural policy
CEE	Central and East Europe
CEN	*Comité Européen de Normalisation*
CENELEC	*Comité Européen de Normalisation Electrotechnique*
CFC	chlorofluorocarbon
CIPE	*Comitato Interministeriale per la programmazione economica*
Comecon	Council for Mutual Economic Assistance
COREPER	Committee of Permanent Representatives
DIN	*Deutsches Institut für Normung*
DoE	Department of the Environment
DÖV	*Die öffentliche Verwaltung*
DVBl	*Deutsches Verwaltungsblatt*
EBRD	European Bank for Reconstruction and Development
EC	European Community
ECJ	European Court of Justice
ECOSOC	Economic and Social Committee
ECR	Reports of the European Court of Justice and Tribunal
EEA	European Economic Area
EEC	European Economic Community
EIA	environmental impact assessment
EIS	environmental impact study
EPA	(US) Environmental Protection Agency
EPA	Environmental Protection Act 1990 (UK)
ETSI	European Telecommunications Standards Institute
EU	European Union

EuGRZ	*Europäische Grundrechts-Zeitschrift*
EURATOM	European Atomic Energy Community
FAO	Food and Agriculture Organization (UN)
FoE	Friends of the Earth
GATT	General Agreement on Tariffs and Trade
GMO	genetically modified organism
GNP	gross national product
HMSO	Her Majesty's Stationery Office
IDHEAP	*Institut de Hautes Etudes en Administration Publique*
ILO	International Labour Organization
IRPTC	International Register of Potentially Toxic Chemicals
ISO	International Standards Organization
IUCN	International Union for the Conservation of Nature
JO	*Journal Officiel* (see OJ)
JZ	*Juristenzeitung*
KTA	Committee for Nuclear Technology (Germany)
LCA	life cycle assessment
MAK	*maximale Arbeitsplatzkonzentration* (maximum workplace concentration)
MIK	*maximale Immissionskonzentration* (maximum environmental concentration)
NEPA	National Environmental Policy Act (US)
NGO	Non-governmental organization
NJW	*Neue Juristische Wochenschrift*
NVwZ	*Neue Zeitschrift für Verwaltungsrecht*
OECD	Organization for Economic Cooperation and Development
OJ	Official Journal of the European Communities
PCP	pentachlorophenol
PIC	prior informed consent
RJE	*Revue juridique de l'environnement*
SEA	Single European Act
UNEP	United Nations Environment Programme
USL	*Unità Sanitarie Locale*
VVdSTRL	Veröffentlichungen der Vereinigung der deutschen Staatsrechtslehrer
VwVfG	*Verwaltungsverfahrensgesetz*
WE	Western Europe
WHO	World Health Organization
WTO	World Trade Organization
WWF	Worldwide Fund for Nature

List of Contributors

Gyula Bándi	Professor of Public Law, Eötvös Loránd University, Egytem tér 1-3, H-1053 Budapest.
Antonella Capria	Istituto per l'Ambiente, Milano.
Pieter Glasbergen	Professor of Environmental Studies, Policy and Management, The Open University, Herleen, and University of Utrecht, Postbus 80115, NL 3508 TC Utrecht.
Gretta Goldenman	Advocate, Oppenheimer, Wolff & Donnelly, 110 Rue Washington, B-1050 Bruxelles.
Malcolm Grant	Professor of Law, Director, Department of Land Economy, 19 Silver Street, Cambridge CB3 9EP.
Jan Jans	Professor of European Law, Director, Europa Institut, University of Amsterdam, Postbus 19123, NL 1000 GC Amsterdam.
Jerzy Jendroska	LL.D., Environmental Law Group, Polish Academy of Sciences, ul. Kuznicza 46/47, 50-138 Wroclaw.
Michael Kloepfer	Professor of Public Law, University of Lausanne and W. v. Humboldt University, Unter den Linden, D-10117 Berlin.
Peter Knoepfel	Professor of Administrative Sciences, University of Lausanne; Director, Institut de Hautes Etudes en Administration Publique, Routes de la Maladière 21, CH-1022 Chavannes-près-Renens.
Ludwig Krämer	Dr. jur., LL.D., Head of Legal Matters and Application of Community Law, DG XI, European Commission, Avenue de Beaulieu 5, B-1160 Bruxelles.
Karl-Heinz Ladeur	Professor of Law, University of Hamburg and European University Institute, Villa Schifanoia, Via Boccaccio 121, I-50133 Firenze.
Claude Lambrechts	Research Fellow, Centre de Droit International de l'Environnement; Editor, Revue Juridique de Droit de l'Environnement, 11 Rue du Maréchal Juin, F-67046 Strasbourg.

Richard Macrory   Professor of Law, Barrister, Director, Environmental Change Unit, University of Oxford, 1a Mansfield Road, Oxford OX1 3TB.

Albert Mumma   Senior Lecturer in Law, University of Nairobi, P.O. Box 30197, Nairobi.

Eckard Rehbinder   Professor of Economic and Environmental Law, J.W. Goethe University, Senckenberganlage, D-60054 Frankfurt/Main.

Gerd Winter   Professor of Public Law, University of Bremen, Universitätsallee GW I, D-28359 Bremen.

Series Foreword

TEMPUS TEXTBOOK SERIES ON EUROPEAN LAW AND EUROPEAN LEGAL CULTURES

The Trans-European Mobility Scheme for University Studies (TEMPUS) is part of a broader programme of the European Communities for economic reform in Central and Eastern Europe (PHARE) and supports 'Joint European Projects' between academic institutions in order to improve university education in Central and Eastern Europe. Within this programme two academic institutions of the Community (International Institute for the Sociology of Law, Oñati/Spain, and Zentrum für Europäische Rechtspolitik, Bremen/Germany) and the Law Faculty of the Eötvös-Loránd University, Budapest/Hungary, collaborated during a period of three years for the publication of a textbook series on European Law and European Legal Cultures.

The series consists of collections of (original or reprinted) texts on European Legal Cultures, Economic Law, Environmental Law, Agrarian Law and Labour Law and will be eventually complemented by other volumes. They have been elaborated and discussed by multinational teams from different Western and Central European universities which have put together a large quantity of material in order to represent most legal systems and legal cultures of the area.

The conception of the series is based on three *Leitmotive:*
First, legal education in a period of rapid globalization must enable future practitioners to deal with foreign legal systems, to understand different regulatory structures in their own right and to defend their own positions in cross-cultural negotiations. Legal knowledge and familiarity with legal cultural differences together with a sufficient mastery of the English language are necessary elements.

Second, modern legal education is an interdisciplinary exercise where theoretical and empirical knowledge play an equal part and where neighbour disciplines like Economy, Sociology, Political Science and Psychology are not excluded. Students together with their intellectual training in legal reasoning must understand the law in action, its effects and the problems of its implementation. This knowledge enables them to criticize law and push for reform and legal change.

Third, legal education in the second half of the 1990s must account for the fact that the Berlin wall and all other political, economic and social barriers between East and West have fallen and that a legal community is going to be created which goes far beyond the EU, the EFTA and the EES. Whereas law reform in the beginning was and still is directed predominantly from West to East, scientific discourse takes place in a climate of equality and openness to learn. Consequently also students all over Europe (in its largest geographical definition) should be socialized as early as possible within this climate of mutual curiosity and recreate something that centuries ago was a reality: a common European Legal Culture.

Volkmar Gessner   Armin Hoeland

Foreword

This volume was originally designed to provide academics and practitioners in Central and Eastern Europe (CEE) with an overview of environmental law in Western Europe (WE). However, the assumption underlying this project – that as a part of their transition to market economies and pluralist democracies, the CEE societies would be required to adopt new environmental law wholesale – proved (in a double sense) to be somewhat simplistic. First, as chapters 21 and 22 by Jerzy Jendroska and Gyula Bándi show, the former communist states were well endowed with quite sophisticated environmental protection law, mostly (but certainly not exclusively) of the command and control type, the effective implementation of which was, however, obstructed by the close proximity of supervisory to economic structures. Consequently, CEE law-makers have found that they might be quite selective vis-à-vis Western models of environmental protection. Second, a closer look at WE environmental law – and at these societies in general – reveals that their law (and above all the perception of that law) has itself also undergone a significant change, namely from traditional command and control structures to cooperation and self-control.

Ironically, now that the 'East' might be prepared to learn how to turn regulatory law into effective command and control practice the answer found in the 'West' seems increasingly to suggest that regulatory law should no longer be relied upon and that environmental protection should instead be pursued using instruments based on market mechanisms. A market has, however, hardly had time to develop in the East. I am inclined to say (but do not feel all my learned co-authors would agree with me) that command and control (or, to put it in a more preferable way, democratic regulation and its loyal implementation) is still worth establishing, if adapted to more modern needs of bureaucratic flexibility and societal autonomy. This is all the more so as the environmental law of the European Union still follows a regulatory pattern which on the whole will also require existing and future Member States to 'go regulatory'.

Although the messages passed amongst the players in the East, in the West and 'above' in Brussels may point in different directions, they must, in any case, be based upon reliable information about the structures and the developing trends in environmental law and practice. To furnish some of this information is the more modest aim of this volume and may indeed also be of interest in other parts of the world.

xiv *European Environmental Law*

Chapter 1 puts environmental law into the wider perspective of broader policies and the law designed to implement them, which in the first instance contribute to environmental deterioriation and are to be adapted, or even internally remotivated, in the environmental interest.

Chapter 2 explores to what extent environmental protection has become the object of fundamental rights, in particular how the triangle between such third-party rights, the polluters' economic rights and the state's obligations to protect these rights is constructed.

Seven chapters characterize Western-style regulatory environmental law, as regards its substantive and procedural patterns: the substantive criteria of environmental protection (Chapter 3); the scope of instruments (Chapter 4); the environmental impact assessment as the major database for decisions (Chapter 5); the involvement of the public in environmental administration (Chapters 6 and 7); standard-setting as a typical phenomenon between legislation and individual decision (Chapter 8); and judicial review including the crucial issues of third-party standing and density of review (Chapter 9).

Two further chapters (10 and 11) highlight the regulatory approach, one examining the implementation deficit and its causes in one particular state (Italy), the other building up a normative model of effective environmental administration; a model which is clearly informed about the political and organizational substructure of the regulatory approach.

In four chapters these deficiencies are taken as starting points for more radical alternatives. These might comprise what is called network management (Chapter 12), the use of various financial incentives (Chapter 13), an improvement of liability schemes under private law (Chapter 14), and a rich scope of (more or less law-inspired) self-regulation by the industry oriented towards consensus-building, information of the market, and reorganization of the firm (Chapter 15).

Four further chapters investigate the major characteristics of EC environmental law – its rise (Chapter 16), its objectives and principles (Chapter 17), its decision-making structures (Chapter 18) and its competences (Chapter 19).

Chapter 20 deals with environmental law in regard to international transactions, an approach focusing on the control of the export and import of dangerous goods as regulated by international and EC law.

Finally, three chapters (21, 22 and 23) analyse environmental law in transition in the CEE states, both as it stands now and will develop, and as it will be required to adapt to EC law. Poland and Hungary are used as examples.

A number of people deserve particular thanks for their assistance in the management of this project: Gyula Bándi, Malcolm Grant and Michel Prieur for valuable advice in its early stages, Volkmar Gessner and Armin Hoeland, the overall editors of the Tempus series of books, for their encouragements and advice, but also for their setting of deadlines, the publisher for not taking the deadlines too seriously, the co-authors for eventually meeting them despite their other often heavy workloads, Tara Diedrichsen and Andrea Gavriel for translating some of the texts (Chapters 2, 3, 4 and 8), Martin Hession and the publisher's reader for excellent editing, Sabine Ahlers for the management of the project and, finally, Andrea Gavriel, Gretchen Herzfeld and Balkrishna Isvaran for their skills in production.

Gerd Winter
Bremen, April 1995

Part I
General Questions

1 The Scope of Environmental Law

Richard Macrory

Table of Contents

I INTRODUCTION

Academic and practising lawyers in nearly all European countries now recognize that environmental law represents a distinctive and significant body of law and legal principle. Yet, when it comes to trying to define the boundaries of the subject, it is clear that there is little in the way of agreement. Certain commonly agreed elements exist such as the regulation of polluting activities by man and the protection of natural assets such as wildlife or landscapes, and these fields of law are what many environmental lawyers would describe as their core concerns. However, it is equally clear that there are many other areas of regulatory law such as health and safety at work, land-use planning, the protection of the manmade cultural heritage, and consumer protection law which have substantial environmental implications, even if environmental protection, as many would understand it, is not their sole focus. Looking further afield, the principles upon which apparently unconnected areas of law, such as competition or trade law, operate may be far from neutral in their potential impacts on the environment.

The need to integrate an environmental dimension into areas of policy hitherto largely unaffected by such concerns is one that is increasingly recognized by many countries, although the task is far from easy to achieve. In this chapter, I outline a number of legal considerations that appear to be involved in the challenge of integration. My underlying argument is that those who study and practise environmental law should be wary of limiting their attention to boundaries of law that are so narrowly confined that they fail to address what may prove ultimately to be far more significant issues of concern.

II INTEGRATED POLLUTION CONTROL

In the context of environmental law and policy there are different notions of what can be implied by integration. A significant element of environmental law is the regulation of industrial pollution, most commonly by means of various forms of consents or permits. The development of this type of pollution legislation has taken place at different times in different European countries, with examples in some countries to be found in the nineteenth century but with a rapid growth in scope and complexity in the last 30 years. The initial driving force behind such pollution controls was often a concern for the protection of human health and, at a later stage, the incorporation of wider environmental considerations. But common to many national legal systems is the extent to which such pollution laws regulate discharges into the environmental media of air, water and land on a quite distinct legislative basis, with different laws often being developed at different times. The UK, for example, had legislation regulating industrial discharges into the atmosphere dating back to the mid-nineteenth century, while a detailed regulatory system controlling discharges into waters did not appear until the early 1950s. No specialist controls over waste disposal on land emerged until the 1970s. These specialist controls are frequently enforced and applied by different agencies. The drawback of such a legal structure is that it may lead to inconsistent decision-making and ignore or fail to consider the cross-media impact of control strategies, leading to results which are sub-optimal from an environmental perspective.

In 1975 the UK Royal Commission on Environmental Pollution identified these concerns, and coined the term, the *Best Practicable Environmental Option* (BPEO) as an appropriate criterion for the goal of all pollution control strategies.[1] It took some 15 years for the Commission's legal and institutional recommendations for the implementation of this approach to be fully taken on board by government. Part I of the Environmental Protection Act 1990 introduced the concept of *integrated pollution control* under which discharges of pollutants from specified industries into water, air and land are regulated by a single licence issued by a single authority.

---

[1] Royal Commission on Environmental Pollution, *Air Pollution Control – An Integrated Approach*, 5th Report, London: HMSO, 1976. See also the Commission's follow-up report, *Best Practicable Environmental Option*, 12th Report, London: HMSO, 1988.

Other countries, such as the Netherlands, have introduced 'one stop' licences for industrial discharges, and in 1993 the European Commission proposed European Community legislation which would introduce integrated pollution control throughout the Union.[2] The main aim of the proposal is to protect water, air and land against pollution from certain types of industries by introducing an integrated permitting regime and, as an underlying harmonizing principle, requiring industry to employ the 'best available techniques' of pollution prevention. At the time of writing the proposal has still not been agreed by Member States, and it is likely to be some years before the type of integration required by the proposed Directive is converted into a legal requirement throughout Member States.

But even where distinct legislation has existed for different pathways of industrial discharges, the obligation to conduct environmental assessment procedures for new projects, as required under the 1985 European Community Directive on the subject[3] has inevitably required a degree of integration. Where the Directive applies, the type of information generally required as part of the assessment process before consent is given for the project to proceed includes, *inter alia*, 'an estimate, by type and quantity, of expected residues and emissions (water, air and soil pollution, noise, vibration, light, heat, radiation, etc.) resulting from the operation of the proposed project'. The Directive does not oblige Member States to establish a single, unified consent procedure for projects subject to environmental assessment, but at the very least requires them to ensure improved coordination between decision-making agencies.

In countries such as the UK, where the assessment procedures were largely integrated into an existing land-use planning consent system rather than the specialist regulatory controls over pollution, the link between land-use planning and the pollution implications of land-based developments has been strengthened by the requirements.

Improved coordination between different pollution control agencies, the reorganization of such bodies into unified agencies[4] and the establishment of 'one-stop' pollution consent procedures are developments that are now likely to take place in many jurisdictions, and represent one form, though a limited one, of integration.

---

[2] Proposal for a Council Directive on Integrated Pollution and Control, Com(93)230, 14 September 1992.

[3] Council Directive 85/337 of 27 June 1985 on the assessment of the effects of certain private and public projects on the environment, OJ L 175/40, 5 July 1985.

[4] See, for example, the creation of the French environmental agency, the Agence de l'Environnement et de la Maîtrise de l'Energie in 1990 and the establishment of the Irish Environmental Protection Agency in 1990.

III CODIFICATION

A further development of the concept of environmental integration may now be seen in a trend towards the codification of environmental legislation. At the very least, this may involve an updated restatement of existing laws into a single body of law and the removal of the more overt inconsistencies. For example, it was only recently that the European Community passed legislation which attempted to introduce a greater degree of harmonization and standardization concerning the requirements under various Community environmental Directives for Member States to provide regular national reports to the Commission containing the results of monitoring in the sector covered by the Directive in question.[5] Previously there were some glaring inconsistencies between different items of legislation even within the same general field; for example, Member States had an obligation to make regular reports concerning the state of bathing waters under the Bathing Water Directive, but no similar obligation in respect of drinking water under the Drinking Water Directive.

But, as Kiss and Shelton note: 'Codification involves more than the reproduction and restatement of applicable statutory texts; instead it constitutes a systematic consolidation and revision of the law, a major legislative effort.'[6] Examples of a moderate form of integration can been seen in the type of framework legislation adopted by Portugal in 1987, the Lei de Bases do Ambiente. Current work in Belgium, undertaken by the Interuniversity Commission for the Revision of Environmental Law in the Flemish Region, represents a more ambitious approach towards codification seeking to articulate underlying principles as well as consistent procedures.[7]

Yet, however laudable, even this approach towards codification generally restricts itself to the more familiar boundaries of pollution and nature protection legislation. This is not to underrate the intellectual challenges involved in such a task but, again, it by no means represents the full implication of environmental integration.

---

[5] Directive 91/692 OJ L 377, p. 48 1991.

[6] A. Kiss, D. Shelton, *Manual of European Environmental Law*, Cambridge: Grotius Publications, 1993, p. 49.

[7] A Conference on the Codification of Environmental Law was held by University of Ghent in early 1995.

IV INTEGRATION INTO OTHER POLICIES AFFECTING THE ENVIRONMENT

1 Article 130r Treaty of Rome

In 1985 the European Commission proposed to the heads of states and government that, as a basis of Community environmental policy, 'Protection of the environment is to be treated as an integral part of economic and social policies both overall (at macroeconomic level) and by individual sector (agricultural policy, industrial policy, energy policy, etc.); the point must be made that an active policy for the protection and improvement of the environment can help economic growth and job creation'.[8] This proposal eventually led to the insertion into the Treaty of Rome, following the Single European Act 1987, of the provision that 'Environmental protection requirements shall be a component of the Community's other policies'.[9] The requirement was altered and, I would argue, strengthened under the version of the Treaty as amended by the Maastricht Treaty, and coming into force on 1 January 1993, and now reads, 'Environmental protection requirements must be integrated into the definition and implementation of other Community policies'.[10] Similar integration requirements concerning culture have been introduced under Article 128 of the Treaty which requires that 'The Community shall take cultural aspects into account in its activities under other provisions of this Treaty', and concerning public health where, under Article 129, 'Health protection requirements shall form a constituent part of the Community's other policies'.

This environmental provision under Article 130r clearly represents a far more ambitious notion of integration than either the moves towards the coordination of pollution control or the codification of environmental laws described above. It is a challenging statement of principle and legal obligation which has yet to be replicated in the national legislation of many countries and has been described as perhaps the most important of all the environmental provisions contained in the European Treaty.[11] Yet, as Ludwig Krämer noted in his commentary on the 1987 version, '...the medium- to long-term consequences of this principle for the Community are a matter of speculation for the moment'.[12] Certainly, if one looks at the potential environmental impacts of important aspects of the Community's sectoral

---

[8] *Bulletin of the European Communities*, No. 3, 1985, p. 101.

[9] Second para., Art. 130r, European Treaty (pre-Maastricht).

[10] Third para., Art. 130r, Treaty Establishing the European Community as amended by the Treaty on European Union.

[11] N. Haigh, *EEC Environmental Policy and Britain,* (2nd edn), London: Longman, 1987, p.11.

[12] L. Krämer, *EEC Treaty and Environmental Protection*, London: Sweet and Maxwell, 1990, p. 65.

policies such as fisheries and transport, it is far from clear that any serious move towards environmental integration has yet been made. The longer-term environmental implications of those policies remain immense.

2   Principle of law or policy?

To a large extent such a statement of broad principle, even though expressed in legal language, is bound to be more a expression of policy aspiration than a specific legally binding requirement capable of enforcement by conventional legal routes.[13] Provided policy-makers take at least some account of potential environmental consequences, courts are unlikely to wish to become overinvolved in determining the extent to which this should take place. Nevertheless, this does not mean that such a principle is devoid of legal consequence.

3   Legitimizing environmental integration

An important area of potential legal dispute within the European Community concerns the identification of the correct Treaty legal provision on which to base subsidiary legislation. The choice of the legal basis is especially significant since it will determine the political procedures that must be followed for the adoption of the proposed measure, and different provisions in the Treaty provide quite distinct procedures giving differing voting requirements and differing degrees of influence to the Community institutions, notably the European Parliament.[14] Despite the political implications of the choice of legal basis, the European Court of Justice has consistently held that this choice must be based on objective factors amenable to judicial review rather than consideration of politics.[15] In *Greece* v. *EC Council*,[16] it was argued by the Member State that a Community regulation restricting imports of agricultural products from third countries following the Chernobyl nuclear accident should not have been adopted under Article 113 of the Treaty, dealing with common commercial policies, but should have more appropriately been based on either the express environmental provisions under the Treaty or

---

[13]   See L. Krämer, *EC Treaty and Environmental Law,* (2nd edn), London: Sweet and Maxwell, 1995, p. 59.

[14]   See M. Hession, R. Macrory, Maastricht and the Environmental Policy of the Community: Legal Issues of a new Environmental policy, in D. O'Keefe (ed.), *Legal Issues of the Maastricht Treaty*, London: Chancery Publications, 1994. See also J. Jans in Chapter 19 in this volume.

[15]   *Commission* v. *Council*, (1987) ECR 1493.

[16]   (1990) 1 ECR 1527.

under the parallel Euratom Treaty dealing with nuclear matters. The European Court upheld Article 113 as a correct legal basis, and rejected the idea that, because there was a clear environmental dimension to the measure, it should have been treated as part of the Community's express environmental programme of action. In so doing, the Court invoked the integration requirement in Article 130r: 'That provision which reflects the principle whereby all Community measures must satisfy the requirements of environmental protection, implies that a Community measure cannot be part of a Community action on environmental matters merely because it takes into account those requirements.'

4   Ensuring environmental integration

Such a legal analysis supports the legitimacy of environmental integration where it takes place. Policy-makers who produce legislation in other sectors with strong environmental associations, such as transport or agriculture, will find their action less vulnerable to legal challenge on the grounds that such considerations were not legally relevant. But one task for environmental law in the future is to devise suitable provisions and techniques which will help to ensure that this process continues to take place to a far greater extent than at present, rather than to merely enable it to take place when policy-makers so wish.

a)   Implementing environmental integration principles

One approach is to supplement broad general statements of principles with far more express environmental requirements in subsidiary, 'non-environmental' legislation. For example, Article 7 of Regulation 2052/88, governing the distribution of structural funds within the Community, provides that

> measures financed by the Structural Funds or receiving assistance from the European Investment Bank or from another existing financial instrument shall be in keeping with the provisions of the Treaties, with the instruments adopted pursuant thereto and with Community policies, including those concerning the rules on competition, the award of public contracts and environmental protection.

This is clearly an important requirement which attempts to ensure greater consistency between policies on financial aid and the environment although, in reality, it has not proved easy to implement, not least because structural funds are given on the basis of regional programmes prepared by Member States whereas identifiable environmental impacts are often associated with specific projects which emerge from such programmes, probably at a later date.[17]

Nevertheless, the requirement provided the basis for a legal challenge by environmental groups before the European Court of Justice in 1994 – the first time that such a case had been brought. In Case T-461/93 *An Taisce* (the national Trust for Ireland) *and Worldwide Fund for Nature* v. *European Commission*,[18] two associations were concerned about the environmental implications of the proposed construction of an interpretative centre in a National Park which was to be financed under structural funds already approved by the European Commission under a Programme for Tourism submitted by the Irish government. The groups had alerted the Commission, and challenged what they alleged to be the Commissions' decisions not to withdraw the structural fund support on the grounds that the proposals were inconsistent with the requirements of the Structural Fund Regulation concerning compliance with Community environmental programmes. In the event, the Court decided that the Commission had not in fact taken any decision not to withdraw funds and that they were entitled to do so at any time, even after completion of the works. Since the case was rejected on its facts, the Court therefore did not have to determine whether the applicants had legal standing before the Court to bring such a case – clearly an extremely significant issue. However, despite the result of the case, it did underline the extent to which the integration requirements within the Structural Fund Regulation potentially have real legal purchase.

b)   Enriching procedures

Another legal technique that may be employed to ensure improved integration is the use of procedural requirements in connection with policy and similar proposals in other sectors. The 1985 Community Directive on Environmental Assessment is expressly limited to proposals for projects such as industrial works and road schemes, but there has been considerable discussion concerning the possible extension of such assessment requirements to cover a much broader category of plans, policies and programmes. To date, any further development on such proposals appears to have been resisted within the European Commission, and would almost certainly be opposed by a number of Member States.

However, in dealing with policies at EU level, the parties to the Maastricht Treaty noted in one of its Declarations 'that the Commission undertakes in its proposals, and that the Member-State undertakes in implementing those proposals, to take full account of their environmental impact and the principle of sustainable

---

[17]   See Krämer (1995), *op.cit.*, p. 29.
[18]   Judgement of the Court of First Instance, 23 September 1994.

growth'. In June 1993 the European Commission adopted internal administrative practices which were aimed at assisting the meeting of those goals; the measures included a commitment by the Commission to describe and justify the significant environmental impacts of proposed legislation, and the appointment of officials within each Directorate-General of the Commission with a specific responsibility to ensure that their Directorate takes on board the principle of environmental integration.

This sort of administrative management has been reflected at national level. In 1991 The UK Department of the Environment published a document intended to encourage other government departments to assess the environmental implications of their policies in a more systematic manner than had hitherto been the case,[19] and so-called 'Green Ministers' were nominated in each department. The document was followed up in 1994 with a series of case studies illustrating how such environmental appraisals were being carried out.[20] Yet the reality of the extent to which such a greening of government has genuinely taken place, against the background of such initiatives, has been consistently challenged.[21] To take one example, the 1994 report of the Royal Commission on Environmental Pollution on Transport and the Environment[22] provided a powerful critique of the extent to which UK transport trends were environmentally unsustainable in the longer run, and took to task the Department of Transport for failing 'to provide this country with an effective and environmentally sound transport policy'.[23]

c)   Forming environmental integration principles

Another example of a legal technique designed to ensure greater environmental integration across departmental interests is the imposition of general duties concerning the environment. An early example to be found in British legislation is the provision in section 11 of the Countryside Act 1968 that 'In the exercise of their functions relating to land under any enactment every Minister, government department and public body shall have regard to the desirability of conserving the natural beauty and amenity of the countryside'. Although the parliamentary debates during the discussion of the provision displayed a surprising degree of pas-

---

[19]   Department of the Environment, *Policy Appraisal and the Environment*, London: HMSO, 1991.

[20]   Department of the Environment, *Environmental Appraisal in Government Departments*, London: HMSO, 1994.

[21]   See, for example, J. Hill, M. Jordan, The Greening of Government: Lessons from the White Paper Process, *ECOS*, **14**, 1993.

[22]   Royal Commission on Environmental Pollution, *Eighteenth Report: Transport and the Environment*, Cm. 2674, London: HMSO, 1994.

[23]   Ibid. para. 13.65.

sion and conflict,[24] the blandness and generality of the duty has meant that it is effectively unenforceable in law, and it is difficult to pinpoint any real effect that it has had on decision-making over the years. Nevertheless, such broadly based duties, even if non-enforceable in a conventional sense, may still, as Ross Cranston has noted, give 'legitimacy to aspirations ... and can provide a backdrop against which specific decisions with legal consequence can be made'.[25]

In the mid-1980s there was an extended period of political controversy in Britain over the environmental implications of modern agricultural practices, criticism being focused on the relevant government department, the Ministry of Agricultural, Fisheries and Food, which was perceived to have sacrificed environmental concerns in favour of agricultural productivity. As one response, the government eventually introduced legislation which imposed a general duty on the minister to endeavour to achieve a reasonable balance between conservation, rural and agricultural interests.[26] Again, such a duty may be perceived as more of a gravitational rule rather than a enforceable legal obligation legitimizing internal shifts of resources and priorities within a department. Certainly discussions with officials can frequently reveal the very real significance that such a duty can have on the internal administrative workings of such an organization. But the difficulty with the implementation of such duties is not to devalue them by overuse, and in their drafting to achieve a sensible balance between being overgeneralized (and thereby ineffective or open to too many differing interpretations) and so specific that they lose the power to inject an environmental dimension across a broad area of activity.

V   INTEGRATION INTO POLICIES WITH REMOTE ENVIRON-MENTAL IMPACT

In reality there is no single or optimum solution that will ensure greater environmental sensitivity across different industrial and economic sectors. A combination of broadly based legal principles, procedural requirements and the types of administrative restructuring described above must all contribute to reinforcing aspirational goals which are easy to state but infinitely less so to achieve.

But the challenge for environment law can go further. The types of measures so far taken to ensure integration tend to focus on the policies and decisions of non-

---

[24]   See R. Macrory, *Loaded Guns and Monkeys: Responsible Environmental Law*, London: Imperial College Centre for Environmental Technology, 1994.

[25]   R. Cranston, *Law, Government and Public Policy*, Melbourne: Oxford University Press, 1987.

[26]   Agricultural Act 1986, s. 13.

environmental departments (whether at national or Community level) which demonstrably have significant physical impacts on the environment, energy, transport and agriculture being clear examples. Effective integration, however, goes deeper and implies that other areas of law must now be examined to determine the extent to which they are environmentally neutral or incur actual benefits or disbenefits.

The potential conflict between free trade and environmental protection is one that is familiar at international level, and within the Community has had to be tackled by the European Court of Justice. In the landmark 1988 case of *Commission* v. *Denmark*[27] the European Court expressly permitted a Member State to introduce legislation concerning the recycling of drink cans even though it would have had some restrictive impact on the fundamental principle in the European Community Treaty concerning the freedom of movement of goods. A later case upheld the right of a regional authority to restrict the import of wastes from other regions and countries into its area on the grounds that such unrestricted free movement would have severe environmental consequence.[28]

Competition policy must similarly be examined. Article 85 of the European Community Treaty contains a general prohibition of price-fixing and similar agreements between competitive undertakings, but permits certain agreements which contribute 'to improving the production or distribution of goods or to promoting technical or economic progress, while allowing consumers a fair share of the resulting benefit'. The European Commission has now had to consider to what extent these latter conditions were fulfilled where environmental aims were involved, and in at least one case has confirmed this to be the case.[29] Ludwig Krämer[30] has also noted that the application of competition law principles to the types of voluntary environmental agreements and covenants between industry and government bodies, as favoured in some countries such as the Netherlands, is a new area of potential conflict that has yet to be fully explored.

In the search for integration, however, one can take a more profound approach which demands that the underlying rationale for principles that govern a much broader spectrum of law is examined to determine to what extent they are consistent with the contemporary challenge of the environment. Gerd Winter[31] has noted the extent to which modern environmental law takes an interventionist, regulatory form which has been imposed upon, and restrains, 'the inventiveness and energy

---

[27] Case 302/86 (1988), ECR 4607.
[28] Case C-2/90 *Commission* v. *Belgium* (1992), 1 ECR 4431.
[29] *XXIInd Report on Competition Policy 1992*, European Commission 1993.
[30] Krämer (1995), *op.cit.,* p. 30.
[31] See G. Winter, Perspectives for Environmental Law – Entering the Fourth Phase, *Journal of Environmental Law*, 1 (38), 1989.

of the individual'. The encouragement and release of such inventiveness had been one of the driving forces behind many developments of the law, particularly in the nineteenth century in countries such as Germany and the UK, and can be found in such diverse areas as patent legislation, corporation law and the promotion of freedom of trade. He argues that, set against the scale of environmental problems now facing society, the regulatory, interventionist approach cannot wholly succeed, and that it will be necessary to re-examine those underlying and pre-existing areas of law to ensure that they are more environmentally sensitive: 'The emancipatory law must therefore be inoculated with ecological considerations.'[32] This approach to integration has taken us a long way from the tentative moves towards seeking greater consistency between laws regulating the discharges into water and air. Yet, ironically perhaps, the argument reflects, at a deeper level, the debate that has already taken place in the much narrower context of pollution control where the heavy reliance on 'end of pipe' solutions as a means of controlling discharges is seen ultimately to have only a limited role, and the fact that it is preferable to examine the total industry process to ensure improved waste minimization and an eventual reduced burden on the environment. Environmental law, as it is conventionally written about and analysed, may represent a discrete and bounded field of law, but one role of the true environmental lawyer is to be prepared to re-examine all fields of law from an environmental perspective – ultimately, this is implication of the integration principle.

---

[32]   Ibid. p. 45.

2 Environmental Constitutional Law

Karl-Heinz Ladeur

Table of Contents

I THE EMERGENCE OF INDIVIDUAL RIGHTS TO ENVIRONMENTAL PROTECTION

1 Access of the public to nature

Despite the differences evident in the constitutional traditions of the individual European states and uncertainty arising from the recent adoption of the liberal-democratic model of constitutional politics by the central and eastern European states, an historical trend towards the emergence of a common European constitutional law can be found,[1] which may contribute to the moulding of new forms of legal institutionalization of complex reciprocal relationships with nature.

Environmental constitutional law is a relatively new area of legislation for all European countries, although individual aspects have found a place within the constitutions of a number of countries for some time now. An early variant is the rights to the enjoyment of nature in various forms. In the past these rights have had a more social or distributive function: scarce nature, which cannot be infinitely reproduced, could only be subjected to the exclusive effect of private property in a limited manner, so that the access of the general public might be maintained. Such rights of public access to nature (even if this is in private hands) can be found, for example, in several constitutions of the German *Bundesländer*.

However, as a result of the dominance of their distributive goals these rights hardly provide a guarantee to protect nature. Such rights can only guarantee the enjoyment of nature as long as nature persists, but not its maintenance (protection). In addition it is very difficult to reconcile such rights with the constitutional protection of land ownership. In particular, when the right in question is defined not as a right of access to certain parts of the countryside (forests, lakes and so on), but as an unspecified right to rest and recovery in nature, the problem of determining its limits arises: to what extent may it be limited by rights of private property? For example, in cases of conflict, the Bavarian constitutional court has focused on the reasonableness of the restriction – a criterion which is difficult to put into concrete terms.[2]

From an ecological perspective a further and separate problem arises from the fact that the right to enjoyment of nature may endanger the environment itself, but that the necessary restrictions in the interest of the environment can only be based on the interest of the property-holder.

Therefore, a right to the protection of nature, rather than access to nature comes closer to the point.

2   Fundamental right to human health

A fundamental right framed as an individual right to the protection of nature, its integral parts and the environment in a wider sense of the word has been the sub-

---

1 Cf. Peter Häberle, Gemeineuropäisches Verfassungsrecht, *Europäische Grundrechts-Zeitschrift*, 1991, pp. 261, 268.
2 Bavarian Constitution Art. 141 s 3; cf. Richard Bartlsperger, Das Grundrecht auf Naturgenuß, in *Festschrift für Klaus Obermayer*, Munich: Beck, 1986, p. 3 ss.; Bayerischer Verfassungsgerichtshof, *Neue Zeitschrift für Verwaltungsrecht* (NVwZ), 1986, p. 633 ss.

ject of legal and political constitutional discussions for several years now.[3] Indeed, such a fundamental environmental right has been adopted into the constitutions of several Western and, in particular, Central and Eastern European countries.

In determining its normative content, one must first distinguish between the right not to be harmed by the carriage of pollutants through the medium of the environment to individual protected interests (such as health and property) and a right to the protection of nature in the sense of an interest in the maintenance of a healthy, or even clean and intact, environment. In the first variant, the fundamental environmental right would require a specification of the defensive individual right to health which, although it does not belong to the traditional stock of liberal rights, is contained in a number of modern constitutions. This right has great significance for environmental protection (see below, section VI) because, and to the extent that, going beyond the traditional mode of rights, it forms the basis for a state's duty to protect against ubiquitous dangers or dangers arising from individual third parties.

3   Fundamental right to a healthy and intact environment

Stressing the protection of a healthy environment, however, increases the existing problems with respect to limitation which exist even with respect to the more narrowly defined right to health: the question arises, how much must the concept of environment be extended to encompass a guarantee of protection to the individual.

The extension of the protective area of a fundamental right to a clean (and not merely a healthy) environment would render limitation problems even more acute: the link to the individual right to health would be further loosened and the transition to an unspecified right to environmental protection would become complete. Such a right would have as its primary object the protection of the environment as an aesthetic object of individual interest or as a collective good, which could be asserted by an individual as a form of trustee. Here, the protection of individual health could only serve as a secondary objective. The right would thus take on more of the character of a right to participation in environmental protection, the extent of which would be difficult to determine. In so doing, a particular problem would arise as to whether, and to what extent, the public interest could be consid-

---

3 Michael Kloepfer, *Umweltrecht*, München: Beck, 1989, s 2 No. 1, 9 ss.; Hoppe, Beckmann, ibd. (fn. 3), s 4 No. 8; for the European development cf. Ida Koppen, Karl-Heinz Ladeur, Environmental Rights, in: Antonio Cassese, Andrew Clapham, Joseph Weiler (eds), *Human Rights and the European Community: The Substantive Law*, Baden-Baden: Nomos, 1994, p. 1 ss.; cf. also the overview of Otto Kimminich, Umweltverfassungsrecht, in Heinrich v. Lersner, Peter Storm (eds), *Handwörterbuch des Umweltrechts*, vol. 2, Berlin: E. Schmidt, 1988.

ered to coincide with the individual civil right. The literature on such a fundamental environmental right included as a positive right in individual constitutions shows that appropriate legislative reservations have inevitably developed.

However, if parliament is empowered to impose restrictions, what might be the constitutional limits to such a legislative reservation embodied in ordinary legislation?[4] The effectiveness of the constitutionalization of a subjective *right to environmental protection* depends also upon the extent to which a particular constitution explicitly guarantees legal protection. Even where the substantive restriction of a fundamental environmental right is permissible, actions based on the right may generally continue to be admissible.

II   THE FUNDAMENTAL RIGHT TO ENVIRONMENTAL PROTECTION

In the European constitutional discussion the demand for a fundamental environmental right emerged in the 1970s. Initially an anthropocentric point of view dominated (the right to an environment corresponding with human dignity),[5] although a formulation without reference to humanity was introduced later into the debate. In the meantime, the fundamental right to environmental protection has become a part of a number of European constitutions.

1   Delimiting the protective scope

No matter how the protective scope of the fundamental environmental right is formulated its structure brings about a number of doctrinal problems, not the least of which is defining its limits. Even taking into account that the protective scope of all fundamental rights is poorly defined around the edges, the collective element

---

4 For the doctrinal construction of 'positive' rights cf. Kloepfer (1989), *op.cit.*, ibd. s. 2 No. 9; idem., *Zum Grundrecht auf Umweltschutz*, Berlin: Duncker & Humblot, 1978; Hans Hugo Klein, *Ein Grundrecht auf saubere Umwelt, Festschrift für Werner Weber*, Berlin: Duncker & Humblot, 1974, pp. 643, 646; idem., *Die Grundrechte im demokratischen Staat*, Stuttgart: Kohlhammer, 1974, p. 35, 54; Herbert Schambeck, *Grundrechte und Sozialordnung*, Berlin: Duncker & Humblot, 1969; Georg Brunner, *Die Problematik der sozialen Grundrechte*, Tübingen: Mohr, 1971; cf. the proposition of the 'Green' members of the German Bundestag (BT-Drs. 11/663, 4/8/1987; cf. also Ernst Benda, *Verfassungsrechtliche Aspekte des Umweltschutzes, Umwelt und Planungsrecht*, 1982, p. 241; Hansjörg Dellmann, Zur Problematik eines 'Grundrechts auf menschenwürdige Umwelt', *Die öffentliche Verwaltung* (DÖV), 1975, p. 588.

5 Cf. generally Werner Hoppe, Martin Beckmann, *Umweltrecht*, Munich Beck, 1989, s 4 (8).

of the environment as a subject of a right poses particular problems for constitutional doctrine because 'environment' forms a complex 'network of networks' of
partially social and partially natural interrelationships which are difficult to describe and even more difficult to reduce to attributable and individualized
'parcels'. Since traditional doctrine is not adapted to a normative area which is so
difficult to structure, making the protection of such a complex structure of effects
the subject of a fundamental right requires that new meta-rules of argumentation
and decision-making be created. The novelty of the environmental fundamental
right is not so much evident in its collective rights aspect, which is also a feature
of a number of other social fundamental rights which do not conform to the classical conception of individual rights but which are nevertheless very familiar to us,
such as the right to an education, but is rather in its new level of complexity which
is characterized by the fact that environmental protection demands the setting of
priorities that are essential to deal with the complexity of the underlying problems
it seeks to address. However in a parliamentary system, such priorities must be
formulated by parliament, government and administration in harmony with other
competing interests and financial restraints on the state and private individuals,
rather than be set by the courts.[6]

2 Designing multi-polar relationships

In addition there is a further doctrinal problem: traditional liberties (such as occupational liberty) are directed against the state. This is most clear where these liberties take the form of a defensive right against state interference. But even when
interpreted to include a right to receive a benefit, they still conform to this bipolar
constellation of rights because these, too, are aimed against the state. Greater
problems confront constitutional law in structuring multi-polar legal relationships
in the form of fundamental rights: this task arises not only when different interests
must be taken into account in balancing decisions (for example, state financial
support for either environmental protection or social concerns), but also when
different forms of protection of fundamental rights conflict with each other.

a) Direct effect on private law relationships?

Such conflict emerges when the fundamental right to environmental protection is
constructed to have direct effect on third parties,[7] in the sense that the distinction

---

6 Eckard Rehbinder, Grundfragen des Umweltrechts, *Zeitschrift für Rechtspolitik*, 1970,
   pp. 250, 252.
7 For Greece see Glykeria P. Sioutis, Greece, in Edward J. Kormondy (ed.), *International Handbook of Pollution Control*, New York: Greenwood, 1989, p. 173.

between public and private law is eliminated through fundamental rights claims private (affected) persons would then possess against private persons (for example, plant operators). This would supersede the traditional concept according to which there are private law remedies such as an injunction against interference with property or health. This problem can also be found in relation to other fundamental rights and is overcome in practice through a variety of solutions (in particular through interpreting general civil law clauses in accordance with the basic 'objective' values inherent in the fundamental subjective rights, thereby reorienting the private law claims. This solution may be more appropriate also to rights to environmental protection, because a direct effect of fundamental rights which gives protection against private persons (who themselves are bearers of liberties) seems slightly oversophisticated.

b)   Objective obligation of the state to protect third parties

Even if the fundamental environmental right were only aimed against the state, the problem of moulding multi-polar legal relationships through individual liberties would still have to be dealt with, since most environmental hazards are caused by private persons rather than by the state. Such a right could only be effective if extended to include a right to governmental protection against private activities which are hazardous to the environment. At the same time, a problem would arise in attempting to balance the polluter's defensive right against state interference and the state's protective duties in the interest of the third party. The novelty of this constellation derives from the fact that the state is no longer merely asserting the 'public interest' against private interests, but must itself assert the rights of affected third parties as well. This particular constellation of rights arises when a firm applies for a permit to release hazardous substances, and thus embodies the 'negative' liberty to pursue a livelihood, and, at the same time, fearful neighbours insist on the priority of their protective rights. In this case freedom from public interference could then even be transformed into a delegated power to impose risks on other persons giving rise to the question: if a new highrisk technology (say genetic engineering) is put into practice, can it be restricted because of the risk or does it need an explicit legal authority to proceed?[8] A number of traditional rules of argument and decision-making exist to deal with the first constellation, but not for this new type of conflict.

---

8   G. Winter, *Grundprobleme des Gentechnikrechts*, Düsseldorf: Werner Verlag, 1993, p. 23 ss.

c) Procedural consequences

On the procedural side the detachment of this fundamental right from the individual interest would also require a broader conception of legal standing, causing particular difficulty in cases resulting from legislative inaction.[9] A restriction through procedural admissibility requirements, such as a legally protected individual interest, would be contradictory to the assertion of a substantively extended fundamental rights protection. Another procedural problem which arises – for example, under German law in this context – is that an objection to an encroaching administrative act has, in principle, a suspensive effect; if, however, the freedom of a citizen is no longer only to be weighed against the state and the public interest defined by it, but must instead be balanced with fundamental rights of third persons (to the protection of the environment) which have equal status in principle, this particular procedural hierarchy will be questioned. Much the same goes for other procedural legal institutions: the large circle of potentially affected bearers of fundamental rights can make administrative decisions much more unpredictable.

3 Normative or symbolic value of constitutional rights?

The problems described above arise in any case when fundamental rights are allotted to a relatively strict normative force, making them directly binding for the legislator, administration and courts, as is largely the case in German law. Certainly other forms and functions of the constitution should be considered, particularly those with exhortatory and integrative effects on the process of forming public opinion and will. In countries with a new constitution especially, it is very difficult to estimate the extent of the harmonization of the state powers with each other; and, similarly, the normative status of a constitution is shaped by this process.[10]

---

9 Cf. Kloepfer (1989), *op.cit.*, s. 2 No. 22; *Bundesverfassungsgericht (BVerfGE)*, 1989, **56, 54, 70** (noise of airplanes); *Neue Juristische Wochenschrift (NJW)*, 1983, p. 2931 (damage to forests).

10 Cf. Art. 55 s. 1 Bulgarian constitution: 'Right to a healthy and pleasant environment in conformity with existing standards and norms'; cf. Emil Konstantinov, Die neue bulgarische Verfassung von 1991, *Recht in Ost und West (ROW)*, 1993, pp. 35, 40; Art 35 of the Charter of Fundamental Rights and liberties of the CSFR: 'Right to life in a favourable environment'; cf. Mahnlena Hosková, Die Charta der Grundrechte und Grundfreiheiten der CSFR, *Europäische Grundrechte-Zeitschrift (EUGRZ)*, 1991, p. 369 ss.; similarly, Art. 29 of the Declaration of Rights and Liberties of Man of the USSR (cf. *EUGRZ*, 1991, p. 433 ss., and Art. 72 s. 1 of the Slovenian constitution; cf.

Scepticism concerning the practical difficulties in implementing a basic right to environmental protection is undoubtedly based upon a perspective that is determined by the relatively continuous development of environmental law on the one hand and the generally stable coordination of the differentiated functions of state powers and executive and judiciary legislation on the other. Due to the courts' limited resources legal action can be effective only at certain points, and there is little scope for the judiciary to deal with complex problems of environmental decision-making under such conditions, particularly if additional requirements including differentiated instruments and high financial demands are adopted. However, with regard to Central and Eastern European reform, states (in common with some developing countries) must grapple with major problems regarding the coordination of different state powers and, simultaneously, great leaps in economic development and an inability to assess the consequences. Given these possible sources of error, in the field of legislation and administration, constitutional control which serves as a kind of institutionalized 'emergency brake' could assume quite a positive role.

This can be demonstrated by a recent decision of the Hungarian Constitutional Court which has pronounced the privatization of nature and landscape components to be incompatible with the constitutional requirement of environmental protection insofar as there are insufficient nature conservation regulations to set private owners boundaries of use in the interest of public welfare.[11] The Supreme Court of India took the role of an institution of social protest when it pronounced the passivity of the state in the face of continuous transboundary air pollution to be incompatible with the right of environmental protection guaranteed by the constitution.[12] Nonetheless, it remains doubtful in such cases whether the judgement of a constitutional court can provide any significant compensation for an incoherent division of labour among the institutions of a given state.[13]

Ivan Kristan, Verfassungsentwicklung und Verfassungsordnung Sloweniens, *Zeitschrift für ausländisches öffentliches Recht und Völkerrecht (ZaöRV)*, 1993, p. 322 ss.; cf. also Christian Baumgartner, Die Verfassung der Slowakei vom 1.9.1992, *ROW*, 1992, p. 375 ss.; Sabine Kofmel, Die neue Verfassung der Republik Estland vom 28.6.1992, *ZaöRV*, 1993, p. 135 ss.; the existing literature interprets these norms more as 'principles' than as binding law. Cf. generally Woyciech Radecki, Jerzy Rotko, *Entwicklung des Natur- und Umweltschutzrechts in Mittel- und Osteuropa*, Baden-Baden: Nomos, 1991; Pawel Czechowskie, Reinhard Hendler (eds), *Umweltrecht in Mittel- und Osteuropa*, Stuttgart: Boorberg, 1992.

11 Cf. the details given by Gyula Bándi (Chapter 22 in this volume).

12 Cf. Nandan S. Nelivigi, M. G. Poojitha, Armin Rosencranz, The Judiciary and the Environment: Recent Trends and Developments, *Environmental Policy and Law*, 1993, p. 102 ss.

13 Cf. generally Marcelo Neves, *Verfassung und Positivität des Rechts in der peripheren Moderne*, Berlin: Duncker & Humblot, 1992.

III THE ASSOCIATION ACTION: NATURE'S 'OWN RIGHTS'

In many countries, associations (particularly those for environmental protection) may exercise a right of action independent of any individual right with respect to environmental hazards according to various procedural forms (and based either on substantive rights granted specifically to them or a special procedural capacity to make an application).[14] It should be considered whether such a so-called association action (*Verbandsklage*) might be institutionalized at the constitutional level so that several of the concerns about the adoption of a fundamental environmental law mentioned above could be alleviated. This would, however, entail the loss of the particular 'pathos' of the individual protection of fundamental rights.

The constitutionalization of a 'personal right' possessed by nature itself could play a similar role.[15] This too ultimately involves a variant of the association action, since nature would need someone to bring a suit on its behalf and to assert its 'own right' in any legal procedure.[16] The concept of a 'fundamental right of nature' is very questionable. In its favour is the symbolic recognition of the autonomy of development possibilities for nature transcending considerations of social expediency. Against it is the fact that the right is difficult to define, particularly in terms of which parts of nature such a 'personal right' can be recognized, making the formulation of certain anthropocentric categories unavoidable. The complexity of this new institution (the environmental right) is, in any case, a good reason for the introduction of a legislative reservation – and it needs to be a wide one. The necessity of creating a legal infrastructure (delimitation of standing, trusteeship, substantive limitations and so on) for such a right goes against the constitutionalization of an 'own right' of nature. Considerable implementation problems must also be anticipated, as experience upon which to assess this institution is limited and it is hard to determine the compatibility of such a right with an individualistic legal system. Here also, the possibility of accepting these problems and trusting in the symbolic effect of such an ecocentric approach should be considered.

---

14 For association actions see Kloepfer (1989), *op.cit.*, s. 10 No. 103; for France cf. Michel Prieur, *Droit de l'environnement*, Paris: Dalloz, 1984, p. 158 ss.; for Italy cf. Karl-Heinz Ladeur in Gerd Winter (ed.), *Öffentlichkeit von Umweltinformationen*, Baden-Baden: Nomos, 1990, p. 249 ss. See, further, Chapter 9 by A. Mumma in this volume.

15 Cf. Kersten Heinz, Die geplante Staatszielbestimmung Umweltschutz – Ein Weg zu einem besseren Grundgesetz?, *Zeitschrift für Umweltpolitik*, 1988, p. 1 ss.; for the European discussion see Koppen, Ladeur (1994), *op.cit.*, p. 18 ss.

16 Christopher D. Stone, *Should Trees have Standing? Toward Legal Rights for Natural Objects*, Portola Valley: Tioga, 1974.

The possibility of making ecological damages liable for compensation, regardless of their economical valuation, should also be considered in this context. Several constitutions have express provisions to this effect.

IV   PROCEDURAL RIGHTS TO PARTICIPATION IN DECISIONS RELATING TO THE ENVIRONMENT

The complexity of the environment and of environmental protection as described has not only a substantive dimension, especially with respect to the definitional limits of the appropriate normative scope and the necessity of balancing interests, but also a procedural one: the collection and generation of knowledge for decision-making under complex conditions is itself of considerably greater significance than it is with respect to other processes. Therefore the question arises whether, instead of a substantive fundamental right to environmental protection (or in addition thereto), a procedural right to citizen participation in decisions related to the environment, as well as a right to information independent of any decision to be made vis-à-vis the administration, can and should be constitutionally guaranteed.

In principle, there is much to be said in favour of inserting these rights into the constitution, since in this way the basis of the knowledge necessary to decision-making might be extended. To an increasing extent, the administration must rely on mere partial knowledge and experiment with its measures, because it can no longer fall back on knowledge based on general or generalizable experience. Procedural rights to participation include such rights as a right to information and to the co-construction of new policies and co-assessment of their implementation. Such participation is of particularly great importance because the constructive nature of decision-making under complex conditions is selective in character.[17] On the other hand, a number of competing rights and interests present themselves, which must be balanced by the law individually – for example, the protection of commercial and industrial secrets. Such a right needs an elaborated legal structure and must therefore be coupled with a legislative reservation. Much the same applies to a right (independent of any decision) to information, the assertion of which is also dependent on conditions to be laid down by the law.

---

17 Cf. Koppen, Ladeur (1994), *op.cit.*, esp. p. 38 ss.; for environmental information see EC-directive of 23/6/1990 (ABl L 158/56) and the contributions in Winter (ed.) (1990), *op.cit.*; Amdedeo Postiglione, *Legislation on Environmental Information, European Environmental Yearbook 1987*, p. 190 ss.; idem, Informazione, segreto e ambiente, *Rivista giuridica dell'ambiente*, 1986, p. 325 ss.; some of the new constitutions of eastern European countries grant rights to environmental information.

V ENVIRONMENTAL PROTECTION AS A STATE GOAL

The limits of a subjective right to environmental protection have led to the suggestion, as a more practical alternative, that environmental protection be adopted as an objective state goal[18] in order to give direction to the formal powers possessed by the legislature in terms of reservations to individual fundamental rights (such as property). The establishment of a goal has a binding effect which not only enables action, but also imposes a duty on the state to take action. Unlike a reservation enabling the legislative assertion in favour of the general welfare (including competence rules, especially in a federal state) and unlike a mere non-binding 'programme', the provision of a state goal – depending on its wording – actually guides the legislature, the executive, and the judiciary.[19]

Depending on the organization of the constitution as a whole, such a constitutional norm can also have a more symbolic and exhortatory character and, if a constitution contains other programmes and state goals in addition, there is much to be said in favour of including an important goal such as environmental protection.

Conversely, when the constitution incorporates a high normative claim, special attention must be paid to the goal's precise binding effect and the harmonizing of the relationships between one constitutional court and other state powers. A general obligation on the state with respect to environmental protection will lead the judiciary to derive the necessary solidification of principle directly from the consti-

---

18 Cf. Wilfried Brohm, Soziale Grundrechte und Staatszielbestimmungen in der Verfassung, *Juristenzeitung (JZ)*, 1994, pp. 213, 217 s.; Eckhart Wienholtz, Arbeit, Kultur und Umwelt als Gegenstände verfassungsrechtlicher Staatszielbestimmungen, *Archiv des öffentlichen Rechts (AöR)*, 1984, p. 533 ss.; Karl-Heinz Ladeur, Kann es eine 'Umweltverfassung' geben? Zur Diskussion um ein Staatsziel 'Umweltschutz' im Grundgesetz, *Jahrbuch Ökologie,* 1994, p. 166 ss.; Peter C. Mayer-Tasch, Hans-Martin Schönherr-Mann, Der Staat als 'Naturstaat', *Jahrbuch Ökologie,* 1994, p. 157 ss.; in some European countries a principle of environmental protection is deduced from other constitutional norms; cf. the Italian Corte di Cassazione (criminal section) Decision No. 2687 of 10/11/1982; Corte Costituzionale Decision No. 184 of 9/6/1983; cf. Amedeo Postiglione, *Manuale del'ambiente*, Rome: La Nuova Italia Editrice, 1986, p. 19; for the international development cf. Alexandre Kiss, *Le droit international de l'environnement*, Paris: Pedone, 1989, p. 20 ss.; cf. also Prieur, *op.cit.*, p. 190: the right to environmental protection may serve as integrative principle; cf. also *Le droit à un environnement humain*, Berlin: E. Schmidt, 1973.

19 See, for example, the new Art. 20a of the German Grundgesetz:
   The State protects, taking responsibility also for the future generations, the natural fundaments of life, in the framework of the constitutional order, through legislation, and, in accordance with law and justice, through the executive and the judiciary.
   For the French discussion see Prieur, *op.cit.*, p. 190.

tution. The provision of a state goal can also serve as an interpretative guideline to the application of ordinary laws and grant environmental protection greater weight in the process of balancing different interests.

Indeed, uncertainty regarding the consequences which follow from the incorporation of such a goal in the constitution could be productive and lead to a new harmonization of the division of state powers. For a long time now the distribution of state functions has no longer been characterized by the distinction between the power to set long-term rules on the one hand, and case-by-case control on the other: to a large extent the legislature itself makes decisions under conditions of uncertainty and by experiment. In this context the judiciary can take on a more cooperative role, by observing the productiveness of the experimental design and by providing stimuli for its 'improvement'.[20]

Readiness to experiment and a flexible rearrangement of the division of powers between the legislature and the judiciary can, however, become problematic if a strong judicial activism develops alongside it. Such a development severely constricts the legislator's freedom to shape complex policies. But fears of judicial activism are largely exaggerated, and it is very unlikely that the courts would prejudice the decision-making competence of the legislator to an unreasonable degree. In any event the legislature has too broad a strategic decision-making power for this to occur and, for their part, the courts must rely on a certain readiness to cooperate on the part of the legislature as, in the absence of cooperation, a finding by the court that there has been a breach of the constitution would have no effect.

Reducing the vagueness of the state goal by the incorporation of a reservation to the legislative power[21] or a clause prescribing a balance between different goals could be considered. But neither of these two suggestions is really compatible with the formulation of environmental protection as a state goal: the former does not lead inevitably to the legislator being legally bound (apart from suggesting a boundary to the abuse of power); on the other hand, the necessity of weighing and balancing other state goals against a particular environmental goal is inherent in any state goal. The linking of a state goal with a legislative restriction thus appears problematic.

---

20 For the role of the constitutional justice in Germany see Alfred Rinken, *Alternativ-Kommentar-Grundgesetz*, (2nd edn), Neuwied: Luchterhand, 1989, 'General Remarks' concerning Art. 93, 94 No. 4 ss.; for Italy, see Enzo Cheli, Giustiza costituzionale e sfera parlamentare, *Quaderni Costituzionali*, 1993, pp. 263, 265; for France, see Bernard Genevois, La jurisprudence du Conseil Constitutionel est-elle imprévisible?, *Pouvoirs*, **59**, 1991, pp. 129, 134; for Eastern Europe see Georg Brunner, Die neue Verfassungsgerichtsbarkeit in Osteuropa, *ZaöRV*, 1993, p. 819 ss.
21 Cf. the wording of Art. 20a of the German Grundgesetz (note 19).

Nonetheless, the state goal of 'environmental protection' can act as a guideline for the interpretation and coordination of the many undefined legal terms in environmental law, and it is here that it will play its most substantial role!

Against the introduction of a state goal provision, it might be argued that – unlike the rule of law, liberal fundamental rights or other traditional constitutional principles – the principle of environmental protection is insufficiently legally defined for it to be promoted to the status of a constitutionally binding state goal. However, in so far as ordinary statutory law has produced a pattern of legal terms, it does provide a structure and opportunity for the construction and further development of indefinite state goals in constitutional law – as has been the case with other less traditional state goals such as the social state principle – and thus limit the risk of overpoliticization or arbitrariness in relation to constitutional judicial decisions.

In legal systems in which the infrastructure of ordinary law with a framework for the interconnection and development of environmental law principles generated by individual decisions does not exist, the state goal 'environmental protection' might particularly be justified as a guideline for judicial interpretation, even though its influence on the legislator might be difficult to assess.

While the significance of the resulting environmental obligation of the state must not be overestimated, the possible exhortatory and integrative function of an appropriate constitutional norm should not to be ignored. The constitutional upgrading of restrictions on the exercise of fundamental rights (property, occupational liberty and so on) to the level of positive requirements can give the public interest sharper contours and a greater weight in relation to competing private ones.

From a democratic perspective it is also conceivable that the allocation of certain decisions to the legislature itself (as opposed to a delegation to the administration) which follows from a general legislative reservation might also gain a greater significance in the sphere of environmental protection.[22]

VI   THE FUNDAMENTAL RIGHT TO HUMAN HEALTH

1   Defensive dimension

A (defensive) *right to health*[23] or (with an appropriate wide interpretation) to undisturbed personal development may also provide protection against environ-

---

22 Cf. only *BVerfGE*, **49**, 89, 127; Kloepfer (1989), *op.cit.*, s. 2 No. 40; for Italy, Cheli (1993), *op.cit.*, p. 272.
23 Georg Hermes, *Das Grundrecht auf Schutz von Leben und Gesundheit*, Heidelberg: C.F. Müller, 1987.

mental hazards.[24] This relates in particular to pollution and noise from public infrastructures (streets, airports and the like).

However, the legislator must be allowed a margin of discretion in the difficult problem of weighing up interests when deciding what is tolerable for the affected person. In addition, a number of procedural problems (legislative reservation, certainty of regulations, relationship between experts, legislature, and administration, the binding of the judiciary by 'standards') arise, which are discussed in more detail below.

2   Protective duties of the state

The extension of fundamental rights by the additional dimension of protective duties plays a large role, especially with regard to the fundamental right to health. According to this doctrinal construction the state must actively further the maintenance of health and defend it against the encroachments by private third parties. The protective duty is aimed primarily at the legislator who must pass new protective laws and improve old ones. According to German constitutional interpretation this is an 'objective' constitutional principle, the concretization of which must be left to the prerogative of the legislator. Only in special cases does this objective protective duty turn into a subjective right.[25] This is of particular importance not only for the control of the constitutionality of the laws but also for the admissibility of constitutional complaints, should a constitution make provision for this possibility.[26]

The obligatory protective nature of the fundamental right also plays a role in the legal regulation of individual claims for damages or compensation.

It is not easy to determine in detail what risk prevention, in its role of protecting the health of the population from danger, can be constitutionally required for the fulfilment of this objective protective duty, or where we are merely dealing with what is required by ordinary law rather than by the constitution itself. The constitutional law of individual countries will weight these aspects differently and therefore shape the intensity of constitutional control by the judicature.

Here, too, the question of legislative freedom and restriction in the light of uncertainty must be considered. This question is not only raised in relation to the substantive law, but suggests that procedural variants of a differentiated structure of the decision-making problem should be developed, in particular through systematic duties of observation and, if necessary, of subsequent improvement of leg-

---

24 For Germany see *BVerfGE*, **49**, **89**, **140**; **53**, **30**, **57**, **56**, **54**, **73**.
25 Cf. Kloepfer (1989), *op.cit.*, s. 2 No. 17.
26 Cf. Koppen, Ladeur (1994), *op.cit.*, p. 13 ss.

islative decisions. The significance of procedural law is enhanced with relation to environmental law. This can be seen in the fact that the components (such as those developed in the German jurisprudence) of a fundamental protective duty also have a procedural dimension:[27] Many risks which are difficult to describe are almost impossible to evaluate for affected third persons if the stock of knowledge about risks obtained through proceedings for an administrative decision is not made accessible for the public. On the other hand, various affected interests and rights must first be made known to the administration. Procedural rights to information, to the inspection of files, to be heard, and so on must be legally created to this end.

The question of whether, and to what extent, procedural law may serve the fulfilment of constitutional protective rights has particular consequences for the issue of admissibility of a constitutional complaint to a constitutional court: A breach of ordinary procedural law can become a breach of fundamental rights where the ordinary law contains a concretization of the pertinent fundamental right.

VII FUNDAMENTAL RIGHTS OPPOSING ENVIRONMENTAL PROTECTION

So far, we have analysed fundamental rights and corresponding state obligations to protect the environment or, as a part of this, human health. It has already been said that such rights and obligations are in potential contradiction to other fundamental rights (including related state obligations) which amount to utilizing the environment thereby tending to oppose environmental protection. In the following sections we ask how such guarantees of utilizing the environment are shaped and, in particular, in what way they may be adapted to environmental protection needs.

1 The fundamental right to property

The fundamental right to property is the most prominent of those rights which are frequently the subject of state interference and general restrictions in the interest of environmental protection. Constitutions differ in the extent to which the state is bound in this respect. In German fundamental law, for example, the state is empowered not only to expropriate private property (against due compensation), but also to restrict the utilization of individual property and even generally to determine what kinds of object may or may not be capable of becoming private prop-

---

27 *BVerfGE*, **58**, **30** (Mülheim-Kärlich); Kloepfer (1989), *op.cit.*, s. 2 No. 41.

erty.[28] As a result, extensive legal intervention over the use of property is made possible. Although the fundamental right is focused on the protection of 'settled' property, in particular guaranteeing longer time periods for adjustment in these cases to allow for the amortization of the value of investment, the freedom of the legislator to interpose with respect to future property rights is generally recognized in modern constitutions.

This applies in particular to uses of property, the permissibility of which is subjected to a licensing procedure and remains subjected to 'subsequent orders' in the future. Such orders are certainly compatible with property protection, if obviously dangerous effects are at stake, although situations of uncertain risks are more problematic. Of course, the permissibility of restrictions could be founded on a general environmental duty of proprietorship, but this is of little significance so long as the use of private property and the public burden of argumentation is not called into question. The legislator finds himself confronted with the difficult problem of weighing up political and legal considerations when uncertain future risks must be balanced with present economic advantages. Priorities must be set.[29] Weighing up the different factors is also difficult when, as is often the case, the uncertainties of different temporal and factual dimensions must be compared with each other. Recourse can, however, be taken to the assessment prerogative of the legislator (for example, concerning the importance to be attributed to uncertainty in environmental decision-making). Here the courts exercising judicial control of constitutionality would have to adopt particular reserve due to the lack of definitive criteria, or because the criteria conflict with each other.

Conversely, the superiority of the legislation would simultaneously, have to be compensated for through new procedural requirements governing legislation under *conditions of uncertainty*. These would have to make greater allowance for improvised experimental decision-making and the compulsory generation of new knowledge.[30] The standard of proportionality can only be made operational under conditions of *uncertainty*, if the legislator facilitates the possibility of transition to new requirements through the generation of new knowledge, financial support for adaptation and a guarantee of transitionary periods. Due to the complexity of environmental problems, the emphasis in the future will lie not, however, in decisions on the superiority of private or collective interests but with the harmonization of conflicting interests.

---

28 As the leading case see *BVerfGE*, **58**, p. 300 ss.
29 Cf. Karl-Heinz Ladeur, Vorsorge und Prioritätensetzung im Umweltrecht, in *Jahrbuch des Umwelt- und Technikrechts*, 1994, p. 297 ss.
30 Cf. Karl-Heinz Ladeur, Berufsfreiheit und Eigentum als Grenze der staatlichen Kontrolle von Pflanzenschutzmitteln und Chemikalien, *Natur und Recht,* 1994, p. 8 ss.

2   The fundamental right to occupational and entrepreneurial freedom

The question has recently been raised as to whether and to what extent the state may alter the conditions for the exercise of this fundamental freedom through use of measures which do not 'interfere' with so-called 'classical' rights (such as the provision of environmental information through ratings, positive or negative discrimination between products and, in particular, public warnings). The maintenance of coherence and uniformity in the legal order is in question, when, on the one hand, an activity (the distribution of a product) is permitted by law while, on the other hand, it is discriminated against by official or officially supported warnings. In principle, this can be regarded as permissible, provided the legislator has a constitutional basis for such action. Beyond this, however (especially when no standards for accuracy are available) it seems difficult to grant the government a discretionary margin of judgement with respect to a kind of public advertising, particularly in the case of distant health risks where this could possibly have a stronger effect than an absolute prohibition.[31] However, the problem here concerns more the harmonization of influencing measures with the requirements which the constitutional system places on state intervention measures. This is principally a question of the extent of legislative reservation which is handled differently in the different constitutional systems.

Ultimately we are talking about an aspect of the global tendency away from regulatory restrictions on private property, and towards systems of incentives which do not prohibit environmentally risky activities, but rather discriminate against them through the imposition of financial sanctions or, conversely, favour environmentally-friendly activities (through subsidies, and the like). In principle this should be permissible within general constitutional requirements. One must be aware of the consequent problem, however, which may arise from the necessity of harmonizing the imposition of contributions and discriminatory taxes with regulatory restrictions as this, too, can cause constitutional concerns as to fair procedures, proportionality and so on.

VIII   PUBLIC PROPRIETORSHIP OF 'ENVIRONMENTAL MEDIA'?

The possibility of treating environmental media (air, water) or eco-systems as public property, subject to special state control (at least to the extent that concrete parts thereof have not already been made the subject of any property rights) should also be considered. This would draw a new limit on private property: Restrictions

---

31 Cf. Udo di Fabio, Grundrechte im präzeptoralen Staat, *Juristenzeitung,* 1993, p. 689 ss.; *BVerwGE,* **87**, p. 37.

on emissions would then no longer be examined as a restriction on property by the state, but rather quite the opposite: the asserted use of the environmental medium, being public property, would require a permit.[32] Such a regime of public management does actually exist under German Water Law,[33] which subjects the introduction of sewage into water to the requirement of a permit, to which (most importantly) there is no right as such. In contrast, the provision of a right to obtain a permit under commercial law (upon fulfilment of certain safety requirements) reflects the traditional liberal and constitutional system. In principle, such a management regime is conceivable but, if it is extended to all 'environmental interests', its compatibility with a system of individual liberties becomes doubtful. An extensive management/planning discretion would not be incompatible; limits would be found in the principle of proportionality here, although attaching a stronger weight to environmental interests would certainly be permissible. At the same time this would also mean that more distant risks (appropriately weighted) could legitimate state restrictions.

IX   ENVIRONMENTAL PROTECTION THROUGH PROPRIETORSHIP

The exercise of fundamental rights to property (ownership) are not only the potential subject of state restrictions but, to the extent that parts of the environment are propertied interests, this rights protection can itself also serve the environment.[34] The fundamental right to property is ambiguous from the point of view of environmental protection. An example of this is the encroachment on forest proprietorship through air pollution.[35]

The German judiciary has extended the defensive elements of traditional liberties through an additional dimension of a duty to protect,[36] and this also applies to property. In principle this appears to be appropriate. Formally, however, the fact that the obligation to protect needs to be concretized by the law cannot be avoided, and a certain discretion in the legislator which allows for a balancing of factors will therefore have to be recognized and respected by the judiciary.

---

32 Cf. Dieter Murswiek, Privater Nutzen und Gemeinwohl im Umweltrecht, *Deutsches Verwaltungsblatt*, 1994, p. 77 ss.
33 For household water see *BVerfGE*, **58**, p. 300 ss.
34 Walter Leisner, *Umweltschutz durch Eigentümer unter besonderer Berücksichtigung des Agrarrechts*, Duncker & Humblot: Berlin, 1987.
35 For proprietorship of forests see Bundesgerichtshof, *NJW*, 1988, p. 478 ss.
36 Hans Dieter Jarass, Grundrechte als Wertentscheidungen bzw. objektive-rechtliche Prinzipien in der Rechtsprechung des Bundesverfassungsgerichts, *AöR*, 1985, pp. 363, 382.

X   CONSTITUTIONAL REQUIREMENTS FOR STANDARD-SETTING

The legislator inevitably uses largely undefined legal terms, the content of which the person affected thereby may find difficult to estimate – a problem that has consequences for the determination of the relationship between the legislature and administration on the one hand, and the judiciary on the other. Terms such as 'danger', 'risk', 'considerable', 'substantial', 'reasonableness' and so forth are all characteristic of environmental law. This is largely unavoidable, but also acceptable if and to the extent that a process of concretization can be established which has the capacity to learn from new situations and evaluations.

To this purpose the law sometimes refers to various existing forms of professional procedures and organizations of standardization, although this may raise constitutional problems.[37] For instance, the 'state of the art' referred to by a law affects the constitutional principles of certainty of legal norms and democratic legitimation. Such reference must nevertheless, in principle, be regarded as permissible, even though certain procedural requirements should be observed by which constitutional guarantees are reflected in the procedures and organization of setting the standards. A most important requirement would be the guarantee of plurality within the relevant expert committees.[38] At the same time a consequent problem arises, namely that of the distribution of competence over interpretation: does the establishment of standards form part of the administration's prerogative or are we talking about the 'application' of legal norms, which forms the basis for complete judicial control? These questions are very contentious, and their answer certainly depends on the concrete constitutional system in question.

Furthermore there is the issue as to whether and to what extent the traditional rules for delegating legislation apply here, whether the standards themselves must be formulated into rules or whether informal variants of legislation through internal administrative guidelines or reference to private norms is permissible (and which binding effect these different variants might have, as the case may be, for the courts). The practice varies greatly in different countries but cannot presented here in any detail.

XI   CONCLUSION

Environmental protection as a constitutional issue is somewhat ambiguous because it is related to structural problems of the balance of powers, the coordination of

---

37 See further Erhard Denninger, *Verfassungsrechtliche Anforderungen an die Norm-setzung im Umwelt- und Technikrecht*, Baden-Baden: Nomos, 1990.

38 See further the Chapter 8 on standard-setting by G. Winter in this volume.

conflicting rights and of different dimensions of protection (substantive, procedural, 'negative' and 'positive'), not to mention the problem of transforming state
competence to impose limits on the use of civil liberties into substantive constitutional duties of individuals (or firms). If these problems are taken seriously new
conceptual approaches to the constitutional management of complexity have to be
developed. Otherwise the constitutionalization of environmental protection will
end up in another exercise in the art of legal lyrics.

Part II
The Administrative Model

3 Substantive Criteria of Environmental Protection

Gerd Winter

Table of Contents

I INTRODUCTION

Whenever it has to be determined whether a potentially harmful activity can be tolerated in terms of environmental protection, substantive criteria are needed. By them a society decides what impact on the environment it is prepared to accept and what it is not.

Legal cultures vary as to who exactly takes this decision. Some leave it basically to the administrative agencies thereby trusting in the latter's expertise and effectiveness in persuading or forcing the addressees to comply. The supervision of the agencies by democratic mechanisms may then be widely absent (as in France) or established through the parliamentary responsibility of the competent minister as well as through participatory decision-making procedures (as in the UK). In other legal systems (such as the German) substantive criteria are formulated in parliamentary statute. Such a course implies that, if the courts are invoked in respect of a particular administrative decision, they can take a hard look at both the facts and the agency's reading of the law because it is their task to guarantee that the executive abides by the legislator's will. On the other hand, if the establishment of substantive criteria is left to the agencies' discretion, the courts cannot but confine their judgement to whether there was 'arbitrary and capricious' action.

This rough picture must, however, be qualified. Recent years have shown a certain convergence between these countries. In France and the UK, legislation has become more active in criteria-setting, and the courts have adopted a practice of denser control whereas in Germany the legislature has introduced more flexible balancing tests and the courts have developed a more reserved attitude.[1]

Turning to the substance of the criteria under consideration it seems appropriate to distinguish between different routes of potential environmental impact, that is:

- pollution from stationary sources;
- pollution from mobile sources;
- impact through waste;
- encroachment on nature; and
- impact through dangerous substances.

The substantive criteria to be found in many legal systems tend to vary depending on these routes.

II   POLLUTION FROM STATIONARY SOURCES

Pollution from industrial installations has long been a focus of environmental protection law. Therefore it is understandable that the related legislation and its doctrinal elaboration is rather sophisticated.

In order to understand the criteria of delimiting intolerable impact, two questions should be answered:

1. What kinds of environmental impact must be envisaged?
2. What kinds of environmental impact does the law prohibit, and by what means?

1   Environmental impact described

It is established custom to distinguish between an envisaged harm and the probability of the occurrence of the harm.[2] The probability, in turn, has two components; the frequency of the event (the occurrence of the harm) and the level of certainty that the event takes place. For instance, an event may, to our certain knowledge, be very infrequent or its frequency may be very uncertain.

In the first case, one has no difficulty in speaking of a *low probability*. But in the second case, which is often also taken as a variant of 'low probability', this is doubtful since further investigation may prove that the event is in fact highly fre-

---

[1]   See Chapter 9 by Albert Mumma in this volume.
[2]   Michael Kloepfer, *Umweltrecht*, Munich: Beck, 1989, p. 77 *et. seq.*

quent. In this case, one can speak of low probability in terms of what is 'probed' in a given society: events which are not 'probed' are not probable. In any case, this difference must be appreciated when it comes to understanding what kinds of impact a society is willing to tolerate.

As to the harm, one may distinguish between the deterioration of an environmental medium (air, water, soil) and protected *end points* such as human health, in particular, but also animals and plants. The probability of a harmful effect will generally differ depending on what category of harm is looked at. The introduction of cadmium into a river has a 100 per cent probability of polluting the water, but may affect the fish at a much lower rate and the fish-eating population even less.

From another angle one may distinguish between harm done to individual organisms and harm arising to biosystems. A system – for example, a given biotope – may be more sensitive than the single organisms of which it consists, but it may also be more resistant because it is able to replace one organism or even function with another.

From yet another perspective grave harm may be distinguished from less serious harm. For instance, death is more grave for an organism than sickness. If gravity of a particular harm is related to collective entities rather than individuals, grave harm means that a high level of the population is affected, and minor harm that only few individuals (possibly the more sensitive ones) are affected. For instance, a concentration of 80 μg/cbm sulphur dioxide in the air will cause health problems only to those who suffer from bronchitis, the tolerance limit for the average person lying around 140μg.

These distinctions must be kept in mind when it comes to understanding or framing substantive criteria for prohibiting or authorizing an environmental impact. As the framing of every aspect would be too complicated the legal language uses more condensed terms. German law and doctrine, for instance, draws a line between hazards and risks. Hazards (*Gefahren*) can be defined as grave harm of a sufficient probability (frequency, certainty). The Immission Control Act counts even mere nuisances and disadvantages (which, however, must be highly probable) as hazards. On the other hand, traditional police law holds that harm which is of low probability constitutes a hazard if its gravity is extreme – for instance, if a nuclear catastrophy is considered.

By contrast, an environmental impact is defined as risk if the harm is minor and/or the probability of its occurrence is low.[3]

---

[3] The term is differently defined by scientists. They take it to denominate the product of probability and gravity of harm, the different levels of risk being expressed by appropriate adjectives like high or low risk (for example, high probability of grave harm and the inverse, respectively). The legal use as outlined above corresponds better to the ordinary understanding ('the investment seems secure, but there is a risk left').

Situations where the probability is so low and/or the harm is so minor that what is left is negligible are termed as a residual risk (*Restrisiko*)[4] by German doctrine.

2   Environmental impact regulated

The degree to which hazards and risks are acceptable or not must be determined by legislation or the administration. In most legal systems the law prohibits the causation of hazards. No installation may be authorized if it will cause hazards. This can be understood as an expression of 'the polluter pays' principle, to be sure one where the pollution is 'reinternalized' into the polluter's sphere by prohibitive regulation rather than by financial means.[5] For instance, the German Immission Control Act formulates hazard prevention as follows:[6]

> (1) Installations subject to licensing shall be established and operated in such a way that
>
> 1.   this does not involve harmful effects on the environment or other hazards, significant disadvantages and significant nuisance to the general public and the neighbourhood,
>
> 2.   precaution[7] is taken to prevent harmful effects on the environment, in particular by such emission control measures as are appropriate according to best available technology.

There are cases outside the area of the authorization of hazardous installations where the law does tolerate hazards. As to existing installations, even the rather stringent German Immission Control Act does not force but only empowers and urges, the responsible agency to impose orders for eliminating the hazards.[8] More importantly, the peculiarity of a project may be such that it requires sacrificing parts of the environment – in other words cause a hazard. A road, for instance, cannot be built without the destruction of the plants growing on the route. We shall see later on that the law sometimes establishes further requirements which justify or mitigate the hazard in those cases.[9]

---

[4]   See, in the context of preventing nuclear power catastrophies, the Kalkar-decision of the Constitutional Court, BVerfGE, **49, 89** (137).

[5]   See for this principle and its two expressions (that is, qualitative and financial) Michel Prieur, *Droit de l'Environnement*, (2nd edn), Paris: Dalloz, 1991, p. 125 *et. seq.*

[6]   Art. 5, para. 1, No. 1, Bundesimmissionsschutzgesetz (BImSchG).

[7]   *Vorsorge.*

[8]   Art. 17, para. 1, BImSchG.

[9]   See Chapter 4 in this volume.

If hazards are generally prohibited the same is not true for risks. Risks, by definition, cannot be excluded because there will always remain a small probability of possible minor harm. Risks can, at best, be minimized. If the law prohibits action not merely to avoid hazards but to abate risks it establishes what is known as the *precaution principle* which requires the reduction of the extent, frequency and/or uncertainty of harm. There are numerous examples of how this can be secured. In particular, environmental quality objectives can be set at a level below the threshold which demarcates the line between hazard and risk, leaving the entrepreneur to find ways and means of how to meet the standards. If the entrepreneur fails to meet them the authorization of the installation can be refused. Another method is to prescribe *best available technology* (BAT – *Stand der Technik*), a criterion from which emission limits or specific technical installation requirements may be deduced.[10]

Some, particularly the British, have objected that the BAT standard, being blind to environmental effects, causes inefficiency because it may lead to costly abatement technology even if there is no anticipated hazard or significant risk. Thus, particularly in the water pollution area, they have therefore preferred an approach which is oriented towards the effects of pollution, using water quality objectives as a guide for controlling waste water discharge.[11] Yet, at least in the not-too-rare situation where knowledge about possible harm is lacking, the BAT standard is a sensible precautionary tool and can prove very efficient if better knowledge reveals that the impact would have been harmful. For this reason and others, the UK has adopted the BAT approach in the Environmental Protection Act (EPA) 1990, although qualified by cost considerations[12] (*best available techniques not entailing excessive cost* (BATNEEC)).

Another precautionary tool is to prevent the shifting of pollution from one environmental medium to another. This covers cases where each of several relevant media is affected up to, but not above, the hazard threshold, but where the overall risk to the several media may be seen to be more objectionable than a hazard affecting only one medium. The tool the British law provides in these situations is called the '*best practicable environmental option*' (BPEO). It is formulated in s. 7, para. 7, EPA:

> The objectives referred to in subsection (2) above shall, where the process (a) is one designated for central control; and (b) is likely to involve the release of substances into more than one environmental medium; include the objective of

---

[10] For further details on standard-setting see my contribution in Chapter 8 of this volume.

[11] Ss. 104 to 105, Water Act 1989, as annotated by R. Macrory. See Richard Macrory (ed.), *The Water Act 1989. Text and Commentary*, London: Sweet and Maxwell, 1989, p. 104 *et. seq.*

[12] See s. 7, para. 4, EPA.

ensuring that the best available techniques not entailing excessive cost will be used for minimizing the pollution which may be caused to the environment taken as a whole by the releases having regard to the best practicable environmental option available as respects the substances which may be released.

III   POLLUTION FROM MOBILE SOURCES

Substantive criteria, possibly specified by quantified emission limits, could also be used for drawing a line between accepted and intolerable air pollution from mobile sources. However, if they exist at all, they are frequently vaguely framed or totally inadequate. This is probably due to the fact that pollution from traffic is so common and serious that clear legal language would have to admit that the hazard threshold is exceeded in many parts of the country. This would require immediate and far-reaching action which is very costly due to the economic importance of unhindered transport and the socio-psychological value of individual mobility.

Instead of regulating traffic under the ordinary requirements of environmental protection the law has used more indirect measures. Among these figure emission limits for motor vehicles, prohibition of certain toxic substances in gasoline, tax incentives for catalytic converters and so on.

German law provides examples where substantive criteria in the above sense are in fact established, albeit rather vaguely.

- According to Article 45 of the Road Traffic Regulation (*Straßenverkehrs-ordnung*) traffic may be restricted on certain roads 'for the protection of the neighbourhood against noise and exhaust'. Against exactly what kind and amount of noise and exhaust protection is seen to be needed is not specified.
- Article 40 para. 2 of the Immission Control Act allows the restriction of the traffic even in whole areas of a community. Measures can be taken on the basis of the balancing of the aim of reducing or preventing harmful air pollution against the traffic needs and city planning considerations. In this case, the substantive criterion consists in a balancing requirement.

In particular, if a 'smog situation' (low air circulation) arises, air emissions may have hazardous environmental effects (*schädliche Umwelteinwirkungen*), and traffic restrictions can be imposed for parts or the whole of a *Land* (Article 40 para. 1 Immission Control Act). The *Land* is empowered to set the relevant emission thresholds by regulation. Most of the *Länder* have done this for carbon monoxide, nitrogen dioxide, sulphur dioxide, and some also for ozone.

IV   POLLUTION THROUGH WASTE

Substantive criteria may be set in order to prevent pollution (in particular the contamination of the soil and groundwater) from discharged waste. In most cases they will lead to more concrete requirements as to the geology and the insulation and sealing of the disposal site. The stipulation of certain kinds of pretreatment and conditioning of the waste also plays a part in this approach.

More sophisticated systems regard the waste itself (or, more precisely, waste which is not, or not harmlessly, degradable) as a nuisance, the deposit of which should be reduced to a minimum. These systems establish recycling and avoidance duties which cannot be framed in absolute terms due to the technologal and cost implications. For instance, the new German Recycling and Waste Act (*Kreislaufwirtschafts- und Abfallgesetz*) provides as follows:[13]

> The duty of recycling is to be observed insofar as this is technically feasible and economically tolerable and, in particular, there exists or can be created a market for the recovered material or energy.

The same Article makes a further qualification. The priority of recycling over discharge is not maintained if the discharge is the environmentally more benign solution.[14] This avoids a requirement to recycle where the process for treatment of the waste for recovery purposes causes more pollution and/or energy consumption than the conditioning and deposit. This qualification can be understood as a second version of the BPEO principle cited above from the British Environmental Protection Act 1990.

Since this chapter is not about waste law I shall delve no deeper into the much discussed definition of 'waste'. But a methodological parenthesis may be worthwhile. The way in which the legal systems define 'waste' teaches us that policy decisions are contained not only in the express directions of a law but also in the definition of legal terms. If, for instance, a law establishes that the local authority is under a duty to collect and dispose the household waste and defines waste ('subjectively') as anything the possessor wants to get rid of, the result is a dead-end of ever higher waste mountains. Consequently, this subjective definition has been termed the waste definition of the throw-away society.

Yet overly semantic discussion regarding definitions can demonstrably be fruitless. In the example above the definition of waste could certainly be narrowed, but the duties connected to the term could also be made more complex by, for example, introducing a duty to primarily recycle the (then broadly defined) waste. A functional approach is preferable. The legislator should begin by devising a consis-

---

[13]   Art. 5, para. 4, sentence 1.
[14]   Art. 5, para. 5.

tent set of duties (avoidance, recycling, disposal), sort out the categories of objects to which these duties should be connected, and give these categories a name. If the duties are carefully formulated, it is of secondary concern whether the law uses a broad notion of waste (as EU law does) which is then subjected to the various duties, or whether the law defines as 'waste' only substances which must be disposed of, calling those substances which can be recycled 'secondary raw material', and using 'residues' as the generic term for both 'waste' and 'secondary raw material'.

V   ENCROACHMENTS ON NATURE AND LANDSCAPE

Consumption of space by the construction of buildings, roads, airports and so forth is a further path of environmental deterioration. Its extension has led the legislature and the courts in a number of countries to develop substantive criteria by which space-consuming activities are controlled.

Many countries have aligned their planning laws to this purpose. For instance, in 1987 the French Code de l'Urbanisme was amended by a clause requiring the protection of nature and landscape. Interestingly, a requirement to manage the space in an economic way was also introduced.[15] In the UK, the courts have established a power of the planning authority to refer a proposed development to an alternative site on the ground (among others) that this leads to less harm to nature and amenities.[16]

By contrast, German law which also recognizes the concepts of balancing, economizing and alternative testing in planning law,[17] has built into its Nature Protection Act a rather more refined set of substantial requirements, which have to be observed both in planning decisions and decisions under any other law authorizing encroachments on nature and landscape (*Eingriffe in Natur und Landschaft*).[18] Such encroachments must, in the first instance, be avoided as far as possible, and if an encroachment is unavoidable, it must be compensated in kind. For instance, if a wetland area must be sacrificed for the project, a similar biotope must be installed in the neighbourhood or, if a biotope of this kind already exists, it must be put under a special nature protection regime. If adequate compensation measures (*Ausgleichsmassnahmen*) are not feasible, the resulting encroachment on

---

[15] Art. 110, Code de l'Urbanisme (Article 22 Loi No. 87-565 of 22 July 1987). The importance of this clause is stressed by Michel Prieur (1991), *op.cit.*, p. 589.

[16] See Michael Purdue, Eric Young, Jeremy Rowan-Robinson, *Planning Law and Procedure*, London: Butterworths, 1989, p.219 *et. seq.*

[17] See Art. 1, Construction Code (*Baugesetzbuch*).

[18] Art. 8 Federal Nature Protection Act (*Bundesnaturschutzgesetz*); M. Kloepfer (1989), *op. cit.* p. 555 *et. seq.*

nature must be balanced against the benefit arising from the project. If the local natural environment is considered to be more important the project will have to be abandoned. In the other case the project may be given consent but only on the condition that substitute measures (*Ersatzmaßnahmen*) are taken. These may consist of establishing a biotope which is also valuable but may be different and situated at some distance from the one destroyed. Finally, if substitute measures prove unfeasible, a compensatory payment may be required, although this is not made obligatory by federal law. The *Länder* may provide for this in their nature protection laws. Some have done so; others have desisted from this tool for fear that, in practice, most developers will press the authorities to agree to lump sum compensation payments in order to forego the organizationally and financially more burdensome compensation in kind.

VI   ENVIRONMENTAL IMPACT THROUGH DANGEROUS PRODUCTS

Products can cause environmental harm while being used or after their use (that is, as waste). Prevention of such harm can be targeted by disposal/recycling requirements once the product has become waste. It can also be strived for through requirements for the use of the product (for example, the regular checking of automobile exhaust). Whereas this kind of regulation intervenes at a rather late phase in a product's life cycle, other kinds are tied to earlier phases, making them more effective. The most frequent approach is to regulate the marketing of the product. Two strategies are to be found in most legal systems: information requirements and positive restrictions. The law may require the supplier to inform the customers about the risks entailed by the product – for example, by labelling the package. Alternatively, it may fix quality conditions such as limits for the concentration of toxic substances in products, or it may prohibit outright the marketing or even production of certain products, preparations and substances.

What substantive criteria does the law establish for determining what kinds of products are environmentally tolerable and what are not? There is a multitude to be found in the various product-related laws which are still awaiting doctrinal systematization and simplification. I shall confine myself to the chemical substances laws. The laws themselves are normally not very specific, merely postulating that no environmental harm should arise from chemical substances, preparations and products. Sometimes, as in the German case, the *precaution principle* is added, which provides that grounds for suspecting a risk suffice in respect of regulatory measures where scientific certainty is lacking.[19] These legal standards

---

[19]   Art. 17, para. 4, Chemical Substances Act (*Chemikaliengesetz*).

must be concretized in order to be manageable in practice. In this respect, guidance is given by an EC Directive,[20] which basically posits a two-step evaluation:

First, the innate hazard of the substance is determined by identifying the relevant dose-response-relationships. From this it may, for instance, result that a concentration of 1 mg/kg in a human being leads to nausea. Second, the predicted exposure of human beings (be they consumers, workers, the public and so on) is investigated. If the predicted dose is higher than the threshold deemed to be tolerable on the basis of the dose-response curve there is sufficient ground for the regulation of the substance, be this a total ban or merely requirements as to the handling of the substance. Measures of the latter kind depend on whether the substance will be available to end consumers or only to professional customers of whom one can expect a more cautious attitude.

Besides environment-related criteria less transparent ones are applied in regulatory practice. Prominent amongst these are economic concerns connected with the restriction of the substance (cost for consumers of purchasing alternative substances, loss for the producer of the substance, cost of developing a substitute substance). Another consideration that can be observed in practice is the need for, or benefit taken from, the substance. If the benefit is small, the regulator will be more inclined to react even in cases of uncertain or insignificant harm caused by the substance, while in cases of high benefits (when there is also no substitute available) such smaller risks may be accepted. In this context a question arises as to whether these 'factual' considerations should be left to the discretion of the regulator or rationalized (and possibly cut back) by explicit legislation. Insofar as need aspects are concerned, German law has indeed made this explicit. For instance, the authorization of the marketing of both pesticides and products consisting of, or containing, genetically modified organisms has been made dependent of a *benefit–risk assessment*.[21]

---

[20] Directive 93/67/EEC of the Commission of 20 July 1993 on the evaluation of risks from notified substances, OJ L 227/9 (1993).

[21] See Art. 15 Pesticides Act (*Pflanzenschutzgesetz*) in the interpretation by the Federal Administrative Court (BVerwGE 81, 12 *et. seq.*) and Art. 16, para. 1, No. 3 Genetic Engineering Act (*Gentechnikgesetz*). See Gerd Winter, Regelungsmaßstäbe im Gefahrstoffrecht, in idem (ed.), *Risikoanalyse und Risikoabwehr im Gefahrstoffrecht. Interdisziplinäre Untersuchungen*, Düsseldorf: Werner Verlag, 1995.

4 Instruments of Direct Behavioural Regulation

Michael Kloepfer and Gerd Winter

Table of Contents

I GENERAL

Direct behavioural regulation conclusively prescribes a particular type of behaviour (to act, to tolerate or to refrain). *Indirect behavioural regulation* approaches the government aim but by a roundabout route: it primarily influences the motivation of the addressee and leaves him or her a broad area of discretion. If, in the latter case, the state formulates a behavioural expectation at all, a behaviour which frustrates this expectation remains lawful (however unwanted and possibly made subject to such burdensome consequences as, for example, the payment of a charge). This is different from direct behavioural regulation, where the addressees' behaviour against the expectation is unlawful. The addressees only have the possibility to bow to the administrative demand or to give up the regulated activity completely. The performance of the direct behavioural demand can be different from the indirect behavioural expectation, in principle induced by means of coercion and its non-performance punishable by sanctions.[1]

In contrast to the indirect form of regulation the direct behavioural regulation has, on one hand, the disadvantage of a certain inflexibility and abruptness but, on the other hand, the advantage of clarity under the rule of law. The flexible and soft indirect behavioural regulation clouds this clarity under the rule of law because it qualifies the border between legality and illegality by having in-between categories with less sharp outlines (of the unwanted but not forbidden or of the wanted but not advisable behaviour). Additionally, judicial review in the interest of the 'second' party (that is, the applicant, addressee and so forth.) or affected third parties is geared to the direct behavioural regulation (for example, the administrative act) whereas, in contrast, it only incompletely grasps the behavioural expectation of the indirect type of regulation.

Admittedly in the comparison between instruments of direct and indirect regulation there is no sharp edge of delimitation but an ideal typical difference. Numerous in-between forms exist: The indirect regulation can therefore have the effect of a clear-cut prohibition if the intensity is sufficient – as, for instance, when a pollution charge is enormous. Conversely, the instruments of the direct behavioural regulation usually precede an informal agreement process with the addressee.

Instruments of direct behavioural regulation include the following:

* supervision;
* prohibitions and rules;
* obligation to notify;
* permission requirement.

As a rule, these instruments are intended for the enforcement of laws which prescribe a certain standard of environment protection in general terms. For example, a law may require that damage to environmental goods is to be avoided and precautions against the coming into being of such damage are to be taken, as well as that environmentally dangerous activities are obliged to gain permission so that it can be examined whether they obey the requirements of the law. Between these general legal requirements and the specific conditions laid down in the individual permits, intermediate steps can be taken. This is possible by standardization of the requirements[2] or by planning. (See the explanation at the end of this chapter).

---

[1]   See on these and other differences Chapter 12 by P. Glasbergen, Chapter 13 by G. Bándi and Chapter 15 by E. Rehbinder in this volume.

[2]   See Chapter 8 on standard-setting by G. Winter in this volume.

II SUPERVISION

State supervision fulfils a double aim in environmental protection: First, it serves to control individual activities with regard both to whether they comply with the requirements of the environmental laws and the concrete terms of the permits or prohibition (compliance control). Second, it has the more comprehensive function of continuous environmental monitoring of the development of the environmental situation sector by sector. In this case it serves the planning preparation and individual administrative measures which can produce a further compliance control at a later stage. In this way a proper supervision cycle can form.

The individual competences of supervision include the authorities' right to enter premises and to inspect, the right to look at files and documents, rights to extract test samples, to take own measurements and make inspections as well as the authority to demand information and active support. Sometimes the supervisory authority is also entitled to enter works without prior announcement.

The regulation of the bearing of the costs for measuring and testing is of considerable significance for the authorities. One example is the German Federal Immission Control Act:[3] the plant operator bears the costs of the investigation into the emissions and immissions only when it emerges that he has violated the permit conditions or when the severity of ecological damage justifies additional conditions independent of those already existing.[4] As most authorities only have low budgets allocated to them for examinations, this regulation may hinder active supervision. At least in dangerous installations which necessitate a special emissions licence, the operator should, in any case, carry the examination costs, when there are grounds necessitating an examination and also when the grounds are not confirmed by the examination results.

Supervision can be implemented by the appointment of a state registered private supervisory organization as well as through self-supervision by the firm or by its participation in a semi-voluntary environmental audit.[5]

In the official practice of many countries it is observable that the supervisory activities are *cura posterior* and frequently lack a systematic approach with the setting of priorities and planning of the order of supervisory action.[6] The authorities generally only become active after complaints from neighbours and therefore only in cases in which the ecological damage is visible. As a rule the largest part of the workload is connected with the granting of permission for new installations

---

[3] Bundesimmissionsschutzgesetz.
[4] Art. 52, para. 4.
[5] See Chapter 15 by E. Rehbinder in this volume.
[6] See Chapter 10 by A. Capria in this volume.

and activities.[7] A reason for this is that in some countries – as in Germany – the operators' subjective right to permission is set against the authority's discretion in the observance of its supervisory authority. Accordingly the authority does not act illegally if it refrains from supervision; it does, however, if it does not grant a permission – provided that the legal conditions are fulfilled.

In order to escape this incongruity it has been suggested that supervision should be formulated as an obligation of the authority.[8] An additional possibility exists in giving third parties a right to intervention by the authorities against the cause of ecological damage. When the supervision is within the authority's discretion, this third-party right cannot nevertheless be directed at a specific measure but only at the judicial review of the use of the discretion. If the third party has, for example, made an application stating that the authority should take measures against an installation which exceeds the emissions limits and if the authority has refused to intervene because, according to its view, these limits have not been exceeded, the third party can institute proceedings and obtain a judgement. In this, the court orders the authority to decide anew upon the application in accordance with the court's factual and judicial observations. If it has emerged from the trial that the level of emissions has actually been exceeded, the authority must find and state other reasons if it still wishes to desist from intervention.[9]

III   PROHIBITION AND RULES

Prohibitions and rules can be contained in a law which is directly effective upon the behaviour of the individual and need not be tailored to the concrete case by an administrative act, for example, a permit. There is, for instance, in the German nature conservation law, a prohibition on destroying especially valuable biotope.[10] This must be observed by force of the law. No concretizing prohibition or rule by an agency is necessary.

Laws very frequently contain rules or prohibitions to be drawn up by executive regulations. This is normal, for example, in the German Chemical Substances Law. Accordingly the limitation of the usage or marketing of dangerous chemicals will be expressed by regulation.[11]

---

[7]   See Introduction in G. Winter (ed.) *German Environmental Law. Basic Texts and Introduction*, Dordrecht, 1994.

[8]   G. Lübbe-Wolff, Vollzugsprobleme der Umweltverwaltung, *Natur und Recht*, 1993, p. 217.

[9]   See German Administrative Court case BVerwGE 11, 95. For the legal position in England see Chapter 9 by A. Mumma in this volume.

[10]   See Art. 20c, Nature Conservation Law.

[11]   Cf. Art. 17, Chemical Substances Law.

Sanctions are mainly imposed if anyone violates the prohibitions or rules which have been laid down by laws or regulations. These consist of criminal prosecution only in serious cases. Many legal systems have special administrative sanctions in the form of a monetary fine. In addition there are official enforcement measures. In German law these consist of the authority first to order, by means of an administrative act, the deviant behaviour back into harmony with the legal rule or prohibition (basic order). To do this, the law must contain a special authorization for such an order, the simple prohibition or rule directed to the individual is not sufficient for this. If the special law does not contain such an authorization police law remains as a starting-point. The injury of a material prohibition or rule is valid as an injury to the public safety, endangerment of which authorizes official intervention under police power laws.

Where there is no special authorization provided, other legal systems instruct the authority to refer to normal legal court action which of course will delay the enforcement of the law itself.

If a basic order has been made and the operator is still not abiding by it, according to German law, three kinds of enforcement measure are available to the authority, namely:

- coercive fine (*Zwangsgeld*);
- substitute performance (*Ersatzvornahme*);[12]
- direct coercion (*unmittelbarer Zwang*).

The offender must be warned by the agency before these enforcement measures can actually be applied.

If the offender believes that he has not violated the legal prohibition or rule, he can appeal against the authorities' basic order. If he neglects to do this within a certain time period the order becomes final and absolute. There is also legal protection against the enforcement warning and measures but, at this stage, it can only be directed against the method of enforcement not against enforcement in general.

Alongside rules or prohibitions deriving directly from laws or regulations there are ones which are laid down by individual administrative acts. According to the principle of the rule of law, a legal authorization must be in existence for the enactment of such an administrative act. For example, according to the German Chemical Substances Law (Article 23) the competent regional authority can enact temporary measures to limit the marketing of a substance, if grounds for a considerable hazard are resultant and the normal method of enactment by the federal government (*Bundesregierung*) is too prolonged.

---

[12] In this case the authority appoints a third party to carry out the required activity and burdens the injurer with the costs of this measure.

Otherwise legal authorization for such rules or prohibition orders are frequently connected with permits. A permit allows a certain degree of ecological damage but prohibits going beyond the permitted limit.

IV   THE OBLIGATION TO NOTIFY

The *obligation to notify* comes essentially in two variants: as an alternative to the requirement of permission (notification replacing a licence); or as a supervisory instrument be it in view of the compliance with the permit conditions, or of compliance with the direct legal rules and prohibitions (notification for supervision).

1   Notification replacing a licence (*Mitteilung als Ersatz für Erlaubnisvorbehalt*)

As an instrument to control the beginning of ecologically damaging activities the obligation to notify represents the mildest method. German environmental law provides an obligation to notify, for instance, in the Chemical Substances Law where a duty to notify the marketing of new dangerous substances is established. Through this type of notification the administration should obtain the information it needs in order to be able to intervene if necessary. The extent and intensity of the obligation to give information are governed very differently in individual laws, whereby the Chemical Substances Law, which is inspired by the relevant EC Directives, makes the highest demands in which it combines notification with demanding obligations on the applicant to examine and of proof. A far-reaching obligation of this type can (in the individual case) lead to effects whose intensity of intervention is comparable to a reservation of permission.

The notification replacing a licence is sometimes connected with a waiting period, within which the reported activity may not be carried out. The Chemical Substances Law is also an example here: the authority must be given the requested data to examine, six weeks from the time of notification, before the notified substance may be brought into circulation.

There are various reasons for introducing notification instead of requiring a permission. In the Chemical Substances Law the argument is that the reservation of permission would have led to considerable economic losses because the granting of permission takes so long. Whilst this delay represents is a burden on the economy, in the concept of the obligation to notify it is a burden on environmental protection. Nevertheless this is only tolerable when it can be assumed that the operator (as a rule) puts no ecologically damaging material on the market of his own accord.

2   Notification for supervision (*Mitteilung zur Überwachung*)

The rule in Article 27 of the German Immission Control Act may serve as an example of the obligation to notify for supervision:

> The operator of an installation subject to licensing shall be liable to provide the competent authority within a period to be fixed by such authority or on the date which has been fixed in the regulation issued pursuant to para. (4) below with information on the type and volume and spatial and temporal distribution of air pollution emitted from such installation within a specified period, including the conditions governing such emissions (emission declaration); he shall update the emission declaration at regular intervals of two years each.

V   THE PERMISSION REQUIREMENT (*ERLAUBNISVORBEHALT*)

Permission requirements prohibit the commencement of certain activities (for example, the operation of an industrial installation) before official inspection and permission. The opposing concept is the fundamental permit with a prohibition reservation that only allows for an administrative monitoring with a possible prohibition.

1   The subject of permission

The subject of permission can be an installation or an activity. If it is an installation it is of significance whether the term 'installation' is narrowly or broadly defined. With a narrow definition a plant may need several licences because it may consist of several installations. For example, for a power station a licence could be necessary for the kiln, a further one for the machine room with turbine and a third for the cooling tower. A broad definition of the term has the advantage that the whole factory complex can be judged as an interrelated system. The benefit of viewing the complex as a whole will, however, be lost when with especially large installations the permit is granted in partial steps – the so-called partial licence (see below, section 4).

From another point of view an installation can have simultaneous effects on several environmental resources – for example, the air, water and soil. In this case several permits geared to the respective media are necessary. In a system of integrated environmental licensing these various permits will be drawn together into one permit.[13]

The most important example of a permission requirement referring to an activity is connected to the usage of waters. Nevertheless, the environmentally most significant case being the discharge of sewage the relevant activity will often be connected to installations. The corresponding permit will therefore be granted, as a rule, in connection with the licence for the installation.

Licences referring to installations are principally formulated as *real concessions* – that is, they refer to the installation and not the applicant in person and their validity will therefore be unaffected by a change in individual operator. By contrast the person-related permit is not transferable because it is connected to such personal qualities as the reliability, capability and knowledge of the applicant. In environmental law combinations of both forms are frequent. The permit for constructing an atomic power station, according to German law[14] is geared to the safety of the installation on the one hand and the reliability of the applicant staff on the other.

When a type of installation or product is repeatedly constructed or marketed it is considered that its environmental safety, in so far as it is inherent in the installation or product, can be ascertained once and for all by a type of construction or model authorization. Permission for construction or distribution in the individual case can then be limited to individual questions of space and time. With an installation licence these are mainly locational problems. With larger, complex installations, however, each installation is still developed specifically because the location and, moreover, the continuous progress in technology so require. A *standard type permit* is not recommended for large installations. Apart from this it is also difficult to carry out a formal procedure with public participation for standard type licences because the public's usual first interest in a project lies in its realization at a particular location.

2   Supplementary regulations to a permission (*Nebenbestimmungen*)

Permits are frequently connected with supplementary regulations. In particular there exist impositions which prescribe certain behaviour or omissions for the operator (for example, compliance with an emissions limit), the fixing of the permit's expiry date and delaying or resolving conditions which make the taking effect or continued existence of the permission dependent on a defined event (for

---

[13]   The EU is preparing a directive which provides for these effects of integration. See below, section (e).

[14]   Art. 7, Nuclear Energy Law.

example, the availability of waste disposal for a nuclear power plant). A further supplementary regulation is the *reservation of revocation*.

Supplementary regulations are a flexible instrument for focusing the permission on the features of the individual case. Since they can potentially undo the whole grant of the permission as, for instance, in the case of an unlimited cancellation reservation, German law[15] limits the permissibility of supplementary regulations in certain ways. With administrative acts, supplementary regulations may only be enacted in order to secure the legal requirements of the grant of the permit. For administrative acts which are within the authority's discretion, the area of discretion is larger but is nevertheless limited by the fact that the supplementary regulations may not be contrary to the aim of the law regulating the permit.

In earlier German cases an operator could separately appeal against a burdensome imposition, leaving the permit itself untouched. The court had to repeal the imposition if it proved to be illegal. This applied even in those cases where the permit would probably not have been granted without the condition had the agency known that the condition was illegal. According to more recent case law the condition must be understood as part of the administrative act, so that a cancellation of the condition may only be considered when the permit would have been granted without the condition.[16]

3   Types of permission according to the scale of programming

The granting of permission can be programmed more or less strictly by law. How strictly the administration is bound by law is influenced by the national constitutional traditions, in particular on whether the parliament bases its control of the administration completely on the responsibility of the competent minister – in which case exact material instructions can be dispensed with – or whether the parliament considers these controls to be insufficient and therefore issues such material instructions. The legal programming is especially dense in those legal systems which focus on the protection of subjective rights and correspondingly establish a right to permission by the applicant. The variations become clear when one compares English, French and German formulation of the criteria for the grant of a licence for dangerous installations:

Section 6 of the British Environmental Protection Act 1990 provides:

---

[15]   Art. 26, para. 1, sentence 2 and para. 3, Administrative Procedure Law.

[16]   See H.-U. Erichsen in Erichsen, Martens (eds), *Allgemeines Verwaltungsrecht*, (9th edn), 1992, para. 15 II 3.

1. No person shall carry on a precribed process ... except under an authorization granted by the enforcing authority and in accordance with the conditions to which it is subject.
2. An application shall not be granted unless the enforcing authority considers that the applicant will be able to carry on the process so as to comply with the conditions which would be included in the authorization.

In section 7, standards are formulated from which the conditions should be derived. These aims are very concretely formulated. For example, the prescribed standard is the *best available techniques not entailing excessive cost* (BATNEEC).

The legal technique is such that a negative barrier is erected for the authority – namely, permission is only granted under specific conditions. The authority is, however, not positively compelled to grant permission, and possesses the discretion to refuse this even when the named conditions are able to be fulfilled.

In French Law No. 76-663 of 19 July 1976 concerning classified installations Art. 3 states:

Installations which present significant dangers or nuisances for the interests named in Art. 1 [i.e. the well-being of the neighbourhood, the health, the safety and hygiene of the public, the protection of nature and environment, the conservation of the landscape and of monuments] are subject to authorization by the prefect.

The authorization can only be granted if these dangers or nuisances can be prevented by measures which are specified by prefectoral decision.

The law specifies no aims for such measures. From the legal-technical standpoint we are again concerned with a negative barrier: the conditions must prevent damage and nuisance, but the authority is not positively obliged to grant the permit. This differs from English law in that the conditions to be arranged are not rewritten precisely as regards to content.

In Article 4 of the German Federal Immission Control Act it is stated that dangerous installations require a special licence. Article 5 lays down so-called basic obligations which each operator must observe independently of the framework laid down in the permit. Hazard avoidance and precaution rules belong to these obligations. That means, as in Article 6, that:

The licence is to be granted when (1) it is guaranteed that the obligations ensuing from Article 5 and regulations enacted by virtue of Article 7 are fulfilled, and ....

This demonstrates the two ways in which German legal technique differs from the English and French: First, the authority retains no discretion but is positively obliged to grant permission when the demands in Articles 5 can be fulfilled ('The licence *is to be* granted'). Second, the demands are not formulated as criteria for conditions to be attached to the licence but, as previously stated, as basic obligations which are primarily directed to the operator and which, by reference, become preconditions of the granting of a permission (which does not, in practice, exclude the fact that they are also framed as supplementary regulations (conditions or special terms), to the licence).

The technique of establishing a negative barrier with remaining official discretion is put into effect in German law in the water law for example. According to Article 6 of the Federal Water Act (*Wasserhaushaltsgesetz*) the authority must refuse permission when damage to water is expected, especially when it serves as drinking water. However, even if no damage is anticipated the authority is not obliged to grant permission since the permit may still be refused for reasons of water management – for example, in order to keep parts of the self-cleaning capacity of the water open for other uses.

In German law there is yet another type of permission in which the authorities' discretion is especially broad – namely, plan approval (*Planfeststellung*). This relates to larger infrastructure projects which affect a great many, different interests and are mostly connected with expropriation and destructive encroachments on nature – categories which include roads, airports, waterways, dams and railways. Here, the competent authority will essentially only balance the affected interests. Due to the possible consequences of expropriation it is furthermore necessary that the project is required in the public interest.[17] This prerequisite of public interest itself also simultaneously justifies possible encroachments on nature.

In most legal systems the granting of permission for projects requires that a formal procedure with public participation has been carried out and furthermore that the project has been the subject of an environmental impact assessment.[18]

4   Permission in steps

The licence for large and complex installations frequently follows partial steps. Through this it is possible to select decisive problems and deal with them in sections. A single licensing act is replaced by successive layered licensing processes.

The layering can be carried out in two ways: By advance licence (*Vorbescheid*) in which individual licence requirements are declared in advance to be given, such as the suitability of the installation's location or the overall conception of the

---

[17]   Art. 14, para. 2 of the German constitution only permits dispossession when they serve the general good.

[18]   See Chapter 7 by C. Lambrechts in this volume.

plant; or by partial licence (*Teilgenehmigung*) which permits the realization of an actual part of the installation or a distinguishable phase of the project.

The advance and the partial licence become more permanent if no legal action against them is taken, and are therefore binding. If, later, a further partial licence is granted which refers to another part of the installation, should a complaint be launched against this partial licence the legality of the earlier partial licence may not be examined. This kind of preclusion of objections should not to be confused with the preclusion of arguments which could be raised, but were not raised in time, by objection in a formal administrative procedure.

The possibility of advance and partial licences is problematic in that parts could be granted with no consideration for the whole project. The realization of a part could also prejudice follow-up decisions, thus hindering the free consideration of subsequent applications for partial licences. In German law, in order to limit this danger a requirement in the granting of advance and partial licences a so-called preliminary overall assessment (*vorläufiges Gesamturteil*) of the project is demanded.[19] This examines whether 'a temporary assessment results in there not being, from the start, any insurmountable obstacles in the way of erection and operation of the whole installation, in view of the licensing requirements'.[20]

For its part, this preliminary overall assessment exhibits a certain binding effect. In the test of subsequent partial licence, the authority must keep to that which has been tested at the preliminary overall assessment. Only if the specific circumstances or the legal regulation has changed since then is the overall assessment not binding. If the authority, for example, has accepted previously that the installation is technically so equipped that scarcely any emissions are to be expected, but closer examination of the installation technology at a later date has shown that emissions will in fact be considerable, the authority is not bound, for example, to grant the subsequent partial licence for the kiln from which the emissions escape.

The inner tension characterizing all these partial decisions lies in the conflict between interests of continuity (primarily of the applicant) and interests of flexibility (primarily of the licensing authority). On the one hand the applicant should receive relative security for his planning and investment; on the other hand the licensing authority cannot completely commit itself at the time of the partial decision because the details of the project's realization are still by no means definite. Nevertheless, the authority can be asked for a certain loyalty and consistency of direction in the enactment of any further decisions developing out of the relevant partial decisions. Large-scale changes of direction (without the removal of the earlier decisions – whose withdrawal remains possible, but is nevertheless bound to the general conditions of the withdrawal of administrative acts) in the later de-

---

[19]   See, for example, paras 8 and 9, Immission Control Act.
[20]   Art. 8, para. 1, No. 3, Immission Control Act.

cisions are permissible only on the grounds of such circumstances arising, which at the time of the partial decision were not yet sufficiently recognizable or had not yet been tested by the authority.

Incidentally, it is frequently difficult for concerned third parties to retain an overview and to know which part of the installation and which licensing conditions have been covered by which partial or advance decision. This is particularly the case when, as is not infrequent, a number of step-by-step decisions are enacted, which might, in the course of the licensing proceedings, even be retrospectively modified or altered. In this situation a third party might appeal against one of the later partial licences but may be turned down on the ground that the specific controversial point had already been decided by an earlier partial licence which, having not been challenged within the appeal period, had already become final.

Furthermore, according to some environmental laws, the applicant can, under certain circumstances, begin to realize the project even before the granting of the licence (the so-called authorization of a *premature beginning*). This possibility clearly serves the interest of the applicant in accelerating the procedure but has the great disadvantage that factual pressures are created by the realization of the project, which means that, even if the plan proves to be illegal, the courts can *de facto* prevent the permission which has been granted from being quashed. On authorization of the premature beginning therefore, certain preconditions are set. According to Article 15a of the German Immission Control Act these preconditions comprise the following:

1. the final decision is expected to be in favour of the person(s) responsible for the project,
2. there exists a legitimate public interest in the earlier establishment including the trial operation of such installation because of the anticipated enhancement of environmental protection,
3. the person(s) responsible for the project undertake(s) to indemnify any damages suffered in connection with the establishment including the trial operation of such installation pending final decision and to restore the status quo ante in case of rejection of the project.

According to Article 15a, para. 2, the authorization can be revoked at any time and be subject to a reservation that subsequent conditions are imposed. Furthermore, according to section 3, the authority can demand the lodging of a security.

5· Effects of the permission

Primarily a licence permits the undertaking of a defined activity (the building of an installation, the marketing of a product, and so on). In addition, it gives a judicial structure. This means that the legal relationship between the developer and others (particularly third parties), which is only roughly outlined by the underlying law, is put in concrete terms for the individual case. This implies, for example, that the third parties are compelled to tolerate the project. This particularly applies to those laws and duties which are derived from public laws. In addition, however, a licence can develop private law effects. In this case existing private law protection claims of third parties are excluded from further court action through the licence (the so-called *preclusion of claims* under private law – *Präklusionswirkung*).[21] Through this, third parties are compelled to proceed against the licence if they do not wish to lose their private-law rights.

Such a preclusion of claims under private law can only then be provided for if the licence is granted in formal proceedings, so that the third party bears witness to the proceedings and enables them to assert their objections.

A third effect of the licence is the so-called *integration effect* (*Konzentrationswirkung*). As complex proceedings frequently require several licences – for example, separate licences complying with the Immission Control law, Water law, Waste law, Construction law, Epidemic law and so on – the various licences are sometimes combined into one in the interests of simplifying the proceedings. At the granting of the integrating licence, however, the responsible authority must observe each of those requirements set by the individual special law.

In German law the plan approval has the most extensive integration effect within it.[22] The licence for dangerous installations has a partial integration effect[23] and includes, for example, the licence under Construction law and under Waste law, but not that under Water law, reflecting the special position of public waters which traditionally demand care from separate authorities.

One problem with extending integration is that the weight of the authorities who are responsible for individual media is reduced. Although cross-section examination when making a plan is desirable insofar as the displacement of the ecological damage from one medium to another is avoided and an optimum solution can be sought, it does so at the expense of the in-depth examination with regard to the individual media. The factory inspectorate, for example, is presumably not in a position to see and to coordinate completely all future burdens on a stretch of water. A solution to this dilemma may lie in making the granting of the integrated licence subject to the agreement of the authorities in charge of the most important media (water authority, nature conservation authority, waste authority).

A further problem of the integration effect arises in the supervisory framework after the realization of the project. Although the respective specialist authorities are certainly responsible for this supervision at any one time, they are hindered

---

[21] An example in Art. 14, Immission Control Act.
[22] See Art. 75, Administrative Procedure Law.
[23] Art. 13, Immission Control Act.

from making a quick reaction, however, by the fact that they themselves may not take measures which contradict the integration effect of the licence. They can only suggest to the officials responsible for the integrated licence that they alter the licence or that they equip it with additional orders.

6   Subsequent changes to the permission

The granting of licences is counterpointed by the possibilities of subsequent change to licences, which are particularly highly developed in environmental law since they secure flexibility. There is a difference between the revocation of the licence on the one hand and additional orders on the other.

The revocation is the more traditional instrument. In German law a difference is made between the withdrawal of a licence which has been illegal from the outset, and the revocation of a legitimate licence. This differentiation is provided by the general administrative procedure law,[24] and is taken up and, in certain ways, refined in the environmental law. Put crudely, the withdrawal is more easily possible since, because of the illegality, the beneficiary of a licence is only granted a small protection of legitimate expectations, while the revocation presupposes that the situation or legal position has changed and that the person concerned be paid compensation, in so far as his confidence is worthy of protection.

In practice, the revocation of licences is rare – not least because of the duty of compensation. Additional orders are the common instrument of adjusting an installation to the new recognition of risks, new factual circumstances and new legal positions. This instrument is provided for in a multitude of laws and is most precisely illustrated in Article 17 of the German Federal Immission Control Act.

The additional order shows a type of legal reservation which differs from the conventional reservation in that it must not be included in the licence as a supplementary requirement, but is valid in every case.

The additional order stands in a tense relationship with the protection of vested rights and of legitimate expectations. The protection of vested rights is particularly restricted by the fact that additional orders are usually not connected with compensation. To a large extent, laws such as the said Article 17 does not even have to demand that the ordered measure is economically viable for the individual firm. It merely demands that the measure is proportionate; in other words, that a less costly measure is not discernible and that the ordered measure is also not out of proportion to the additional environmental protection which can be achieved.

---

[24]   Cf. Art. 48 and 49, Administrative Procedure Law.

Additional orders are – at least theoretically – an appropriate opportunity for so-called offset agreements. Although such informal agreements, because they are concluded in the shadow of the formal law, tend to evade legal control there is a regulation in Article 17, para. 3a of the German Immission Control Act. This regulation runs as follows:

> The competent authority shall refrain from giving any such subsequent orders to the extent a plan submitted by the operator provides for technical measures to be taken at such operator's or any other parties' plants resulting in a reduction of emission levels which is significantly higher than the aggregate of reductions which might be attained by issuing such subsequent orders for the performance of the obligations ensuing from this Act or from any regulations issued hereunder, thus promoting achievement of the purpose referred to in the Article 1 hereof. This shall not apply to the exent the operator has already undertaken to reduce emissions by the issue of a subsequent order under para. (1) above or by the imposition of an obligation under Article 12, para. (1) hereof or to the extent such subsequent order is to be issued pursuant to para. (2), second sentence, above. Compensation shall only be permitted among substances of the same type or substances having a comparable effect on the environment.

In German administrative practice, this option is rarely used.[25]

---

[25]   For the problem of offset agreements see Chapter 15 by E. Rehbinder in this volume.

5 Environmental Impact Assessment

Claude Lambrechts

Table of Contents

I INTRODUCTION

This chapter analyses the environmental impact assessment rules of the European Union and of some of its Member States from a comparative law perspective.

Environmental impact assessment (EIA) was introduced into EC law by a Directive[1] adopted in July 1985, after many years of negotiation and quite a number of preliminary drafts. Its purpose is to ensure that the consequences of environmentally sensitive projects are properly considered before they are authorized or carried out. Thus it confirms the principles 'laid down... and repeatedly expressed'[2] by the European Communities that the best environmental policy consists of preventive, rather than remedial, action and that it is necessary to identify,

---

[1] Directive 85/337, JO L 175 dated 5.7.85. See, on its elaboration, chapter 18 by L. Krämer in this volume.
[2] L. Krämer, *Focus on European Environmental Law*, London: Sweet and Maxwell, 1992.

at the earliest possible stage, the likely damage to the environment of a particular project or action.

Some European countries, following the stance of the USA, had already adopted legislation providing for prior environmental assessment while others claimed to have comparable requirements. But great differences in conditions could still be observed between the various Member States, so that the application of strict environmental standards by some countries would result in unfavourable competitive conditions, detrimental to the achievement of the common market.

Although the protection of the environment was not yet one of the objectives of the Treaty establishing the European Economic Community, the first programme of action on the environment adopted in 1973 had declared that 'the improvement of the quality of life and the protection of the natural environment were among the fundamental tasks of the Community', and a legal basis was found in articles 100 and 235 of the Treaty.[3]

II   THE ESSENTIAL REQUIREMENTS OF THE DIRECTIVE

The Directive requires Member States to include in their decision-making procedures a process of evaluation of the environmental impacts of public and private projects likely to have adverse environmental effects. Its aim is primarily procedural; it does not purport to govern the legitimacy or correctness of the the final decision, but merely to guarantee that the decision was made after the competent authorities and the public were given the opportunity to have adequate information.[4]

But it goes a little further in its specification that information provided by the impact assessment 'must be taken into consideration in the development consent procedure'. This might be understood as a substantive, as well as a procedural, requirement, and the meaning attached to this phrase will depend on the scope of judicial review of decisions made by national authorities (see below).

---

[3] An indisputable legal basis has been provided by the Single European Act in Art. 130 r, which emphasizes the prominent role of environmental protection among the EC objectives. 'Environmental protection requirements shall be a component of the Communities other policies' (Art. 130r (2)). For a detailed commentary on the Treaty see L. Krämer, *EC Treaty and Environmental Protection*, (2nd edn), London: Sweet and Maxwell, 1995.

[4] As a procedural tool, it has been said 'merely to prohibit uninformed – rather than unwise – agency decision'. See J. Jendroska, Environmental Impact Assessment in Poland in the Light of EC-Directive 337/85 and NEPA, *Jahrbuch des Umwelt- und Technikrechts*, 1993, p. 209–25.

In its present state,[5] the Directive is a mixture of rather broad guidelines and a few specific prescriptions, which allows for problems in implementation. Directive 85/337 is, with the exception of Directive 79/304 on the conservation of wild birds, the Directive which has raised the greatest number of infringement procedures and complaints to the European Commission.[6]

1 The scope of the EIA procedure

Being mainly a procedural tool, the Directive has a limited scope. It applies to projects for which the decision-making procedure requires consent or permission, but not to plans and programmes.[7] The projects to be subject to an environmental impact assessment are those that are 'likely to have significant effects on the environment by virtue, inter alia, of their nature, size and location ...' (Article 2). However, Article 1 contains two general exemptions: the first concerning 'projects serving national defence purposes'; the second, 'projects the details of which are adopted by a specific act of national legislation, since the objectives of this Directive, including that of supplying information are achieved through the legislative process'. The reasons given to justify this second exemption are not very persuasive. Even if it is to be assumed that the legislative process warrants a measure of democratic information, it is doubtful that it takes special care of the environment. Consideration of the environmental impacts of legislative prescriptions is not yet a reality with most national parliaments.

It should be added that the general statement contained in Article 2 is immediately qualified by the provisions of Article 4 which divides relevant projects into two categories: those which are listed in Annex I and for which an EIA is mandatory (except those exempted under Article 2 (3)), and those which are listed in Annex II and 'shall be subject to an assessment ... when Member States consider that their characteristics so require'.

The first category covers industrial plants and infrastructure developments which are obviously most harmful to the environment. Their list is very limited at the moment;[8] even so, a possibility of exemption is provided by Article 2(3) which

---

5   Proposals concerning the modification of the Directive have been presented to the Council, on 21 April 1994, see JO C 130, 12.05.94.

6   As reported in the 10th report on the implementation of EC Law. See Rapport sur l'application du droit communautaire dans le domaine de l'environnement – 1992, taken from chapter G, *Dixième rapport annuel de la Commission sur le contrôle de l'application du droit communautaire*, COM(93), 320/2.

7   Jendroska (1993), *op.cit.*, p. 213.

8   They are classified into nine groups:

allows Member States 'in exceptional cases, to exempt a specific project in whole or in part'. In such a case, however, the Member State must consider whether another form of assessment is appropriate and give the 'public concerned' 'information relating to the exemption and the reasons for granting it'. It also must communicate this information to the Commission prior to granting consent. The Commission, in its turn, has to inform the other Member States and to report to the Council.[9]

The list of projects belonging to the second category is more elaborate. It is divided into twelve groups concerning different types of activities:

1   agriculture;
2   extractive industry;
3   energy industry;
4   processing of metals;
5   manufacture of glass;
6   chemical industry (if not included in Annex I);
7   food industry;
8   textile, leather, wood and paper industries;
9   rubber industry;
10   infrastructure projects;
11   'other projects' – that is, related to tourism, waste disposal, various noxious industrial activities not included in the previous categories;
12   modifications to development projects included in Annex I and projects in Annex I undertaken exclusively or mainly for the development and testing of new methods or products and not used for more than one year.

---

1   crude-oil refineries (excluding undertakings manufacturing only lubricants from crude-oil) and gas installations (over a certain capacity);
2   thermal power stations (over 300 megawatts) and nuclear power stations and reactors (with some exceptions);
3   installations solely designed for the permanent storage or final disposal of radioactive waste;
4   integrated works for the initial melting of cast-iron and steel;
5   diverse installations for extracting or processing asbestos;
6   integrated chemical installations;
7   transport infrastructures (motorways, long-distance railway lines, airports...);
8   trading ports and inland waterways and ports (for vessels of over 1,350 tonnes);
9   waste-disposal installations for the incineration, chemical treatment or land fill of toxic and dangerous wastes.

The proposals for modification add new categories.

9   Information is lacking about how and when this power has been exercised by Member States.

For all works and projects belonging to this second group which comprises all sorts of extremely polluting activities, it is provided by Article 4(2) that Member States may designate certain classes of projects or develop criteria and thresholds to determine which projects will be considered as requiring an EIA. In so doing, they will have to take into account the nature, size and location of the concerned development.

The wording of the Directive is so ambiguous that it is not clear whether there is a strict obligation for Member States to take specific implementation measures in this respect. Most European states seem to have implicitly considered that there was not. According to the tenth report on the control of EC law, all Member States, except France and the UK, have been satisfied with a minimal transposition of the Directive, providing for mandatory EIA procedures only for Annex I projects and leaving Annex II projects to be dealt with eventually on a case by case basis without any formal definition of guidelines. In such cases, the Commission considers that the Directive has not been properly transferred into national legislations and that the Member States are in breach of Community law.

The modifications recently adopted by the Commission aim to ensure a better enforcement of the Directive for Annex II projects. It proposes to establish common criteria based on the size and location of the project, the type of waste produced, the risks of accidents, and to require an EIA for all projects likely to affect significantly special protection zones.[10]

A tightening of existing rules is all the more needed as the Commission receives a great number of individual complaints arguing that developments likely to cause significant and even irreversible damages to the environment are being authorized without any preliminary impact assessment.[11]

2 The content of the EIA

On the whole the Directive leaves broad discretion to the Member States concerning the form and content of the EIA. Here again we find the same mixture of minimum compulsory elements and of broad requests posing problems in interpretation.

Although the Directive does not include a definition of the environment, its Article 3 gives a quite comprehensive description of the impacts to be taken into account when making an EIA. These include 'the direct and indirect effects' on

- human beings, fauna and flora,

---

[10] COM(93) 575.
[11] *Dixième rapport annuel de la Commission, op.cit.,* para. 3.

–   soil, water, air, climate and the landscape,
–   the interaction between the factors mentionned in the first and second in-
    dents,
–   material assets and the cultural heritage.

Annex III gives further details about what is to be understood by 'direct and indirect' effects which may include cumulative, short- and long-term, permanent and
temporary, positive and negative impacts.

Article 5(2) determines the minimum content of the EIA while Annex III details the information referred to in the Directive itself. The Annex is not simply
explanatory, it adds new elements not mentioned in the Directive, and the legal
value to be attached to it is not very clear.

The EIA includes at least a description of the project, its location, size and design, a description of the measures envisaged to minimize and eventually remedy
its adverse effects, the data required to identify and assess the main effects the
project is likely to have on the environment, and a non-technical summary of the
first three items. Annex III adds two essential elements:

1   an outline of the main alternatives envisaged by the developer and of the
    reasons for his choice from an environmental point of view;
2   a description of the significant effects that the project is likely to have on
    the environment in terms of use of natural resources, emissions of pollut-
    ants, creation of nuisances, and waste disposal.

It also explicitly asks for compensation for adverse effects of a project.

There is some controversy as to the legal value of Annex III. Are the informa-
tions prescribed by it to be supplied in every case by the developer unless he is
exempted, which seems to be the view of the Commission and of some Member
States, or are they optional and left to the discretion of Member States? Since Article 13 of the Directive reserves the right for the States 'to lay down stricter rules
regarding scope and procedure', the reasons for optional provisions are unclear.[12]

On the form of the EIA, the Directive is rather concise; it only requires that it
should be presented 'in an appropriate manner'.

---

[12] Substantial modifications of Art. 5 are proposed by the draft: Art. 15(1) would be
completely revised and Art. 15(2) would be deleted. The content of the EIA would be
determined through a scoping procedure between the applicant and the consent
authorities and by reference to Annex III. Only relevant and reasonable data – considering the state of the art and of scientific knowledge – would have to be required from
the applicant.

3 The author of the EIA

The Directive designates the developer as the person who has to supply the necessary information (Article 5) about the project but leaves open the question of who is to sign the final document. It could be the developer himself, or the administration in charge of the consent procedure, or an independent body or expert. Neither does it specify at what stage of the administrative procedure the EIA should take place. Different kinds of solutions may be imagined: the EIA could be made after the consultation of authorities having specific environmental responsibilities or not. It could incorporate public comments or not. Various solutions have been adopted by the national legislations as will be seen below.

4 Administrative consultation and public participation

The Directive is more explicit concerning consultation and public participation requirements, although, on close scrutiny, many questions remain unanswered. Rightly, the Directive insists on the need for administrative coordination and on the consultation of the authorities 'likely to be concerned by the project by reason of their specific environmental responsibilities' (Article 6(1)). They must be given the opportunity to express their opinion, but without any specification about when (that is, at what stage of the consent procedure) this opinion is to be requested. Adequate arrangements are to be made by Member States.

Public participation, too, is an essential requisite. The public must be informed of any request for development consent and information gathered pursuant to Article 5 must be made available to them. The public 'concerned' must also be given the opportunity to express an opinion before the project is 'initiated'. But who is the public concerned? When is a project initiated? The Directive gives no answer to such questions.

Article 7 refers explicitly to transfrontier pollution and requires that 'where a Member State is aware that a project is likely to have significant effects on the environment of another Member State or where a Member State likely to be significantly affected so requests', the Member State in which the project is to be undertaken has a duty to provide the other Member State with the same information as to its nationals. It is then up to the concerned neighbouring Member State to inform its own citizens. [13]

---

[13] One of the main objectives of the revised Directive is to set EC legislation in conformity with the Epsoo Convention on Environmental Impact Assessment in a Transboundary Context signed by the Member States and the Community on 25 February 1991. Obligations concerning mutual information and cooperation and public participation of foreign citizens are strengthened in the new draft of Art. 7.

III   PROBLEMS IN IMPLEMENTATION BY MEMBER STATES

The EC Directive had to be transferred into national legislation within three years of its notification – that is, before 8 July 1988. Most Member States were late in its implementation, which led the Commission to bring judicial proceedings against some of them. Various factors made it difficult to transfer the Directive, in particular constitutional problems and the allocation of competences between federal and national or regional levels. This was the case with Germany and Belgium.

It should also be remembered that the national legal background differed widely between countries. France, for instance, had formally introduced the 'Environmental Impact Study' for public and private projects by an Act of 1976 relating to the protection of nature. In other European countries – in the UK for instance – procedures already existed, which were considered as almost equivalent, particularly procedures for considering environmental effects in planning decisions. Another Member State of the European Communities, the Netherlands, had made long and detailed preliminary studies without reaching any positive result.

So it appears that the question of the environmental assessment had already been much debated, but that this idea was not easily accepted by all concerned. This may be why the Directive leaves such a broad discretion in matters of implementation: ' ... the Directive is drafted in broad and vague terms'[14] so that, although its interpretation has to conform to that of the European Court of Justice, it allows for a variety of choices in specific implementation procedures. Article 2 (2) expressly provides for flexibility when stating:

> The environmental impact assessment may be integrated into the existing procedures for consent to projects... or failing this into other procedures or into procedures to be established to comply with the aims of this Directive.

It can be observed that there is a marked difference between the French and the other European systems; this is probably due to the fact that France had introduced the Environmental Impact Study nearly ten years before by an Act of 1976 relating to the protection of nature. As required by the French constitution, this Act only set the general legal framework and left detailed implementation to regulatory instruments. This was done by a first decree of 12 October 1977 completed and amended by a decree of 25 February 1993.[15] Thus, there is a single set of regula-

---

14   J. Alder, Environmental impact assessment – the inadequacies of English law, *Journal of Environmental Law*, **5**,(2), 1993, pp.203–20, at 205.

15   This last decree purports, at last, to place French regulations in complete conformity with EC Law. At the time when the Directive was passed, France already had a rather progressive legislation concerning EIA, and the French government probably considered that there was no need for specific implementation measures. In fact conformity was lacking in several important respects (analysis of indirect and secondary effects,

tions modifying nearly all the relevant administrative procedures with a view to inspiring the bureaucracy with a new perception of environmental issues. Hopefully, the Minister of the Environment saw in it 'a quiet revolution'.

In the UK, as in Germany, EIA was introduced in domestic law in order to implement the Directive, with some reluctance and even some delay. The Directive seems not to have been fully implemented in Germany where the formulation of administrative guidelines is still in process.

Further differences appear between these three systems: they concern all the core questions posed by environmental assessment procedures; the definition of projects subject to EIA; the content and preparation of the EIA and its effects on the decision; and public participation.

1   Options in implementing projects requiring an EIA

Following the lead of the Directive, all Member States, except France, have opted for a positive listing of projects to which the procedure applies either mandatorily or under specified conditions. This method is considered as easier and simpler and leaving no doubt to concerned people as to legal requirements. In fact, on closer scrutiny, this is not the case as is evident from a comparison between the English and French systems.

a)   The British approach

In the UK, the Directive was transferred into domestic law by means of several statutory instruments whose aim was a strict transposition of the European provisions.[16] The main one, issued by the Department of the Environment, is the Town and Country Planning (Assessment of Environmental Effects) Regulations 1988 which applies only to developments requiring planning permission. Other statutory instruments had to be issued for works or projects outside the scope of Town

---

summary in clear language...) and pressure from the Commission and from conservationists (through a number of judicial actions) helped to force the government into compliance.

On EIA in France see in particular Etudes d'Impact, special issue of *Revue Juridique de l'Environnement*, 1981, (2); C. Huglo, Etudes d'impact écologique, *JurisClasseur Environnement*, Fasc., pp. 190, 191; M. Prieur, Les études d'impact en droit français, *Environnement et Société*, (5), Arlon, Belgium: FUL, 1990; Les études d'impact et le contrôle du juge administratif en France, *RJE*, (1), 1991, p. 23.

[16]   On EIA in the UK see Alder (1993), *op.cit.*; M. Grant, Environmental Assessment in the United Kingdom: Implementation of the EC Directive, *Environnement et Société*, (5), Arlon, Belgium: FUL, 1990.

and Country Planning legislation and for which an EIA appeared necessary: afforestation (financed by grant or loan); land drainage improvement works; salmon farming works in marine waters; highways; harbour works; electricity and pipeline works and so on.

The Town and Country Planning (Assessment of Environmental Effects) Regulations determine in Schedules I and II the types of developments which require an EIA. Schedule I, which is the almost literal translation of Annex I of the Directive (except point 12) draws the list of works and developments for which an EIA is mandatory. Schedule II lists the types of developments for which an EIA may be required as they are likely to have significant effects by virtue of such factors as their nature, size or location.

The questions remain: What is a significant impact? Who is to decide and by reference to what criteria? A DoE circular (15/88) proposes general criteria:

> EA will apply to the second class of projects where they are major and of more than local importance, or irrespective of size, they affect particularly sensitive or vulnerable locations, or where they have unusually complex and potentially adverse consequences making it desirable that a detailed, expert analysis of those consequences take place....

It also gives some detailed instructions and guidelines,[17] but the decision ultimately lies with the local planning authority.

In practice, a rather complex and time-consuming machinery has been set up. First the applicant has to ask the local planning authority whether the proposed development is one to which the EA procedure applies by virtue of Schedules I or II. The request must be accompanied with a plan showing the location of the project, a brief description of the nature and purpose of the development and its possible effects on the enviroment, and any such other information as the applicant wishes to provide. The authority, having eventually asked for further information, has to answer within a period of three weeks (or more if agreed). If they consider, in case of a Schedule II development, that an EA is required before granting planning permission, they have to deliver their opinion in 'a written statement giving clearly and precisely their full reasons for their conclusion' (SI 88/1199, s.5). When planning permission is requested with no mention of an environmental statement, the local authority can notify the applicant that such a statement is required, giving full reasons for their opinion. In either case, the applicant may appeal to the Secretary of State for direction on the matter.(The applicant may also submit an environmental statement on his own initiative.)

These arrangements leave broad discretion to the administrative authority which ultimately has to decide whether or not an assessment is required. Its deci-

---

17   For a clear description of this machinery see ibid.

sion could be challenged in court, though, apparently, with very little chance of success. It seems a well established doctrine that, except in case a of complete ir-rationality, the local authority would be considered by the court as having exclusive jurisdiction over the matter.[18]

In conclusion, it appears that a method of lists without clear and compulsory criteria is open to criticism for at least two reasons:

1   It is lacking in certainty and transparency, first for the developers, and even more for third parties, especially when the authority considers for reasons of its own (which have not to be explicit) that there is no need for an environmental assessment. Only the decision requiring that an EIA be made has to contain a statement of reasons. A negative decision need not be justified, and so cannot be challenged by third parties.

2   This uncertainty is not favourable to an early consideration of the environmental effects of a project and to the research of alternative solutions.

b)   The French approach

The French take a quite different approach. The general idea is not to rely on lists but to adopt other criteria – that is, financial and ecological criteria.

The rule laid down by the 1976 Act is that all important works or developments and all works or developments likely to have significant impacts on the natural environment must be subject to a preliminary environmental study in order to assess their impacts. Although the principle is quite simple its implementation proved to be complicated and resulted in an intricate system of exemptions concerning:

•   maintenance and repairs whatever the works concerned;
•   certain categories of works or developments , either because their impact on the environment is considered as negligible (these are listed in Annex I to the decree) or on the assumption that their environmental impact has been separately considered under planning regulations (these are listed in Annex II);
•   works or developments whose cost is less than 12 million Fr. (the original figure was 6 million Fr. in 1977, but was raised to 12 million Fr. in February 1993). But, in order to correct the potentially harmful effects of this wide-ranging exemption, some categories of works considered as likely to have damaging impacts on the natural environment are subject to an environmental impact study (EIS) whatever their cost. They are listed in Annex III to the decree and comprise industrial plants known as 'classified installations', mining and quarrying works and so on.

---

[18]   See Alder (1993), *op.cit.*, p. 210.

Finally, Annex IV lists categories of works exempted from a comprehensive impact assessment but subject to a lesser form of environmental scrutiny (*notice
d'impact*). This machinery is probably unduly sophisticated and despite its ambi-
tion, it introduces questionable exemptions. However, after a period of adjustment
it seems to have been rather well understood by all concerned and it makes clear
exactly when an EIA is required. The main problems in interpretation have occurred in relation to questions of cost. For global projects to be realized progressively (or in successive stages) developers are tempted to divide the cost in order to
remain below the financial threshold. In such cases, it is the total amount of the
project which is to be considered. This has been confirmed by the 1993 decree as
well as by judicial interpretation. For instance, in a recent case, the High Administrative Court (*Conseil d'Etat*) considered that the construction of a road to reach a
new cross-country skiing station formed part of a global project which included
providing access, car parks, ski trails and other associated facilities (restaurants,
shops and so on). Permission to build the road should not have been delivered
without a preliminary impact assessment of the whole project, and the authorization was quashed at the request of a local opposition group.[19]

It is essential to know whether or not an EIA is required, as the lack of it, when
required, has significant legal consequences. In urgent proceedings brought in an
administrative court, the judge must order a temporary stay of execution of the
decision made without the required EIS. This is a quite exceptional provision as it
leaves no choice to the judge, demonstrating the high value attached to this procedure by the legislator. The judge may also quash the decision itself as not complying with a substantial procedural requirement.

2   The environmental assessment: author, elaboration process and content

Other differences are also to be seen in this respect between French, German and
English regulations. French legislation has a fixed and uniform approach while
Germany and the UK show more flexibility and a greater cooperation between the
applicant, the consent authorities and, eventually, the public.

a)   *The French approach*

In France the environmental impact study (EIS) is usually undertaken by the applicant or the public or private developer, unless the law provides by decree that it
must be made by a public person for some particular works or developments. He

---

19 Conseil d'Etat, 24 February 1993, Melle Descours, *RJE*, (2), 1993, p. 279.

may engage professional consultants to assist him and, since the 1993 decree, the name and complete designation of the author must appear on the final document. The important point is that there is no administrative or independent control over the EIS before it is handed over with the application to the responsible consent authority. It is eventually submitted, in the course of the consent proceedings, to various public authorities that are to be consulted on the application. During this phase, the Minister of the Environment may call up the EIS on his own initiative or at the request of a private or public person. From the day he has received the file, the Minister has a term of 30 days to give an advisory opinion on the EIS. Apparently, the only legal effect of this measure is to compel the responsible authority to wait until the end of the prescribed term to open the public inquiry or to make the final decision. It should be mentioned that the Minister is not given any explicit powers, such as asking for further information or giving any directions to the consent authorities. As a result, the only control exercised upon the EIS is by way of judicial review of the consent decision in administrative courts.

The EIS must comprise five 'chapters':

1   a description of the initial state of the site and of its environment, in particular natural resources, agricultural lands, forests;
2   an analysis of the direct and indirect, temporary and permanent effects of the project, in particular effects on fauna and flora, sites and landscapes, soil, water, air, climate, natural areas and ecological balance, the protection of the cultural heritage, and, if relevant, on the neighbourhood, and on public health and safety;
3   the reasons for which the project has been retained among other options. The French law does not use the word 'alternatives' which would have a precise meaning, but the word *parti* (option) so that this requirement has a limited scope, merely amounting to the necessity for the developer to give the reasons why he has chosen one particular option among other posibilities envisaged by himself. There is no obligation to examine other more environmentally friendly alternatives proposed by third parties during the public enquiry on the project;[20]
4   the mitigation measures envisaged by the applicant and their cost. The measures proposed by the applicant can be imposed as a condition of the delivery of the permit or licence;
5   a description of the predictive methods used and of the problems met of a scientific or technical character and a non technical summary (added in February 1993).

---

[20]   For instance for the passage of a motorway: Conseil d'Etat (section), 17 June 1983, Commune de Montfort, *RJE*, 1984, p. 53, Conclusions Pinault.

The lack of one of the elements required or their gross inadequacy has frequently been construed as non-compliance with a substantial procedural requirement, leading to the decision being quashed. When the EIS is grossly inadequate, it may even be considered as totally missing.[21]

Although the format of the EIS is quite standardized, the law provides that it should be in relation to the importance of the project. This gives the applicant some discretion in view of the particular circumstances: the nature and character-istics of the project, its location and so on. In case of judicial review, the court will consider each case on its merits, and assess whether the administrative authorities and the public had the means to be fully informed.[22] If not, the EIS will be consid-ered as inadequate and the decision quashed. Administrative courts exercise close scrutiny over the content of impact studies and do not hesitate to enter into very technical considerations. Defence groups often rely on 'bad impact assessments' to obtain the annulment of controversial authorizations. This may not be ultimately very efficient as, after being obtained on procedural grounds, the decision may be reversed once the EIS is amended.

Finally, beyond its procedural effects, the impact study may have a substantial influence on the decision itself and serve to appreciate its legality. Administrative courts are competent to review the content of administrative decisions (though not to substitute their own decision or give injunction to the administration). They ensure that the law has not been misunderstood or misapplied. The data provided by an environmental impact study may serve to establish that public authorities have obviously been mistaken[23] in granting a permit or in licensing an activity. For instance, the permission to work a quarry on a site where protected species of plants could be found was considered as in violation of the law.[24]

---

[21] The case law is very important and has been analysed by specialized writers, in particu-lar C. Huglo and M. Prieur. Deficiencies considered as substantial frequently concern the analysis of the effects of the proposed activity on the fauna, the flora, the land-scapes and the natural resources, but the main bulk is furnished by impact assessments which omit to propose or evaluate adequate mitigation measures.

[22] CAA Nancy, 4 November 1993, SA Union française des pétroles, *RJE*, 1994, p. 71.

[23] In French, 'erreur manifeste d'appréciation'.

[24] TA Amiens, 20 November 1992, Association Aisne-Environnement, *RJE*, 1993, p. 577 (note: P. P. Danna et E. Valette). See also the decision of a municipal council to authorize in its local plan future urban development in wetlands well known for their ecological and biological value, TA Orléans, 29 March 1988, M. Jacques Rommel et autres, *RJE*, 1989, p. 209.

b)   Other approaches

Germany and the UK both have different, though not similar, approaches concerning the making of the environmental assessment. They have in common a closer cooperation between the applicant and the public authorities and a greater flexibility concerning the content of the EIA.

In the UK[25] it seems that the local planning authority (or the other responsible authority for projects outside the scope of planning permission) have the principal responsibility for determining the content of the EA and its adequacy. There are minimum requirements: there must be a written statement submitted by the applicant which must comprise the 'minimum specified information', but further information may be required by the local planning authority upon consideration of the location, the nature, the importance of the project and the quality of the existing environment. The distinction between the minimum requirements and what further information may be requested roughly follows what is indicated in Article 3 and Annex III of the Directive. There is an informal 'scoping' procedure consisting of a dialogue between the applicant and the consent authority about the information that is to be supplied. It may be assumed that there is no 'environmental statement' if the minimum requirements are not met, and that, as a result, the authority has 'no jurisdiction to determine the application to which it relates'. The applicant can lodge an appeal to the Secretary of State against the local authority's decision to ask for further information if this is considered excessive or inappropriate.[26]

As pointed out by M. Grant,[27] some considerations plead in favour of good impact assessments: in particular, the importance of the process for the determination of the application and the possibility of cross-examination at a public inquiry that forces the applicant to respond to objections.

Germany gives the example of a methodical and integrated approach.[28] At a preliminary stage, the developer informs the responsible authority of the planned project. The required information is determined through a 'scoping' process. The responsible authority, after consultation with the applicant, interested agencies, experts and environmental associations decides the methods, content and scope of the EIA and informs the applicant in writing of the documents he has to produce. The authority may also require the applicant to describe the configuration and environmental effects of project alternatives he has considered.

---

25   Grant, *op.cit.*
26   For a detailed analysis of existing case law, see Alder (1993) and Grant (1990), *ops cit.*
27   Grant (199), *op.cit.*, P. 21–2.
28   Cf. Gerd Winter, *German Environmental Law, Basic Texts and Introduction*, Dordrecht: Martinus Nijhoff, 1994, p.14 *et seq.*

A summary description of expected impacts of the project is drawn after the necessary information and data have been collected and a public hearing has been held. Thus public participation is integrated in the evaluation process. Then comes the proper evaluation of the environmental impacts which is made by the responsible authority. Whether the evaluation should be based on purely ecological grounds, or whether other interests should be considered is a controversial matter.[29] Anyway, the decision, with a statement of reasons, is made available to the applicant and to the public – especially to the members of the public who have raised objections.

3   Information and public participation in the EIA procedure

Information and public participation are essential ingredients of the environmental assessment procedure,[30] but their implementation has been subject to severe criticism by the Commission,[31] the Directive and implementing measures having failed to achieve a real public participation of European citizens in decisions which most directly concern them. Individual complaints are steadily increasing and frequently point to similar deficiencies: information comes too late to the citizens, public consultation is merely formal, and objections and opinions are not taken into account especially if they bear on environmental issues.

These general statements have to be qualified although, obviously, how public participation is organized and integrated in the evaluation process is a condition of its efficiency and credibility. There are three degrees in integration of the public:

1   The public is excluded from the procedure until the end of the preliminary stage, and sometimes until the decision has been made.

In France, for instance, the EIS is available to the public only when the public inquiry on the project is opened.[32] Although not all projects liable to EIS are liable to a mandatory public inquiry the requirements are tending to harmonize. Nevertheless, some projects require an impact statement but are not subject to public inquiry, so that some special publicity can only be

---

29   Ibid.
30   See Art. 6(2), (3) of the Directive.
31   Dixième rapport annuel de la Commission, *op.cit.*, para. 1.7.
32   Art. 5 of the 1977 decree. The EIS forms part of the documents that must be made available to the public for his information during the whole public inquiry. On public inquiries, see Public Participation.

organized after the decision has been made, although before the project's implementation.[33]

2 The public is informed in the course of the preliminary proceedings and is at least given an opportunity to express its opinion before the EIA is completed (and to participate in a public inquiry whenever one is held).

This is the case in the UK for projects requiring an EIA under the planning or other consent procedures.[34]

3 The public is involved in the evaluation process from an early stage and may intervene in a public hearing which forms part of the process of information gathering, as in Germany.

On the whole, it appears that public participation is organized much in the same way whether or not there is an environmental impact assessment. No special device seems to have been set up to encourage public involvement when an environmental evaluation is to be made.

IV CONCLUSION

Environmental assessment is tending to become a major tool in the proactive management of natural resources and its importance is steadily increasing as it is required in a growing number of international treaties and national legislation.[35] This chapter has attempted to give concrete exemples of the main problems met in drafting legislation about environmental assessment. Some important matters have not been considered – although they probably should have been – for instance, the questions of the liability of the author(s) of the statement, of the need for better methodological tools.

It might be interesting to consider the goals assigned to environmental assessments. Currently it is chiefly oriented towards preventive action, but it could also become an instrument for the monitoring and improvement of the quality of the environment in the neighbourhood of polluting installations or a basis for the negotiation of voluntary agreements or other forms of self-regulation.

---

[33] Art. 6 of the 1977 decree. The public is entitled to look at the EIS after 'the decision of authorization, confirmation or execution' has been made and adequate publicity is required. It still leaves an opportunity to challenge the EIS through judicial proceedings.

[34] For instance, developments proposed by local planning authorities and works coming under the new system of Integrated Pollution Control contained in Part I of the Environmental Protection Act 1990. On IPC, see S. Ball, S. Bell, *Environmental Law*, London: Blackstone Press Ltd, 1991, ch. 10.

[35] In some countries the number of impact assessments made every year is already very high: 6000–7000 in France for instance as it is required for small as well as big projects, against 70–80 in the UK (figures given by M. Prieur and M. Grant).

6 Freedom of Environmental Information[1]

Gerd Winter

Table of Contents

I NATIONAL VARIATIONS

Comparative examination can establish that the particular resistance to, or pro-pensity towards, freedom of information in a given country is influenced by its specific constitutional history. For example, in Germany, access to official files has traditionally been restricted to persons whose individual substantive rights may be affected by an imminent administrative decision. The right to know is seen as an essential element – indeed the primary element – of the legal protection of the substantive rights and it is not designed to guarantee participation in public decision-making. Historically this can be explained by what is called the German *Sonderweg* (peculiar path) towards parliamentary democracy. Eighteenth-century German absolutism was basically benevolent and did not provoke strong demo-cratic opposition as it did in France. The German bourgeoisie, afraid of the politi-cal potential of the rising working classes, compromised with the nobility to es-tablish a constitutional monarchy rather than a parliamentary republic. They wanted parliamentary and other participation in governmental decision-making where they deemed their individual rights to personal freedom and property were affected, but let the monarch rather than the parliament decide about other politi-cal issues, thereby hampering the development of a full democracy.

In the UK, in principle at least, those whose individual rights may be affected have, until recently, had a right of access to official files, though subject to impor-tant qualifications. In contrast to Germany, free public access has frequently been

---

[1] This chapter is based on the introduction to Gerd Winter (ed.), *Öffentlichkeit von Um-weltinformationen*, Baden-Baden: Nomos Verlag, 1990.

provided to final administrative decisions and a number of registers containing official information. However there is an overall reluctance to allow extensive participation in the governmental decision-making process prior to the decision itself. At first sight, this may appear surprising given John Locke's influential definition of government as the 'trust' of society. While this construction is indeed taken seriously in British constitutional doctrine, it is not the public at large but rather parliament (which represents it) to which the executive branch is made responsible. Given the multitude of factual circumstances of which a minister may remain ignorant, and given the quasi-autonomy of many administrative bodies, a minister has in fact little direct control over day to day decision making, so that in reality ministerial responsibility to parliament has become little more than a fiction. Nevertheless, this fiction has served as an argument against access to information outside parliamentary channels.

France provides an example of how a country with a highly professionalized and centralized administration can abandon official secrecy. The relevant legislation is the Act of 1978 on access to administrative documents which was part of a group of laws enacted in the late 1970s designed to promote public participation in administrative decision-making. On the one hand the policy behind the legislation flowed from a broad democratic movement pushed by the student rebellion in the 1960s and reflecting, in a broader sense, more radical French democratic traditions. On the other hand, it may also be traced from the French Orleanist tradition of benign autocracy. From this second perspective the Act can be seen as a gift from above, from the enlightened bureaucratic élite searching for greater legitimacy at a time of intensified technocratic intervention. These two strands in the relaxation of administrative secrecy have combined in the effort to alter bureaucratic routines, and the seriousness of the undertaking can be shown by the establishment of a supervisory commission charged with the implementation of the Act, the *Commission d'Acces aux Documents Administratifs.*

In the USA absolutism has not been an historical and symbolical phenomenon against or through which the public has had to struggle and establish itself. Certainly, as elsewhere, bureaucracy in the USA has a real tendency towards secrecy, but distrust of bureaucracy has led to the need for public participation becoming established as an undisputed societal value in America. Ministerial responsibility to parliament is not a viable alternative as an important part of the administrative branch of government – that is, the many regulatory agencies are neither responsible to a particular ministry nor derive full legitimacy from Congress. As a result these agencies must establish public approval directly, and this in particular explains their participatory rule-making and adjudicatory procedures and the acceptance of open access to information.

An examination of socialist configurations completes our overview of the various national variations. In the German Democratic Republic, before its unification with the Federal Republic, no right of access to administrative information was provided by law, but neither did a legal principle of official secrecy exist. According to the official socialist conception the state and the people were identical. The state was constructed as the people's 'committee'. In practice this resulted in the attitude that the people did not need to have individual rights of access because, by implication, they had access collectively. Equally, the state did not need to establish secrecy by law because, as the state *was* the people, there was in fact no official secrecy. Of course, this vision of popular and state 'identity' contradicted the actual clash of the interests between the state and the citizen. This tension finally contributed to the 1989 November revolution.

In this respect, Poland was more realistic, preserving some of its pre-war tradition of the rule of law and pluralist democracy even during the socialist period. Much as in West Germany it established a right of access to files for those who are aggrieved with respect to their individual rights through action of the administration. To this a socialist component was added so that so-called societal organizations, ranging from labour unions to environmental associations, were also given a right of access and of participation in every administrative procedure. However, as these organizations were closely supervised by the state they could not develop as a real opposition.

II EMPIRICAL OBSERVATIONS

Before turning to concrete legal forms of access to official information, I would like to make some empirical observations concerning the consequences of the introduction of access laws.[2] There is, however, a caveat to be made. The impact of new legislation on actual practice cannot be measured precisely. A new law will most probably have some effect, but many other factors are necessary in order to direct society and government towards the envisaged aim: in our case, making bureaucracies open-minded and inducing the actual exercise of rights of participation by the public may depend more on the general information-culture than on the law. As a result, much remains to be done once access laws have been adopted. Nonetheless, laws are indispensable in that they can operate to preserve a culture of openness in time of decline, and to strengthen it in a time of growth. Our data shall be presented in the form of answers to arguments against freedom of information legislation:

1 **'Free access leads to an additional workload for public officials'**
There are enormous differences between individual states and agencies in respect of frequency of requests and the workload arising from responding to

---

[2] The following information draws on an empirical investigation reported in ibid.

these requests for information. For instance, the US Consumer Product Safety Commission handles about 13,000 requests for information per year, to deal with which 16 full-time posts have been created. On the other hand, a French department which supervises 1,500 classified factories receives only about three to four requests per year. This reflects, among other things, the differences in the information cultures already mentioned. But where a heavy workload results the solution must be to appoint more personnel. If open administration is considered desirable a society, logically, must be prepared to bear the related cost.

2   **'Freedom of access will be perverted as a means through which business will gather information about competitors'**
Whereas in the 'open systems' we researched – that is, France, Sweden, the Netherlands and Canada – most requests in the environmental and consumer protection fields came from concerned persons and associations, access rights in the USA are, it is true, used much more frequently by businesses and even specialized companies, which make a business out of conveying freedom of information services to clients. For instance, of the 41,500 requests received by the Food and Drug Administration in 1987, 80 per cent were filed by regulated and other industries, 6 per cent by the press, 4 per cent by private persons and 1 per cent by public interest groups. Indeed, why should competitors in a market economy, whose very concept relies on the free flow of information, be refused information (not legitimate trade secrets, of course) about their fellow competitors? Many requests are from companies seeking to establish whether they are being treated equally by the agency; others come from businesses wishing to sell technology to companies with a low environmental performance. These, I believe, are perfectly legitimate goals.

3   **'Business will become more reticent in voluntarily providing agencies with information'**
In open systems, business develops greater awareness and caution with respect to sensitive information so that, in the interaction with administrative bodies, more information is declared to be a trade secret. Cases have been reported in Sweden and the Netherlands where firms have refused to give voluntary information about an environmental aspect of their processes and products (even if this information could not be deemed a trade secret), when the relevant agency failed to agree not to disclose the information. Yet, although such a change in attitude may be an unavoidable cost of opening up two-tier relations with third parties, the consequences could be mitigated and, in particular, the giving of information could be made obligatory rather than voluntary. For its own part, the agency could secure the confidence of the information

suppliers by careful appraisal of secrecy claims, and this could be reinforced by reliable practice.

4 **'Business will be harmed by frequent disclosure of trade secrets'**
Although we asked all our respondents both in private business and administrative agencies about this point not one single concrete case was mentioned where a firm was economically harmed by the disclosure of information. Those who make this claim ignore the fact that most agencies almost overanxiously either accede to the firms' initial secrecy claim or give them a prior notice for possible comment before they release potentially sensitive information.

5 **'Access rights are covertly counteracted in practice'**
This argument is frequently put forward by environmental associations in France, Germany, Italy and Greece but less so in Sweden and the Netherlands. In the USA it is made with regard to some, but not all, agencies. Obstacles to access experienced by associations include high requirements as regards specifying the requested document, delayed responses on the part of the agency, intolerable reading conditions within the agency, lack of copying facilities, high charges, broad interpretations of exceptions to disclosure and so on. Yet, quite obviously, these experiences do not mitigate against stricter access legislation.

6 **'Formalized free access will cause informal sources of information to dry up'**
Odd as it sounds, this argument is not too far-fetched. Certainly, informal channels of information do exist in the shadow of formal official secrecy. To a growing extent third party networks are infiltrating into bureaucracies to 'whistle-blow' (that is, give clandestine telephone information) and 'brown-bag' (that is, mail information in brown paper bags). Also, substantive legal protection rights are sometimes traded for the voluntary provision of information. For instance, when the German chemical company Hoechst planned to build a new pesticide manufacturing factory in Frankfurt, a neighbouring objector withdrew his complaint, which would have delayed the realization of the project considerably, in exchange for the firm's promise to release process- and product-related information otherwise not accessible to him.[3] The argument goes that formalization of information flows might, by channelling its wilder flows, make such interactions more effective as far as non-sensitive information is concerned and, at the same time, more restrictive for sensitive

---

[3] See the case study presented by M. Führ, Umweltinformationen im Genehmigungsverfahren, in G. Winter (1990), *op. cit.*, p. 149.

information. I doubt that this expectation is correct. The US example shows that formalized free access and additional informal communications can go hand in hand. In any case, nobody who would make this assumption would seriously oppose free access rights.

III   FRAMING FREE ACCESS RIGHTS AND EXEMPTIONS

In the following I shall take the perspective of a law-maker who devises a new access law under EC Directive 90/313 on Free Access to Environmental Information[4] and takes the different national laws and experiences into account.

The Directive establishes an access right independent of showing an interest. Access shall be given to environmental information. The Directive defines what this is and states exceptions to the access right. It also requires that the right be legally protected. For the transformation into national law it should be noted that, as the Directive is based on Article 130 s of the EC Treaty, Article 130 t is applicable, which allows the Member States to go further. For instance, the national legislator may want to open access to more information than that which the Directive rather narrowly defines as environmental information. Also, the legislator has some discretion – and may exert it in favour of greater public access or public secrecy – in concretizing the exemptions to the access right (the protection of trade secrets, privacy and governmental deliberations). In this there is a risk that the doors which are to be opened by the basic right of access lead ultimately to rooms which have been carefully emptied through a broad definition of the exemptions.

1   Prerequisites of access rights

As mentioned above, the right must be framed as a general right open to everybody. *No specific legal interest has to be shown.* Foreign citizens are included, no matter whether they belong to a state inside or outside the Union. This may confer advantages on those searching in a more open foreign state for information not accessible in their own state. The USA has been used as such a source. For instance, expert reports on environmental pollution and its effects have generously been made available by the Environmental Protection Agency to foreigners. On occasion, this information has even concerned a situation in the country of the foreign requestor which was not accessible there.

So far as the *object of access* is concerned it makes a difference whether the agency selects the data or whether this is left to the requestor. Selection costs

---

[4]   OJ. L 158/56 of 23 June 1990.

worktime but is linked also to the power to determine what will be released and what will not. He who selects the relevant information also defines the dividing line between secrecy and openness. Little power remains with the agency when the object of access is the entire file, as is the case in the USA, Canada and Sweden. There, a requestor not only receives information concerning the matter enquired about but also concerning the handling of the matter by the authorities – whether it was delayed, formed part of a trade off, was treated seriously, pushed through and so forth. This 'operative' information is useful in respect of possible legal action and more generally contributes to effective participation. Most operative information remains secret when the object of access is a public register, as was formerly the case in the UK, or administrative documents, as it still is in France, because operational information emerges from the whole of a file rather than from a single datum or document. The EC Directive leaves it to the Member States to decide how the information should be made available. German law, for instance, gives the agency discretion to grant access to the files or to hand separate documents to the requestor.[5] Even more broadly, English law refers to 'such form, and at such times and places, as may be reasonable'.[6]

The *scope of accessible information* is, in principle, not limited in those legal systems (such as the USA, Canada, France, the Netherlands, Denmark and Sweden) which have introduced general freedom of information legislation. It would be interesting to know why, in the other European countries, the debate about introducing a general access right has focused on *environmental information* rather than on other or more general categories of information. It could be that, for most such categories (possibly excluding the area of consumer protection information which also requires access legislation), an interest-bound access right is sufficient. This can be shown by the fact that in those countries which have an interest-free access right most information requestors do in fact have an individual interest to accede to the information.[7] For these persons the interest-based legal systems provide access equally well. By contrast, environmental information is an exemplary case of the kind of information which is very often not only of individual but of collective interest. Given its general importance it is unsurprising that a lack of access to information has caused particular dissatisfaction in the environmental field.

---

[5] Art. 4, para. 1, sentence 2 Umweltinformationsgesetz (Environmental Information Act), reprinted in G. Winter (ed.), *German Environmental Law. Basic Texts and Introduction*. Dordrecht: Martinus Nijhoff, 1994.

[6] The Environmental Information Regulations 1992, s. 3 para. 5.

[7] Commission d'Access aux Documents Administratifs, *6ième Rapport d'Activités*, Paris: La Documentation Française, 1990.

The range of information open to public access under the Directive goes beyond simply environmental quality data and includes information about emissions and pollution abatement measures. At first sight, the broad and most important area of product-related data – data about the composition, effects and utilization of harmful substances and products – might seem to be excluded. The Commission proposal for the Directive had expressly mentioned data relating to the 'production and use of dangerous products or substances'.[8] This passage does not reappear in the final version.[9] But as these product-related data were mentioned as examples of 'activities' which may impair the environment and these activities are retained in the final version, it can be inferred that information about product-related environmental effects is indeed included.

Accessible information must furthermore be delimited according to the *relevant person holding the information*. As access is open to administrative information the problem here lies in the definition of what 'administration', and more specifically environmental administration, means.

First, the *legislature* and *judiciary* are excluded by the Directive. With respect to legislative functions one might ask whether implementing regulations amount to legislation. In German law this is assumed[10] – wrongly so, I believe. The legislative function is excluded from the access to information right because one assumes that it is exposed to the public by its very nature: proposals for new laws are published and debated in parliament. But, this is not the case with a regulation. The subject matter and procedure adopted resemble those of administrative tasks and processes much more than parliamentary decision-making. For instance, in Germany, whether a dangerous chemical substance shall be prohibited is decided by regulation (*Rechtsverordnung*) but could just as well be framed to be decided by administrative order. Under the Act on Access to Environmental Information, however, access is excluded by the mere chance fact that the Chemical Substances Act prescribed a regulation rather than an administrative order as the form of prohibitive intervention for these substances. Therefore, the exemption of 'legislation' from the access right must be understood not to include law-implementing regulation.

The sphere of administrative holders of information subject to access rights must be distinguished from the *private sphere* which is not made subject to the access right. Some legal systems, it is true, recognize the direct right of a private person to information held by other private persons without the intervention of an administrative agency. For instance, under the German Environmental Liability Act an aggrieved person has a right to be informed, by the plant operator, about

---

[8] OJ C 335/5 of 30 December 1988, Art. 2 (a) 3rd indent.
[9] Art. 2 (a).
[10] Art. 3.

the installations, the utilized substances and their effects if there is reason to believe that the plant may have caused the damage. There is also vast legislation at Union and national level prescribing the declaration of process- and product-related dangers. For instance, dangerous substances must be labelled accordingly if marketed,[11] and plant operators must keep the public informed about possible dangerous accidents and their effects.[12]

This kind of information flow between risk-setter and individually or collectively affected private parties must be distinguished from the information flow between private parties and the government. The basic idea of the former is to identify and control specific hazardous causative chains. By contrast, the idea of the latter is to appraise and supplement the government's administrative tasks. Therefore, access to environmental information held by private parties does not form part of the relevant legislation. However, to the extent that private parties perform a *public service* of environmental protection and are, in this respect, subject to governmental supervision the Directive has included them in the list of relevant holders of information.[13]

For instance, a technical expert who is officially mandated to undertake the monitoring of air pollution required by law must be counted as a holder of information. The monitoring data collected by him must be made available, albeit via the supervisory agency, as the Directive distinguishes between the relevant holder of information and the person to whom the information request must be addressed. It is less clear whether scientific and technical advisory bodies also belong to the administrative sphere within the meaning of the Directive. Probably not, since such bodies themselves can hardly be said to perform environmental protection functions and to be supervised by the government. An even more intricate question is whether private or public entities which render a public service in the area of environmental management should be made subject to the access right. For example, the running and managing of a waste disposal facility may be taken as a public service in the field of environmental protection whether it is managed by a private company or public corporation.

A third dimension of identifying the proper addressee of the access right requires that *agencies with environmental tasks* be distinguished from those with other tasks. A narrow conception might include only agencies the main purpose of whose functions is environmental protection. This would exclude almost any access to information in those countries where the environmental protection function

---

[11]   Directive 92/32/EEC of the Council, OJ L 154/1 of 5 June 1992 (Chemical Substances Directive), Art. 23.

[12]   Directive 82/501/EEC of the Council, OJ L 230/1 of 5 August 1982 (Seveso Directive), Art. 8.

[13]   Art. 6.

has not been bestowed to separate agencies but has been left to the general administration or to agencies with other primary responsibilities, such as, for instance, the agency responsible for building permits. But, because there remain a significant number of agencies which would be excluded in other countries, a broader conception which also includes agencies carrying out environmental protection not as a main purpose but in connection with other primary functions is preferable. This must be the proper interpretation of the Directive, one which has been taken up by the English law on access to information.[14]

We have thus far identified the subject, object, scope and (direct or indirect) addressee of the access right. Some national laws add one further delimitation which is to exclude access as long as the agency is conducting certain *proceedings*. To these belong, according to the Directive, investigations, including disciplinary proceedings and 'preliminary procedures'. The latter term stems from the French Act 78-753[15] where it relates to the administrative activities which are carried out in the preparation of court proceedings. By contrast, the English law reads the clause to cover formal public inquiries in addition. While this may be tolerable because such formal procedures resemble court proceedings and draw their own specific regulation of access to information, the German reading appears to stretch the clause too far. In the German law access to information is excluded during any administrative proceedings.[16] Given the fact that the Administrative Procedure Act includes within the concept of proceedings any administrative activity in preparation of an administrative order or contract,[17] access to information is reduced to a minimum. This contradicts the very idea of access to information. It can also easily be misused by the agency merely pretending to have initiated a proceeding.

2   Exemptions from the access right

There are a number of exemptions to the right of access by which various interests in secrecy of the information are protected.

One exemption protects the *decision-making process of the administrative agency*. The Directive takes two measures in this respect. The first deals with the technical side of the process and provides room for undisturbed work. Thus, un-

---

[14] Environmental Protection Regulations 1992, s. 2 (3).

[15] Act on the Improvement of the Relationship Between the Administration and the Public, Art. 6, 4th indent.

[16] Art. 7, para. 1, No. 2. Only information which was not obtained because of the ongoing proceedings is available.

[17] Art. 9.

completed documents or unprocessed data may be excluded from access.[18] For instance, emission data may be retained as long as it is raw, uncompiled and un-analysed. This is acceptable, provided access is given to all information after completion of the document. All national free access laws do so, including the Dutch, French, Danish, Swedish and US, but, remarkably, the Directive does not.

The second exemption concerns the *substance of the decision-making*. Some laws – for example, the French and German – protect documents which are written in direct preparation for the final decision.[19] Others, like the Swedish, require that specific damage arising to the agency must be shown should the information be disclosed. The Directive uses very elusive language in this respect. Access is denied when it affects the 'confidentiality of the deliberations of the agencies' (which, according to a protocol declaration includes the national, regional and communal levels).[20] In addition, 'internal communications' may be protected.[21] Escape clauses could not have been better phrased, all the more so as preparatory information is not expressly made accessible once the decision has been taken.

Trade secrets are the second most important exemption from the access right.[22] Like most of the national laws the Directive does not define the term, thereby perpetuating the interpretative battles raging at the national level. The Directive missed the opportunity to decide some of the issues, of which the most important are whether emission data becomes a trade secret when it allows the inference of information about the production technology (reverse engineering), whether in balancing the firm's and the public's interest priority should be given to the latter, whether the agency shall determine by itself the need for secrecy or has to give prior notice to the secret holder, and whether secrecy protection presupposes a secrecy claim by the information provider.

Interpretation of the term 'trade secret' may become easier if elements which, in one way or another, are common to many legal systems are distinguished. These constitute four filters through which the information must pass in order to qualify as protected secret.

First, the information must directly relate to the technical process or business of the concerned person or firm. Hence, any environmental quality data must be accessible, because such data primarily relates to the environment and not, or only indirectly, to the polluter. An exception may only apply when the actual produc-

---

[18] Art. 3 (3).

[19] In France the secrecy of *documents préparatoires* is extrapolated from the fact that only 'documents' are accessible. For the German law see Art. 29, para. 1, sentence 2, Administrative Procedure Act.

[20] Art. 3 (2) 2, 1st indent.

[21] Art. 3 (3).

[22] Art. 3 (2), 4th indent of the Directive.

tion of the data is such as to make it an intellectual product disclosure which is forbidden to regulatory agencies by special or general national intellectual property law. Information concerning abatement or avoidance measures taken by the polluter, on the other hand, is clearly of a technical nature. There is greater difficulty concerning emission data as it could be said that since the emissions have left the polluter's property such data no longer relates to the polluter's technical process.

Second, the information can only be termed secret if it is not known by more than a small number of persons. According to some laws, the information is also not secret if it could be produced easily by the average professional. Otherwise latent public information which might easily be brought into the open by the public itself would be made private. This means that, even if one assumes that 'reverse engineering' from emission data back to process data necessarily renders that emission data classifiable information, this does not hold if the reverse engineering could be done by anybody up to an average professional.

Third, the concerned person or firm may be required to claim secrecy when submitting information to the agency. Some legal systems do so (for example the US) whereas others, such as the Dutch and the German, by law or in practice, assume a claim to secrecy by the submitters.

Fourth, in many legal systems the interests of secrecy must be weighed against the interests of disclosure on a case-by-case basis. Some legal systems, such as Canada's, give the public interest, as it relates to public health, public safety or protection of the environment, a certain priority. Others require that for the interest of secrecy to prevail it must be shown that the person concerned would suffer loss should the information be disclosed.

The last exemption from the access right I want to mention is the *protection of privacy*. Information about an event or phenomenon may also contain information about a private person, whether this person was involved in the event or phenomenon or whether this person is the sole source of the information – for example, the author of an expert opinion, the author of a third party intervention, or an applicant for a licence and so on. This person may wish to conceal his or her authorship or involvement in the substance of the information while disinterested as to whether the substance, stripped of the personal allusion, is disclosed.

In order to decide under what circumstances privacy shall be protected two questions must be answered. The first concerns the legal technique: should the conflict of interest between protection and disclosure be regulated by the free access law or by the privacy protection law? The former solution is the more frequent, and is indeed more appropriate in our context because regulation specially tuned to environmental information can be devised.

The second question relates to the substantive criteria for the resolution of the conflict of interests. Some legal systems, such as France and Germany, define a narrow sphere of private life beyond which privacy is not protected. Others use a broad definition of person-related information but limit its protection by setting up negative lists of information which, though person-related, shall nevertheless be accessible. A third group prescribes a balancing of interests test. The latter, however, is an unsatisfactory solution because parliament then avoids setting priorities and, also, respect for the public sphere may wither away in the humdrum process of equalizing interests in principle.

IV CONCLUSION

Access to environmental information, if constituted as universal right, is part of, and strengthens, the public sphere. Public democratic debate is the necessary chaos which constantly questions and destroys domination emerging in the private and governmental sphere thus preventing societal sclerosis and resistance to learning. The public sphere is permanently subject to attack and erosion from the ordering powers. In developing states the development administration has been able to avoid the chaos of uneducated debate by believing itself to know better than the public, but has often departed from societal needs and become visibly 'corrupted'. The same is true of socialist states where the bureaucracies have believed themselves to be implementing an historic mission, identifying themselves with an abstract labour class whose needs they thought they knew best. The public sphere is also in constant danger in capitalist states. Although there is a structural place for it – that is, the sphere of transcendence of individual interests for their long-term benefit – and although capitalism has succeeded in establishing the public sphere in the face of feudal and absolutist *arcana imperii*, the force of capitalism itself, combined with the technological potential of the information society, poses new threats.

'Information' – that is, the 'forming' of knowledge through communication (rather than, for example, through force or money) – has, to an extent unknown to date, become a means of production, a commodity and a marketing device in the economic system. The political/administrative system, on the other hand, has learned to use information as a method of power more sophisticated than the traditional method of sanctioned law. What has emerged combines in an attempt to make private what was previously in the public sphere. There are a multitude of legal tools which are used to support this process, including the privatization of telecommunications, the commercial capture of science by joint ventures between universities and private industry and the extension of patent law to extend even to genetic information.

In contrast to this trend the battle over a universal right of access to governmental information has been won by the public sphere, although the victory may turn out to be Pyrrhic as exceptions to the right are framed. Broad definitions of the protection of administrative deliberation and of trade secrets are forceful weapons for regaining territory which has been opened to public access. But privacy protection also plays a peculiar role in this context. Privacy protection is certainly legitimate and is indeed a means of preventing the above-mentioned privatization of interests from not only seizing the public, but also the personal sphere. But because it privatizes information as well, though for different reasons, it is apt to be misused by the more powerful economic and governmental actors as a disguise for otherwise not protectable trade and governmental secrets. Therefore, the protection of administrative deliberation, of trade secrets and also of the private sphere must be critically assessed if the European battle over a public environment shall not finally be lost.

7 Public Participation in Environmental Decisions

Claude Lambrechts

Table of Contents

I   INTRODUCTION

Decisions likely to have an impact on the quality of life and on the environment are usually made by administrative authorities. Particularly in centralized states, like France, they are made by a bureaucracy far removed from any democratic control and acting in a technical capacity. This may not be so evident in countries having a long tradition of local government or in federal states where local and regional problems tend to be regulated at different levels and, hopefully, with more attention to local demands and preferences. But, whatever the political structure of the different states, the general principles governing administrative discretion – whether natural justice, due process of law or principle of legality – require that concerned populations should be given a fair hearing before a final decision that may affect their rights or interests is made.

So it is a general and long-standing practice in democratic states to inform concerned populations about certain projects likely to have an effect on their property rights, or on their enjoyment of the environment where they live, and to allow ob-

95

jectors to make representations. Such consultations must usually occur before public or private projects are authorized, especially when they involve the compulsory acquisition of land in the public interest – for instance, before the construction of highways, airports, power plants, dams, and the like. They are also often prescribed in the case of planning decisions, concerning, for example, the siting of new facilities, the building of a shopping mall or a supermarket, or even of leisure facilities.

These public consultations have often been the forum in which determined environmental groups demonstrate their opposition to such developments or infrastructure projects as nuclear power plants, airports and high-speed railroads and motorways. For these organized groups, public consultation gives the opportunity not only to express more or less forcefully their disagreement, but also to ask for an open discussion about the ecological, economic and social aspects of the pending administrative decision. In fact, the active part taken by environmental associations on some very controversial issues and the strong pressure put on the political body by scientists and conservation groups has been a powerful incentive towards the development of environmental law.[1]

Public participation is now increasingly integrated in environment-related decision-making procedures. It tends to be considered a right of the public and a counterpart of the citizen's general duty to protect the environment for present and future generations.[2] Its purpose is primarily to meet democratic requirements by enabling concerned populations to express their opinions on proposed developments likely to affect either their environment and living conditions or their property rights, or both. It implies a right of access to information and the appropriate means to express opinions or objections and to have them taken into account.

Public participation may also serve the more complex goal of winning the approval of concerned populations for controversial projects in order to ensure that the control of human activities that accompanies it will be more acceptable and better enforceable. The involvement of organized groups in preliminary proceedings may be viewed as a means either to convince or to pacify opponents.

Public participation may take different forms: the best known and most usual is the *public inquiry* (called 'local public inquiry' in the UK, *enquête publique* in France, *Erörterung* in Germany). But other forms of participation are now appearing and are more specific to environmental proceedings: participation of environ-

---

[1]   M. Prieur, *Droit de l'environnement*, (2nd edn), Paris: Dalloz, 1991; R. Romi, *Droit et administration de l'environnement*, Paris: Montchrétien, 1993.

[2]   See Prieur (1991), *op.cit.*, p. 90; M. Prieur, Le droit à l'environnement et les citoyens: la participation, *RJE*, 1988, (4), p. 397; A. Kiss, D. Shelton, *Manual of European Environmental Law*, Cambridge: Grotius Publications Ltd, 1993, p. 37; A. Kiss, La mise en oeuvre du droit à l'environnement, problématique et moyens, *Second European Conference 'The Environment and the Rights of Man'*, Salzburg, 3 December 1980.

mental experts or of organized associations to administrative committees and participation of the general public in preliminary studies or proceedings related to local planning schemes or developments.

Currently, public participation is generally limited to issues immediately affecting private interests such as the granting of permits or local and regional planning decisions. Its scope could be enlarged to encompass matters of public policies, plans and programmes and the setting of regulatory standards,[3] but this is not yet the practice.

II PUBLIC INQUIRIES

1 Definitions and general purpose

'The statutory inquiry is the standard device for giving a fair hearing to objectors before the final decision is made on some question of government policy affecting citizens' rights or interests'. Its primary objective is 'to make sure that the best possible decision is made in the public interest and that the citizen has his objections fairly considered'.[4] These phrases perfectly summarize the aims and the general philosophy of public inquiries.

French law 'relating to the democratization of public inquiries and the protection of the environment'[5] emphasizes the link between ecological control and public inquiry. According to its Article 1, the scope of the statute extends to developments which 'owing to their nature, to their peculiarities or to the character of the areas concerned are likely to affect the environment'. The purpose of the public inquiry is 'to inform the public and to collect his opinions, suggestions and counterproposals, after an EIS has been made where required, so as to enable the competent authority to be in possession of all the relevant information' (Article 2). Formerly, a public inquiry had been required whenever the government policy suggested a compulsory purchase of land in the public interest or to authorize im-

---

[3] For a few examples, see *Manual on Public Participation in Environmental Decision Making, Current Practice and Future Possibilities in Central and Eastern Europe*, Regional Environmental Center for Central and Eastern Europe, Budapest, 1994.

[4] Ibid.

[5] Loi no. 83-630 du 12 juillet 1983 relative à la démocratisation des enquêtes publiques et à la protection de l'environnement. This Act has completely modified the regulations applying to public inquiries. Further amendments have been brought by an Act of 8 January 1993 concerning the protection of landscapes. The categories of works that are subject to public inquiries are fixed by Decree no. 85-453 of 23 April 1985, amended by Decree no. 93-245 of 25 February 1993. However, the ancient legislation has not been entirely repealed and continues to apply to some categories of works.

portant public works . Its aim was to enable the administration to assess the public utility of a project – that is, to balance its social and financial costs against its public interest. The 'ecological cost' of a project was first considered on a par with its financial cost and the infringement caused on property rights by the Conseil d'Etat (Ville Nouvelle-Est) in a decision dated 28 May 1971. This is considered a landmark decision on the law of public inquiries and prompted the much needed 1983 reform. Since then the inquiry has developed towards a more open and pluralist procedure.

The same shift in emphasis can be observed in Germany. In the words of S. Rose-Ackermann, 'German public law recognizes that participation serves other goals than the protection of individuals against arbitrary state-action'.[6]

2   General features

Public inquiries show peculiarities which may be traced back to different legal traditions, although they partly have common purposes.

The British public inquiry – often considered as a model even if badly reproduced – is a prominent feature of administrative law whose primary goal is to ensure 'that administrative power is fairly and reasonably exercised' and that objections from the public are fairly considered. So it has the 'same purpose as natural justice'.[7] Public inquiries developed principally as a mechanism for resolving conflicts between individuals or between individuals and the government, which explains their quasi-judicial character and the emphasis set on procedural fairness. But, because it prepares a political decision, it is also an administrative mechanism. Public inquiries nowadays appear to be more oriented to the collection of information and less restricted to a contest between two opposing parties.[8]

In other countries, especially those where administrative action is subject to judicial control by administrative courts, public inquiries have different purposes. They are mainly directed to the defence of individual rights in Germany. In France, since the 1983 reform, the public inquiry serves a multi-polar purpose: it is still the means for people who object to projects that might impair their individual rights to be heard before a decision is made but it has been reoriented towards the information of the administration and the weighing of conflicting public interest matters.

---

[6] S. Rose-Ackerman, *Controlling Environmental Policy: The Limits of Public Law in Germany and the U.S.*, New Haven: Yale University Press, (forthcoming), ch. VII.

[7] Wade, p. 956.

[8] See P. P. Craig, *Administrative Law*, (2nd edn), London: Sweet and Maxwell, 1989, pp. 129, 142 *et seq.*

These diverse purposes are reflected in the rules applying to standing and to the general conduct of the proceedings.[9]

3 Standing

The *right to participate* may be either totally free or submitted to restricted access.

In France, for instance, every member of the public can participate in a public inquiry. There is no restriction concerning the access of private or public persons, individuals or organized groups and associations, nationals or foreigners. There is no objection either to individuals or groups making representations on behalf of the public interest.

In the UK, the right to participate seems also to be fairly open, although it is doubtful exactly to what extent. Relying on Lord Moulton's opinion in the Arlidge case, W. Wade considers that 'A public local inquiry, and likewise a local inquiry, implies that there will be a right of audience for all persons *in the locality*, who are *genuinely concerned for good reasons*, and not merely for those who have legal rights at stake' (my emphasis).[10] Procedural rules make distinctions between those who have legal rights and other members of the public who may be heard at the inspector's discretion. But, in practice, public inquiries, including planning appeals, 'are open freely to all comers' including 'neighbours, amenity societies and other third parties',[11] which, however, does not mean that they all benefit from the same procedural advantages (see below).

Access seems to be more restricted in Germany where, according to the Administrative Procedure Act,[12] only those 'whose interests are affected by the projects' are allowed to make objections in planning procedures. Also, the oral hearing is not public but restricted to those who have submitted objections. Special provisions have been made to deal with mass objections from individuals combining

---

[9] Only a general outline of procedural rules will be drawn in this chapter as there are, in every country, several (and sometimes many) types of public inquiries each with its own set of rules. For a brief review of the different types of public inquiries in the UK, see Wade, *op.cit.*, p. 984.

[10] Wade, *op.cit.*, p. 975. The quotation of Lord Moulton is as follows:
    The effect of the insertion of the word 'public' appears to me to be that every member of the public would have a locus standi to bring before the inquiry any matters relevant thereto so as to ensure that everything bearing on the rights of the owner or occupier of the house affected, or the interest of the public in general, or of the public living in the neighbourhood in particular, would be brought to the knowledge of the Local Government Board for the purpose of enabling it to discharges its duties in connection with the appeal.

[11] Wade, *op.cit.*, p.956.

[12] VwVfG, para. 73(4).

their efforts to oppose the planning or licensing of very controversial projects, like nuclear power plants, airports.[13] The Administrative Procedure Act of 1976 attempts to regulate this type of situation by requiring that where more than 50 people make identical submissions they must be represented by one individual person.[14] In practice, opponents tend to regroup themselves into loose local citizens' associations (*Bürgerinitiativen*) which acquire a more or less permanent status. Mass objections can thus be expressed under the cover of individual rights since groups are not empowered to speak in the public interest.[15]

Everywhere, the attitude of the public towards public inquiries is rather ambiguous: on the one hand there is a strong demand for participation; on the other hand there is a general feeling that public inquiries are only a mock-consultation – a means to give legitimacy to a decision made beforehand by the responsible authorities. In consequence much attention is paid in national legislation to procedural matters so as to ensure adequate information and publicity and fairness in proceedings.

4   The conduct of the proceedings

No attempt will be made here to enter into a detailed description and comparison of the proceedings except to stress the most significant points relating to preliminary information and publicity, to the hearing itself and the role of the inspector in charge of the inquiry.

a)   The British example

Preliminary information and publicity for the inquiry are essential requisites everywhere. In the UK the general pattern is as follows: the proceedings begin with a notice or written statement giving a description of the project and stating the reasons for it. Publicity for the project is ensured by various means specified by special rules or deriving from general rules of procedure: individual notifications to

---

13   Some projects have met with huge opposition from tens of thousands of objectors, causing much delay and inconvenience: 90,000 opponents to the licensing of the atomic power plant at Whyl in 1974, and 44,000 in 1983. Other significant figures are reported by Rose-Ackerman, *op.cit.*, n. 36.

14   VwVfG, para. 17, 18.

15   See Rose-Ackerman, (forthcoming), *op.cit.*, ch. VII:
Here the paradox of German notions of public participation is clear. Groups claiming to represent the public interest may thereby lose their legitimacy. But groups may intervene so long as they assert that they are merely collections of individuals.

property owners or occupiers; announcements in local daily newspapers and/or in official gazettes, notices posted on the site and/or at the town hall; and inscription on a register. The public must be advised of the place where they may consult the documents and of the time limit within which they will be able to make objections or comments. In the case of statutory inquiries, a period of variable length (21–42 days) is prescribed before the beginning of the hearing stage. In practice, at the request of the inspector, it may even be extended to several months in large-scale inquiries involving complex economical, environmental and technical matters.[16]

The hearing phase of the public inquiry bears a superficial resemblance to a court procedure as it is, in most cases, an adversarial and oral procedure governed by rules of procedure. An oral debate actually opposes the developer (or applicant) to objectors who have legal interests at stake. Both parties have a right to appear, to know the opposite case, to be represented by legal counsels or advisers and to give evidence and cross-examine witnesses. But the public inquiry does not have to obey the same procedural standards as a court of justice. Besides, its purpose is not to regulate conflicts but to collect information prior to making a decision on a matter of public interest.

The main responsibility of the conduct of the inquiry falls on the inspector who decides on essential procedural and substantive matters and benefits from very wide-ranging discretionary powers within the limits of natural justice.[17] For example, he decides who is allowed to appear. The law distinguishes those who may appear as of right, having a legal interest at stake, from third parties who may be allowed to appear if authorized by the inspector. In practice, access could not be refused to objectors without good reason and standing is fairly open. The inspector also has the power to enforce attendance, to require the production of documents, to take evidence on oath and to decide whether an objector is allowed to cross-examine witnesses and if cross-examination is desirable. The refusal to allow an objector to cross-examine evidence given by the applicant is not a simple matter of procedural fairness. Public inquiries are not modelled on court proceedings, and cross-examination is not the only method of ascertaining facts and collecting information[18] so that refusal is not unfair *per se*. Denial is rather linked to the question of the inspector's power to determine the scope of the inquiry and to rule out topics which are not considered as relevant. It is not always easy to draw the

---

[16] As an example, in the Inquiry about the PWR Sizewell B nuclear reactor almost a year's notice was given: T. O'Riordan, R. Kemp, M. Purdue, *Sizewell B, An Anatomy of the Inquiry*, London: MacMillan, p. 95.

[17] See Craig (1989), *op.cit.*, p. 132 'The procedure at the inquiry is, as recommended by the Franks Committee, very much left in the hands of the inspector...'; Wade, *op.cit.*, p.987 'The inspector is master of the procedure...'

[18] See the opinion of Lord Diplock in the *Bushell* v. *Secretary of State for the Environment* case, reported by Craig (1989), *op.cit.*, p. 133.

boundary between matters that may assist the finding of facts useful to make recommendations in a particular case and matters not suitable for discussion at a local public inquiry. In large-scale inquiries pre-inquiry meetings are sometimes
organized to prepare the public hearing and to discuss procedural questions.[19]

After the close of the inquiry, the inspector makes a report consisting of a
statement of facts and of recommendations. An important issue is that of the public access to the inspector's report. In the UK, the government long resisted the
disclosure of the inspector's report.[20] This resistance was finally overcome to the
great benefit of the mutual relations between the citizens and the authorities. Disclosure of the reports led to a better protection of objectors who are thus able to
know how their representations were received and can act accordingly.

The English public inquiry is generally considered as a model of public participation. But this heavy machinery is, in many instances, superseded by more informal written proceedings which are less costly and time-consuming but do not
offer the same procedural safeguards, especially to third parties.[21]

b)   The French example

In France the *nouvelle enquête publique* issued from the 1983 reform seeks to
restore the image of the public inquiry which had come to be considered as a
merely formal step, where the public was neither adequately informed nor heard
and which served mainly to legitimate administrative actions.

The 1983 Act[22] brought some significant changes which consisted mainly in
improving public access and information, in extending the hearing period and,
especially, in giving an independent status and greater investigating powers to the
inspector(s) in charge of the inquiry (*commissaires enquêteurs*). The inspector is
now designated by the President of the Administrative Court, and no longer by the
préfet, which guarantees his independence with regard to administrative authorities. According to the scope of the project submitted to inquiry, a single inspector
or a commission of three or five members may be designated. The inspectors have
been given extensive investigative powers: in addition to the long list of documents that must be provided by the developer, they can ask for further information, make on-site visits and require that a public audience be held either at public
request or on their own initiative.

In fact, most inspectors are not in favour of public audiences, which are usually
requested where there is a serious controversy and which may often prove difficult

---

19   See O'Riordan, Kemp, Purdue, *op.cit.*, p. 96.
20   Wade, *op.cit.*, p. 972.
21   Much criticized by Wade, see ibid., pp. 989-90.
22   See above, note 5.

to manage. In the vast majority of cases, the proceedings are only written and involve no debate between the developer and his objectors.

The usual way for the members of the public to participate in the consultation is to make a written statement on a register kept at the town hall or to address letters or petitions to the inspector. The inquiry is opened during a period of at least one month, during which all relevant documents must be available[23] and to which the inspector may add two further weeks. The public audience, if any, takes place at the end of this period and must be advertised sufficiently early. The proceedings at the audience are quite informal and left to the inspector's own devices. It is generally the only opportunity the public has to meet the developer or proponent of the project who, unlike the inspector, is under no obligation to meet with the public during the inquiry period.

Within one month of the inquiry's closure the inspector makes a report which comprises:

- an analysis of the general reactions of the public and of the remarks and comments made either for or against the project;
- a personal conclusion on the public utility of the project with a *statement of reasons*.

The inspector is under a duty to state clearly whether he is favourable or unfavourable towards the project; he may also express a favourable opinion under explicit reservations. The report is available to the public at the town hall.

5   The role of public inquiries in the decision-making process

In spite of all their differences, some features are common to all public inquiries: their procedural importance; and their advisory character.

a)   Mandatory in procedure

Public inquiries, at least when they are mandatory, form an essential prerequisite of some administrative decisions. In this respect, substantial variations exist between national legislations. In some instances, public inquiries are never discretionary. In France, the law determines all the situations where a public inquiry is required and there is no escape. In the UK, in contrast, there is a great flexibility. Whether a public inquiry is mandatory or discretionary depends on the provisions of relevant legislation. Moreover the government is always free to organize an

---

[23]   The list of the documents is specified by the decree of 23 April 1985, Art. 6 and comprises eventually the EIS.

informal inquiry and may sometimes choose other means to ensure public participation. This flexibility has been criticized as offering fewer safeguards to individual objectors than a formal procedure, although still within the limits of natural justice.[24]

A decision made without a public inquiry when one is required is liable to be quashed. Likewise a decision based on a defective public inquiry would be quashed if challenged in time,[25] particularly if the decision is substantially vitiated – for instance, by the omission of important evidence in the inspector's report.[26] In France, case law concerning public inquiries is particularly abundant as associations often try to obtain the annulment of decisions on the grounds that they were based on defective public inquiries. Only outright violation of the law or 'substantial' irregularities will generally be considered as sufficient ground to quash a decision – for example, the lack of adequate publicity or access to the required information, or if the inspector's opinion is substantiated by badly stated reasons.[27] The gravity of the alleged deficiency is a matter of judicial construction and is often subject to criticism.[28]

b)   Advisory in substance

The inspector's report and his expressed opinions always have an advisory character. In the vast majority of cases, public inquiries are required in situations where the ultimate decision is political as is the case in planning and licensing decisions. The opinion expressed by the inspector at the end of the inquiry is never binding on the competent authority (minister, local government authority, *préfet* and so on).

This does not mean that objections and representations have no practical nor even legal effect. Apart from their moral and psychological impact, they may have concrete and technical consequences and lead to the taking of special measures in order to minimize a project's harmful effects, either in the interest of environmental protection or in the interest of private owners or occupiers. Objectors may,

---

[24]   Wade, *op.cit.*, p. 990.
[25]   'If some part of the statutory procedure has not been properly followed, or there has been a breach of natural justice, there will be no valid inquiry and any order made in consequence, if challenged within statutory time limit, can be quashed by the court', Wade, *op.cit.*, p. 957.
[26]   Reported by Wade, *op.cit.*, p. 973.
[27]   Conseil d'Etat, 10 décembre 1990, Les amis de Port-Ripaille, reported by Romi (1994), *op.cit.*, p.77.
[28]   Law books and articles about public inquiries are fairly abundant in France. See in particular J-C. Hélin, R. Hostiou. *Le droit des enquêtes publiques*, Paris: Editions du Moniteur, 1993; up-to-date bibliography in Romi (1994), *op.cit.*

according to the relevant laws, also have a right to propose counterprojects or alternatives that must be reported by the inspectors.

Occassionally the initial project, submitted to the public, is substantially modified after the inquiry. In that case, French courts have considered that a second public inquiry was necessary, if 'the general structure of the project has been altered'.[29]

The legal effect imparted, in French legislation, to the inspector's report should be stressed. If the inspector, stating his reasons, concludes against the project, the authority competent to decide is no longer the *préfet* (the government's representative in the *département*), but the prime minister, who must first take the advice of the Conseil d'Etat. Where the conclusions are favourable under some express conditions, these conditions must be satisfied before consent is given, or the report is assumed to be unfavourable. This provision imposes a heavy duty and responsibility on the inspectors but, at the same time, gives greater credibility to the procedure. This is the reason why, for highly technical and controversial projects (highways, nuclear power plants, planning schemes in big cities and so on), a commission of three or five members is usually designated and its composition carefully attended by the court.

The rules applicable to public inquiries have been modified and amended many times, in the UK as in France, and further reforms are still envisaged; despite long experience and many adjustments to public demands and the need for procedural fairness, they are still considered unsatisfactory, in particular because they take place so late in the administrative process. It also appears very difficult to achieve the right balance between public involvement and administrative discretion. Other forms of public participation have been experimented with, not as substitutes, but as complements to public inquiries.

III   THE DEVELOPMENT OF PRELIMINARY CONSULTATION (*CONCERTATION*)

Public inquiries, in a formal sense, are often criticized as being held too late and concerning 'fullyfledged' projects that cannot be altered. To remedy this situation, it may be considered expedient to develop early consultative mechanisms, not on a voluntary or informal basis, but on an institutional basis.[30]

During the last ten years, French participation law has thus been enriched with statutory provisions that tend to expand what is labelled 'local democracy'. The

---

[29]   For instance, if a local plan is altered to take account of remarks made during the inquiry.

[30]   See also ch. 12 by P. Glasbergen in this volume.

objective is to associate citizens, local interest groups and professional associations (industrialists, chambers of commerce, farmers and so on) to the preparatory phases of local development projects. For instance, an Act of 18 July 1985 obliges municipal authorities to organize the consultation of local residents and interest groups and of all other concerned people before undertaking certain categories of urban developments, especially if they are likely to substantially modify the environment or the economic activity of the city.[31] The mayor is under a duty to report to the municipal council the results of this preliminary consultation which is about the only legal requirement clearly expressed by the Act.

A similar provision has been introduced in an Act of 1991 on urban policy and management[32] in order to organize the consultation on urban developments which 'owing to their importance or their nature will modify the living conditions of the residents in the districts or areas concerned'. (This procedure is not identical to the one mentioned above.)

Finally, an Act of 1992 on the 'territorial administration of the Republic' authorizes mayors to organize 'local referendums', but only on questions of local interest[33] and with an advisory (as opposed to decisional) purpose.

Far from reducing opposition and litigation, as was expected, these new legal requirements pose a risk of increased judicial challenge of administrative decisions. As the statutes are not very clear and leave broad discretion to the municipal authorities, the types of planning schemes covered and what constitutes a regular consultation are questions subject to judicial interpretation. This may offer new opportunities for judicial action, and already does.[34] The legal effect of these requirements is somewhat difficult to predict. It has been suggested that only a gross inadequacy or deficiency in the consultation could lead to the decision being

---

[31]   Art. 300-2 du Code de l'urbanisme modifié par la Loi no. 85-729 du 18 juillet 1985 relative à la définition et la mise en oeuvre des principes d'aménagement.

[32]   Art. 4 de la Loi d'Orientation sur la Ville du 13 juillet 1991.

[33]   Loi d'orientation n° 92-125 du 6 février 1992 relative à l'administration territoriale de la République , art. 21 modifiant les articles L. 125-1 à 125-7 du Code des Communes. On the interpretation of 'local interest', see Tribunal Administratif de Nantes, 8 février 1993, *Revue Juridique de l'Environnement*, 1993, no.2, p. 297. On the local referendum see J.-B. Auby, La loi du 6 février 1992 et la citoyenneté locale, *Revue Française de Droit Administratif*, 1993, January-February, p. 37.

[34]   A planning decision concerning the creation of an enterprise zone has already been quashed on the ground of an irregular previous consultation: Trib. Adm. de Nantes, 13 December 1990, mentioned by J-C. Hélin, Urbanisme et démocratie, *Actualité juridique-droit administratif*, May 1993, p. 184.

quashed.[35] On the whole, legal commentators are rather sceptical that any real progress is achieved through all these new devices.[36]

IV PARTICIPATION IN ADVISORY COMMITTEES

A last form of public participation will be briefly mentioned: the participation of environmental defence associations or amenity societies to advisory administrative committees. In France, seats are reserved for environmental associations or to qualified persons (who are in fact delegated by environmental associations) in advisory committees which have to be consulted in a great number of administrative proceedings.[37] This is the means for environmental and nature conservancy groups to express objections or give expert advice in the general interest and to develop environmental awareness among the responsible authorities.

The representative role of associations is slowly gaining ground: in Germany, for instance, where associations are often to be heard in rule making committees.

V CONCLUSION

This rapid overview of decision-making procedures leaves the (not very original) impression that some progress has been made towards a better understanding and a better consideration of environmental issues, but that much remains to be done. No legal system presently appears to be able to offer truly satisfactory solutions to this challenge, and this probably cannot be helped. Flexibility and pragmatism lead to a degree of uncertainty and leave many regulatory gaps. Rigidity and over-regulation do not succeed in eliminating gaps and are apt to lead to enforcement problems that make them inefficient. It is highly desirable, and certainly possible, to tend the same goals, but it may not be advisable to use uniform legal tools to achieve them. Each country leans to its own bias; legal instruments form part of traditions and cultures whose diversity cannot, and probably must not, be ignored.

However, in our global village 'there is only one environment and care has to be taken that measures which are taken in one part of this earth do not adversely

---

[35] Morand-Deviller, Jacqueline, Les instruments juridiques de la participation et de la contestation des décisions d'aménagement, *Revue Juridique de l'Environnement*, 1992, no. 4, p. 453.

[36] Morand-Deviller, Hélin, Romi and so on.

[37] For a list of these commissions and their functions see Prieur (1992), *op.cit.*, pp. 109-11; Romi (1994), *op.cit.*, pp. 115-17.

affect other parts of our Eden...'.[38] This implies an active and imaginative legal action in order to prevent environmental deterioration and the enactment and implementation of binding legal rules that can be made efficient. As expressed by L. Krämer:

> In order to discuss environmental matters in an open society – where Governments derive their right to govern from the consent of the governed and where the setting of standards does not consist of transforming shadows of the Platonic idea of Justice into a piece of legislation, but are conceived, scheduled and accepted by way of democratic procedure – a number of conditions must be fulfilled.[39]

To summarize them, they comprise: 'access to environmental information' and 'the possibility of the public – the individual, as well as associations or groups – participating in environmental discussion'. It is indeed essential, in this perspective, not only to give the public better legal tools but to develop environmental awareness and to persuade the public to use existing means and not to underestimate their capability to influence political decisions.

---

[38]   L. Krämer, *Focus on European Environmental Law*, London: Sweet and Maxwell, 1992, p. 275.

[39]   Ibid., p. 281.

8 Standard-setting in Environmental Law[1]

Gerd Winter

Standards are the working level of regulatory environmental law. Environmental law which has not been put into operation by means of standards rarely 'works' in practice, but will often remain exhortative. Standards can be used as a general term which breaks down into process-related technical requirements and maximum threshold values. *Thresholds* are the form of standards most frequently used in environmental law. The thrust of this chapter will therefore be concentrated on these.

The chapter explores:

- what kinds of standards exist;
- in what procedures standards are found;
- how and to what extent standards are given binding force;
- whether and how standard-setting should be improved.

---

[1]   This chapter is based on the introduction to G. Winter (ed.), *Grenzwerte*, Düsseldorf: Werner Verlag, 1986.

I TAXONOMY OF STANDARDS[2]

Thresholds differ first according to their addressees: they are individually set if they are the object of a condition attached to a licence and addressed to only one polluter limiting the emission of pollutant chemical substances from the licensed installation. They are of general validity if addressed to all polluters, for example, through a legislative measure. General standards can be specific (that is, limiting each single pollutant) or they can be summative if covering all pollutants in a given area as a whole.

Thresholds differ also according to the object or goals of protection: human health, animals and plants as well as inanimate nature (such as water) or buildings. For a long time, priority was given to human health; the other entities in need of protection were only indirectly protected by the thresholds directed at human beings (as, for example, plants by means of pollution thresholds) or were merely used as a medium for the protection of human health (for example water quality standards as a precondition for its use as drinking water). However, more and more voices and initiatives have recently been pushing for the recognition of the need to protect nature as such, and to have separate standards set for this purpose. Thus in the amendments to the German Technical Guideline for Air Pollution Control (*Technische Anleitung Luft – TA Luft*) of 1983,[3] special pollution values for carbonate fluoride and sulphur dioxide were established in order to protect particularly sensitive plants and animals.[4] Ultimately, however, this protection also remains oriented towards the benefit which the so-called things (such is the legal classification) offer humans.

There are various, partially intertwined, routes of pollution between the sources of pollutants and the object in need of protection. Thresholds can be distinguished according to the route they are regulating. Pollution at work is regulated by standards for maximum concentrations at the workplace (MAK Standards[5]), called *occupational health standards*. Pollution conveyed by the environment and

---

[2] See, for a similar taxonomy, S. Ball, S. Bell, *Environmental Law*, London: Blackstone, 1991, p. 61 *et.seq.*

[3] An English version is reprinted in G. Winter (ed.), *Environmental Law in Germany: Basic Law Texts and Introduction*, The Hague: Kluwer, 1994.

[4] No. 2.2.1.2 a, subpara. 2 with Appendix A, TA Luft. The threshold is unfortunately specific in the above defined sense – that is, it limits the individual source rather than the total sum of all relevant sources. Summative standards for the protection of sensitive plants and animals were deemed too costly. Only one summative standard protecting sensitive plants and animals is contained in the TA Luft: No. 2.2.1.4 requires sulphur dioxide contamination to be kept to a limit of 0.05 or 0.05mg/cbm air in areas which meet this value.

[5] MAK = Maximale Arbeitsplatzkonzentration.

reaching human beings, for example, in the form of air, soil or water pollution is regulated so-called environmental standards. A third route of contamination intertwined with both of those mentioned above is found during the production of intermediate or end products when pollutants endangering the health of the consumer are incorporated into (or not properly extracted from) the product. Standards dealing with this route usually limit the concentration of such pollutants in the product. Examples are thresholds for pesticides in food or for pollutants in drinking water. We call them *product quality standards.*

In a route of contamination thresholds can be distinguished according to whether they are fixed close to the source, to an intermediate object or to the polluted object. So-called emission thresholds are fixed directly at the source: they limit the emission of pollutants. Examples are the thresholds for sulphur dioxide emissions from coal power stations or minimum requirements for the direct discharge of waste water into public waters under various EC Directives. So-called immission thresholds[6] such as, for example, thresholds for suspended particles in the air or for noise in the neighbourhood, refer to media (that is, to media capable of transporting pollutants such as air or water). In this context, intermediate or end products containing toxic substances or emitting pollutants or noise may be considered as well. The corresponding thresholds have already been introduced above as product quality standards. Finally there are thresholds determining tolerance limits in contaminated objects or better, in receiver organisms, especially such as the so-called biological thresholds for risks from production materials (BAT Standards)[7] in occupational health regulation, which are meant to make it possible to decide whether a worker may be exposed to further toxic substances or if his or her capacity to take in such substances is exhausted.

Why these classifications? They are more than just a game, rather they help to pose questions. Thus a comparison between occupational health values and environmental protection values for pollutants in the air shows that the former are often considerably more liberal than the latter. For instance, the German MAK values for cadmium and lead are 50 and 100 μg/cbm of air, whereas the environmental maximum contamination concentrations (MIK values) are 0.04 and 2 μg/cbm, respectively. This means that the MAK value for cadmium is thousandfold and the one for lead fiftyfold more lax than the MIK value. The same can be observed regarding product quality values: drinking water is, in relation to its heavy metal content, more strictly regulated than vegetable and animal food for

---

[6] The term 'immission' refers to the endpoint where an 'emission' arrrives. Originating in the language of German environmental law, the term is being used also in English legal language where 'pollution' is the more familiar term. Based on the German term one can speak of 'immission standards' instead of what are 'environmental quality standards' in the British terminolgy.

[7] BAT = Biologische Arbeitsstofftoleranzwerte.

human beings, because the ubiquitous background contamination of plants and animals is usually taken as natural baseline. The stepping downwards is once more repeated in relation to animal feed which is even less strictly regulated than vegetable and animal food for human beings.

However, differences in threshold values must not necessarily lead to differences in real damage or risk. Thus MAK values are valid for an 8-hour (workday) exposure of (mainly) adults, while MIK values are valid for a 24-hour exposure of everybody including children. Nevertheless, a closer analysis of the consequences of the American lead thresholds of 50 µ/cbm and 1.5 µg/cbm has shown that the resulting real risks are clearly different, the threshold (which amounts to 50 per cent of the German value) still implying neurologic damage, kidney trouble and light anaemia for about 10,000 employees.[8]

All this shows that it is worth exploring reasons for different strictness of standards in more debth than it is possible here. Variations between standards for different pollution routes or substances will often be more difficult to explain (if not by sheer arbitrariness), than differences concerning the same substance and stages of the same pollution route. For instance, a source-related emission value for substance X should be in line with the pollution value for the same substance fixed on the medium or receiver organisms.

II   STANDARDS AND OTHER INSTRUMENTS FOR CONTROLLING POLLUTION

Thresholds set a framework for behaviour. They leave the decision of how to act to the party being regulated. The entrepreneur, for instance, maintains discretion as to the technology to apply in order to abide by the threshold. The situation is different with process-related standards. They intervene in the set framework and stipulate certain processes for production or waste treatment. Examples can be found in countless regulations of autonomous standard-setting organizations, but rarely in legally binding regulations.

Standards can be formulated as commands which are immediately applicable or as guiding values towards which the actor is oriented without being strictly bound. If framed as commands they leave the operator no choice as to whether to keep within them or exceed them. In this regard the standardizing technique differs from market-simulating instruments.[9] A system of pollution charges would allow such a choice; the higher the emission of pollutants or noise, the more is to be

---

[8]   D. R. Hattis, R. Goble, N. Ashford, Airborne Lead: a Clearcut case of Differential Protection, *Environment*, **24**(14), 1982.
[9]   For a more detailed account of these see G. Bándi (chapter 13 in this volume).

paid. But even such a system could not exist entirely without thresholds, because they have to be used to set the desired quality goals (for example for air or water) in order to enable judgement as to whether the charge is high enough to act as an incentive towards preventing pollution. Something similar applies to a system of environmental certificates or pollution rights that are traded at market prices. In this case quality goals are the basis for deciding how many certificates are to be issued on the market.

A question arising in this context is whether, in connection with market simulating instruments, the problem of an enforcement deficit that can frequently be observed when dealing with thresholds can better be solved. This may be doubtful because administrative monitoring and inspection remains necessary also in the framework of a charges or certificate system. It is furthermore questionable whether the virtue of greater efficiency (that is, pollution avoidance at the least cost) ascribed to the market approach does indeed materialize: also, in a regulatory system reliant on binding standards, the supervisory agencies could focus their enforcement activities on those who can abate pollution at the least cost.

III   HISTORY OF STANDARD-SETTING

Occupational health and environmental protection went hand in hand during the industrialization era in Germany, both legally and in administrative practice. Art. 16 of the Industrial Code (*Gewerbeordnung*) from 26 July 1900 regulated the requirements for environmental protection and in Articles 120 a–c those for protection at work. The Prussian 'Technical Instruction Regarding the Approval of Industrial Plants', dated 15 May 1885, contained requirements for licensing plants which closely linked aspects of protection at work with environmental protection. Thus it can be read, for example, in relation to oil destillation plants:

> Therefore it has to be stipulated upon licensing these plants that they are provided with well equipped, completely impervious distillation devices, which are suited to achieving condensation of vapours which is as complete as possible and that the working areas are fireproof and preferably subject to massive vaulting.

As shown also by the above quotation, the method of regulation comprised mainly instructions regarding plant process technology, care also being given to orientate the instructions towards the desired result ('complete condensation', 'fireproof') and to leave the details of execution up to the operator. Initially, thresholds existed only sporadically, as a means of limiting the risk of accidents, mainly caused by the bursting of pressure containers. For example:

Before being used, collection containers from which distillates are extracted by pressure ... must undergo a water pressure test during which 1½ times the working pressure, but at least 1 atmosphere more than the working pressure is applied.

In the following period the regulations for protection at work and environmental protection developed separately, ending with the separation of the air pollution rules out of the Industrial Code by the Federal Immission Protection Act of 1974 and the setting up of specific work protection ordinances.

In the course of this legal development the societal perception of industrial hazards was increasingly being directed from disastrous accidents to the 'normal functioning' of an installation and the possible harmful consequences arising therefrom, especially through chemicals and noise. The scientific basis for establishing contamination thresholds for the protection of human health was initially provided by workplace medicine the empirical basis of which (the many occupational diseases) was as tragic as it was rich, because at the workplace harm was more serious, more visible and therefore more easily traced back to its causes than was possible in the environment at large. All the while that dose-response research on environmental interrelations was lacking, knowledge derived from the study of occupational diseases was frequently extrapolated to make dose-response assumptions for environmental processes. The usual rule of thumb was to divide the hazardous dose found in the workplace context by a factor of 10–20 to get the tolerable environmental dose.

IV   PROCEDURES OF THRESHOLD-SETTING

There are two versions of descriptions of the procedures by which thresholds are set. One version regards thresholds as derivations from findings of natural and applied science – that is, as a kind of hard science; the other version perceives thresholds as the results from a wide range of cognitive and valuation considerations – that is, as a kind of soft science, or even policy. For a long time the second version was reserved for insiders and critical outsiders, while the first version was intended for the general public, being suitable for justification purposes in contexts up to the jurisprudence of the highest courts, which have, in Germany, understood thresholds as pre-set expert opinions – pre-set in the sense that the courts must observe the expert opinions and need not recheck them in each individual case. In the meantime, and most recently when it became clear, for instance, that the 'experts' responsible for the sulphur dioxide thresholds did not anticipate that those thresholds would allow the emergence of acid rain and forest damage, the second version is penetrating the official and judicial level as well. Some commentators favour pluralistically formed committees and disclosure of value judgements. Others adhere to the concept of expert committees, but also demand at least a higher level of opinion for scientifically unresolved value judgements.

Before the first or second, or maybe even a completely different third, conclusion is drawn, it would seem appropriate to take a clear look at the second version of description which obviously is the more realistic one, since only a precise and realistic threshold setting can justify proposals for reform. In so doing I suggest making a distinction between the perspective deriving from the context of justification of thresholds – that is, the analysis of the participants' patterns of argument – and the perspective deriving from the context of discovery – that is, the analysis of interests and forms of organization during the decision-making process. Both levels relate to each other: an analogy would be the description of a conversation with respect to its contents on the one hand and its group dynamic aspects on the other. If asked for their opinion as to the most convincing participant in the conversation, the argumentation theorists would choose the participant with the clearest and soundest arguments, whereas the social psychologists would tend to identify the participant with the best conversational tactics or the highest authority. Both points of view illuminate important facets of reality and are legitimate in their own right.

1 Patterns of argumentation in threshold-setting

Ideally, the argumentation of scientifically based thresholds develops in three steps:

1 The law forbids contaminations which are harmful to the health.
2 Science indicates at which dosage the symptoms of disease start to appear.
3 This dosage is made the threshold.

In analogy, the argumentation of thresholds (principally emission limits), based on applied science, develops as follows:

1 The law forbids emissions in so far as it is possible to reduce these according to the given state of the art.
2 Engineering sciences indicate what the state of the art is and up to what limit it allows a reduction of emissions.
3 This limit is made the standard.

The reality of threshold-setting is completely different. Three deviations from the picture of exact scientific method can be observed:

a)   In the framework of the relevant natural and engineering sciences implicit speculations or assumptions are made.
b)   The necessity for socio-economic scrutiny is underestimated.
c)   Valuations (for example, the balancing of the virtue of protecting life against the cost of protective measures) are carried out.

These deviations are discussed below.

a)   The role of speculations and assumptions in scientific argumentation

Natural scientists, especially when involved in threshold-setting processes, do not limit themselves to statements that are conclusively proved. In particular, inaccuracies bridged by speculations and assumptions, are to be found in the following areas.[10]

Investigative methods   *Epidemiologic investigations*, for example, into the relationship between certain atmospheric pollutants and diseases are usually of low reliability because the causes searched behind the observed effects frequently differ only little from the 'background noise' of other factors. The isolation of specific causative chains is, among other reasons, difficult because, for instance, the areas marked by distinct effects and therefore selected for comparison show overlapping factors, the rate of response to survey is low, the self-diagnosis possibly demanded by the questionnaire is unreliable and so on.

Animal testing in order to find dose-response relationships are of doubtful evidential value, because it is uncertain whether and to what extent the results can be transferred to human beings. Experiments on human beings made to the same purpose, due to their necessary voluntary nature, allow only a limited formation of characteristic groups for comparison, can only deal with small samples, and are usually carried out over short periods of time.

One usually tries to balance out these inaccuracies by collecting as many studies as possible, comparing the results (regarding, for example, dosages causing a specific effect), sorting out exceptional cases and finally choosing from within the spectrum a value close to the lower (cautious) end. This is a questionable procedure due to the fact that the different studies may all show the same inaccuracy. Errors having the same origin do not neutralize each other. It also happens that experiments with low concentrations which have not found significant correlations are not published just because of the negative outcome and the low esteem connected with such kind of publication.

---

10   See, for the following, the contributions by Pflanz, Koller, Schlipkötter in Umweltbundesamt (ed.), Medizinische, biologische und ökologische Grundlagen zur Bewertung schädlicher Luftverunreinigungen, *Sachverständigenanhörung*, 24 February 1978.

Subject of assessment Not only are the methods of investigation imperfect, but the subject itself is poorly defined. The connections between pollutants and diseases are much more complex and intertwined than the legislation regarding dosage-response envisages and is willing to accept. Thinking along the lines of thresholds for a given response neglects the multitude of effects which only one pollutant might bear, the increase of this multitude through a combination of intervening substances and the biological variability of the receiver organisms. Particularly high uncertainty exists regarding substances causing and intensifying cancer. There is reason to believe that these kinds of substance have effects at extremely low concentrations, a hypothesis which nevertheless can hardly be proved because of the very nature of a low concentration. One is stuck with making extrapolations from tests with higher dosages, which gives them a strongly speculative character. It is important though to understand that the problem of small quantities arises not only with carcinogenic substances but also with other sensitizing substances.

Statistics Ideally, the mathematical depiction of the results of a scientific investigation should precisely mirror the extent of the uncertainty. However, the method of depiction contains inaccuracies in itself. For example, the researcher has a choice between a number of mathematical models for representing the experiment results. Even in ostensibly neutral statistics one can find a hidden tendency towards the acceptance of risks and against cautiousness: when the harmfulness of a substance is being assessed, an error margin of 5 per cent is usually chosen for the correctness of the positive hypothesis. In the case of a negative result, the harmfulness is negated although, according to statistical calculation, a margin of error of up to 95 per cent for the negative result is possible.[11] This consequence can manifest itself especially when dealing with substances (for example, carcinogenic substances) for which the concentration of exposure occurring is extremely low.

Deductions of thresholds from doses Even when a specific dose-response relationship (for example the critical concentration of cadmium which impairs the functioning of kidneys) has been extensively researched, the tolerable pollution value (that is, the admissible concentration of cadmium in the air) is not automatically given. Thus additional research is necessary to determine the intake through respiration, food and drink, reabsorption, excretion, and possible accumulation or decomposition by the affected organism. Such research is usually fragmentary, and once again speculations and assumptions have to fill the gaps.

---

[11] G. Osius, Mathematisierung von Dosis- Wirkungsbeziehungen und statistische Analyse von Beobachtungsdaten, in: G. Winter (1986), *op. cit.*, p. 49 *et seq.*

Taking the example of the German threshold proposed for cadmium,[12] the oral intake of this substance was totally neglected, with only respiration intake being taken into account. Moreover the period of intake through respiration was limited to only 50 years. Therefore the average human being who does not contract a disease due to the threshold resulting from these calculations is assumed to live on nothing but air, and this only for 50 years. On the other hand, out of two values proposed in the literature for the reabsorption period (the so-called biological half-life value), the higher one was taken on – that is, the one assuming a longer reabsorption period. This means that the so-called conservative approach was applied.

Safety factors   The multiple uncertainties found in the subject itself, as well as in the methods used and the conclusions drawn are summarily taken into account by the application of safety factors – that is, by multiplying the resulting threshold by, for instance, 1 to 10, 1 to 100 or even 1 to 1000. The factor used will differ greatly according to the knowledge accumulated about the pollutant under consideration. It is often not at all clear what kind of uncertainty is 'absorbed' by this factor and in particular what is its relationship to the statistical statements regarding confidential areas. The following could be named:

- number of tests performed;
- size of tested sample;
- method of testing;
- steepness of the dose-response curve;
- patho-physiological mechanisms of the pollutant;
- accumulation and degradation of the pollutant;
- severity of the disease effected by the pollutant.

On the other hand it has been asserted that safety factors cover the area of total ignorance, while in areas where even fragmentary information exists, one should work with statistical methods. Besides, the safety factor may not be in the least influenced by considerations of how easy it is both politically and economically to carry through a reduction of each existing level of pollution.

Measurement provisions   Thresholds are understood as limits of pollutants or noise which actually exist and have an effect. The degree of the actual contamination is not evident; rather it has to be measured. Measurements, however, are always constructions of reality, never an exact copy. Inaccuracies occur more frequently, the more strongly the contaminations fluctuate in time and location. Due to the fact that it is impossible to measure everything permanently, measurement provisions must be added to the thresholds in order to deal with these fluctuations.

---

12   See the proposal and its justification by J. Krause-Fabricius in Winter (1986), *op.cit.*, p. 285 *et.seq.*

For instance, when determining short-term pollution values of the German TA Luft the highest 2 per cent of the actually measured values can be disregarded and, for the long-term threshold, an average is taken of the values measured in a (again especially constituted) reference area, leading to a result far from realistic value. This applies even more so if, when approving new plants, contamination prognoses are involved, which are to be extrapolated from emission data about a not yet existing installation and transformed into pollution data by application of often highly controversial simulation models on the distribution of emissions by air and water. In this way, reality is not only scientifically reconstructed, but the relevant science (in this case meteorology) is, in turn, legally reconstructed. The distance from actual contamination and, with it, the uncertainty is thus doubled.

b)   The use of socio-economic argumentation

When a more or less well founded dose-response curve connecting different concentrations with corresponding harmful effects is derived from the natural sciences, it may be asked which point on the curve should be chosen as the threshold. In order to answer this question socio-economic arguments which are often not made explicit or are based on rather rough guesses come into play. It is worth considering whether the relevant sciences – sociology and economics – should not be consulted more. The still rough, but possibly improvable, assumptions used consider, for instance, at which point the benefit derived from the threshold exceeds the costs of its realization. If a threshold is to be achieved which is so strict that the cost of anti-pollution investment is higher than the benefit derived from the saved health care costs, then this would speak against it and in favour of a less strict value.

Later we shall discuss whether such cost-benefit considerations are legally permitted at all (doubts arise because of the non-monetarizable concerns). We are dealing here only with a description of actual decision-making processes, where socio-economic discussion undoubtedly does take place.

An example of a scientific approach is a study which shows that a decrease of benzol emission from certain plants from 0 to 90 per cent costs 2.9 to 3.6 million $ per avoided death from cancer, a decrease from 90 to 97 per cent 32.7 to 40.7 million $ and a decrease from 97 to 99 per cent 32.8 to 94.4 million $. But science cannot truly judge the value of one life.

Even in cases of such apparently exact analysis the question arises as to the limits of scientific methods and the role of speculations and assumptions. Uncertainty and inaccuracy[13] often exist regarding the cost of waste avoidance and

---

[13]   N. Ashford in Winter (1986), *op.cit.*, p. 116 *et seq.*

clean-up procedures or the development of new products and also fail to take account of the fact that

- the required anti-pollution technologies will become cheaper and the more benign products more profitable with the general penetration of the market which will follow a technology-forcing threshold; and
- management will learn to act more efficiently in the newly designed framework.

Regarding the benefit derived from different thresholds there is wide dissent about assumptions on

- the expression of the value of human lives, human health and other basically non-monetarizable goods in monetary terms;
- the comparison of present and future benefit: in particular, how a future benefit can be discounted – that is, be calculated as a current benefit;
- the taking into account of such beneficial side effects of standards, as, for example, the advantages of modernization to be gained in connection with required avoidance technologies;
- the fact that the particular industrial branch might have invested into pollution avoidance technology even without the standard being applied.

c)   Valuations

Speculations and assumptions which fill gaps in the knowledge of the natural and social sciences can, themselves, only partially be supported by scientific findings. Instead, they are heavily influenced by value judgements. Value judgements are even more relevant when it has to be decided for which substances standards shall be set and for which not. For instance, only about ten dangerous substances have been selected for pollution thresholds to be set by the German TA Luft whereas the other hundreds of, sometimes also very hazardous substances, were left unregulated.

Opinions differ widely with respect to such value judgements. The probably most important crossroad leads to the question of the burden of proof when a harmful effect cannot be clearly determined. One side shifts the burden of proof to the causative party and requires the most extensive safety measures until research is far enough advanced to signal the 'all clear'. The other side chooses the traditional path of economic liberalism: as long as damage has not been proven by research, there is no reason to initiate protective measures (or at least not expensive ones).

Criteria for valuations can be brought into play from the relevant laws. These contain hierarchies and exclusions amongst such criteria as human health, natural environment, economic gain, job creation, cost saving and so on.

A good example of the significance of value judgements is the above-mentioned difference between occupational health and environmental protection thresholds. The difference can be explained by the attitude in the cases of MAK standards, which are based on a tradition of compensation for workplace diseases, to think along the lines of diseases and the robustness of the organism, whereas in cases of environmental thresholds which are stimulated by more or less suffering neighbours one tends to look rather from the point of view of indisposition and sensitivity. Behind the differences of criteria that are applied *de facto* and directed by law, lie differences in history and differences in the political power basis of the working and living world. Health protection at work had to emancipate itself from a much higher level of 'normal' incidence of harm to human health than environmental protection, and was supported by the labour organizations which were politically far weaker than the bourgeosie which supported environmental protection.

2 Organization of standard-setting

The way in which thresholds are established cannot be fully understood if only the level of argumentation (with scientific findings, assumptions, value judgements) is examined. The *context of discovery* in other words, the social organization of threshold-setting should also be considered.[14] Utmost significance has been given here, among other things, to the composition of the committees which propose thresholds or actually determine them.[15] As far as individual but not general standards are concerned, the negotiation process between the operator and the authority plays an important role. When considering standard-setting by committees, the qualification and affiliation of their members is of prime importance.

In approaching the issue in terms of the level of argumentation or the *context of justification* it is logical to expect that all sciences relevant for the envisaged topic are represented as, for instance, chemical science, medicine, ecotoxicology, engineering and economics for the establishment of immission thresholds for toxic substances. Experts in moral judgement, for instance theologists, could be added. Furthermore, in this perspective the appointment of persons representing different strands in scientific controversies, for instance as to the risk of fissile nuclear power, would probably be demanded. In fact, standards are indeed often formulated by scientific committees. However, in most cases, experts from the soft sciences (economics, ethics – if they are sciences at all) are missing, and little care is taken to have scientific controversies represented on the committees. In the latter

---

[14] See also chapter 15 by E. Rehbinder in this volume.
[15] See, for instance, M. Böhm, Rechtliche Probleme der Grenzwertfindung im Umweltrecht, *Umwelt- und Planungsrecht,* 1994, p. 132 *et seq.*

respect the Consensus Workshop practised in the USA[16] could serve as a model. In this workshop are represented any scientists who have worked on a certain subject irrespective of whether this work was commissioned or carried out independently, thereby giving a representation of a broad spectrum of opinions. Admittedly, the result may not be a threshold proposal but rather only a summary of what has been researched, illuminated or remains open. But, even then it is valuable material for follow-up evaluation and identification of standards.

Following the logic of the 'context of discovery' one would start off with the assumption that standard-setting is principally influenced by socio-economic interests. Even science appears as an interest in this perspective. The scientific training and professional practice of the scientists do not confer on them an independence, even insofar as university teachers are concerned. Research appointments and grants from external sources which they are always eager to receive may make them less independent than scienstists employed by industry. The fact that scientific affiliation and independence do not go hand-in-hand cannot be emphasized too strongly, particularly in view of the fact that the opposite belief is so widespread. The interest-based perspective would require that the interests affected by the subject envisaged for standard-setting must be represented in the relevant committee including, in the environmental field, environmental associations.

An example of a pluralistically formed committee is the Committee for Dangerous Working Materials at the German Federal Ministry for Work and Social Order. Representatives of the employers, the employees, the authorities and the universities (mostly scientists having a certain affiliation with the pertinent interest group) are equally appointed to this committee. Standards concerning environmental risks, however, are still mainly being developed in committees in which representatives of the associations for environmental protection are completely missing. Thus, for example, the Committee for Nuclear Technology (KTA) at the Federal Ministry for the Interior includes: 20 representatives of manufacturers and operators of nuclear installations; 10 representatives from the supervisory authorities; 10 representatives from expert and consulting organizations, and 10 representatives from other authorities, the institutions for nuclear research, insurances, labour unions and the Deutsches Institut für Normung (DIN). Although there have long been numerous scientists opposed to the exploitation of nuclear energy, none of them has been invited to be a member. Although regulations from the KTA on technical safety are published before their final approval and thus made available for critical comment, this can in no way substitute for working on the committee itself, with access to the background material of the technical regulation and the debates in the committee sessions.

---

[16]   See DiMento in Winter (1986), *op.cit.*, p. 103 *et seq.*

The situation in Germany in this respect still lies behind the concept of 'balanced representation' which is demanded by the US Federal Advisory Committee Act 1972. The scenario is further complicated in the case of international standard-setting. On the international level not only divergent national cultures of risk perception, but also different national economic interests come into play. The European Union has established a peculiar structure to reflect this fact – the so-called comitology. Very frequently, EC legislative Acts delegate powers of technical standardization to the Commission, but with the proviso that the Commission must consult a committee of Member State representatives (mostly experts from the relevant high authorities), and that, if the committee's qualified majority dissents (which proves that the question is not merely technical), the Council may revoke the decision.[17]

I have presented two different perspectives of standard-setting which can intellectually be separated from each other. In the real world, however, it must be decided which path to take. For instance, in the German Act on Genetic Engineering (*Gentechnikgesetz*) a combination of both approaches has been tried: the Committee for Biological Safety (*Zentrale Kommission für Biologische Sicherheit*) which, among other things, gives advice on safety standards for biotechnology, comprises experts from a number of relevant sciences on the one side and representatives of different societal interests on the other. I am not sure that a simple summation of the scientific and the interest approach is a viable solution. It is interesting to note in this respect that the representative of the environmental associations has given up her membership because she did not have the financial means to collect the necessary scientific background information.

It is probably best to differentiate with respect to the subject matter which is to be standardized. Sometimes the problem is primarily of a scientific nature. Then the first approach should be applied, possibly modified by a proviso requiring the appointing minister to consult the relevant interest groups before he nominates the members. If the matter is more political and value-laden a pluralist composition is preferable; this may even include laypersons as possible candidates for membership. In any case it would be advisable to have as a chairperson someone trained in fair procedures, most probably a lawyer experienced in identifying controversial points and separating factual from value arguments.

V   THE BINDING FORCE OF STANDARDS

Having described the creation and development of thresholds, we should now clarify in what way thresholds are binding on those who are to comply with them.

---

[17]   See, for details of the procedural variants, Chapter 20 by G. Goldenman in this volume.

1   Definition of threshold transgression

Regardless of whether or not non-compliance is connected with legal sanctions, non-compliance must first be defined. This depends on the wording of the threshold and may differ according to the area of application.

Thresholds may depict maximum limits that are not to be exceeded, as, for example, emission and immission values in environmental protection; they may be indicative of values that must, on average, be complied with; and they may be approximate values which serve as guidelines for both operators and authorities.

This differentiation raises the question of whether the variability of technical processes and, in particular, the likelihood of minor accidents (for example, in chemical plants) allows for the setting of strict maximum values at all. For this reason, special thresholds are sometimes set for exceptional cases.[18] Alternatively, measurement and calculation provisions can level peak values resulting from minor accidents, or maximum values can even generally be understood such that a modest transgression does not necessarily entail a sanction but gives reason to initiate an investigation into the causes of the transgression.

2   Legal consequences of threshold transgression

When the threshold is legally enforceable, transgression entails legal consequences which vary greatly according to the legal area. For example, the authorization for the construction and running of a plant may be refused or withdrawn, subsequent orders may be imposed (for example, to install filtering devices or observe certain duties as to occupational health), the marketing of a product may be restricted or forbidden, a fine may be imposed.

Alongside legal areas one can furthermore distinguish between legal consequences which demand a certain behaviour from the polluter (for example, reduction of emissions, not to distribute the produce, not to employ young people at a certain workplace) and legal consequences which cause official interventions (for example, denial of a permission, prohibition of product's distribution, enforcement of compliance and so on). The differentiation serves to emphasize that the polluter must comply with standards even if no special official measure is taken; for instance, he must carry out of his own accord any decrease in emission which becomes technically possible and may not, relying on the originally granted approval, wait for a subsequent official order.

Nevertheless, when thresholds are legally binding this by no means signifies that legal consequences will always follow. In practice there are numerous strate-

---

[18]   This is the case with German nuclear power plants for which thresholds for contamination from manageable accidents are set that are higher than the thresholds for the normal operation of the plant. See Art. 28, para. 3, Strahlenschutzverordnung.

gies of evasion. In this respect, thresholds are often merely negotiating positions forming a basis upon which the authority may barter with the polluter.

Yet another differentiation merits consideration: the legal consequences are usually directed at the party causing the emission or immission. Sometimes, however, the victims of the contamination by pollutants or noise are those who are blamed. The German biological tolerance values (BAT Standards) may serve as an example. When the BAT value of an employee for a pollutant is exceeded, this does not necessarily force the employer to improve the working conditions; on the contrary, depending on the applicable law, it may instead allow the employer to transfer the victim to another workplace or even to dismiss him or her. A similar oblique burden affecting the wrong party can be observed when a farmer is not allowed to feed grass if the threshold for lead contents for animal feed are exceeded because of pollution from a nearby lead factory, or when fishermen are not allowed to sell their catch because, due to the polluted sea, the fish meat does not comply with the thresholds of the foodstuff laws.

3 Legal force of thresholds

In order to be legally binding – that is, to cause legal consequences of the aforementioned kinds – thresholds have to be recognized by legal norms which tie such legal consequences to certain conditions, specially on the transgression of certain thresholds. This happens most obviously through the explicit incorporation of a threshold in the text of a law or regulation. One example of this is the German Regulation for Coal Power Plants 1983 (*Großfeuerungsanlagenverordnung*) which contains emission thresholds categorized according to plant type and age.

A weaker form of the legal recognition of thresholds is the so-called reference (*Verweisung*). Here the legal norm refers to thresholds being set by autonomous or administrative authorities for a closer description of criteria outlined verbally by the norm itself. One must distinguish between references which are complementing and references which are concretizing legal criteria. Both kinds of references can be static or dynamic – static meaning that the threshold referred to is already formulated and shall remain the same, dynamic meaning that any future change in the formulation of the threshold is also referred to. References of a law complementing nature which are dynamic are problematic because they delegate power to institutions which are not democratically legitimized. This is why they are held to be unconstitutional by German doctrine.[19] Alternatively, one could postulate the creation of a legitimizing basis for the autonomous standard-setting by requiring certain procedural safeguards as, for example, the representation of the concerned sciences and interests as well as public notice and comment requirements. This could then be taken as a partial substitution for the parliamentary legitimation.

---

[19] P. Marburger, Die Regeln der Technik, 1979, p. 390 *et seq.*

Such a conception would also fit better with the EC level where, on the one hand, law complementing dynamic references is frequent practice and, on the other hand, parliamentary legitimation is a particularly scarce resource.

The weakest form of legal recognition of thresholds are so-called 'hinge concepts' (*Scharnierbegriffe*) – rather vague terms, used in law which are operationalized through quantified thresholds. An example may clarify this.

In German environmental protection law a characteristic double approach has evolved. The first relates its criteria of environmental protection to the possible harm and marks the threshold of the harmful dosage (the so-called *danger threshold*); the second relates its criteria of protection to the available avoidance technology and marks the threshold of the technically possible (the so-called *precaution threshold*).[20] The interpretation of the relevant legal terms should normally allow the definition of what gravity of pollution a 'danger' or at which emission level an inadequate realization of the 'best feasible technology' is to be assumed: for instance, the term 'danger to health' might, by recourse to legal materials or through teleological interpretation, be read to mean 'causing vegetative malfunctioning of the human vegetative system'. This level of language is sufficiently concrete to be related to the level of empirical knowledge which can be obtained from experts through administrative or court procedures. From them one might deduce that the above-mentioned malfunctioning starts to occur from a daily dosage of 100 µg. This value would then be taken as the precise expression of the danger limit.

General thresholds offer the advantage that the point to which the legal consequence (for example, approval/denial of approval) is attached must not be established anew for each case but is established once and for all. Such an operationalization of the legal term could well be carried out by the courts themselves. They already act in this manner as, for instance, in family law when establishing alimony tables and adjusting them periodically. In environmental law, however, the courts do not see themselves as capable of doing so and prefer to take recourse to the thresholds prepared by administrative or autonomous bodies. In the case of 'hinge concepts' where there is no explicit incorporation of, or reference to, a specific standard, standards cannot be called binding by law. Legal doctrine had therefore to invent auxiliary principles which make the transfer of extra-legal rules into the law plausible.

The German Federal Administrative Court in its *Voerde* decision of 1978 decided in favour of a concept of procedural law applying the rule that expert opinions can be taken as evidence for related allegations: extra-legal thresholds may be accepted as evidence if, for their formulation, the available scientific knowledge was extensively taken into consideration. This allows for them to be taken as 'anticipated' expert opinions, anticipated in the sense that they do not have to be

---

20   Compare G. Winter, Chapter 3 in this volume.

reassessed in individual cases. As with all expert opinions they may only be refuted if reasonable doubts exist as to their validity.[21]

This jurisprudence has been widely criticized. In particular it has been asserted that the volitive not cognitive elements of threshold-setting are being overlooked. If applied to our example this critique would probably state the following: first, the threshold of 100 µg contains an interpretation of the norm in setting the danger threshold at vegetative malfunctioning rather than at the more cautious point of indisposition. Second, it contains uncertainties at many points, even where dose-response ratios based on seemingly 'hard' science have been established. These uncertainties are compensated by speculations, assumptions and valuations. Finally, even when the setting of thresholds appears to be made from a purely medical point of view, economical consequences are also being taken into consideration, if only in disguise.

Under pressure from this kind of criticism the Federal Administrative Court came to feel the need to replace the hypothesis of the anticipated expert opinion by a formula which reflects the political elements in the expert judgement. In the *Wyhl* decision of 1985 the Court acknowledged the executive power to possess the capacity for standardization.[22] This doctrinal shift can best be explained in terms of separation of powers: the earlier attempt to trust in science as a source of quasi-legal standardization thereby instituting science as a kind of constitutional power has failed. Looking for another power into which the capacity for standardization could be invested the Court, echoing an earlier decision of the Federal Constitutional Court,[23] found neither the legislative branch nor the judiciary to be equipped for detailed and flexible standard-setting. Therefore, it took recourse to the executive branch.

It is doubtful whether this was an optimal solution. Upon a closer look the executive agencies are often unequipped for providing both the scientific knowledge and the rational evaluation required for standard-setting. Procedures will have to be developed and given legitimate value which activate the participation of expertise and interests. On the other hand the courts should not restrain themselves too much from this field. They have to play a role in checking whether the procedures were followed, whether diverging scientific and technological opinions were not overlooked, whether or not evaluative elements hidden in the scientific and technological reasoning were brought out into the open, and whether or not relevant arguments were left out of consideration.

---

[21] Decision of 17 February 1978, BVerwGE 55, 250.
[22] Decision of 19 December 1985, BVerwGE 72, 300.
[23] Decision of 8 August 1978, BVerfGE 49, 89.

VI   REFORM CONSIDERATIONS

Reform considerations may be based upon four essential findings:

- Thresholds schematize interrelations which in fact follow highly variable and individual courses.
- Thresholds pretend knowledge which in reality does not exist; furthermore they stabilize the erroneous assumption that a potential for harm is to be assumed only when positive scientific scrutinies are at hand.
- Thresholds are influenced by valuations and thus also by interests.
- Thresholds tend to maximize the protection of a medium thereby risking that the pollution is shifted to another medium (for example, from air to water).

In view of these, and other, shortcomings of thresholds one might consider whether the instrument of threshold-setting should be given up altogether, especially thresholds derived from a thinking backwards process from harm to health and nature contaminations. As almost every quantum of toxic or non-degradable chemicals being released must be considered as too much, consequent avoidance, inclusion and recovery is required. In this respect, a proactive approach forcing technological innovations has up to now proved to be especially effective (and then in the form of emission thresholds which usually follow spectacular accidents). But emission thresholds can still be employed in the area of persisting routine, albeit no longer as a permanent marker but rather only as an instrument which has to be revised according to plan and which serves as an instrument for a stepwise reform towards minimal emission.

Nevertheless, immission thresholds also remain essential because the approach of minimizing emission does not exclude the possibility that dangers to health and the environment might appear – due, for example, to the multitude of the sources being individually minimized. But these thresholds must first be understood anew as only first steps (due to the fact that no exact knowledge can be established) which are tightened systematically and regularly not only in light of new positive findings but also because of the uncertainty of their scientific basis. Such utilization of standards implementing substantive law criteria like prevention and avoidance of harmful effects will also be indispensible in future. But the procedure of threshold-setting needs to receive more intensive attention than it has hitherto because standards are never set without the influence of interests. A wider range of scientists must be involved, as well as a provision for greater publicity of the procedure or the incorporation of a lay element in the decision-making committees.[24]

---

[24]   For more detailed suggestions in this respect see H. v. Lersner, Verfahrensvorschläge für umweltrechtliche Grenzwerte, *Natur und Recht,* 1990, p. 193 *et seq.*

9 Judicial Review of Administrative Action

Albert Mumma

Table of Contents

I THE REMEDIES

In their day-to-day determination of the issues before them, courts review the acts and decisions of public authorities and private individuals alike. The phrase 'judicial review', however, refers specifically to court proceedings whose express purpose is to review the legal validity of acts and decisions of public authorities. The procedure under English law is the 'application for judicial review'. In the UK, unlike many other continental European countries, there are no special 'administrative courts' for dealing with judicial review applications; such cases simply come before the ordinary courts.

Provision for judicial review is made in s.31 of the Supreme Court Act 1981 and Order 53 of the Rules of the Supreme Court, which codified the common law. The Act requires an application to be made to the High Court. As a preliminary step the applicant must seek leave of the court, allowing the application to be made. The need to obtain leave enables the court to filter out deserving from undeserving applications; the latter are dismissed without a hearing. The application for leave is typically determined on the basis of affidavits sworn by the parties without an oral hearing of the evidence.

The remedy sought will be any or several of the following orders:

1   quashing a decision by a public body;

2   stopping a public body from acting unlawfully;
3   requiring a public body to perform its duty;
4   declaring the legal position of the litigants; and
5   monetary compensation.

The court may also be asked for an injunction to hold the position of the parties before the matter is determined. It is a requirement that the application be made within three months of the cause of action arising unless there are special circumstances justifying a delay. Indeed the court has the discretion to dismiss an application brought within the three-month limit if it could reasonably have been brought sooner. The above orders are known as *certiorari*, prohibition, *mandamus* and declaration.

1   *Certiorari*

An order to quash a decision of a public body is known as a *certiorari*. It is awarded where the public body has acted:

1   beyond its legal powers (that is, *ultra vires*) – a decision or an act of a public body may be *ultra vires* for various reasons such as the failure to take into account relevant matters or taking into account irrelevant ones;
2   contrary to the principles of natural justice: these require an absence of bias and a fair hearing in decision making;
3   in error of the law.

In awarding an order for *certiorari* the court does not substitute its decision for that of the public body concerned. *Certiorari* simply quashes the unlawful decision, leaving the public body free to make another decision. Judicial review is not an appeal on the merits of the decision challenged: it challenges the legality of the decision. The merits of a decision can only be challenged in appeal proceedings.

2   Prohibition

An order stopping a public body from acting unlawfully is known as 'prohibition'. The award of prohibition stops the public body from undertaking an act or taking a decision which would be unlawful for the same reasons outlined under the discussion on *certiorari*. Prohibition is therefore a pre-emptive remedy which can be resorted to where there is reason to fear an illegal act or decision.

Prohibition is paralleled by the injunction, which serves a similar function both in private law (that is, actions based on tort or contract) and in public law (that is, judicial review applications). The injunction can be temporary, preserving the situation while the matter is determined, or permanent.

3 *Mandamus*

An order requiring a public body to perform its duty is known as a *mandamus*. It is awarded where a public body has failed to exercise a duty to act or take a decision, but not where it has a discretion whether or not to do so. Thus, *mandamus* may be awarded to require a public body to give reasons for its decision if there is a statutory duty to give reasons.

4 Declaration

An order which simply declares the legal position of the litigants without granting some further remedy is known as a 'declaration' or a 'declaratory judgement'. Provision for declaratory judgements is made in Order 15, rule 16 of the Rules of the Supreme Court which states that:

> No action or other proceeding shall be open to objection on the ground that a merely declaratory judgement or order is sought thereby, and the court may make binding declarations of right whether or not any consequential relief is or could be claimed.

But as the court stated in *Gouriet* v. *Union of Post Office Workers and others*[1] 'the jurisdiction of the court is not to declare the law generally or to give advisory opinions; it is confined to declaring contested legal rights, subsisting or future, of the parties represented in the litigation before it and not those of anyone else'. Thus there must be a genuine legal, as opposed to academic, dispute before the court can give a declaratory judgement. Although no action is specifically ordered by a declaratory judgement, a public authority will normally act in the spirit of it. A declaration is therefore as effective a remedy as any of the others.

5 Alternative remedies

The application for judicial review is a flexible procedure enabling the applicant to apply for a combination of the above remedies without having to make a choice. The court, having heard the evidence, is free to award the most appropriate rem-

---

[1] [1978] AC 435.

edy in the circumstances. It may also award monetary compensation in the same proceedings.

However, the application for judicial review is not available in all cases. It does not replace the ordinary private law remedies in contract and tort. There are no clear criteria on the distinction between 'public' proceedings (for which judicial review is the appropriate procedure) and private proceedings (for which it is not). However, one may not choose to proceed by way of judicial review in a private law dispute with a public body for the sole reason that the defendant is a public body. Also, judicial review does not replace the expressly provided statutory remedies against the decisions of public bodies.

The position regarding the availability of private law remedies is illustrated by the recent case of *Equal Opportunities Commission and another* v. *Secretary of State for Employment*[2]. The Employment Protection Act 1978 provided that full-time workers qualified for redundancy payments after two years' employment while part-time workers only qualified after five years' employment. Because the majority of part-time workers were women the Equal Opportunities Commission brought a judicial review application against the Secretary of State arguing that this constituted discrimination against women and was contrary to the requirements of EC law. A part-time worker who had been made redundant by her employer after less than five years' employment joined the action. The court held, in relation to the part-time worker, that this was not the appropriate forum in which to adjudicate on her claim against her employer. Her application was therefore dismissed although the main case succeeded.

The position regarding statutory remedies is less clear-cut. Statutory remedies are typified by the provision in planning legislation which enables those who are 'aggrieved' (dissatisfied) with the decision of the planning authority to challenge the legal validity of the decision by appealing to the Minister (who may set up a 'public inquiry' to consider the appeal) and, if this appeal fails, making an application to the courts. There is a short time limit – normally six weeks after the Minister's decision – within which the application to the courts must be made. The grounds upon which a planning decision may be challenged under the statutory remedy are the same grounds for bringing an application for judicial review, that is, *ultra vires* and the principles of natural justice.

These statutes typically state that after the expiry of six weeks the decision 'shall not be questioned in any legal proceedings whatever'. This mechanism is designed to enable decisions to be implemented quickly without the risk of a legal challenge after money has been spent on new developments. In interpreting these provisions the courts have had to balance the need for developments to proceed expeditiously against the injustice of denying an applicant with a grievance access

---

[2] [1994] 1 All ER 910.

to the courts. The courts have come to different conclusions, at times holding that these provisions protect decisions from challenge[3] while at other times, allowing the applicant to challenge the decision.[4]

II STANDING

The application for judicial review is a public law remedy and is designed to control the validity of the acts and decisions of public bodies. Under s.31(3) of the Supreme Court Act 1981 and Order 53 of the Rules of the Supreme Court, leave to make an application for judicial review can only be granted if the court considers that the applicant has 'sufficient interest' in the matter to which the application relates. Sufficient interest is to the application for judicial review what 'aggrieved person' is to the statutory remedy for challenging planning decisions; both limit the category of persons who may come before the court.

The issue of standing is considered at two stages in the proceedings; at the preliminary stage when the application is made for leave to bring the application for judicial review, and again during the hearing of the merits of the application. At the preliminary stage the question is whether the applicant has sufficient interest to apply to the court while at the main hearing the question is whether the applicant has sufficient interest to be entitled to a remedy, assuming that the case is made out. As the court said in *Inland Revenue Commissioners* v. *National Federation of Self-Employed Businesses Ltd*[5] there may be simple cases in which it can be seen at the earliest stage that the person applying for judicial review has no interest at all or insufficient interest to support the application, in which case he would be refused leave to apply at the outset. This is to prevent undeserving applications from being carried forward. In cases where it is not possible to determine at the outset that the applicant does not have sufficient interest the question has to be determined during the main hearing, as part of the application.

Because standing is considered at two stages in the proceedings, defendants have at times adopted the position during the preliminary stage, of not contesting the applicant's standing but reserving their position on the matter. In *R.* v. *Secretary of State for Social Services ex parte Child Poverty Action Group*[6] the court held that the parties cannot, by consent, confer jurisdiction on the court to entertain the application if the applicant does not have the required standing.

---

[3] *Smith* v. *East Elloe RDC* [1956] AC 736.
[4] *The Anisminic* [1969] 2 AC 147.
[5] [1982] AC 617.
[6] [1989] 1 All ER 1047.

1   Who has standing?

Applicants for judicial review may be one of three kinds; a local authority, a private individual and a representative organization. Under English law the position of the local authority is the most straightforward. Section 222 of the Local Government Act gives local authorities the power to bring proceedings in their own name if they 'consider it expedient for the promotion or protection of the interests of the inhabitants of their area'. Private individuals and representative organizations, on the other hand, face the serious hurdle of 'standing' before they can bring a judicial review application.

The general position is that only the Attorney General can sue on behalf of the public for the purpose of preventing public wrongs.[7] Thus, a private individual cannot sue on behalf of the public. An application for judicial review by a private individual can only be entertained if the unlawful conduct interferes with some private right of his or inflicts on him particular injury over and above that suffered by the public at large. This legal position is represented by the requirement, in relation to the application for judicial review, that the applicant demonstrate 'sufficient interest' in the application and by the alternative statutory remedies, that the applicant must be a 'person aggrieved'.

2   Standing for representative organizations

There is no statutory definition of either of the two phrases, 'person aggrieved' and 'sufficient interest'.

Denning LJ said of the 'aggrieved person':

> The words 'person aggrieved' are of wide import and should not be subjected to a restricted interpretation. They do not include, of course, a mere busybody who is interfering in things that do not concern him; but they do include a person who has a genuine grievance because an order has been made which prejudicially affects his interests.[8]

In modern society the key environmental decisions are taken by public bodies. Thus, the approval of development proposals, decisions regarding environmental assessments, the enforcement of environmental requirements through criminal prosecutions and so on are functions discharged by public bodies. The way in which the public bodies concerned discharge these functions is therefore crucial to the effectiveness or otherwise of environmental protection.

---

[7] *Gouriet* v. *Union of Post Office Workers* [1978] AC 435.
[8] In *A.G (Gambia)* v. *Njie* [1961] 2 All ER 504, 511.

Under English law a public body has discretion whether or not to exercise a power available to it. This discretion is subject to the supervision of the courts through the application for judicial review, which ensures that it is exercised objectively. Where the application for judicial review is brought by an individual whose legal right is (or will be) prejudiced in some way by the action or inaction of the public body, the environmental consequences of the decision challenged are not the primary issue at stake and whatever environmental benefit results from a successful challenge is welcome but only purely incidental.

Alternatively, the application for judicial review or resort to the statutory remedy available may be brought by a third party – someone whose concern lies predominantly in ensuring effective environmental protection. Increasingly, the third party is a professional environmental pressure group or someone acting with the backing of such a group rather than an individual acting on his own. The third party and the environmental pressure group face a serious hurdle in trying to prove that they have sufficient standing or a grievance to enable them to challenge the decision of the public body. The concept of standing therefore represents the principal challenge in the development of judicial review as a mechanism for environmental protection. Whereas there is a clear trend towards judicial recognition of the interest of third parties in environmental protection, the issue is by no means resolved.

Buxton v. *Minister of Housing and Local Government*[9] represents the more restrictive approach to standing. The Minister's decision to overturn the decision of a local authority refusing planning permission to extract chalk was challenged by neighbouring landowners who feared injury to their land from the development. The court denied the applicants' standing on the ground that the phrase 'person aggrieved' in a statute meant a person who had suffered a legal grievance; since the applicants had no legal rights which had been infringed they were not entitled to challenge the Minister's decision.

The ruling in *Buxton* was applied in *Burke* v. *Minister of Housing and Local Government*[10] which has significance for environmental pressure groups in so far as it dealt with a representative organization. The applicant applied for a local authority's compulsory purchase order in respect of certain land and premises to be quashed. He was not, and never had been, the owner or occupier of land or premises comprised in the orders but he was the secretary of a tenants' association to which two persons living in the premises comprised in the orders belonged. He argued that, in these circumstances, he was a 'person aggrieved' by the orders and entitled to make the application. The court dismissed the application on the

---

9   [1961], 1 QB 278.
10   [1957], 8 P & C.R., 25 (Digested in 57, 1583).

grounds that the applicant had not suffered a legal grievance and therefore he was not a 'person aggrieved'.

However, the courts have since moved towards a more accommodating approach, abandoning the restrictive interpretation which insists on there being a legal grievance. In *Turner and Another* v. *Secretary of State for the Environment*[11] the chairman and secretary of a local preservation society who had objected to a proposed development and made representations at the local public inquiry were granted standing to challenge the Secretary of State's decision, a challenge they lost because of a legal technicality unrelated to the question of standing. According to Ackner J.:

> any person who, in the ordinary sense of the word, was aggrieved by a decision, and certainly any person who had attended and made representations at the inquiry, should have the right to establish in the courts that the decision was bad in law ....

Thus, the courts now recognize that representative bodies may have the necessary standing to challenge the decision, arguing that the fact that they have made representations on the proposals gives them the right to challenge in court the decision that follows.

These representative bodies are not, however, motivated primarily by an interest in environmental protection. Typically, they are associations formed in order to pursue more effectively what are private interests, such as interests in land. On the whole the cases have dealt with whether such bodies are aggrieved persons.

The application for judicial review is based on the need to establish 'sufficient interest' and the courts have shown a similar ambivalence in construing this phrase in the context of environmental protection.

In *R* v. *Secretary of State for the Environment ex parte Rose Theatre Trust Co.*,[12] 'the Theatre Company' was formed to preserve the remains of an historical theatre which was discovered during the development of a site. The company's application for the theatre to be protected under the Ancient Monuments and Archeological Areas Act 1979 failed and the company sought judicial review of the Secretary of State's decision. Its standing to seek judicial review was challenged on the ground that it did not have 'sufficient interest' in the matter. The court upheld this challenge on the basis that the company could have no greater claim to standing than its individual members had (and no member had standing).

However, in the more recent *R* v. *HMIP and MAFF ex parte Greenpeace*[13] Greenpeace sought judicial review of the decision to grant British Nuclear Fuels

---

[11] [1973] vol. 288 EG 32.
[12] [1990] 1 QBD 504.
[13] *The Independent*, 30 September 1993.

Ltd permission to test its nuclear plant at Sellafield. BNFL's challenge of Greenpeace's standing failed. Justice Otton held that Greenpeace was an entirely responsible and respected body with a genuine concern for the environment, 2,500 of whose members lived around the plant. Additionally, Greenpeace had the expertise to mount a well informed challenge thereby saving the court's time and resources. The judge distinguished the Rose Theatre case on the basis that the company had been formed for the exclusive purpose of saving the theatre and no individual member could show any personal interest in the outcome.

Similarly, in *R* v. *Secretary of State for the Environment ex parte Friends of the Earth*[14] FoE sought judicial review of the Secretary of State's decision not to take enforcement action against two suppliers of public drinking water for their failure to meet the standards prescribed for the pesticide levels in drinking water. The court held that FoE had standing to bring the application since FoE was 'a company of high repute and accepted as having relevant expertise'.

In these two cases the environmental groups were granted standing primarily because their recognized expertise in the field meant that they could conduct the action professionally and thus save the court's time and resources. This is no doubt important, particularly in an era when environmental protection has become a complex and professional pursuit involving the interpretation of complex pieces of legislation and sifting through technical and scientific evidence. It is self-evident that an individual on his own would not be able to mount the sort of well informed challenge that is often necessary.

R v. *Poole BC ex parte Beebee and others*[15] represents a different trend in thinking. This was an application for judicial review of a grant of planning permission for a housing development on land which the Nature Conservancy Council wished to designate as a 'site of special scientific interest'. Two representatives of the Worldwide Fund for Nature (UK) and two members of the British Herpetological Society (BHS) applied for judicial review of the decision. The BHS had a long established association with the subject sites and much of its work had been funded by the Nature Conservancy Council. Indeed one of the conditions of the planning permission for the housing estate provided that 'prior to any development starting on the site a full season's notice shall be given to the BHS to enable the catching and relocation of rare species known to inhabit the site'. The position of the WWF was that it had made grants to the BHS since 1971 to assist them in carrying on their work and was an internationally renowned environmental organization. The court held that 'the BHS, with its long association with this site, its financial input into the site and its connection with planning permis-

---

[14]   *Times*, 4 April 1994.
[15]   (1991), *Journal of Environmental Law*, **3**(2), 293.

sion by being named therein, had sufficient interest to make the application for judicial review'. The WWF however did not, on its own, have sufficient interest.

This case seems to indicate that, by close association and active involvement with environmental protection issues, particularly at local levels, an environmental organization can acquire sufficient standing to bring an application whose purpose is the protection of the environment. Fully developed this would amount to the granting of standing to an organization to represent environmental interests. Granting standing to some organization as representing particular environmental interests is the closest one can come to giving the 'environment' standing in its own right (that is, the only practical way to respond to the question 'do trees have standing?').

This above case is comparable to the decision of the Dutch Supreme Court in *De Nieuwe Meer*.[16] This case involved an action for an injunction by three public interest groups against the city of Amsterdam for dumping dredgings from canals in an artificial lake, the De Nieuuwe Meer. They sought a prohibition of further dumping on the ground that the environment was being harmed. The Supreme Court granted standing to these groups on the basis of their objectives as set out in their articles of association.

In Germany the position that an association does not have standing prevails, although the *Länder* (regional governments) have the competence to grant them standing, and some have done so.[17] The position varies between European States.[18] Most apply severe restrictions on the ability of associations to bring judicial review action, and the few who allow it, such as Poland, have had few examples of the right being utilized.

III   ENFORCING EU REQUIREMENTS

In the European Union (EU) individuals may force implementation of EU requirements by bringing action in local courts, because a series of European Court of Justice (ECJ) judgements have established the principle that certain EU requirements have 'direct effect' on individuals. This gives individuals a right to sue their state for any damage they have suffered through the state's failure to implement the requirements, or for implementing them inadequately. EU requirements

---

[16] 1986, recounted in G. Betlem, *Civil Liability for Transfrontier Pollution*, London: Graham & Trotman Ltd., ch. 6.

[17] G. Winter (ed.), *German Environmental Law: Basic Texts and Introduction*, Dordrecht: Martinus Nijhoff, 1994, pp 54-7.

[18] See M. Führ, G. Roller (eds), *Participation and Litigation Rights of Environmental Associations in Europe*, Frankfurt: Peter Lang, 1991.

have direct effect only if they are clear and unambiguous, unconditional and not dependent on further action by the EU or the Member State.

The extent to which these conditions can be applied to environmental Directives is still not clear. In *Wychavon DC* v. *Secretary of State for the Environment*[19] a UK court held that the environmental assessment Directive (85/337/EEC) did not meet the requirements for direct effect to apply. But in *Twyford Parish Council* v. *Secretary of State for Transport*[20] another UK court took the view that the provisions of the same Directive were unconditional and sufficiently precise to enable it to have direct effect. Recently, in the Lombardia case[21] the ECJ held that Article 4 of the Waste Framework Directive which requires Member States to ensure that waste is disposed of without endangering human health and without harming the environment does not give individuals rights which they can use to sue in their national courts. The extent to which individuals can claim direct effect in the environmental field would therefore seem to be restricted.

However, where the object which the individual wishes to achieve is environmental protection then the provisions for ensuring the implementation of EU requirements may be relied even although the individual is unable to demonstrate direct effect. Article 169 of the Treaty of Rome sets out the procedure for ensuring that Member States implement EC requirements. If the Commission considers that a Member State has failed to fulfil an obligation under the Treaty, it shall deliver a reasoned opinion on the matter after giving the state concerned an opportunity to submit its observations. If the state does not comply with the opinion within the period laid down by the Commission then the Commission may bring proceedings before the ECJ which may find that the Member State has failed to fulfil an obligation under the Treaty.

A second way in which individuals can force a Member State to implement the requirements of EC law is by commencing action in the national courts. Under Article 177, where a matter of EC law is raised before a national court and the national court considers that a decision on the question is necessary to enable it to give judgement, the national court may request the ECJ to give a ruling on the matter. In *R* v. *Secretary of State for Employment ex parte Equal Opportunities Commission* (above) the Commission applied for a declaration that the provisions of the UK law were incompatible with EC law. The Secretary of State argued that the court had no jurisdiction to declare that the UK was in breach of Community law and that the appropriate procedure was to submit the question to the ECJ. The court rejected this argument and held that a national court was an equally appropriate forum for adjudicating upon whether UK law was compatible with EC re-

---

[19] Times, *7 January 1994.*
[20] *Journal of Environmental Law*, **4** (2), p. 273.
[21] Case 236/92, transcript, 23 February 1994.

quirements and there was no need to refer the question to the ECJ. This judgement enables questions of implementation to be adjudicated in UK local courts, reducing the scope for delay which normally arises when matters are referred to the ECJ.

Whereas the ability to bring judicial review proceedings in relation to the implementation of EC requirements is a useful mechanism which may be resorted to for environmental protection, it would be a retrograde step for the individual to be restricted to the national court and denied the option of seeking to have the matter taken before the ECJ. This is because, on the substantive issue, the ECJ and the national court may come to different conclusions. The ECJ has consistently held that practical difficulties cannot be used to justify the failure to implement EU requirements.

In *Commission* v. *UK*[22] proceedings were brought against the UK for supplying drinking water which breached the standard for nitrates. The Court rejected the UK's argument that the Directives did not impose an obligation to achieve a result but merely required Member States to take all practicable steps to comply with the standard laid down, which it had done. The UK argued that its failure to achieve the standard was due to the fact that nitrate fertilizer was used in agriculture. The Court held that this was no more than a 'special circumstance' which could not be relied on to justify a failure to achieve the standard specified.

In the Friends of the Earth case above, FoE sought judicial review of the Secretary of State's decision not to take enforcement action against two suppliers of public drinking water for their failure to meet the standards prescribed for the pesticide levels. The court accepted the Secretary of State's argument that there were many complexities involved in bringing the water up to the required standard and the applicant had not demonstrated that the approach the Secretary of State had taken was too leisurely.

On balance, therefore, applicants should be able to continue bringing matters to the attention of the Commission with a view to the matter being taken to the ECJ for consideration. However in the UK the Equal Opportunities Commission case has given a boost to the possibility of judicial review action being taken against the UK authorities over their implementation of EU requirements. The court granted the Commission, a statutory body, standing to bring the application on the basis that the statutory duties of the Commission included working towards the elimination of discrimination and promoting equal opportunity between men and women.

The second question was whether the court had jurisdiction to grant a declaratory judgement that certain UK primary legislation was incompatible with EU law.

---

[22]   Case C-337 [1990] ECR 1-2821.

The court answered in the affirmative. This means that an appropriate environmental organization could seek declaratory judgement that certain UK environmental law is incompatible with EU requirements. This is even more likely in view of the Marleasing judgement[23] that national courts must interpret national law in a manner consistent with EU requirements. How soon this will be tested remains to be seen.

IV COSTS

Under English law the general rule is that the losing party pays the costs of the successful party. These can be considerable as they include costs of gathering evidence and calling expert witnesses, in addition to paying the lawyers. Costs are often a deterrent, preventing many individuals and environmental organizations from bringing an application for judicial review.

There is a line of cases indicating that a non-party (such as an environmental organization) who provides financial support for litigation which does not succeed may be held liable for the successful party's costs. In *Singh* v. *Observer Ltd* the court said:

...the court would not be helpless to make an order, should it be proved that an action has truly been kept going purely because of outside financing, and thus to have been maintained, without the maintainer having any interest whatsoever in the litigation, and by persons who hope never to be made liable for a penny of the other side's costs, should their action fail.[24]

This restricts the extent to which environmental organizations can resort to the strategy of using an individual who has standing to bring the action. The court may order the organization to meet the costs of the action, despite the fact that the name of the organization does not appear in the case.

The courts have discretion to waive the general rule as to costs. Increasingly it is argued that environmental organizations who act out of a genuine concern for the environment, rather than for personal gain, should be encouraged by not being made to pay costs should the action fail. This argument succeeded in the Greenpeace case but failed in the Friends of the Earth case. The court in the latter case said that 'while there may be something to be said for subsidy to be given by the tax payer to FoE, this is an inelegant way of achieving that'. The issue is therefore still unresolved and is likely to vary from case to case. Its positive resolution would

---

23 Case C-106/89 [1990] ECR 4135.
24 [1989] 2 ALL ER 751, 756.

assist environmental organizations to exercise actively the right to standing which they seem to be slowly gaining.

10 Implementation of Administrative Environmental Law: a Case Study of Italy

Antonella Capria

Table of Contents

I PREMISES

To date EU environmental policy has materialized in nearly 200 regulatory Acts issued over the last 20 years and based on guidelines laid down in action programmes.[1] This policy has often derived from initiatives of national governments or parliaments, which at the same time form the basis of the national decision-making and implementation process. When a Member State supports, or even initiates, a new EC environmental legal Act this by no means implies that it will be the most eager member to put it into national law and practice. Although it would be interesting to discuss the reasons for such an apparently contradictory attitude (do the national representatives simply show off in Brussels, do they collect bargaining chips there for the enforcement game, are they too remote from actual practice?), I shall concentrate on the subject of national implementation.

The subject acquires particular importance since legislators have adopted the unusual practice of delegating to the administration the definition of much of the substantive law as well as of its context, time and method of application. Often, the reason for this lies in the greater flexibility the local level disposes of, but it

---

1   See Chapter 16 on the development of EU environmental law and policy by J. Jans in this volume.

also translates into a deliberate abstention of the legislature to clearly define and decide situations of possible conflict of interest.

In Italy the well documented failure to implement EC Directives has led to accusations of a 'verbal' and 'liturgical' approach to European commitments. A measure of the low level of implementation can be gauged from the seventh annual report of the European Parliament Committee in which Italy has the worst record in respect of infringement proceedings: it also has the highest number of 'complaint letters', the highest number of 'reasoned opinions' and, until 1992, the highest number of cases before the European Court of Justice. In addition it is the only country where this trend is continuing.

It is also the only country which has some difficulty putting Court rulings into effect: a full 21 rulings under Article 171 of the Treaty.

In the following I shall identify the main obstacles in the path of formal and substantial implementation of EU environment law. This will be done by formulating general observations each followed by one or more exemplary cases.

II   INADEQUATE FORM OF REGULATION

Sometimes it is the form of the implementing measure itself which prevents the application of a Community Act; in the environmental field, frequent resort to implementation by government decree, the application of which is strictly limited by the power of legislative delegation, is the source of the problem. Decrees such as these cannot modify the framework of enforcement so as to introduce an element of greater efficiency into public action unless this is expressly provided in the delegation law. Nor can they allocate greater financial resources, nor introduce administrative and/or penal sanctions capable of guaranteeing the correct application of the rules.

Example: Presidential Decree No. 175 of 1988   This decree on risks of major accidents which implements EC Directive 82/501 has been issued based on a parliamentary delegation law, which sets the limits of competence attributed to the executive power. These limits concern both the subjects over which power to make laws is granted to the government, and time limits within which these powers should be exercised. The choice of this particular legislative instrument means the executive regulation is limited within the bounds of delegated powers and cannot introduce any modification to the existing administrative structures in the text of the decree. As a result neither could insurance obligations for companies and other forms of discipline and control of industrial activities proposed by parliamentary committees of the Chamber and Senate be adopted nor could an interministerial committee necessary to coordinate the different powers of competent Ministries be created. Hence, the implementation by decree is flawed due to the absence of a single coordinating body, which could avoid conflicts on questions of competence and consequent administrative delays.

III OVERZEALOUS REGULATION AND ADMINISTRATIVE OVER-LOAD

Moreover, while government and parliament somewhat overzealously intended to extend the above mentioned Directive's initial field of application even though the Directive had expressly limited objectives and there was apparent uniformity of national texts with the EC ones, the implementation regulations interpret the Directive's obligations (particularly concerning the principles of Community action on prevention, information and control) in a quite restrictive way. In some cases, the provisions introduced at the national level are worse than the corresponding measures already in force at the regional level.

Example 1: Decree No. 175 of 1988   This decree on the risks of major accidents, for example, seeks to 'govern' a wider number of companies than the number required by EC Directive 82/501; unlike the Directive, it does not exclude from its application field plants for toxic waste disposal, and it extends the provisions to companies 'at risk', besides the ones at 'high risk'. Globally, it should be applied to 7000–8000 companies.

In contrast to the very wide application and complex procedures envisaged, the controls on new industrial activities are particularly weak: Article 9 of Presidential Decree No. 175 of 1988 provides that a manufacturer can start a new activity after 60 days have elapsed from the notification to the competent authorities of an expert opinion, written by professionals enrolled in the competent Register, notwithstanding the obligation to file the notification (and related preliminary investigation results) in advance. In this way there is no possibility of administrative intervention during the design phase in respect of an authorization that is given after the plant is constructed. Moreover, there are no penal sanctions available against those who file the notification or the declaration in an inexact and incomplete way.

According to data supplied by the Italian Ministry of the Environment, as of 12 November 1991, 212 notifications relating to 707 plants had been filed. On 211 sites identified as high risk, only 21 preliminary investigations had been started, and only 5 of them had reached the penultimate step in this procedure – an opinion from the Advisory Committee on Health.

The situation with respect to declarations to be transmitted at the regional level is no better. According to data from the Ministry of the Environment, as at 12 November 1991, 766 industries at risk had filed declarations. However the data relating to six regions were missing: Valle D'Aosta, and the autonomous provinces of Trento and Bolzano, Abruzzo, Campania, Sicily and Sardinia. Only two regions (Lombardy and Tuscany) have issued provisions regulating control and intervention procedures on the plants at risk.

Example 2: Presidential Decree No. 203 of 1988   This decree subjects manufacturing enterprises to innovative regulations on air pollution.

In fact, while the corresponding EC Directive requires the regulation of some plant categories, the new regulation, in common with Law No. 615 of 1966, applies to all plants that cause emissions to the air. To avoid being less stringent than the existing law, additional plant categories to those listed in Annex 1 of the Directive have been made subject to the obligation to provide a preliminary declaration, as is envisaged by Article 3.3 of the Directive.

From an approximate calculation based on 1991 data, at least 1 million enterprises are affected by the decree in Italy. As a consequence, it is impossible for authorities to grant (and enterprises to obtain) the authorizations within the procedures and time limits required. In Lombardy, two years after the decree came into force, authorization for existing plants had been requested by nearly 150,000 of existing companies, and the authorization proceedings had been concluded for only 100 of them.

To solve some of the problems created by the introduction of national regulations, the Emilia-Romagna region, with Law No. 36 of 1989, increased the number of bodies qualified to issue the authorizations, harmonizing and simplifying the related procedure: before Presidential Decree No. 203 of 1988 came into force, the said region carried out 150–200 preliminary investigations per year; based on the new regional regulation, in the first quarter of 1992 nearly 600 requests had been filed. The Emilia-Romagna region proceeded also to classify the plants according to production areas, indicating for each class the best available technologies, the threshold values, the analysis methods and, in some cases, also the plant construction characteristics.

These criteria are applied only to new plants; emissions from existing plants are regulated at the national level by Ministerial Decree of 12 July 1992. In some cases, the emission thresholds fixed at the national level are higher than those already indicated by single authorization documents.

In Lombardy, too, the application of Presidential Decree No. 203 of 1988 has produced a worsening of threshold values applied to the existing plants when compared to the regional directives already in force.

IV INCOMPLETE AND DELAYED REGULATION

Almost, no piece of EC environmental legislation is fully operational in Italy: notably, environmental impact assessment is still regulated by provisional legislation; provisions on the prevention of major accident hazards have been inadequately applied; provisions relating to air emissions from industrial plants set standards only for existing plants; and provisions concerning dangerous substances in water were approved in 1992 although implementation regulations are yet to be issued.

Faced with obvious difficulties with application, the government has traditionally simultaneously introduced both the principles and, by postponing the issue of definitive implementation provisions, their factual derogation.

Example: EC Directive 80/778   This Directive on drinking waters has been implemented through a decree of the Prime Minister of 8 February 1985. Later the decree was repealed and substituted by Presidential Decree No. 236 of 24 May 1988. The decree of 26 March 1991 provided for the technical rules to implement Presidential Decree No. 236 of 1988.

According to the provisions of the Directive, the terms set for the observance of limit values can be extended in exceptional circumstances with respect to geographically limited urban areas. The said extension is granted by a decree from Ministry of Health in agreement with Ministry of the Environment, on request of the interested region: the extension request must enclose a technical report and a reclamation plan.

In the case of a serious water emergency, where the supply cannot be guaranteed in any other way, a derogation to the limit values up to a maximum admissible level determined by the health authority can be granted, but such a derogation must not constitute an unacceptable risk for public health.

The regions adopt an action plan according to provisions indicated by the national administration. Ministerial Decree of 14 July 1988 laid down the limits for derogations from quality requirements for water destined for human consumption. The decree established the maximum permissible values for derogation from individual parameters up to 31 December 1991, and also provided for the adoption of regional action plans. Later, Ministerial Decree of 23 December 1991 extended the terms of Ministerial Decree of 14 July 1988 to 16 January 1992, in the absence of a law governing quality improvement action and pollution prevention measures for waters destined to human consumption. Ministerial Decree of 20 January 1992 sets new permissible values for those parameters that can be extended, allowing these for two years for nitrates and fluorine and for five years for ammonia, magnesium, manganese, iron, sulphates, sodium and fix residue after drying. The terms of these extensions start from the drafting of regional action plans.

Based on the above-mentioned Directive, Ministerial Decree of 14 February 1989 sets maximum permissible values for some pesticides that the regional extensions may not exceed (for Piedmont, Lombardy, Veneto, Friuli-Venezia Giulia, Emilia-Romagna and Marche). The decree also provides that extensions may not exceed the term of 24 months.

With Ministerial Decree of 8 May 1991, new extensions to the maximum admissible values for pesticides have been introduced at the request of the Lombardy region; the duration of the new extension could not exceed the term of 36 months. Later, Ministerial Decree of 1 July 1991 granted a similar extension to the Veneto and Piedmont regions.

With Decree No. 16 of 5 February 1990, converted into law on 5 April 1990, n. 71, some urgent provisions for quality improvement and for water pollution prevention have been adopted. These provisions, in accordance with an earlier EC agreement, introduce a range of urgent measures and guidelines – relating to the use and sale of herbicides, to the water drawing system and to the water system networks, to the search for, extraction and use of underground waters – which cover the whole national territory and are subject to enforcement by the public administration. The technical rules to implement the decree have, however, not yet been issued.

V   THE LACK OF HOMOGENEITY IN REGULATIONS

Given the lack of a definitive legislative framework at national level, and in the absence of appropriate implementation regulations, there is a strong possibility that the regions, which have general responsibility for environmental planning and control, will develop inconsistent rules. In principle, the Ministry of the Environment can impose environmental plans and issue operational authorizations over the heads of those regions in non-compliance. It may also issue injunctions where there is a risk of environmental deterioration. It cannot, however, substitute for the regions in drawing up rules and standards or impose sanctions on regional bodies. Some regions delay making laws on subjects within their competence, while other regions draft laws without reference to national legislation and in accordance with policies different from those adopted in other regions.

Example 1   One of the best examples of this is the rules on the storage of dangerous waste: in principle Presidential Decree No. 915 of 1982 on waste requires an authorization to store toxic and dangerous waste; a similar obligation is not provided for disposal of industrial waste. While some regions, in accordance with stricter environmental rules, also require an authorization for the storage of industrial waste (for example, Lombardy), other regions did not require any authorization for the storage of toxic and dangerous waste for some time (for example, Campania).

Example 2 A second example, again concerning waste, involves the control of the so-called secondary raw materials. In some regions this material has been considered material for re-use in production, and is not submitted to any particular obligation on the part of companies. In other regions such material is considered waste in all circumstances, even for the purpose of imposing possible penal sanctions. Consequently, in Friuli, foundry sands are materials to be used to fill quarries, and in Abruzzo they are industrial waste to be disposed of in a landfill.

Example 3 Certain regions (the autonomous provinces of Trento and Bolzano) made environmental impact assessment (EIA) mandatory before Italy had implemented the EC Directive on this subject. When national provisions came into force the coordination of environmental impact assessments based on regional rules, and standards and assessments based on national rules and standards, became (and to a degree remain) a problem. Each system requires a different kind of preliminary investigation and different documents to be filed. In fact as the EIA is structured as a sub-proceeding, it is autonomous from all other proceedings: Constitutional Court Ruling No. 210 of 28 May 1987 (autonomous province of *Bolzano* v. *Prime Minister*) declared that Law No. 349 of 1986 does not interfere with regional competence on the approval or authorization of works since separate procedures are followed: the region may oppose carrying out of the works irrespective of the impact assessment decision and may refuse approval or authorization of the project.

VI THE DEFERMENT OF TERMS FOR IMPLEMENTATION

New legislative acts introduced in Italy to put into effect EC rules and standards simplify the decision making process in parliament, although they do not modify the habitual practice of adopting acts whose force is suspended until technical rules are issued. In this way the implementation is deferred until technical rules are in place and, in their absence, contrasting interpretations and disputes over competence frequently arise.

Example: Directive No. 360 of 1984 on emissions into the air from industrial plants has been put into effect by Presidential Decree No. 203 of 24 May 1987, but the provisions of the decree started to be applied only on 31 July 1990.

For new industrial plants, emission standards, such as the lists of best available technologies and the typologies of combustibles allowed have not yet been determined: the Ministry of the Environment has filed some proposals that the Ministry of Industry has still not approved.

At the regional level, the delay in implementing Presidential Decree No. 203 of 1988 has had an impact particularly on the more advanced regions (see section III, example 2 above).

VII   THE USE OF INADEQUATE TECHNOLOGICAL STANDARDS

One of the biggest criticisms directed at 'first generation' environmental legislation (that is legislation drafted from the mid-1960s to the end of the 1980s) is that it was adopted with little attention paid to the underlying science and technology applicable to pollution and environmental protection. Standards for air and water emissions from industrial plants, based on generally practised abatement technologies for the reference sectors, lead to the introduction of end of pipe technologies without encouraging the development of process integrated and recycling techniques.

Moreover, the sectoral approach that governed first generation legislation failed to improve environment quality in general. While Italian legislation has some unquestionable merits developed from the country's experience of emergencies and environmental disasters, it also has the demerit of underestimating the problem of scientific and technological development: there are too few incentives at the industrial level for the continuous improvement of environmental performances, or the development and use of *ex post* adaptation technologies for integrated pollution control. Can techniques which use fewer raw materials, or less dangerous materials be considered better for the environment in general, although the emissions produced from the plants are slightly higher? In 20 years of environmental legislation, in which thousands of authorization and control provisions have been made, this essential question has neither been posed nor answered.

Example: According to Law No. 615 of 13 July 1966 on air pollution, industries should be equipped with plants, installations or equipments able to contain 'within the strictest limits that technical progress admits' the emission of smoke, gases, powders or fumes that, beside constituting a danger for public health, can also contribute to air pollution. This provision was, however, interpreted in such a way that a high chimney could already be considered an abatement plant!

The decree of 12 July 1990, setting guidelines for the limitation from polluting emissions of industrial plants and the establishment of maximum emission threshold values, created additional problems because for some sectors the plant emission values are less demanding than limit values long established in some regions.

However, the regions, in the absence of regional plans for recovery, protection and conservation, cannot set values stricter than the maximum established in the

Ministerial Decree of 12 July 1990, (see section III, example 2, above). In the opinion of the Ministry of the Environment, the decree of July 1990 on existing plants assumes aims and criteria which can be met within actual production technologies and 'set' according to the economic resources of a strong group of industries, but without any reference to the use of best available technologies (BAT).

Nonetheless, there is a second stage which aims at a higher level of commitment from companies and where the concept of BAT is employed with greater care, taking into account compatibility with economic development and therefore also the costs industries will incur to achieve a higher level of environmental efficiency. However, in any event Italian rules and standards tend to crystallize the resort to best available technologies by the drawing up of lists of appropriate technological devices used when granting the authorization of new plants. While this approach is perhaps necessary to 'discipline' or control company behaviour, it is contradictory with the first assumption, according to which it is necessary to create incentives for the development of new processes, tying industries to given technologies as little as possible.

The proposed EC Directive on integrated pollution control introduces a third phase of environmental legislation, giving technological and scientific research a central role: the best available technologies are all those which are able to prevent or, if this is not possible, reduce to the minimum the emissions into the environment in general; verification of their suitability takes place not only in the authorization phase but also through a periodical revision of authorization conditions, during which more ambitious environmental standards can be imposed if the state of scientific research and practical experience allow it. 'Technology forcing standards' are not imposed but, in the new system, there are significant opportunities where environmental conditions require it, to impose more stringent standards than best available technologies can provide. At present this is allowed only where there are risks to public health, or within areas of our territory protected by regulations at the national or regional level.

VIII   THE INADEQUACY OF PUBLIC ADMINISTRATION

The Commission mentions 'difficulties on the part of regional and local structures in organizing and controlling the application of directives'. The Court of Justice in two rulings against Italy for the non-observance of Directive No. 513 of 1983 on cadmium discharges[2] and groundwater protection[3] highlighted the inadequacy of Italian public administration both in the authorization and control phase.

In this regard, it is noticeable that the number of staff responsible for prevention in Italy is far less than the percentage provided by a CIPE (*Comitato Interministeriale per la programmazione economica*) deliberation dated 20 December 1984, assigning 7.5–10 per cent of the total health personnel to prevention.

The principal reason for this probably lies in the organizational links between preventive health provision and environmental prevention: these activities have been unified for a long time under the same structure (*Unità Sanitarie Locali* (USL)), and, because of the severe restrictions on public expenditure, environmental control services have been relegated to a secondary position. For example, in Emilia Romagna, which is probably the most efficient region from the environmental point of view, each USL inspects 300 stacks per year. Multiplied by nine control bodies existing in the region, that makes about 3000 controls per year on air emissions of industrial plants. However, as some plants have several stacks, inspections are carried out on only 5 per cent of plants each year; in 1990, 1593 controls were conducted out of 2216 waste authorizations. This accounts for about 35 per cent of statutory controls (two per year) and, in the opinion of all the competent officials, is insufficient.

Following a referendum requested by environmental associations, the national Agency for Environmental Protection was constituted by Decree No. 496 of 4 December 1993, converted into Law No. 71 on 21 January 1994. The decree also provides for regional and provincial agencies for the development of technical-scientific activities of regional interest and of other technical prevention activities, including surveillance and control.

The Agency has been attributed technical-scientific functions, technical coordination as well as advisory functions to the Ministry of the Environment and other public administrations. The positive aspect of the reform consists in the separation of technical and administrative controls – a new departure in Italian environmental legislation – and in the different weight given to the first with respect to the latter.

One might wonder why the legislator did not take stronger action and use this as an opportunity to simplify administrative proceedings on environmental matters as this has been the subject of prolonged discussion and is already provided for by different sections of the Annex to Financial Law 1993, and the reorganization of

---

[2] Judgement of 13 December 1990, Case No. 89 of 1970, *Commission* v. *Italian Republic.*

[3] No. 68 of 1980 (ruling of 28 February 1991) in Case No. 360 of 1987, *Commission* v. *Italian Republic.*

environmental competences, still distributed among different levels of local and central government.

The delay with which the state is proceeding in the elaboration of application rules and standards and the delay with which the regions are proceeding to set up regional agencies shows some indecision at the administrative level, probably due also to the confusion of the present legislation.

IX   LACK OF COORDINATION

Too many subjects and procedures are involved in the application phase, creating major coordination problems both at central and local levels. The coordination problem exists both at the horizontal level, among the different authorization procedures, and the vertical level, inside the single procedures.

Example 1   To open a chemical plant the following requirements must be met:

1   The promoter must notify the project (if necessary) to the Ministry of the Environment, to the Ministry of Cultural Heritage and to the region where the plant is to be located. The region where the plant is located is only required to express an opinion. Within 90 days of consultation with the region involved, the Ministry of the Environment, in consultation with the Ministry of Heritage, issues a decision on the project's environmental compatibility.

   As some regions have established provisions on environmental impact assessment, their particular procedure may be necessary before their final opinion can be issued. This opinion is sent to the Ministry of the Environment before the latter issues its decision as to environmental compatibility. The assessment is therefore a sub-procedure of works approval and/or authorization procedures.

2   Under Decree No. 175 of 1988 concerning high risk plants the promoter forwards a notification to the Ministry of the Environment (to an administration other than the one competent for EIA) and the Ministry of Health. The Ministry of the Environment, in concert with the Ministry of Health, formulates conclusions relating to the safety report and indicates, where appropriate, integrating or modifying measures and time limits within which the manufacturer must comply. These conclusions are then transmitted to the competent region and prefects. On the other hand, if the industrial activity considered is subject to mere declaration, the regions are the relevant authorities.

   The 'competent body' at regional level varies from region to region (for example, in Emilia-Romagna information is collected by *Assessorato alla sanite protezione civile*, while in Lombardy the same information is collected by a *Servizio prevenzione del rischio industriale* instituted within the *Presidenza della Giunta Regionale*.

3   Prior to the construction of a new plant, or a substantial modification of an existing one, an application for air emission authorization must be presented to the region. A copy of the application must also be transmitted to the Ministry of the Environment and another enclosed with the application for the building permit sent to the mayor.

In some regions the administrative function has been delegated to provinces (for example, in Emilia Romagna). In other regions, such as Lombardy, application for authorization has to be addressed to the regional environmental department (*Assessorato all'ambiente*).

4   According to Decree No. 133 of 1992 on water discharges, application for authorization concerning discharges containing dangerous substances must be submitted to the province or to the authority responsible for the sewerage and purification services if discharges flow into the public sewerage (consortia).

5   According to Law No. 319 of 1976, industrial water discharges must be authorized by municipalities or by the authority responsible for the sewerage and purification services if discharges flow into the public sewerage (system).

It is worth noting that two different authorization procedures overlap: one for discharges, according to Law No. 319 of 1976, and one for single polluting emissions, each the responsibility of a different level of authority – namely the municipalities and their consortia, and the provinces respectively.

At a regional level, a solution has been sought in some cases (for example, in Emilia-Romagna) by centralizing the two types of authorization in the provinces; but, in most cases, the competences have not been unified.

6   The authorization for the storage and disposal of toxic and dangerous waste is granted by the regions. However, competence on waste tends to be delegated to provinces. This process is taking place in Emilia-Romagna; in other regions authorizations are still granted at a regional level.

7   Applications for authorizations for direct and/or indirect discharges of dangerous substances into groundwater must be submitted to the province.

8   Authorizations on plans for noise reduction are granted by the regions (based on the Prime Minister's Decree of 1 March 1989).

9   Before opening the plant, the mayor has to grant an authorization for unhealthy manufacturing processes, based on the Single Text on health laws and the system of licences for use.

As can be seen, in Italy there is no comprehensive assessment of the impact of a new industrial plant on land and environment; competence is extremely fragmentary and no institutional or operational form of coordination among competent authorities exists. In addition, authorities frequently carry out their task inadequately. The difficulties are not merely those of finance or of manpower but, as has been shown, lie also with the design of legislation at the national level, which increases the administrative workload considerably.

Example 2 The procedure provided for by Presidential Decree No. 175 of 1988 on risks of major accidents involves three ministries, the regions or autonomous provinces, the municipalities, USL, the prefects, four technical bodies and two advisory bodies.

At the regional level, the structures involved in the decision-making process change in a significant way between the council presidency and various health councillors, and coordination with land or environmental councillors is provided.

Presidential Decree No. 175 of 1988 provides only some procedural linkage between town planning and health regulations, subordinating the granting of different authorizations to the fulfilment of the procedures provided by the same decree.

In some cases, communication and intervention is duplicated, as in the case where the notification ex Article 216 of the Single Text on health laws is additional to the declaration or notification requirement in respect of unhealthy industries.

In Lombardy a Regular Technical Committee (*Comitato Tecnico Consultivo Regionale*), with consultative and technical assistance duties, has been established. Currently, due to difficulties in coordination between the different sectors and lack of equipment and staff the Technical Committee has neither been formalized nor instituted. Therefore, although it issues specific regulations, the region has failed to comply with them, as far as investigation on applications for licences is concerned. For this reason, manufacturers who present a signed report, as required by Article 18 of Presidential Decree No. 175 of 1988, may start their activities after 60 days from the submission of the project without any response being given by the region.

11 How to Organize Environmental Administration

Peter Knoepfel

Table of Contents

I FOREWORD

The ideas presented in the following pages are based on comparative research – mainly international in scope – which the author has undertaken since the late 1970s into three areas of environmental policy (maintenance of clean air in proximity to stationary sources of pollution,[1] maintenance of clean air in proximity to mobile sources of pollution,[2] and water protection in agriculture[3]) in Western European countries. Although principally based on the author's postgraduate course on environmental policy and management in the Institut de Hautes Etudes en Administration Publique (IDHEAP) of the University of Lausanne, experience gained from Swiss environmental policy will also be drawn upon. Since the mid-1980s the author has participated in training officials in the Swiss federal, cantonal and communal administrations having responsibilities in relation to the environment. The discussion on observation of the environment is based on the groundwork accomplished since 1988 by the Swiss Commission for Observation of the Environment (*Schweizerische Kommission für Umweltbeobachtung*) of which the author is Chairman.[4]

An effective environmental policy presupposes the existence, from the outset, of clarity with regard to the precise manner in which participants from social and governmental circles act in furtherance of the policy (Section II). Moreover, such a policy, as compared with those in other areas, must necessarily rest on a relatively broad range of scientific findings which have to be systematically developed. Accordingly, precise analyses of the nature and evolution of pollution are essential (Section III). It is only on the basis of these findings that clear operational programmes – within the framework of which the specific administrative measures

---

[1] Peter Knoepfel, Helmut Weidner, *Luftreinhaltung (stationäre Quellen) im internationalen Vergleich*, Berlin: Sigma, 6 vols, 1986.

[2] Peter Knoepfel, Rita Imhof, Willi Zimmermann, *Luftreinhaltung im Verkehr: Analyse von Vollzugsprozessen in der städtische Umweltpolitik mittels Massnahmenplänen gemäss Luftreinhalte-Verordnung Art. 31 ff.*, Final Report of Project, Nr. 40228112, of the (Swiss) National Research Programme on Town and Traffic, (No. 25), 1993.

[3] Peter Knoepfel, Willi Zimmermann, *Gewässerschutz in der Landwirtschaft. Evaluation und Analyse des föderalen Vollzugs*, Oekologie & Gesellschaft Series, vol. 7, Basel: Helbing & Lichtenhahn, 1993.

[4] Schweizerische Kommission für Umweltbeobachtung (Swiss Commission for Observation of the Environment): *Konzept für die Einführung eines Beobachtungssystems*, Final Report, Schweizerische Akademie der Naturwissenschaften, May 1993.

can be properly coordinated – can be drawn up (Section IV). The creation of efficient management structures and of clear divisions of competence between the central government and regional or local organs are of particular importance for the implementation of environmental policy (Section V). It is only when these fundamental conditions have been met that the efficient carrying out of the above-mentioned operational programmes can be put in train. In this connection it is worth noting that some useful experience has already been acquired as to how best to structure such implementation (Section VI). Finally, it must be emphasized that an environmental policy cannot be pursued independently of other policies in the public domain. Some aspects of this desideratum are considered at the end of the present chapter (Section VII).

II   THE MAIN PARTICIPANTS

1   The iron triangle

Until well into the late 1970s, environmental policy was, for all practical purposes, carried out by two parties in a bilateral context. One was constituted by the official administrations concerned with environmental management. From the beginning of the 1970s onwards, these became integrated – first with the central government apparatus and then progressively with the regional and local authorities – in every country of Western Europe. Facing these administrations was the other party, which was supported by organized lobbies and may be divided into industrial and artisanal enterprises having an interest in particular environment-related activities (for example, protection against pollution of the air and of water supplies and disposal of waste), private households (sewerage, air pollution, waste), agricultural interests (water and soil pollution, protection of nature) and those concerned with elements of the national infrastructure such as roads, railways and airports (air, noise and soil pollution, protection of nature). A wide variety of relationships between the state and these various lobbies came into existence. Thus, the state authorities regulated pollution levels of concern to the pressure groups by a wide range of procedures involving the fixing of maximum permissible levels of specific types of pollution, as well as outright prohibition: these procedures regularly culminated in the issue of individual and specific orders and prohibitions. On the other hand, the pressure groups participated in drawing up the pertinent regulations and, specifically, in the establishment of the permissible levels of pollution. They were represented in numerous official commissions, where they were in a position not only to contribute their knowledge of the latest technological developments but also to ensure that the standards finally adopted would, to the maximum extent feasible, meet the interest of the lobby in question.

From the mid-1970s onwards this bilateral cooperative relationship was increasingly brought into question. New interests came knocking at the closed doors behind which the discussions between the regulators and the regulated had been taking place on a confidential basis. Since the beginning of the 1980s these new interests have succeeded in making a breakthrough in most Western European countries: the erstwhile bilateral set-up was expanded into a trilateral arrangement in which the organizations dedicated to the protection of the environment were henceforth recognized as having an equal right to have their say. This is true not only at the national level in the drawing up of the relevant programmes but also, and especially, in carrying them out by means of publicly accessible administrative procedures in which the environmental organizations came to acquire the status of political parties. Today – rightly – the implementation of every environment-related policy has to be accomplished in harmony with this trilateral reality.

The following relationships can be perceived within the triangle:

a)   Relations between commercial pressure groups and the authorities responsible for the environment

As already mentioned above, the pressure groups bring their technical knowledge, their economic interests and their determination to bear when pollution control programmes are being drawn up, so that as far as possible the official standards which are ultimately adopted do not affect commercial competitiveness. As a general rule, important undertakings and economic sectors, operating on a country-wide basis, tend towards the adoption of detailed standards while groups representing small-scale and artisanal businesses tend to opt for the adoption of general aims which allow for local variations in application. In such dealings official administrations mostly endeavour to achieve the strictest possible standards in which context they take account of the practice of the most progressive firms. When so doing, however, they must avoid establishing, as an official standard, one which is exclusively based on the technology evolved by a single firm which dominates the market: otherwise, governments would, in practice, be furthering the creation of monopolies and cartels in matters of standards, with questionable effects on fair competition in the marketplace.

For the proper carrying out of an environmental policy, commercial pressure groups must be compelled to furnish the requisite technical and other data. Firms which do this may, in turn, find themselves well placed to influence the administration in formulating the regulations relating to particular standards. Negotiations in this context prove, in practice, to be less concerned with the details of maximum permissible pollution levels than with the fixing of deadlines and with transitional measures. Such bargaining has long been accepted in Western European countries as forming part of the process leading to the adoption of environmental standards. The high-handed and unilateral official proclamations of yester-year are giving way to agreements which, in many cases, are the outcome of informal negotiations.

b) Relations between the authorities responsible for the environment and environmental organizations

In all the countries of Western Europe, environmental organizations (for example, Worldwide Fund for Nature, organizations for the protection of nature and of the national heritage, Greenpeace and numerous types of foundations) have become increasingly significant in the national arena and now form an important environmental pressure group. Their political clout stems from their consistently high degree of organization and thus their capacity to bring public pressure to bear on national governments. It is because of this factor that these organizations are often the authorities' most important 'clients', whose resolve they strengthen in confrontations with the commercial pressure groups. For their part, the authorities increasingly appreciate the support which they receive and regularly involve these organizations in the preparation of protection programmes and, when deciding on specific aims of environmental policy and on the texts to be adopted for their realization, draw upon the high-level expertise and the wealth of experience which these organizations have acquired.

Authorities greatly value the contribution which these bodies make in the many instances in which they take the initiative in securing public acceptance of protective measures and in launching publicity campaigns towards that end. What was an initially sceptical, not to say dismissive, attitude on the part of some public authorities towards the environmental organizations has now undoubtedly become largely a thing of the past.

When it comes to the practical implementation of environmental policy, local groups dedicated to protecting the environment are without doubt the most alert watchdogs, in a position to supply the authorities with valuable details of on-the-spot pollution levels. These local environmental associations also take upon themselves functions – such as alerting public opinion and monitoring the behaviour of major commercial interests – which the official administrations could not carry out on their own; and, today, no environmental management policy, if it is to be really effective, can do without the backing thus afforded by such local groups. All kinds of group dedicated to such protection participate more and more in checking on the environment's level of pollution toleration. In most countries they are allowed to state their case when permissible limits of pollution are being adopted and are accorded right of audience in any subsequent legal proceedings which may be taken to invalidate the limits set. Certainly, trouble can occur when it comes to practical environmental action, if these bodies are not brought into the procedures at any early stage or if they are not really taken seriously. Today, in negotiations between the authorities, commercial interests and environmental protection bodies, resort is increasingly made to 'mediation procedures' with a view to reaching a consensus without following strict and formal legal procedures.

c)　Relations between commercial interests and environmental organizations

Since the end of the 1980s direct relations between commercial lobbies and environmental organizations have undergone considerable change in the Western European countries – largely without official intervention. The days of heavy confrontations between, for example, commercial firms, industrial sectors, farmers and the protective bodies may well be past. Firms have come to appreciate the value of a good relationship with the community in which they are located, as well as with these bodies. They also make a point of voluntarily keeping the pollution levels they create below officially permitted maxima and, within the context of self-regulation, adopt a pro-environmental stance in dealing with any 'black sheep' within their ranks. Legal agreements between protective bodies, local authorities and particular firms, providing for the voluntary reduction of noxious emissions, are no longer unusual today. The same holds for public monitoring of products, technological processes and plant layout – topics once jealously guarded as commercial secrets. Today, effective management of the environment can scarcely dispense with such cooperation from local communities and protective bodies, even if it to some extent renders governmental actions superfluous. The environmental policies of many large commercial undertakings, as well as some medium-sized firms in Western European countries, now provide as a matter of course for the possibility of the agreed suspension of a process, for moratoria and for agreed compensation, mainly relating to waste disposal, air pollution and to protection of the soil.

2　Squares and pentagons

As is well known, government services do not consist exclusively of environment management administrations. In particular, countries with a strong official participation in the national economy are, in many cases, equipped with separate sectoral bureaucracies for industry, trade and agricultural affairs, each of which naturally seeks to promote the economic sector in question whether it be wholly or partly state-run, or merely state-regulated. These bureaucracies usually also see fit to ward off what they consider as excessive ecological demands upon 'their' sectors. When there are such bureaucracies, the concept of a triangle no longer fits: that of a square or even of a pentagon becomes more appropriate, with the bureaucracies participating with the three parties already mentioned in matters of the environment. As a rule, these bureaucracies tend to be the 'natural' allies of the polluter pressure groups, the result being a polarization between two camps. One consists of the bodies dedicated to protecting the environment and of the official administration for environmental management. The other is that of the anti-active pressure groups, who can now mobilize 'their' official bureaucracy in support of their stance in the political power game. The stronger such official sectoral bureaucracies become the more difficult it becomes to implement effective policies for the environment. There is thus in practice a connection between privatization and environmental policy: privatization means the disappearance of the sectoral bureaucracies concerned, which accordingly no longer exist as a protective screen for the polluters. A further outcome of privatization is that all special regulations and exceptions which had been made in favour of a state-run sector of the economy – which, for instance, determined matters in the former socialist republics of Eastern Europe – should lapse.

It must be added, however, that it has not proved possible to prevent the existence of such quadrilateral scenarios, even in the market economies of Western Europe, in a particularly important field – that of the 'public works lobby'. Entrepreneurs, whether building roads, airports, waste incineration plants or in charge of state-run energy production were almost always implementing one public policy or another, for which powerful backing was available from within the official administration concerned. The officials in question were, and still are, in a position to shield public works for the national infrastructure from environmental regulations which they deem to be unduly strict. The result has been that, in many cases, special regulations were made allowing lower standards of environmental protection, in such works, than those applicable to undertakings in the private sector or in trade. When official administrations for environmental management are being set up, care should consequently be taken that protection vis-à-vis the long-established administrations concerned with public works is effective enough to ensure that the latter will have to meet the same environmental requirements as are applied to the private sector.

III   PREPARING THE SCIENTIFIC BASIS

1   Monitoring the environment

Precise knowledge of the nature and levels of pollution is the first prerequisite for an efficient environmental policy: only when it is known which sources give rise to which pollution can any meaningful regulations be prepared. The mapping of pollution surveys based on verified statements or, if necessary, on remote sensing techniques is essential for the control of air pollution, waste disposal and of water and soil protection in particular. The author considers that the making of such maps is of greater importance than the simple recording of general pollution levels present in an extensive area since the latter merely illustrates the need for reme- dial action without, however, pinpointing precisely *where* that action is to be taken. In any case, the implementation of established environmental policies will require the creation of networks for monitoring pollution in zones of greatest con- centration. These serve in particular to locate the priority areas needing remedial action, to identify situations of acute danger (for example, smog concentrations) with a view to the launching of emergency measures, as well as to provide a check on the effectiveness of the policy followed. There is, indeed, a long-term need to monitor the effects of pollution on flora, fauna, mankind, buildings and the land- scape.

Data on the local, regional and national scales must ultimately be correlated so as to bring out the essential structure of the pollution 'scenario' and to show pre- cisely where political and administrative action can best be initiated. Thus, for example, endeavours can be made to link data concerning traffic patterns, urbani- zation and air pollution so as to develop strategies to maintain good air conditions in the principal cities and in peripheral satellite communities in heavily polluted areas. On-the-spot data on the ozone level must be correlated with those for vola- tile organic compounds and nitrogen oxides in order to locate the areas in which this secondary nuisance originates. Finally, it must be pointed out that, if it is to provide a basis for practical action, environmental monitoring must, rationally, take the whole ecosystem into account. There is no 'national quality of the envi- ronment': everywhere, different harmful substances affect variously structured ecosystems in quite specific ways.

2   Monitoring technologies

So that the benefits of the most appropriate pollution prevention technologies may be secured, environmental authorities, as well as individual sectors of the econ- omy, must be informed of what relevant environmentally sound technologies are on offer. Such 'state of the art' knowledge is required not only for the development of environmental programmes but also for their practical implementation; pollu- tion-creating undertakings have to be made aware of the relevant technologies and techniques available for environmentally sound operations. That such monitoring presupposes research on environmental technologies is just as evident as the fact that the interstices between research and practice must also be covered. The scope of such monitoring embraces not only technology in its narrower meaning, but also observation of behavioural patterns, of the motivations which cause them and of the underlying attitudes of the public. It also covers sociological research on the organizational, sociological and administrative requirements for the meaningful adoption of desirable new techniques and patterns of behaviour. Indeed it is known that an environmental technology, wrongly applied, often proves more dangerous than no technology at all: the trouble-free application of a specific technology depends on prior awareness of the reactions and behavioural patterns of the social groups affected as well as on appropriate social engineering.

3 Monitoring policies

The methodical implementation of an environmental policy presupposes the continuous monitoring of its performance. The politically responsible programme managers, governments and executive authorities must have access to the data necessary to enable them to assess just how the policy is working out in practice and what difficulties it encounters. The first questions to be asked relate to precisely where, when and what specific action in furtherance of the policy was taken by the authorities charged with its execution. A compilation of the resulting data enables a map to be drawn for each region of the country, giving an overall view of the policy's impact – or absence of impact – and provides a basis for setting new priorities. Such (electronically assembled) databanks, moreover, enable the exact content of current regulations to be reproduced at a later date as an act of political memory. However, even in Western Europe, such policy output mapping systems are still rare.

It is recommended that, at a later stage, the monitoring of environment policy be extended to cover the major official policies in other fields (for example, agriculture, the infrastructure, the national economy and town-and-country planning), since these policies are often responsible for yet more pressure on the environment.

IV THE MANAGEMENT PROGRAMME

Experience has demonstrated the need for the basic legal documents – for example, laws, decrees and official circulars – relating to environmental management to manifest the greatest clarity when prescribing the solutions to specific problems, in order that uncertainties in execution and the consequential losses in efficiency may be avoided. These problems arise in the following five components that a management programme should contain:

1   Specified quality standards for individual substances (that is, maximum permissible thresholds for pollutants)

As a rule these are expressed in terms of the maximum permissible average concentrations of a given harmful substance during a specified interval of time (mostly as mg/m^3). They serve as the basis for the qualitative assessment of the environmental component concerned and for prescribing the threshold levels to be incorporated in the relevant policy. In Western Europe such thresholds have been set for various harmful substances in water, air and soil, as well as for noise pollution. In general, the thresholds are arrived at partly by means of empirical eco-toxicological findings as to the levels which can be tolerated by humans, animals, plants and by the ecosystem as a whole, and partly by politically influenced estimates of the risks involved. The latter factor causes thresholds prescribed to vary – often considerably – from country to country. A decision as to the threshold to be adopted is rendered all the more difficult when subjective considerations of particular groups influence their assessment of the pollution load in question. A typical example of the impact of such considerations is afforded by noise thresholds. In respect of some fields of application of environmental policy – for example, natural beauty spots and landscapes – maximum permissible thresholds are expressed in quite imprecise terms, while in yet other fields specific thresholds apply to quite small numbers of substances only, thresholds for the remaining substances being left for fixing in the light of on-the-spot eco-toxicological findings.

2   Measurement techniques and networks, and criteria for evaluation

The extent to which permissible pollution thresholds apply in practice depends on how the methods and arrangements for making relevant measurements and on how the criteria for assessing violations of the specified thresholds have been arrived at. Depending on just how the management programme prescribes these criteria and the requisite measurement procedures, violations which set off remedial action will 'occur' with greater or lesser frequency. Thus, the precise manner in which these points are dealt with in the basic texts – and which, despite its technical nature, is of major political significance – can tend to strengthen, or alternatively weaken, the practical effect of the thresholds prescribed. In matters of the environment as in other contexts, the old saying that 'he who wants to chance his arm can get away with it' holds true. It follows that, as a matter of political reality, the ostensibly purely technical question of just how pollution thresholds are to be articulated has manifestly assumed what might, in all innocence, be considered an improbable sensitivity.

3   Pollution output thresholds and product standards

These stipulations constitute the legal basis for a wide range of official documents and thus establish the legal obligations imposed on the commercial interests concerned. They are accordingly the subject of diverse negotiations between governmental authorities and the pressure groups in question. Standards for pollution output and product standards assume key importance in the setting of maximum limits of pollution input, since they must be expressed in such a way that they cannot be exceeded even if each of a multitude of polluters releases the permitted volume of noxious material. Otherwise, excessive levels of pollution would automatically occur in congested areas – a state of affairs directly due to inherently faulty management programming and not to any shortcoming in the actual execution of the programme. Such a faulty correlation between the standards for pollution output, processes and products on the one hand and, on the other, the core of the programme itself – namely the maximum permissible level of pollution input – must be viewed as a preprogrammed failure, resulting in an inevitable loss of effectiveness in implementing the programme. Each threshold prescribed for pollution output must be reviewed to establish to what extent the limits for pollution input can be retained if it is to remain unchanged. It has become the established practice in various Western European countries for national pollution output thresholds to be reduced when their application does not, in practice, prevent those for pollution input being exceeded.

4   Organization and financing

Any programme for environmental management, however coherent and comprehensive it may be, with prescribed standards for pollution output, industrial processes and products, will remain a dead letter if it does not specify precisely who is to be responsible for carrying it out. The same holds true if adequate funds for the inevitably costly investigations entailed in its execution are not provided when the programme is launched. An insufficiently financed executive agency, or one not truly responsive to environmental concerns, will never be able to translate substantial standards into reality. Every legislature concerned with environmental matters must take full account of this interaction between the substantive and organizational aspects of a programme. If a legislature dodges its responsibilities in this field, failure in implementing the programme is inevitable.

5   Management tools and procedures

In addition to allocating responsibilities for its implementation, an environmental management programme must, at least, also clearly designate the instruments from which it derives its authority. For a state based on the rule of law this presupposes that the implementation of a programme will be in accordance with procedures which can be ascertained in advance, and that commercial interests as well as environmental organizations will have their say. The legal basis for the management procedures concerned, together with the legal texts to which the parties involved may have recourse, must therefore be codified. This applies to the tools for control of the programme (such as periodic controls by the executing agency itself, controls by independent inspectors and rights of access), to the procedures leading to the award of licences (such as that for ensuring legal protection against contamination when licences are issued, with or without provision for controlling the environment's capacity to tolerate the proposed pollution, as well as to approvals of plant layout) and to the tools for the initiation of curative measures (such as curative decrees addressed to individual polluters or to entire groups thereof). By the same token, the right of access of the parties to the law courts must also be specified. The clarity with which these various aspects of the procedures to be adopted are set out determines the extent to which the management programme concerned is effectively capable of achieving its goals (constituting the 'core' of the programme). Excluding the environmental organizations from the procedure for the award of permits can damage this 'core' just as much as it can be strengthened by appropriate intervention on the part of these organizations.

V   MANAGEMENT STRUCTURES

The experience gained in building up environmental management bodies in Western European countries may be summarized in the terms of the following nine suggestions, which have been more fully elaborated by the author elsewhere.[5]

---

5   Cf. in particular P. Knoepfel, New Institutional Arrangements for the Next Generation of Environmental Policy Instruments: Intra- and Interpolicy-Cooperation, in Bruno Dente (ed.), *New Environmental Policy Instruments*, London: Gower, (forthcoming); Peter Knoepfel with the collaboration of Rita Imhof, Les cycles écologiques et le principe de légalité – De la nécessité d'assouplir les liens de causalité, Cahiers de l'ID-HEAP, (72), Chavannes-près-Renens: IDHEAP, 1991, 32 pp.

1   First suggestion: keep monitoring separate from administration

Monitoring the performance of a particular agency should be entrusted to another body with a relatively independent legal status. Such an arrangement ensures that the monitoring cannot be suspected of a self-indulgent bias and it also guarantees the continuity, stability and professionalism necessary for collecting and analysing data – activities which should not be disrupted by immediate political considerations. Monitoring the environment is, by definition, a long-term exercise, requiring continuity and scrupulous adherence to procedure. The trend to separate monitoring agencies from the general administrations responsible for environmental management has been evidenced both at the level of the European Union (where an environment agency has been set up) and at the national level (as in France, Germany and Switzerland). It is nevertheless noteworthy that in practice monitoring agencies are under frequent internal temptation or external pressure to accept and exert also management functions. This should be resisted.

2   Second suggestion: structure the environmental authorities on a component-by-component basis

Since the early 1970s the concept of structuring environmental management authorities on an environmental component-by-component basis has become generally accepted in most Western European countries. This fosters within the authority the progressive accumulation of the requisite expertise with regard to such different components as air, noise, soil and water. In most cases this development took place in the wake of the progressive enactment of environmental legislation which was itself component-specific, generally starting with water protection and, from the mid 1970s, successively dealing with the other components – air, soil, the biota (including fauna and flora) – as well as with the landscape. Administrative departments were next set up to deal with pollution by noise, radiation and chemicals. The validity of this basic tenet for the structuring of environmental management has proved itself in practice. It has been the traditional, component-by-component approach to environmental regulation in the majority of industrialized Western European countries. This approach led to the adoption of different environmental policies in response to the impact of emission-creating activities on the different environmental components. As these activities, when they impact on the components of vital importance to human beings, animals and plants, become immediately evident, governments enjoy ever greater political support for protecting the components concerned.

3   Third suggestion: a responsive administrative structure focused on emissions

This component-by-component approach first becomes evident on the environmental quality side and is not primarily concerned with the causes of the pollution in question.[6] There exist totally immission-oriented strategies, in the pursuance of which component-specific remedial activities are undertaken, without going back to the emissions themselves or to those responsible for them. Several concrete examples may be cited: a phosphate-polluted lake is revitalized by an influx of oxygen; the quality of nitrate-polluted drinking water is improved by mixing with water low in nitrate content; dying trees in a forest are replaced by more acid-resisting species; the concentration of harmful substances in the main sewer of a local community is reduced by the mixing-in of rainwater. Such immission-oriented strategies were central to the growth of component-specific environmental management administrations during the 1970s.

Today, however, the validity of these strategies is being queried: after all, they do nothing to reduce the pollution load; they merely distribute it differently. When these strategies gave way to emission-oriented environmental policies, corresponding changes in management structures became necessary. Within component-specific administrative divisions, emission-oriented subdivisions were set up. Thus, for example, in a water protection division, subdivisions for community drainage (sewage treatment), industrial effluents and agriculture are now to be found. Similarly, in a clean air division, subdivisions for industry and trade, households and traffic have come into being. Such a responsive structure of administrative divisions fosters increased knowledge of the sources responsible for the emissions in question, and of the technologies available for avoiding the emissions. It also facilitates close and ongoing communication between the members of those groups and the specialized administrative unit concerned; and in general it provides those responsible for protecting the particular environmental component with greater insight into the causes of the pollution affecting it. Depending on the component, separate subdivisions should be envisaged to deal with industry and trade, households, agriculture, traffic and public works.

---

[6]   Hereafter, as elsewehere in this volume, the impact of pollution on environmental quality is also termed 'immission' whereas the flowing of substances from a source is called 'emission'.

4 Fourth suggestion: link activities relating to different components of the environment (intra-policy cooperation)

Once a subdivision structure, focused on the sources responsible for pollution, does come into being for each component of the environment, the linking of the different subdivisions corresponding to the several sources or to the track of particular noxious substances through successive stages is only a matter of time. Such integration is, indeed, essential for the efficient control of the different sources responsible for emissions, and facilitates cooperation with the related actors. Instead of each polluter having to deal with a different official in connection with controls or discussions relating to each specific component of the environment, it makes more sense to group the regulations applicable to each category of polluter, so that air, water and the landscape are dealt with together. The jump from tackling matters for each component separately to dealing with them collectively on an integrated basis, which took place in environmental administrations in most countries of Western Europe towards the end of the 1980s was indeed a requirement of rational, ecologically responsive environmental policy. Here, priority is given to controlling and managing the pollution loads on entire ecosystems, rather than to controlling and managing individual components of the environment. Ecosystems, after all, interact with each of the permanent components of the environment, and their management accordingly calls for an integrated approach. Ecological cycles cannot be split on a component-by-component basis.

The networking of component-related environmental management recommended here presupposes the incorporation, within the administrations, of 'horizontal' structures for cooperation between the different source-related subdivions. This can be achieved by the creation of a number of 'horizontal' divisions as part of the administrative matrix. Thus, component-specific divisions would be supplemented by the setting up of 'horizontal' subdivisions corresponding to the importance of the main polluter groups. The entire range of environmental components to be affected by a proposed industrial plant must necessarily be taken into account in each case when the tolerance of the environment is being tested and the issue of a permit is under examination. It is in the light of this fact that considerations of intra-policy cooperation have long had a bearing on the internal routing of files when applications for licences are being processed within authorities charged with implementing environmental policy.

5   Fifth suggestion: networking environmental authorities with those dealing with other policies relevant to the environment (inter-policy cooperation)

As was been indicated in Section II. above, government policies frequently share the responsibility for pollution creation. Thus, an agricultural policy aimed at maximizing production can result in soil and surface pollution; the all-out implementation of an energy policy may be accompanied by significant air pollution; road construction policies fostering the development of one branch of transport regularly cause air and noise pollution; while sector-specific industrial policies can lead to heavy water and soil pollution. Since the beginning of the 1990s, those concerned with environment protection in Western Europe have become increasingly aware of the extent to which practical policies for such protection are thus subject to other policies which are not primarily concerned with the environment. Rather than attempt the interminable task of coping with the side effects of these other policies, the environmental authorities are becoming increasingly determined on open confrontation with those policies at the national programming level, and likewise at the implementation stage. Towards this end, bridgeheads were – and rightly continue to be – established within official administrations so as to promote such inter-policy cooperation. Among the possibilities being considered in this connection, mention may be made of interdepartmental working groups, stationing 'satellite' officials of the environmental authority in other ministries, and of incorporating elements of non-environmental policies in those for the environment.

In each design for a new environmental management authority, in-depth consideration should be given to the incorporation of structures which will facilitate inter-policy cooperation: an environmental policy cannot be ecologically successful unless these other policies are made subject to the overriding exigencies of ecology. An ecological policy is therefore not to be considered as merely one governmental policy among many: as was noted in the Single European Act of Luxembourg 1987, the requirements for the protection of our ecological balances must form an integral part of all other policies, such as those of the European Union.

6   Sixth suggestion: networking of structures by means of established procedures

The management structures described above lend themselves to the detailed specification of each task which is to be undertaken by the different administrative subdivisions and component-specific and 'horizontal' divisions. The required networking of a component-oriented with a polluter-oriented stance, or with an overall approach having special regard to the ecosystem can, by contrast, hardly be accomplished by specification of the administrative structures to be adopted for discharging the tasks in question. Networking must permeate procedures: it cannot be ordained merely by what a text may prescribe. There is, accordingly, a need for this networking concept to be put into practice through down-to-earth measures to ensure that appropriate administrative procedures are always followed. The famed 'beaten paths', daily trod by all concerned, have demonstrated their indispensability. Such mechanisms for the routine correlation of policies on a day-to-day basis can be arrived at in a variety of ways – by built-in procedures for the circulation of files relating to important matters through the different divisions and other appropriate administrative units; by periodic meetings of those involved in a given project; by setting up joint working parties to deal with particular topics; or by prescribing procedural rules covering matters such as obligatory consultation, exchange of information and discussion. Experience has also shown the value of other informal channels for cross-communication in strengthening such in-house networking of different policies. Finally, mention must be made of how very important it is for the authority as a whole that it should acquire and maintain its own corporate identity, that all its services should set a good example, and that its basic strategies should be periodically reviewed.

7 Seventh suggestion: separation of programme planning from execution

While sorting out environment-related functions, an administrative separation took place during the 1970s in most[7] countries of Western Europe between the authorities responsible for programming and those charged with carrying out the programmes adopted. This even holds true when a single authority is responsible for the two functions. Despite some shortcomings (such as insufficient feedback between the two functions, or unrealistic and impracticable task-programming), this separation has widely justified itself, and the concept should not lightly be abandoned. It has the advantage of relieving the front-line executive authorities, in a politically objective manner, of the manifold political pressures to which they would otherwise be exposed, and of providing similar political relief to the programming authorities which, when they are engaged in preparing programmes, are no longer harassed on each particular point. They are thus rightly freed to take a broader view and to take objective account of scientifically valid criteria. A further advantage lies in the fact that they can work on the basis of really important parameters relevant to the country as a whole.

---

[7] Notable exceptions: the UK and, to some extent, France. These are characteristically unitary states, marked by a high degree of centralization.

It must be added, however, that – as discussed in connection with management programmes in Section IV.2. above – such separation cannot be achieved in an orderly fashion in all cases. Despite the increasing volume of regulations governing the relevant management programmes there will, in practice, always be some cases which are not covered. In such cases, which were frequent during the early years of these programmes, the executive administration has to take an ad hoc decision on just what has to be done – in other words, to do the requisite programming itself. This means that, for such individual cases, the executive authority must be in a position to acquire the knowledge necessary for reaching an ecologically meaningful solution – knowledge which may well prove useful in dealing with future cases of a similar order. This, indeed, often happens when new harmful substances have to be dealt with. While, theoretically, it should be possible to submit such cases to the appropriate programming body, in reality there is often pressure for them to be dealt with quickly so that, in most instances, an ad hoc solution is indicated.

8 Eighth suggestion: implementation on a regional basis

Programme formation is manifestly the responsibility of the central environment authority. In almost all Western European countries,[8] however, the principle of regional implementation of programmes has become accepted. Implementation by the central authority is now mainly confined to chemicals (approval of substances), transport (vehicle equipment and fuels), air pollution (the importation and production of propellants), radiation protection and the control of the internal and cross-border transport of dangerous substances and wastes.

The advantages of implementation at the regional level, in line with the principle of 'subsidiarity', are manifest: it facilitates the correlation of national aims with the requirements of the regional or local environment, and takes account of the economic and social realities of the regions concerned. To these advantages must be added: close contact with the population; specialized knowledge of the local scenario; and the possibility of associating the networks existing for the implementation of other, non-environmental, state policies ('political carpets') with the carrying out of the environmental programme. But the assignment to the regional level of responsibility for the implementation of these programmes is generally said to entail the risk of greater vulnerability to local or regional economic and political pressure. As has been pointed out under Section V.7. above, such pressure can be countered by the manifest separation of programming and execu-

---

[8] Sole exception: the UK. Today, even in Italy and France, the national environment policies envisage substantial regional participation in their implementation.

tion, by the clearest possible wording of management programmes when dealing with contentious matters (see Section IV.1. above), and above all by mobilizing proactive support from the ranks of the environment protection movement (see Section II.1. above).

It should be noted that regional implementation is not communal implementation. The high degree of technology involved scarcely warrants local authorities (other than those of major cities) being saddled with this responsibility. A communal authority set up to cope with it would be inefficient and all too costly. This should not be taken to mean, however, that there is no role for communal authorities in the carrying out of environmental policy. On the contrary, without the active collaboration of these authorities, no regional body could cope. In those cases in which, in the interests of local industry, a communal authority actively obstructs a regional body, there is little that can be done. A proactive communal authority can, on the other hand, alert the regional body concerning any nuisances within its territory rather sooner than a passive one may do.

9   Ninth suggestion: staff training

Environmental policy is manifestly technical in nature. Neither lawyers nor administrative functionaries can conceive or implement it. Thus it has come about that in Western European countries since the 1970s such policies have led to a significant trend towards the professionalization of those bearing responsibility for conceptualizing and carrying them out. This in turn led to the creation of new academic courses and to options for further education at the university and non-university levels. New profiles came into being for new professions – those of the environmental chemist, the environmental biologist, the environmental engineer and the environmental economist. Today, without such staff, no environmental policy could be carried out. It is therefore not only a scientific imperative but also, and in particular, a managerial necessity that such courses be set up in the various university and non-university institutions. This provides yet another example of how public policies have contributed to the creation of new professions and new educational opportunities.

This professionalism must not, however, be confined to the ranks of environmental management: it must also permeate the other two sides of the 'iron triangle' mentioned in Section II.1 above. It is, indeed, in the interest of protecting the national environment that such ecology-oriented professionalism should be made welcome in industry, in trade, in agriculture and in the bureaucracies in charge of public works. Because of their key importance (also referred to at Section II.1 above), the same holds for the environmental organizations.

VI   IMPLEMENTATION[9]

The experience gained by Western European countries in implementing environmental management programmes may be summarized under the following four headings.

- Implementation means politics
- The regional plan of action
- Executing individual decrees
- Evaluation.

1   Implementation means politics

The implementation of environmental policy is a technical, carefully focused operation *and* an act of political will. Both these elements are present and not infrequently combine to create an explosive mixture. Both are equally necessary: if sheer political pigheadedness is allowed to carry the day against technical good sense, the consequences can be just as bad as when implementation is based on exclusively technical desiderata but fails to obtain general acceptance by the authorities and the parties concerned within the community. Effective implementation is essentially a matter of repeatedly reconciling these two elements with one another.

While, thanks to the desirable homogeneity of the staff entrusted with implementation, the technical, carefully focused operations themselves vary little from one part of the country to another, there are marked differences from region to region in the quality and emotional implications of the acts of political will. It may therefore be assumed that, even in centralized states, there will similarly be differences in actual implementation as regards the assiduity with which emissions are monitored, and in particular in connection with the progress of remedial action both in time and in different parts of the country. This is confirmed by experience in Western European countries as well as by considerations of plausibility, as presented hereunder. For the act of political will is the net outcome of a variety of estimates, within local and regional milieux, of the risks run, as well as of differences in environmental awareness which demonstrably exist within a given country, as also conceivably between North and South or across linguistic frontiers.

---

[9]   See, for further information on this topic, Chapter 10 by A. Capria in this volume.

2 The regional plan of action

Before the regional authorities tackle the drafting of individual decrees, they must first set their priorities: no authority can be continuously omnipresent when it has to discharge its task in a scientifically sound manner and if it is not to engender political antipathy on all fronts at one and the same time. In the countries of Western Europe it has, in most cases, proved feasible to establish territorial priorities by identifying areas of heavy pollution as revealed by pollution measurements. At all events, it is a fact that when excessive contaminations create acute danger for human beings, animals and plants in a given area, the authority is well advised to concentrate its (generally modest) analytical, financial and staff resources on the area in question. Such territorial concentration, as compared with attempts at simultaneous countrywide implementation, has the advantage that it lends itself to the creation among interested parties of local networks which can enable informal understandings (in the sense of Section II.1. above) to be reached between the parties, thus leading to the speeding up of implementation.

As a rule, territorial priorities are linked to priorities in time. The concentration of administrative attention on a particular polluted area implies that measures to remedy emissions outside the area are initially deferred. Such chronological staggering can, however, also take place independently of the setting of any territorial priorities – when, for example, a decision is taken to deal in sequence with remedial action for different sectors of the economy. Such a course is, indeed, to be recommended, particularly because investment in any given sector tends to follow a cyclical pattern: remedial action can conveniently be timed to coincide with the writing-off of plant or with the launching of new technologies on the market.

The last case to be discussed in the present context relates to the setting of priorities for remedial action on a function-by-function basis, as is also feasible in connection with other sources of emissions – for example, agriculture, households and public works. As in the case of chronological priorities, functional priorities may be disrupted due to the political niceties of what might be termed 'parallelism in sacrifice'. For, in many instances, action affecting a given sector of the economy can, in practice, be taken only if corresponding action is taken simultaneously with regard to other sectors. Well known examples of this phenomenon are those relating to water protection and to the maintenance of clean air in the context of transport: farmers are reluctant to consider reducing their use of fertilizer as a contribution to water protection until their communal authorities stop discharging their untreated sewage into the waters in question. Automobile associations – which enjoy much political clout in Western Europe – insist on action being taken against excessive NO_x emissions by local industry in return for acquiescence in traffic restrictions aimed at improving air quality.

Action plans entailing such 'parallelism in sacrifice' can result in an earlier willingness to change and thus in greater efficiency: they stem from an act of political will, which in certain cases may not mesh with purely scientific considerations. Such a case shows that the 'monitoring of technology', referred to in Section III.2. above, must always accompany the preparation of action plans and the setting of priorities. It also poses the question of how ready the interests concerned are to change their attitudes and, consequently, to agree to the curative measures proposed. The preparation of action plans will accordingly be seen to require not only technical expertise but also the ability to achieve a public consensus. Thus, for the implementation of environmental policy, and in addition to such technical expertise, there is a growing need for social engineering.

If the construction of an action plan is not to meet the same end as the building of a sand castle, the environmental authority must endeavour to bring into a consensus all the other authorities which will be affected by the set priorities. The wide-ranging and early participation of these other authorities in the planning process will make it easier to obviate any resistance on their part when it comes to drafting individual decrees. Thus, for example, when priorities are being set with a view to curbing air pollution – largely caused by traffic – in the worst affected zones of Western European cities, it is essential to involve the authorities in charge of road construction, traffic control and town planning in the process. The same holds for corresponding curative measures in heavily polluted areas in Eastern Europe, for which close cooperation with the regional authorities responsible for industry, energy and town and country planning is required. In order to deepen the involvement of the 'other' participating authorities in the plan of action, it is advisable for a binding document to be prepared, setting forth explicitly how individual measures will be implemented in due course. The structure of the body which prepares and takes these implementation decisions should, in so far as practicable, be the same as that which elaborated the plan of action. By this means, any subsequent opting out on the part of a particular 'other' authority is at least made more difficult.

3   Executing individual decrees

When the plan of action has been drawn up, the authority responsible for its execution proceeds to implement the various measures set forth therein. Here the authority will respect the agreed procedures for implementation, as well as the entitlement of the commercial interests and of the environmental protection bodies (see Section II.1. above) to their legal rights. Official instruments for implementation may take the form of the classical act of management – that is, an individual, concrete official decision, including injunctions and prohibitions applicable to every potential polluter and set forth in permissory terms and/or in decrees requiring the taking of specific remedial measures. When several polluters are concerned by a single decree, or by similar ones, a 'general-concrete' plan may constitute an appropriate instrument. Such a plan enables the labour-intensive preparation of several separate decrees to be replaced by a collectively applicable decree conforming to the general requirements of legal protection, thus allowing quicker implementation. Plans and collective injunctions of this kind are particularly apposite in dealing with agriculture – for example, when several farms within the catchment area of a groundwater course are required to reduce their use of fertilizers. Similar collective decrees are in common use with regard to town and country planning and (in the form of generally applicable detailed requirements concerning traffic signs) in the context of an environment-oriented transport policy.

It must be said that no authority will survive a campaign of curative measures which is exclusively confined to the promulgation of formal decrees: for one thing, the sheer volume of work would be overwhelming. In most Western European countries, therefore, practical implementation is increasingly effected by informal means.[10] These include, for example:

- verbal agreements between the authority, the environmental protection bodies and the commercial interests concerned (both collectively and at the level of an individual firm);
- offers of advice (particularly in agriculture and in the waste disposal sector);
- the organization by the authority, in collaboration with industry-specific associations, of events to impart information and training; and
- the dissemination, by means of informal procedures, of texts of regulatory agreements likely to be accepted by a consensus – for example, within the context of events held with a view to mediation.

It is clear, however, that such low-key methods are applicable only when there is a practical prospect of securing the voluntary collaboration of the commercial interests and of the environmental organizations, and thus the uncontested implementation of the legal requirements. If informal procedures should, however, fail, the authority can, of course, always fall back on the promulgation of a formal decree. Depending on the legal system in a given country, such a formal decree may be subject to judicial review in an administrative court.

---

[10] See, on this, Chapter 12 by P. Glasbergen and Chapter 15 by E. Rehbinder in this volume.

4   Evaluation

The final stage of any procedure for implementing an environmental policy should consist of an assessment of the real value of the various measures taken. Towards this end the regional authority responsible for implementation examines, on the basis of monitoring data furnished by an independent body (as discussed in Sections III.1. and III.3. above), to what extent the measures prescribed in the plan of action and put into effect by means of specific decrees have actually led to changed behaviour by the industrial interests in question (for example, as regards emissions) or even to an actual improvement in the quality of the environment (for example, as regards pollution) or in the effects of pollution on the recipients of the policy in question (human health, animals and plants). In practice such evaluations are hampered by numerous obstacles. Experience shows that environmental authorities tend to ascribe to their own actions any improvement in the environment which has happened as a by-product of another, non-environmental, policy or which has come about quite independently – for example, as the result of a recession. Such evaluations should therefore be carefully scrutinized. It is, indeed, in the manifest interest of a regional authority to avoid any such exaggeration of the impact of environmental policy. Outside experts could therefore usefully be associated with the making of such assessments – or could in fact be put in charge of the exercise.

The findings of such assessments must be made accessible to the public. This is a matter of major interest to the non-environmental authorities which have participated in the programme, as well as to the commercial interests and the environmental protection bodies. Moreover, evaluation reports present useful environmentally relevant data, such as the results of monitoring. These are, indeed, supposed to be published within the European Union, pursuant to the guideline[11] of 7 June 1990 on free access to environmentally relevant information. In the light of the public debate thus set in motion, the regional authority will be able either to rectify its plan of action or to set other priorities in the context of its ongoing preparation of a new plan. If an evaluation should reveal any shortcomings in the central government's environmental programme, the programme management must be brought into the picture.

---

[11] EC Guideline 90/313/EEC dated 7 June 1990 on free access to information concerning the environment, OJ 1990 L 158/56. See for comparative research in environmental information systems Helmut Weidner, in: Helmut Weidner, Roland Zieschank, Peter Knoepfel (eds), *Umweltinformation: Berichterstattung und Informationssysteme in zwölf Ländern*, Berlin: Sigma, 1992, 320 pp.

VII CONCLUSION

The recommendations set forth in this chapter have all been evolved in the light of the most recent experience of the environmental policies of the Western European countries. The author has presented them as a whole, in response to numerous questions from Eastern European colleagues about how to organize an effective environmental policy in their countries. In all the discussions which he has had, however, he has been at pains to stress that his limited knowledge of the countries in question does not enable him to assess the extent to which Western European experience can be applied in the context of Eastern European realities. He now wishes to reiterate this reservation at the conclusion. It may well be that, in view of the dramatic levels of pollution in these countries, resort may, as a matter of principle, have to be made to environmental policies other than those thus far applied in Western Europe. The author does not consider himself at the present juncture to be in a position to put forward any concrete proposals for such policies which – in the light of the gigantic social upheavals accompanying the transition from a 'socialist' to a market economy – will presumably have to bite deeper before accomplishing a transformation (thus far by no means achieved in the capitalist countries of Western Europe) into a truly ecological market economy. Fundamental rethinking along such lines would imply leaving behind the emission-focused programmes which have hitherto held sway, and embracing instead the vision of an entirely new regime, based on the concept of dedicated resource management. A discussion of this topic would, however, exceed the scope of this chapter.

Part III
Instrumenting Self-Control

12 From Regulatory Control to Network Management

Pieter Glasbergen

Table of Contents

I INTRODUCTION

Many current social problems, including environmental issues, require government involvement. Yet the capacity of the authorities to govern proves to be limited. It lags behind the need for intervention. A weakness at the core of this administrative issue is the limited mobilization capacity of government bodies. This is revealed in their lack of ability to rally support for environmental issues among both public and private organizations.

The continuing process of rationalization has had an influence on the allocation of government activities which are increasingly spread over diverse governmental bodies. Each of these bodies generally maintains contacts with private organizations working in the same area. This fragmented field must be prodded into action if the approach to environmental issues is to become effective. The field must be motivated to change in two respects. First, the parties involved should not only identify with their own interests; they should feel committed to the wider issues. They should recognize the extent of the problem and acknowledge their responsibility to do something about it. Second, the actors should be mobilized as vehicles of policy implementation. This means that every organization, alongside and in conjunction with other organizations, must feel accountable for policy. They should actively want to contribute to the preparation of policy and help carry out the measures agreed upon.[1]

Government's limited mobilization capacity comes into focus when we consider its approach to the environmental problems that arise, for instance, in intensive agriculture. This is well illustrated by the approach to the issue of manure usage. In many countries this is one of the main causes of the acidification and pollution of groundwater. An international comparative study (of the Netherlands, France and England) reveals that policy will most likely be formulated in three stages and will thus always lag behind developments. In the first stage, recourse is taken to spatial measures such as zoning, with the aim of protecting watersheds for drinking water extraction. This is generally accompanied by an appeal to farmers to help resolve the issue of acidification on a voluntary basis. Meanwhile, the drive to intensify agricultural production continues with the result that these preventive measures have to be supplemented. In the second stage, measures to promote environmental hygiene are formulated. These include regulations on spreading manure and technical specifications for livestock stalls. As the trend to intensify agriculture continues, these measures also prove inadequate, which calls for a discussion of volume measures – that is, the need to impose restrictions on further intensification has to be assessed. All three countries included in the comparative study prove to have gone through these three stages. This process may be called the 'iron law of agro-environmental policy'.[2] At present, the Netherlands is in the third stage, France is in the second stage, and England recently made the transition from the first to the second stage.

To explain the systematic shortfall in the development of policy, we must consider the closed organization of the agricultural sector. Agrarian organizations in each country are usually supported by a powerful political lobby and maintain close contact with the respective ministries of agriculture. These organizations operate as closed circuits. Their sole aim is to raise productivity. Time and again, they are able to rally resistance to a meaningful environmental policy.

This kind of experience with environmental policy leads us to ask whether the present administrative systems can cope with the environmental issues. A telling example is the overview in the report by the Council of the Club of Rome entitled *The First Global Revolution*. That report posits that the main characteristic of modern administrative systems is their increasing obsolescence. The structures

---

1   P. Leroy, Geïntegreerd gebiedsgericht milieubeleid: gestuurde maatschappelijke mobilisatie ten behoeve van het milieu? in M.J. Mastop (ed.), *Gebiedsgericht milieubeleid belicht*, Publikatiereeks gebiedsgericht beleid, no 8, 's-Gravenhage, 1993.

2   P. Glasbergen, Agro-environmental policy trapped in an iron law? A comparative analysis of agricultural pollution control in the Netherlands, the United Kingdom and France, in *Sociologia Ruralis*, **XXXII** (1), 1992, pp. 30–48.

were designed more than a century ago to serve societies that were much simpler than the present ones. The report points out that, although changes have indeed been introduced, they are only marginal or form an extension of existing features. Moreover, as government intervention in the social system increased, these changes were accompanied by more bureaucracy and inefficiency. This report takes the standpoint that a close relationship exists between environmental protection and administrative reform. In fact, the relationship is so close that without administrative reform, it will be impossible to protect the environment effectively.[3]

II CHARACTERISTICS OF THE REGULATORY MODEL OF CONTROL

Modern environmental policy emerged at a time of deep-seated belief in a society susceptible to directed change. This conviction is expressed in the way Western democracies approach problems; the same pattern occurs virtually everywhere.[4] New environmental goals are translated into legal rules, each of which specifies conduct in which people should or should not engage.

The standpoint underlying these rules is that government must be understood as the provision of leadership for social developments by one institution that is above the parties to be governed. This is known as the command and control approach. The government's aim is to achieve certain environmental goals. Accordingly, it views its social and physical surroundings as objects of control. Government by command and control is grounded in a set of hierarchical relations; this structure is found not only within the administration itself but also between public authorities and society.

This approach is clearly manifest in the so-called regulatory model of control that has been developed for environmental policy.[5] It assumes that people choose to behave in the way they are compelled to behave and that this element of force should be constructed according to the rules with which people's behaviour must comply. The rules are formulated in terms of prescriptions (what one must do) and proscriptions (what one must not do). If the rules are not followed, negative sanctions are applied.

The key instrument of regulatory control is the permit. Technically, this instrument operates as follows. The law prohibits a given activity unless a permit has been issued. Usually, the law concerns setting up and/or performing an indus-

---

[3] A. King, B. Schneider, *The First Global Revolution*, Club of Rome, 1992.
[4] A. Weale, *The New Politics Of Pollution*, Manchester: Manchester University Press, 1992.
[5] See chapter 4 by M. Kloepfer and G. Winter in this volume.

trial activity. Rules stipulate the standards that must be met in order to apply for a permit. The permit itself specifies the regulations that will apply to the industrial activity in question. The first permit systems were more or less ad hoc developments. They were not based on a comprehensive set of rules for environmental protection but were generally linked to sectoral legislation – that is, to legislation concerning specific environmental compartments, such as air, water and soil. To some degree, the legislation did follow a sequence. A system of permits was first developed for those activities whereby the detrimental effects on the environment were most visible.

Furthermore, the legislation that regulates the granting of permission is still highly instrumental in this stage. Hardly any normative stipulations are provided in the environmental laws. These Acts merely create a legal framework in which the agency that grants permission is assigned the authority to perform its duties. As a consequence, the norms that should apply are generally determined for each application.

In most countries, there is a considerable gap between the actual situation and the situation that should exist on the basis of the regulations. In many instances, firms do not have the required permits but, even if they do have the right permits, infractions are frequently tolerated.[6]

III   CHANGES IN THE REGULATORY MODEL OF CONTROL

The basic pattern of the regulatory model of control has remained unchanged. Yet in those countries where it was developed, some adjustments have been made in the course of time. These adaptations are largely due to the need for transparency in an expanding juridical framework. As the number of laws grows, the legal framework becomes unwieldy, and the sectoral approach threatens to make the legislation complicated. Separate environmental acts differ from each other in unspecified ways, sometimes overlapping, but also leaving gaps in coverage. Accordingly, the next stage of application of the regulatory model of control is characterized by technical adjustments in the legal code that will gradually gain more content. Although this process warrants a more elaborate discussion than we can give it here, we can briefly review its characteristics in the Netherlands. It may be described in a number of steps.

First of all, accompanying the process of continued expansion in sectoral legislation, a second legislative process begins. Here the aim is to harmonize diffuse and mutually distinct regulations. For instance, an integral environmental permit,

---

[6]   Th.G. Drupsteen, Het juridische sturingsmodel, in: P. Glasbergen (ed.), *Milieubeleid; een beleidswetenschappelijke inleiding*, 's-Gravenhage: VUGA, 1994.

specifying rules for nuisance, air pollution, waste disposal and so on, is introduced. Under this new configuration, a firm needs only one permit to cover all aspects of environmental protection. The diverse bodies that grant the permit must collaborate, so that the applicant has to deal with only one agency.

Second, the content of the permits changes. A shift occurs from the regulation of means to the regulation of ends. Initially, the permits stipulates precisely how a firm is to set up its production process in order to attain set goals (regulation of means). Later, the regulation of ends is introduced to give firms the opportunity to search for solutions according to their own insights and in the most efficient way. These solutions are intended to allow firms to comply with the set goals.

Third, the permit requirement is dropped for those relatively homogeneous branches of industry that generate a low environmental load. Instead of an individual permit, general rules are formulated with which the entire branch must comply. The permit requirement is replaced by a duty to report its intent to the authorities prior to initiating an activity.

Fourth, the permit systems are grounded in planning and buttressed by standardization. This pertains to certain groups of emissions as well as to certain aspects of environmental quality. The national environmental policy plans are involved in the performance of this task.

Over time, these adaptations strengthen an administration that operates according to the regulatory model of control. At present, a more integrated and easier to maintain system of rules for environmental protection is available. As more improvements are made to the system, however, a sense of doubt starts to grow under the surface. In practice, improvements in the quality of the environment can only be made utilizing other modes of control. Continuing with the current mode means that further deterioration can only be halted. The shift in thinking that is now taking place with regard to control is primarily due to a fundamental doubt that the regulatory model of control provides for effective environmental protection. The limits of this model have gradually come to light.

IV   LIMITATIONS OF THE REGULATORY MODEL OF CONTROL

To achieve far-reaching social changes, the utility of juridical control has only a limited capacity. These limitations are inherent in this sort of instrument.

First, let us consider a fundamental question: what instrumental use can and may be made of jurisprudence? Policy operates according to charts of means and ends which are translated into legal measures. This exercise raises numerous normative questions about legal rights and the due course of law. Although control is accepted by jurisprudence, this control can nevertheless only take place under the independent function of the law in the context of a society's judicial institutions. The function of law is to safeguard fundamental freedoms in a market economy. In view of that function, law is not only an instrument of control, it also serves to define the limits of control. The body of law puts the one-sided pursuit of social goals into perspective. Generally speaking, law also restricts control.

Second, and tying in with the preceding question, law cannot go beyond the point that it is felt to be legitimate, since law is a collection of rules of conduct and the effects intended by such acts, and those rules of conduct must correspond to the legal consciousness that prevails in a society. A considerable degree of social consensus is necessary regarding the content of the policy and the rules of conduct predicated upon that policy. In other words, legal rules can only be effective when there is a general awareness that they express how things should be. A greater number of, and more stringent, rules lead to greater efforts to maintain order, and when there is a high level of social resistance, this can undermine the legitimacy of government authority. In this way, a regulating government can even put its own future as a regulatory body in jeopardy.

A third factor limiting the controlling capacity of the regulatory model relates to (in)efficiency. Juridical control is tied to some guarantees because of its exercise of power. When a juridical system is established by taking into account all the stipulated precautions, its development will be slow. Thus, it will be reactive in character. Almost by definition, a system like that will always show some rigidity. Any change will have to take the same slow route. Enforcement of rules is also somewhat rigid. To illustrate this point, let us review the constraints of a normal activity within this system: the issuing of regulatory permits as a way to reduce environmental load. Consultation is certainly required to achieve the aim, and assistance may also be needed in drawing up the permit. In addition, the permit can only be granted by taking certain procedures. The parties affected can always appeal the decision. For each installation, the entire process has to be completed. All this requires a great deal of effort on the part of civil servants and government officials. Once the permit is granted, the regulatory control does not encourage the parties to go beyond the formal requirements to protect the environment. Policy efficiency is not the predominant standpoint of regulatory control: the process of regulations is much more concerned with administrative accuracy, conformity to rules and legal certainty.

The discussion of the points raised above demonstrates that there are limits to enforcement of the regulatory model of control. Of course, these limits are not absolute; they represent shifting boundaries that are closely tied to the society's degree of environmental awareness. This environmental awareness, in turn, is linked to the amount of attention demanded by competing policy issues. For instance, environmental awareness proves to be strongly related to economic prosperity. Apparently, in a period of economic boom, more opportunities are created for environmental legislation. On the other hand, when an economy is in recession, the social climate is less amenable to environmental regulation.

The regulatory model of control is made less effective by one task in particular: to enforce rules of conduct that affect specific target groups while certain measures may be considered legitimate by society as a whole, those groups directly targeted by the policy will not necessarily agree. The regulatory model of control has to rely on the law-abiding citizen. When people are not very willing to comply with rules, the effectiveness of the model has to rely on another group: the agents of enforcement. The greater the effort they are willing and able to make in enforcing the rule of law, the more effective the control will be.

V TOWARDS AN INTERACTIVE MODEL OF CONTROL

We have already stated that the regulatory model of control is grounded in a command and control approach which has as its underlying principles the centrality and exclusivity of the (national) government in the social system.[7] These are the principles that we are subjecting to close and rigorous scrutiny here. In fact, the present discussion centres on the limitations of the mobilization capacity of governments. By reviewing the role of government in social control, we can bring new characteristics of the control situation into the picture.

First, it becomes clear that environmental policy should be seen as one of many factors in a social process that is based on a high degree of autonomy. Many forces impact upon the social processes underlying the environmental issue, including production and consumption. Government policy is one such force, representing attempts at active control, but is not an exclusive and dominant controlling factor. Government policy often plays a minor role in shaping social development.

Second, the fragmented capacity for solving environmental problems is seen as an important characteristic of context. No single government body can take control. Instead, the work and competencies are split between many government bodies. In addition, government authorities share areas of control with special interest groups which also try to exert influence. Of course, sharing responsibility brings out the divergent perceptions of the problem held by the parties involved. Accordingly, the capacity of government to exercise control is largely determined by the extent to which the field of actors can be motivated to cooperate with the policy.

A third observation is that environmental policy is only part of a wider government policy relating to the quality of the environment. Equally important to

---

7   A.J.A. Godfroy, N.J.M. Nelissen, *Verschuivingen in de besturing van de samenleving: bevindingen, kernconcepten en perspectief*, in: A.J.A. Godfroy, N.J.M. Nelissen (eds), *Verschuivingen in de besturing van de samenleving*, Bussum: Coutinho, 1993.

environmental quality is policy in various other sectors: agricultural policy, traffic and transport policy and economic policy, for instance. These 'other' government policies do not always run parallel to the aims of environmental policy, although the policy for other sectors is actually often more important to the quality of the environment than environmental policy itself. Not surprisingly, then, environmental policy proper can only contribute in a limited sense to its purported aim – namely to achieve a satisfactory degree of environmental protection.

In light of this new appreciation of the importance of context, control is gradually being redefined. This new perspective shows that the role of government is relative; and that it therefore should also be redefined. Control is increasingly perceived as a joint activity of various levels of government and civil organizations. We refer to the new model of control as network management,[8] an interactive form of control which attempts to get interaction and communication going among the actors involved in handling a problem. In turn, these processes facilitate a joint effort to formulate a common definition of the problems which would then form the basis for harmonizing the fragmented problem-solving capacity. In this kind of control, government acts more as a facilitator of the policy process than as an autonomous administrator. Policy development is primarily aimed at mobilizing relevant actors. The directions in which solutions should be sought are not fixed; they only emerge in the course of the interaction and communication processes. The actors involved must learn together how to achieve results that meet disparate aims. The outcome must be a step in the direction of the environmental goals, but will also have to do justice to vested interests, which are often clearly present in environmental issues.

The environmental policy of the Netherlands demonstrates several examples of this innovative strategy of control. One is the so-called target group policy; another is area-specific environmental policy. In the following sections, we will briefly relate a few experiences with these innovative forms of control.

VI   TARGET-GROUP POLICY

Target-group policy is intended to translate national goals for the reduction of emission levels into accepted and attainable norms and regulations for a branch of industry. This intent is achieved in a structured consultation among representatives of the industry and delegates from relevant government bodies. The consultation is based on the principle that all partners are equal. It is unusual in that it diverges from the norm of non-committal informative and motivational discus-

---

8   P. Glasbergen (ed.), *Managing Environmental Disputes. Network Management as an Alternative*, Dordrecht: Kluwer Academic Publishers, 1995.

sion. In the case of target-group policy, consultation is also expected to result in binding agreements on the content of the policy and the way in which it will be conducted. An effort is made to reach mutual agreement on the policy aims, as well as on the ways and means of achieving them. The private sector commits itself to performing various activities within the framework of the policy. The government bodies make a commitment to support the policy and to shape their policy around it in the future.

Target-group policy requires all government organizations that deal with a target group to harmonize their activities. This means that separate authorities have to take each other's plans into account. At the same time, they must gear their policy to the aims formulated by the target groups themselves. Consequently, in this form of control, accountability lies largely with those branches of industry that are partly responsible for carrying out the policy.

Diverse target groups have been involved in this type of control. Up until now, these have been mainly refineries, the energy sector, the construction industry, traffic and transport and the retail sector. The consultations involve representatives from the branches of industry, delegates from various ministries, including both the Ministry of the Environment and the Ministry of Economic Affairs, as well as representatives of regional and local authorities. Occasionally representatives of environmental organizations, nature conservation groups and trade unions also take part.

The procedures are systematically broken down into four steps, as described below.[9]

1   The first stage entails making an inventory of the current environmental load and formulating aims for its reduction (especially regarding emissions) for each target group. Together, the participants set a timetable for achieving each of these reduction aims.

2   The second stage consists of signing a covenant in which the parties confirm the agreements made during the consultation. For instance, these agreements might concern activities that the parties will undertake, the reciprocal exchange of information and expertise, or investigations, if deemed necessary.

3   In the third stage, information is disseminated by mounting publicity campaigns and deploying other tactics. The information is directed toward individual firms and (government) organizations that are involved in the policy. In this way, agreements that were made at a central level are communicated to individual members of the target group and to separate government bodies.

---

[9]   P-J. Klok and S.M.M. Kuks, Het doelgroepenbeleid, in: P. Glasbergen (ed.), *Milieubeleid een beleidswetenschappelijke inleiding*, 's-Gravenhage: VUGA, 1994.

4   The fourth stage revolves around implementation of the agreements. It entails formulating plans to limit the environmental load, carrying out these plans, and monitoring the outcome. The actual implementation is the task of the individual members of the target group.

This overview of the stages reveals some characteristics specific to target-group policy, distinguishing it from the classic model of control.

One characteristic of the policy is its openness in regard to content, which is particularly evident in the stage of consultation. Consultation is only meaningful when the policy is not yet worked out in detail and there is thus still an opportunity for negotiation and discussion about the perceptions of the problem, interests, uncertainties and possible solutions. At that point, it is still possible to make a firm agreement that particular issues require further investigation or consensus-building. The policy is seen as a continuous (learning) process in which the firms themselves indicate how they can contribute to product innovation, waste prevention and energy conservation.

Another characteristic of the policy is that long-term agreements about the timing of implementation can be flexible. Agreements regarding policy aims usually cover a long period. In this way, firms retain a high degree of freedom to determine which measures they will take to achieve the goals and when they will do so. Accordingly, government authorities can regulate matters that would be much harder to handle by invoking legal procedures.

A third characteristic of the policy derives from the fact that the consultation is conducted by representatives of organizations. Unlike the case in traditional forms of control, these representatives can be more than the mouthpiece of the vested interests which form their constituency. In practice, the special interest groups are expected to contribute to the implementation of the national environmental policy so that their cooperation is thus an indispensable link in the policy process. Accordingly, the procedures strongly promote support for the environmental policy in society at large.

The keystone of the policy process is the covenant which is a written agreement between various parties serving to elucidate the results of consultation. This clarity has a substantive aspect (what was agreed?) and a normative aspect (what do the parties expect of each other?). The parties may be more or less committed to the covenant, depending on its content and the intent of those involved. The contract may vary from a compulsory agreement to a relatively non-committal statement of intent. Currently in the Netherlands, the number of modern covenants runs into double figures, most of them being still in the first stage of implementation. One such covenant arranged with the printing industry stipulates a drastic reduction in hydrocarbon emissions by the year 2000 – 75 per cent less than the 1990 level. To achieve this and other goals for this branch, a model system for environmental care has been developed and is now being implemented. A further example is an agreement with the packaging industry which has as its main thrust the limitation of the use of packaging materials and the promotion of recycling. Yet another example agreed with the wood-processing industry is aimed at reducing the exploitation of tropical hardwoods stipulating that, as of 1996, only wood from forests managed as sustainable resources will be imported. Interestingly, this covenant makes the weakness of the target-group policy eminently clear. After the covenant had been closed, a discussion arose about what 'sustainable' meant in this connection. As far as the parties know, wood that meets the conditions is not available in sufficient supply.

A definitive assessment of the results of the target-group policy in terms of net gain for the environment would be premature at this point. So much depends on whether or not the signatory organizations are able to impose discipline upon their constituencies and that, in turn, will depend upon the degree to which the necessary investments are both technically and economically feasible. Thus, we venture to say that the effectiveness of the target-group policy should be assessed by tracing its intricate patterns.

There is a place for target-group policy as long as it does not run counter to existing legislation. This means that the classic command and control approach circumscribes the scope of this policy. As long as no rules have been formulated in the context of the classic regulatory model, there is leeway to work with covenants. But as soon as those rules appear, the target-group policy will primarily have to supplement existing rules. In addition, it is also accepted that a covenant is a precursor of future legislation. The application of this form of network management should thus be seen as a preliminary step aimed at reaching agreement between equal partners. It prepares the way to tackle a situation in accordance with the classic model of control. In this light, target-group policy can be conducted in isolation or in tandem with other policy. Both approaches are found in current practice.

VII   AREA-SPECIFIC ENVIRONMENTAL POLICY

Area-specific environmental policy is similar to target-group policy in many respects, but it actually goes a step further. In so doing it tackles a much more complex issue. The object of area-specific environmental policy is to address both environmental problems and socio-economic problems simultaneously at the regional level. This policy, which is still experimental, was developed around 1990 in ten or so regions which, together, cover more than one-third of the total area of the Netherlands. In a few of these areas, development had been stagnating for years due to conflicts of interest. Diverse government bodies, each supported by special interest groups block each other's decision-making. A good example is the region surrounding the national Schiphol airport. For over 25 years, the pros and cons of expanding the airport have been debated, the discussion being focused on how to deal with the environmental problems that expansion would generate (particularly noise). Another example can be found in the region around the port of Rotterdam which is not only the world's biggest port facility but also the country's prime industrial area. Here too, the question is how to combine two priorities: economic development and environmental measures. It is striking that in these cases, a new perspective would theoretically be advantageous to both government authorities and the private sector, which wants security for the future.

In area-specific policy – an initiative of the Ministry of Environment – an attempt is made to mobilize public and private actors by drawing them into a project organization. The Ministry's goal in forming this temporary group is to forge a development perspective for the region. That perspective should do justice to the national environmental goals while serving specific regional interests and, accordingly, environmental goals are placed in a development perspective. New opportunities are sought for those interests in the region that are threatened by the environmental goals. Ultimately, the intention is to put together a package deal – consisting of win-win outcomes – serving the interests of the parties included in the project organization. Like the target-group policy, this package deal is formalized in a covenant.

Various regions take an innovative approach. In other publications, we have analysed a number of the cases extensively.[10] Here, we limit the discussion to a brief sketch of two cases in one agricultural and one industrial region in the Netherlands – giving an impression of the methods used. Although the same basic principles have been followed, the methods are different in each of the regions.

The agricultural region known as the Gelre Valley (Gelderse Vallei) covers 40,000 hectares. Here, livestock farming accounts for excessive manure production which has led to severe soil contamination, as well as to the pollution of groundwater and surface waters. Furthermore, nature reserves surrounding the area are endangered by acidification, due to the ammonia released from the manure. However, it is not only nature that is under threat; the agrarian sector is also in trouble. There are about 5000 farms in the area, most of which are (too) small in size, and the income level of many farmers leaves much to be desired. A project organization was set up in this region to serve a dual purpose: to improve the agrarian sector while improving the environment. The participants in the project organization represented the entire agrarian sector – various ministries, provincial and

---

[10]   P. Glasbergen, P.P.J. Driessen, New strategies for environmental policy, in: *Dutch Crossing*, (50), Winter, 1993, pp. 28–45.

municipal authorities, agrarian interest groups, agribusiness, environmental groups, and the bank to which most of the farmers are tied. This Valley Commission developed a three-pronged approach to the problem, in open communication with the region. The first track was the 'think line', along which this line, research was conducted, perspectives were formulated and directions for solutions were elaborated. Members of the Valley Commission worked out partial perspectives for the various aspects of the issue. The second track was the 'do line', along which small-scale projects were carried out to strengthen the infrastructure of the region. These were started even before the plan was ready for implementation. In this way, the Commission showed the region that it was not just a debating club and demonstrated its capacity to get plans for concrete improvements off the ground. The last track was the 'communication line' aimed at building up confidence in the region.

The meetings of the Valley Commission were open to the public and held at different places in the region each time. The Commission had its own logo and its own newspaper, which appeared regularly. It set up information booths in public libraries and, in addition, held numerous public hearings and information meetings. After a few years, they worked out a plan that contained measures to improve both the agrarian structure and the environmental situation. The implementation of the plan is now underway.

The second case is that of an industrial port area: the Zeeland-Flanders Canal Zone. The area covers 318 sq km and contains a large chemical industry as well as a nature reserve. The residential areas in the region are subject to a severe degree of environmental nuisance (noise, stench, dust, hazard and air pollution). Because the environmental situation does not come up to national standards, firms are forced to take expensive measures at source in order to minimize the nuisance as far as possible. Industries are confronted with restrictions on expansion; the current environmental norms make it difficult for them to expand on their present industrial estates, nor are there sufficient new sites to which industries can relocate. This has negative repercussions on the opportunities for development. The policy that was carried out in the past had a narrow focus, dealing with only certain aspects of the overall problem, and had little effect. In this region, too, it was decided to take the new approach that was based on the principles of region-specific environmental policy. A project organization was set up, including representatives of the private sector, several ministries, delegates from lower levels of government (a province, the municipalities) and the environmental organization for the province. Here, too, a dual goal was set: to improve the economic structure and the environmental situation. The planning process in this region got off to a slow start, being hampered by widespread mutual distrust. On top of that, a long time was spent looking for procedures that would produce results. Eventually, a very practical procedure was selected. It started with an inventory of the bottlenecks that the parties had run into, listed according to a sequence of priority. Then, representatives of industry were asked to look for solutions for the environmental problems and representatives of the environmental interest groups were asked to look for solutions to the problems of economic development. In this way, the parties slowly came to appreciate the others' standpoint. In further negotiations the parties gradually progressed towards formulating points for decision-making. Eventually, a plan, comprising concrete environmental regulations, the planning of a new industrial estate, measures to protect the nature reserve, and so forth, was worked out. In contrast to the Gelre Valley case, negotiations took place in private: the project organization only made the results public when a draft of the plan was ready. The plan was discussed in public hearings and in the board meetings of those organizations that took part in the development of the policy. At that point, the environmental group had to drop out of the project organization due to objections from its membership. Now they watch how the implementation of the plan is proceeding from a distance. In this region, too, progress is being made in resolving the problem. In fact, the project is considered a success.

Evaluation of the area-specific environmental policy suggests that this policy is effective. Stagnation has been broken, and new developments have taken root in regions where the method has been applied. A crucial factor in the success of the approach is the attitude of the parties involved. They have to consider the current or anticipated situation to be undesirable. As no single party is capable of solving the problems on its own, the mutual dependency of the parties must be clearly acknowledged. By making a package deal, which serves multiple interests, actors with entirely different aims are able to work together. The method used in the projects has demonstrably led to the formation of a common definition of the situation, to active forms of joint decision-making, a wider range of options and ultimately, a coordinated approach to complex problems. The national environmental goals play a controlling role in the background. The development of the plan was set within a time of two or three years, forcing the parties to take an efficient and task-oriented approach to the problem.

VIII   CONCLUSIONS

In this chapter, we argued that administrative reform is imperative if we are to develop a more effective approach to environmental issues. We defined administrative reform as an issue of control. This reform should primarily concern procedures: the method by which government authorities can implement their policy. In our opinion, when authorities only have recourse to the model of regulatory control, the degree to which they are able to achieve an adequate level of environmental protection will be insufficient. The operation of the classic model of control depends upon the input of a large and expensive legislative, executive and enforcement apparatus. In addition, this model puts some restrictions on the capacity for control. A review of the characteristics of the control situation led us into a discussion of network management. This is a form of interactive control that seems to offer opportunities to mobilize special interests to support environmental reform. This control corresponds with recent changes in political culture, yet does not adopt the rhetoric that masks political and administrative powerlessness. The review then turned to a discussion of two applications of this kind of control.

Network management is an umbrella concept that denotes a form of control with the following characteristics:

- Environmental interests are not the only ones taken into account. Network management also considers the interests that are forced to adapt and reorient their activities to accommodate environmental goals. Instead of making the usual distinction between environmental and economic goals, this kind of control seeks to amalgamate the two.
- Government aims are not the only policies taken into account. Network management also focuses on the policies conducted by organized special interest groups. This kind of control seeks to develop new forms of public-public and public-private cooperation in order to tackle environmental problems.
- The approach to the problems is process-oriented. Policy-making is viewed as a goal-seeking process. The actors involved in such processes bring their disparate interests to the table. Jointly, they then identify the diverse goals and try to weave these into a coherent programme.
- This kind of control attempts to break down the traditional division between formulation and implementation of policy. The stages of problem analysis, goal formulation, and instrument selection are concurrent. Thus, while policy is being formulated, parts of it are already being executed.
- The actors involved in the development of policy cannot be non-committal. All parties have to abide by the outcomes. Their commitment to the selected approach is formalized in covenants. Progress of the policy process is monitored by the parties jointly.

Network management will not entirely replace the application of the regulatory model of control. Interactive forms of control either precede the classic form of control or supplement it once it is in place.

Prerequisites seem to be:

- a set of national environmental standards;
- a minimum of a regulatory framework;
- an open and well structured administrative system;
- prior experience in participation in decision making;
- negotiating skills.

When these prerequisites are fulfilled the new model of control allows parties to reach goals that are unattainable with regulatory control. Therefore, if we are to tackle environmental problems effectively, we must build a new relation between regulatory control and network management.

13 Financial Instruments in Environmental Protection

Gyula Bándi

Table of Contents

I   THE IMPETUS FOR FINANCIAL INSTRUMENTS

Since the beginning, and increasingly from the middle, of this century environmental protection has evolved as a state function with the basic purpose of protecting society and humanity. The protective function of the state is implemented for the most part through the ordinary methods and mechanisms of public administration – that is, through 'command-and-control' mechanisms or direct methods.

Command-and-control mechanisms take effect as legal rules which regulate, by individual decision, the conditions under which activities with a possible environmental impact may continue. Licensing, the imposition of conditions on a permit and fines are among the most popular and useful of command and control methods. And, of course, these direct techniques are continually improving – for example, permitting has been coupled over time with environmental impact assessment and public participation requirements. Such requirements can contribute

201

to protect environmental interests, but nonetheless incorporate an external approach in that these administrative or direct measures do not require the fundamental agreement of the regulated community; they require only compliance.

All the while that environmental problems were considered limited in scope this approach was arguably entirely satisfactory. However, since environmental degradation has been demonstrated to be a general and global problem, such an attitude has proved untenable. Although the economy and economic growth are now recognized as the chief sources of environmental pollution, in the apparent absence of other options to resolve the problem, the interventionist or external approach of the state has remained the prevailing concept. A general criticism of command and control methods is that these measures do not aim at inherent changes in polluters' behaviour, but rather provide the conditions upon which the behaviour can continue.

Environmental degradation gives rise to a number of harmful effects, all of which incorporate some element of damage or cost in relation to their remedy. Effects on human health lead to lost working days and health care costs; air pollution damages crop production or corrodes the fabric of buildings. Equally, the loss of species, and of natural habitats, or a decline in fish population each has a financial consequence. The main problem as regards the financial consequences is the lack of evaluation systems to measure and allocate the costs. Moreover, in most cases the harmful consequences of environmental pollution arise only over long distances or by way of delayed effects. If we take the example of a waste disposal site, the possible harm may only become visible some years after the abandonment of the site. Consequently, the damage, harm and cost of remedy have less or even no effect on the person who causes them, but nonetheless usually affect neighbours or more distant victims.

> When costs are imposed on others without their being fully compensated or when benefits are received by others for which these beneficiaries do not make full payment, an economic externality, spillover or side-effect exists. These are a frequent cause of market failure especially as far as activities affecting the environment are concerned.[1]

A typical example of an externality is a chemical factory which, by polluting the water and the air in a given region, damages agricultural production. Unless regulation recovers the cost of the damage incurred the pollution is a pure externality for the chemical company. While command and control measures may require the restructuring of business activity or even limit, suspend or arrest the polluting activity, the externality question remains unsolved. In our example,

---

1   Clement A. Tisdell, *Economics of Environmental Conservation*, Barking: Elsevier, 1991 p.45.

while the chemical facility may have a permit with pollution limits described within it, the permission procedure still fails to accommodate all the possible damages and costs. The number of possible externalities being very great, it is almost impossible to deal with each and every one by way of direct measures alone. It is not surprising, then, that in most countries smaller polluting activities are not always required to have a separate permit but instead must meet more general conditions. Furthermore, while pollution standards represent an 'acceptable' level of pollution, they do not necessarily reflect the whole range of pollution. Regulatory conditions and administrative decisions in themselves may be insufficient to provide stimulus for the introduction of cleaning equipment or the adoption of cleaner technologies. Therefore much of the extra cost of preventing or compensating resulting damage comes to be paid by downstream or neighbouring agriculture.

Externalities as signs of 'market failures' with respect to environmental problems can be reflected in financial tools, provided these are sophisticated enough for their assessment. Turning to our example again, if clean water or clean air was not free but the user had to pay for them, the extra costs would become visible in the accounts and more generally in the prices set by the chemical company, and so might consequently have an effect on the marketing of its products. However, externalities do not automatically appear as internal costs, they must be internalized through specific measures which it is not always easy or possible to create. The market frequently does not reflect environmental values because, often, there is no market for the damaged environmental good.

A market in water rights and water use has, it is true, occurred historically because water has generally been a scarce resource. However, this market and the conditions governing it are connected simply with the right to use the water and rarely with the purity of the water supplied. Clean air on the other hand has no history as a marketable product, and has no proprietary background – air has always been considered as a 'free' commodity. As a result water uses may be sold but the cleanliness of water or clean air cannot. Therefore, an artifical value is to be assigned to the particular kind of externality.

The main difference between the principles underlying direct and market instruments is the mechanism by which they influence economic processes. Command and control measures influence, or try to influence, economic processes directly. If an activity requires a permit, that activity may not commence without it. Where permit conditions are broken, the public administration may impose positive and negative obligations, and the activity may be stopped or limited. Beyond this there is a great variety of sanctions designed to impose liability. An administrative or judicial order may limit the activity, attach certain conditions to its continuance, suspend or even suppress it. All varieties of direct measure assume immediate compliance with their terms. As most critics agree, direct measures do not require an understanding of or agreement with the objective pursued, but rather try to develop a general attitude of compliance.

Market instruments are based on a different approach to influencing polluting activities. This method is more indirect, as the idea is to build environmental requirements into market conditions by steps internalizing the externalities involved. Thus the polluters' freedom of action is not limited through direct regulations, but differing consequences are tailored for different behaviour. The polluter may choose a relatively more polluting, energy-demanding, waste-producing way of action, but the financial conditions are less favourable than if clean technologies, energy-saving methods and recycling technologies were adopted. This kind of influence, being less direct, has a more remote or delayed effect on the polluting economy, but possibly a better chance of achieving revised economic management systems.

In the development of market instruments or financial incentives the clarification and careful consideration of environmental, economic and, last but not least, the enforcement consequences is vital. Seemingly favourable market forces are not necessarily helpful to environmental improvement, nor are they necessarily enforceable. The difference between what is economically desirable and what is administratively manageable may prevent the implementation of some market instruments. Additionally what amounts to a working market incentive in a developed country with an effective environmental enforcement system may not have the same effect in a less developed or developing country with a greater need for economic development and a less effective environmental enforcement system.

As a result, we do not propose to prioritize the different market instruments in the following section, but to list them mentioning certain advantages and disadvantages as well as certain conditions for their better implementation along the way.

II   TYPES OF FINANCIAL INSTRUMENTS

1   Classifications

As economic instruments have evolved over time, the borderline between these instruments and so-called traditional instruments has remained quite uncertain. The same is true with respect to any attempt to categorize the different economic instruments themselves.

There are several accepted methods of classification for economic instruments or incentives. One 'classic' categorization is contained in a 1989 OECD publication, which suggests five groups – charges, subsidies, deposit-refund systems, market creation, and financial enforcement incentives – with several examples for each of these groups of instruments.

Charges in this publication are considered as a 'price' to be paid for the pollution. There are various types of charges, namely:

- effluent or emission charges;
- user charges;
- product charges;
- administrative charges; and
- tax differentiation.

Subsidies is used as a general term for various forms of financial assistance, including:

- grants;
- soft loans; and
- tax allowances.

Deposit-refund systems are defined as laying a surcharge on the price of potentially polluting products, which is refunded should the product be returned on the market or for recycling.

Market creation means that actors must buy 'rights' for actual or potential pollution. Several forms exist, in particular:

- emissions trading;
- market intervention; and
- liability insurance.

(Financial) enforcement incentives may be considered as a legal, rather than an economic, instrument. There are two major types:

- non-compliance fees; and
- performance bonds.[2]

Another categorization has been proposed by an EU working group:

Instruments could be categorized as 'economic' in so far as they affect through the market mechanism costs and benefits of alternative actions open to economic agents, with the effect of influencing behaviours in a way that is favourable for the environment. These are inter alia:

– Environmental charges and taxes;
– Tradeable emission permits;
– Deposit-refund systems;

---

2   OECD, *Economic Instruments: a Classification*, Paris: OECD, 1989, pp. 14–16.

– Enforcement incentives;
– Financial aid;
– Industry agreements;
– Environmental liability.[3]

Although the creation of market incentives and instruments is always primarily a matter for the state, we identify two basic types of economic measures according to the actor performing the active role. The leading role could be undertaken, on the one hand, by the state or, on the other hand, by national and international financing institutions. Within the group of state-designed instruments there are some measures closer to the state's enforcement capabilities than others which leave more room for individual activity. In any event regulatory power lies with the state in both these options, and the state also has an influence over instruments where the leading role is taken by financial institutions.

2 Schemes managed by governments

The state is the main player assuming a direct enforcement role in the case of

- charges;
- subsidies;
- pricing;
- enforcement incentives;
- state property and services.

Substantial assistance of the economic actors is required in the case of

- deposit-refund systems;
- market creation;
- offset approach;
- compulsory insurance.

a) Charges

Charges generally imply different forms of permanent payment for the impact on the environment, based on some quantitative and qualitative aspects of the given impact. The plant or facility pays charges on the basis of the characteristics of its pollution. Charges are also present as fees or taxes. In the understanding of the

---

[3] *Report of the Working Group of Experts from the Member States on the Use of Economic and Fiscal Instruments in EC Environmental Policy*, XI/185/90., p. 7.

economic essence of these terms, fees are connected more directly to a public service, while taxes are taken as general revenues of the state with less, or no, earmarked constraints for expenditure.

Charges fall somewhere in between fees and taxes. The permit to use environmental resources could be seen, in very broad terms, as a kind of public service. In addition, the revenue flowing from the charges is sometimes directed to specific purposes such as the construction of purification plants and so on.

Emission or effluent charges are laid on the discharge of pollutants into environmental media. They are calculated according to the quantity and quality of the pollutants. These should be given particular consideration in the case of stationary pollution sources and where there is a greater feasibility of monitoring or controlling the results of self-monitoring.

User charges are payments for using natural resources, like water. The pollution element thus is not so closely linked as in the case of effluent emission charges, but rather more reflects the scarcity of the resources. User charges also have a clear revenue-raising purpose. They have been defined as payments for the costs of collective or public treatment of effluent.

Product charges are levied on products that are harmful to the environment when used in production processes, consumed or disposed. While effluent or emission charges are closely connected with stationary sources, product charges on the other hand try to cover those cases where the use or consumption is not limited to a particular area or number of users.

Administrative charges are mostly fees paid for administrative procedures and services – that is, for registration or disclosure of information. According to recent developments in the area of access to information, requestors representing the public interest pay only the reasonable costs, while requests related to business activities pay charges or a kind of price.

Tax differentiation may lead to more favourable costs for, and prices of, environmentally-friendly products and vice-versa.

Customs duties as a special taxation means may influence the transboundary movement of environmentally-friendly or, conversely, environmentally-devastating technologies. Their influence on prices may be the same as that of tax differentiation.

b) Subsidies

Subsidies are usually financial support given by the state, mostly based on the existing special environmental budgets or funds to help the polluter defray the cost of compliance.

Grants are the non-repayable forms of state financial assistance, given under certain circumstances to support environmentally important investments or supplies in cases either where the environmental interest is greater than usual or where the recipient has limited financial resources to repay the subsidy.

Soft loans are offered by the state as funds to subsidize similar investments in environmental protection as above. The major characteristic of these loans is that the interest rates are set below the market rate.

Financial guarantees are a less direct form of providing financial assistance. With guarantees the state does not really provide material assistance but assists in obtaining bank loans.

A less direct form of subsidy is *tax allowances* which allow, for instance, accelerated depreciation for environmental protection investment thereby reducing the tax debt of the relevant actor.

From the point of view of state budget, charges are preferable , as they add to the state revenues, while subsidies lead to less state revenue or increased state expenditure. Subsidies can also be considered as a more specific market intervention by the state, as they can be geared to specific singular projects.

c)   Pricing

Price systems and the pricing of certain natural resources or services should also be mentioned as forms of market influence. Although, in a market economy, prices are formulated by the market rather than artificially set by the state, there are some cases where the state formulates the limits and controls the level of prices. Limits may mean upper limits or framework prices, while price control has a more market-friendly character. Pricing is more relevant with respect to state-owned enterprises.

A pricing system also has a special importance in that it gives rise to the possibility of marketing pollution rights. The use of a pricing system to value the environmental cost of pollution units forms the basis of this system. These prices should not be determined by the market, but must derive from a state pricing system.

d)   Enforcement incentives

To complete the picture, enforcement incentives should be mentioned and, within this, the primary role of non-compliance fees or fines and performance bonds. These instruments can be considered to be legal measures rather than economic tools, but nonetheless they influence polluter behaviour in much the same way as charges. For example, administrative sanctions, the most frequently used measure being the environmental protection fine, are generally based on a given acceptable limit for pollution or the breach of direct obligations. Although the main reason for using financial sanctions is to provide for liability with respect to an unlawful activity, sanctions may also serve as a source of income. If there are no other consequences with respect to the infringement of particular requirements than a fine or levy, then the government interests stated to be secondary are in fact the most important. The income derived from these sanctions is either placed in special funds, or alternatively perhaps in the same fund as income from the fees. The fine may be considered to be a measure to protect the general interests of the environment. If a polluter pays a fine, he still may be required to pay compensation for damages or may be subject to criminal penalties and so on.

Fines share some common elements: they are always imposed on the polluter by the authorities responsible for environmental protection; they represent a kind of strict liability, requiring no fault or negligence; they are is always based upon a measurable quantity – either a standard or quantity of polluting materials or the size of the affected land or nature conservation area; they can be individualized by using different modifying factors according to the circumstances of harm or pollution; in most cases they are progressive if the same activity is repeated; and funds deriving from fines are accumulated in an environmental protection fund.

If the fine is to be considered a real sanction two major steps must be taken: it should represent a large sum of money and be adjusted for inflation, and the standards, the breach of which gives rise to liability for a fine should be raised every second or third year.

Performance bonds are mainly payments to an escrow account set in the polluter's budget, where the bonds are set aside for use in improving environmental quality, but the concept of performance bonds also includes those payments to authorities guaranteeing and in expectation of compliance with regulations.

e) Use of state property and services

A special, less incentive-like but ultimately market-oriented way of influencing environmental interests is to use state property and state services. This can be distinguished from the administrative charge, as the use of property and services involves the sale of parts of the state's output. Thus there is a difference between charging fees for access to information for different purposes and charging fees for use of the state institutions' data banks. The first covers public interest information; the latter is more related to a private interest. Charges for the use of public land is an even more clear example of this option.

f)   Deposit-refund systems

A given product appears on the market with a deposit which is refunded on return of the product by the buyer or a collector. The deposit is paid on potentially harmful polluting products. When pollution is avoided by returning the products or waste relating to that product, a refund follows. This particular instrument has typically been adopted with respect to beverage containers because of the relative frequency of use of such containers.

Nowadays the use of deposit-refund systems may be desirable as part of the integrated life cycle management of certain products to ensure efficiency of resource input. The system should be considered in respect of products or substances which can be re-used, recycled or if it is advisable for the product to be returned for destruction.

g)   Market creation

Market creation is probably the biggest change in the system of market instruments. It consists in offering polluters tradeable permits which allow them to trade permitted emission rights with other companies. These are environmental quotas, allowances or ceilings on pollution levels that, once initially allocated by the appropriate authority, can be traded according to a set of prescribed rules. Their primary advantage is that they can reduce the costs of securing compliance and guarantee that pollution avoidance is carried out at the least cost (because those who can avoid pollution at low cost will refrain from purchasing a tradeable permit). However, the system always requires an underlying set of basic positive legal conditions.

Two basic types of marketable rights have been suggested by the contemporary literature, and these have been, to some extent, already put into practice. The first is the 'bubble'. This means that, in a given geographic area, a maximum pollution limit is fixed. Whenever a firm plans to enter into, or expand, a polluting activity which exceeds the limits it must buy a permit from another firm which may not need its pollution option because it can abate pollution at lower cost than the price the first firm is willing to pay. The second type is production quotas, where levels of production of a certain product are assigned. Production quotas have been used for sulphur dioxide and chlorofluorocarbons on an international scale.

These marketable rights also need a sophisticated enforcement system which is capable of efficiently monitoring the routes of pollution bargaining. Without such a system the use of uncontrolled market forces can easily lead to general confusion.

h)   Offset approach

The offset approach resembles market creation but differs in that the agreement stays within the same facility or plant. With this approach the facility may propose various approaches to meet the environmental objective and may then be allowed to emit more of one pollutant substance, trading this for a lower emission of another. This approach must condition the balancing of different pollution options in order to ensure that some pollution units can be compensated by others being avoided. This is a difficult approach as not only the given polluter but also the general environmental quality of the given region should be taken into consideration.

i)   Compulsory insurance

The economic efficiency of the polluting firm may be influenced by requiring compulsory liability insurance or, as a possible variation, by requiring the creation of pools or mutual funds: both requirements in order to provide guarantees in respect of possible liability. This kind of requirement should not be unlimited, but restricted to certain specified activities.

3   Schemes managed by national and international financing institutions

When discussing market instruments and the effect of different financial incentives on the market, we should not forget the role of national or international financing institutions. These institutions can easily influence the efficiency of environmental protection decisions of businesses or the market through some of the techniques already mentioned as instruments managed by the state. Lending operations, guarantee policies and interest policies all have a great impact on the freedom of choice of market players.

The World Bank and the European Bank for Reconstruction and Development (EBRD), for example, have both developed strategies for their role in environmental protection. The EBRD even states in its foundation agreement that the bank should 'promote in the full range of its activities environmentally sound and sustainable development'.

Both national and international financial institutions may use the following methods:

- developing specific lending policies to private ventures;
- investing directly, taking an equity share;
- using their discretion to give or refuse financial guarantees; and

- providing technical advice and training – especially in the case of the international financing institutions.

A new concept in the field of financial institutions is the 'debt for environment swap' pursued by lender states with debtor states. This incentive stands somewhere in between real state budgetary considerations and the policies of international financing institutions. States which lend money to other states are similar to other lending organizations – they ask for interest and wish to influence the behaviour of debtor countries.

There is a good example of such a new and international market incentive which was introduced for Poland in 1992. At the time Poland could achieve a 50 per cent reduction of its foreign debt, but the lending countries of the Paris Club also agreed that an additional 10 per cent of the debts could be swapped in a series of bilateral agreements between Poland and the creditor countries if the money was used for investments in environmental improvements.

III   THE SOURCE OF GOVERNMENT MEANS FOR ENVIRON-MENTAL PROTECTION

Both direct involvement of the state and regulatory involvement in environmental protection require considerable financial resources. Direct involvement means that the government must finance its own projects, which involves more than merely the running costs of public administration. Regulatory involvement will have stronger support if some regulatory objectives are also supported by financial means – for example, through funding or credits and the like.

Therefore a vital question relates to the source of government funding for environmental protection. State revenue can be collected as a single sum and allocated according to different requirements of state expenditure. Occasionally revenue is collected and especially earmarked to satisfy environmental interests. The principle sources of revenue for the environment can be listed as follows:

- the state budget and the division of tax income;
- different charges for the use of environmental resources;
- financial sanctions for activities which infringe environmental requirements;
- loans and credits;
- voluntary donations.

The state budget is the simplest source of government resources, where income is not altered particularly for environmental reasons. When the government has no special interest in environmental protection it only separates part of the budget necessary for the running of the environmental administration and those other projects connected with the management of state property. The structure of the budget does not necessarily give a sufficient guarantee only to use certain financial resources always for environmental reasons.

Special charges for the use of different environmental resources have been described above. They serve two functions: they act as economic incentives and at the same time provide a financial basis for further environmental programmes.

The revenues collected from sanctions are different from charges as they also amount to a negative classification of a particular activity which infringes basic environmental requirements,

Loans and credits are given to the government, mostly by international banks, foreign governments and other funds, to fulfil environmental obligations and must always be accounted for through subsequent government actions. These loans and credits can be managed separately or can be added to special funds.

Voluntary donations are not given directly to the government but may be given to funds run by governments. These days the likelihood of such donations is very small.

The next question concerning the government resources is how to use these resources: in particular, what are the conditions of their use and to what extent must these be connected to specific environmental objectives? The second question also determines whether it is possible to use the money designated to environmental assignments for other purposes, and under what circumstances. From this perspective, regulation of these resources is of primary importance. Regulation may limit or guide the government's ability to reallocate or redistribute funds. The environmental part of the state budget is the most vulnerable in this respect as it is the element most likely to be used for other purposes.

Special environmental funds designated for specific purposes, projects or media or one comprehensive fund – methods may differ – are more visible, and regulations governing these funds usually make it impossible to use their resources for reasons other than environmental protection. How these funds are classified (whether as separate specific funds or one large central fund) is partly determined by the division of environmental protection jurisdiction among the different administrative organs. One determining factor in this can be the method of control over the utilization of funds where public participation may have a decisive role. The greater the publicity given to the reports on utilization of the funds, the less chance the government has to misuse them.

IV   MARKET INSTRUMENTS AND THEIR RELATIONSHIP WITH TRADITIONAL METHODS

A most exciting problem for the present and future development of environmental protection, and particularly environmental law, is not only to find the proper place of market incentives, but also the proper relationship between market instruments, traditional command and control techniques and self-regulatory devices.[4] All three of them should be combined, not only because they can hardly be neatly distinguished from each other, but mainly because they can have synergetic effects.

If we carefully analyse market forces, it becomes apparent that, in a great number of cases, legal regulation plays the greatest influence on market behaviour. Legislation governing the company type and main structure, regulations concerning consumer protection, the limits of dumping or monopolies, labour regulations and, last but not least, existing environmental regulation are all manifest in the market. No market economy can live without regulation: an absolutely free market does not exist. The regulatory element is even greater in the field of environmental protection than in other regulatory areas. The reason for this lies principally in the special importance of environmental protection and the need for effective and unquestionable protection. This protection is the primary responsibility of the state.

First of all the environmental quality objectives are exclusively regulated by the state. The setting of these objectives requires a careful analysis of different effects and components – among others not only environmental but also social and economic factors. To this it must be added that, increasingly, environmental objectives are at least influenced, if not settled, by the international community (consider the examples of ozone depleting substances, climate policy requirements and so on). Under a traditional direct regulatory scheme, emission standards must be developed in order to clarify the role of each of the polluters in implementing quality objectives. But, this part of standardization might also be provided by the market. A good example of this is the marketing of pollution rights. It should not be forgotten that, even in this case, basic pollution rights, and consequently emission standards, must be set down in a state regulation and market regulation that can be introduced only after the state allocates initial quotas.

Another aspect of the same problem is the need for permitting, licensing and, associated with this, environmental impact assessment. Market forces fail to incorporate the concept of prevention insofar as applies to operations in the process of planning, since they are introduced into the environment protection system only late in the day. Market intervention is even less capable of handling the precautionary principle, where there is even less certainty than in the case of prevention. Permission and its accompanying mechanisms may also include public participa-

---

[4]   See, on these, chapter 15 by E. Rehbinder in this volume.

tion as both a procedural and substantive element. Consumer influence is not sufficient to replace public participation.

In both cases the relative inability of the market to set long-term objectives with respect to environmental media which are not fully incorporated in the market system is clear. The lack of a traditional property and pricing system in connection with environmental media is the main handicap here.

From an alternative viewpoint, state regulation and environmental management are not capable of determining the technology which will serve environmental goals most effectively. The vague term of 'best available technology' (BAT) is a good example of this. While the state must determine the quality objective, the market may be the proper forum for selecting the most appropriate technology which achieves the required standard in the least costly way. State regulation cannot decide the appropriateness of particular technologies in a market situation.

Environmental charges or fees may help by bringing environmental values closer to those of marketable goods. The difficulty, however, is that environmental values have no clear proprietary consequences and so their market price is an artificial consequence of setting up a charge system.

The use of market forces is almost impossible in the sphere of such environmental 'goods' as aesthetic values, as these cannot really be charged nor can they form a part of the market economy. Protected species will not be utilized in production chains in the same way as water is used nor are they polluted as constantly as clean air. This aspect of environmental protection – nature conservation requirements – cannot be marketed or sold. The only method available to is to protect these species and their habitat directly.

One underlying condition for developing market incentives is the need for democratization of traditional regulatory schemes. In the process of democratization as well as in the process of developing market instruments strong consideration is given to the active and passive forms of providing environmental information. Public control or in a broader context – again – public participation is strictly connected with the new struggle for using market forces. Information rights and participation rights could never be implemented without legal regulations that serve here as a means of guarantee.

The arguments for and against market mechanisms could be listed over several pages, but the above examples probably suffice to demonstrate that the use of market incentives depends upon an existing regulatory and enforcement system, and, more probably, on an existing market. If most of the market instruments described above are examined it should be clear that the market-based approach is itself a legislative and administrative management product.

Thus, traditional or regulatory devices and market forces or financial incentives should complement each other. This kind of structure has a number of advantages for the protection of the environment. Actual experience in using market devices also proves that there are some imperfections in these instruments which will prevent them from replacing command and control mechanisms in the long run. Some of these present failures are listed below.

- The market itself has some glaring imperfections. One example of this can be found in the different management systems for existing state property and private businesses. An other example is the market's failure to solve social problems.
- Market instruments need certainty in measurement and values. Environmental charges and prices for the sale of pollution rights are calculated by the state. The market cannot handle the measurement of environmental values and their relationship to quality objectives, and requires state intervention in this respect.
- There are problems of political acceptability. Given the present delicate environmental situation it is difficult to get society to accept the concept of pollution 'rights', and it is just as difficult to make the market accept artificial values put on public goods.
- The underlying legal regulations are not always complete.
- Internal market regulations are far from satisfactory.

Market instruments therefore need introduction by state regulation and also require the assistance of state enforcement. Summarizing what has been stated previously, the state should

- set the environmental quality objectives;
- arrange the first distribution of prices and tasks, based upon the quality objectives;
- regulate the framework of both market instruments and their relationship to other existing devices;
- serve as a source of public information;
- monitor the environmental conditions and also control the fair use of market instruments;
- influence the market through its own resources;
- punish derogation from environmental standards.

It may be useful to consider the following criteria when choosing these instruments:

- effectiveness from the environmental point of view;
- availability of some experience in practice (deposit-refund systems or charges, for example);
- economical efficiency of market instruments;

- the provision, by market forces, of a proper basis for the allocation of environmental resources;
- avoidance of differentiation between market participants;
- suitability;
- cost-effectiveness;
- the consent of those involved.

Finally, reference must be made to the specific situation of the Eastern and Central European region. According to Frances Cairncross, the environmental editor of the *Economist*:

> Any sets of standards will only be as good as its enforcement. Use of the market, through taxes, charges, or tradable permits, will work only if the market works. Eastern European countries, the dirtiest in Europe, have elaborate arrangements for regulating and penalizing polluters; yet the fines are uncollected.... It makes no sense to fine a firm when it cannot buy good anti-pollution equipment because its importation is restricted. Nor does it make much sense to charge an enterprise for pollution when it is a monopoly and can simply pass on the entire increase in costs to its customers. Countries with highly controlled markets will find it harder to use market-based incentive to tackle pollution. In general, regulations and economic instruments are likely to be employed together, on reinforcing the other. This approach will be most justifiable where market functions worst.[5]

---

[5] Frances Cairncross, *Costing the Earth*, Harvard Business School Press, 1992, p. 109.

14 Environmental Liability

Malcolm Grant

Table of Contents

I INTRODUCTION

Over the past five years there has been an upsurge of interest in systems of environmental liability throughout Europe. The principal reasons for this are that conventional regulatory systems for forestalling environmental harm are perceived to be inadequate for the task as are conventional liability systems designed to ensure restoration once environmental harm has occurred. Europeans have also been uncomfortably aware of the US experience under the Federal Superfund programme, which has stretched concepts of civil liability well beyond those conventionally understood in Europe by imposing a system of liability which is not only 'no-fault' and retrospective in effect, but which also holds defendants liable not only for their own acts but also for those of all other defendants.

What are the weaknesses of conventional regulatory systems? Their common form is that of 'command and control'. A simple example is a law which prohibits the discharge into water of specified substances except in accordance with a permit which will prescribe such conditions as the maximum quantity, concentration and temperature of discharge. This model works best with discharge at source, but is less effective in dealing with diffuse discharges because its enforcement depends upon proper monitoring. Hence, effective regulation demands a multiplicity of approaches to controls over products, substances, processes, wastes and the containment of hazards. Environmental legislation tends therefore to be highly technical in content yet not necessarily comprehensive in extent.

Command and control can nonetheless achieve a great deal if it is actually observed in practice, and it is by far the most common method of environmental protection. It has great potential for clarity, certainty and equity; and its value as a principal tool is in no way undermined by the current interest in the use of supplementary economic instruments. Yet, in itself it is imperfect. There is often little enthusiasm to enforce environmental regulations, enforcement being a problem not only at national level but also between nation states. The poor record of effective transposition of EU Directives has now become a major scandal and, although there have been some significant improvements in the quality of national legislation over the past ten years, there is still remarkably little harmonization between states. The Commission's enforcement machinery has proven hopelessly inadequate and too open to political interference. Member States have regularly agreed solemnly to adopt environmental measures, with no apparent intention of putting them into effect. At national levels, enforcement agencies are often underfunded and tend to be 'captured' by the industries that they are regulating.

One way, therefore, of making more effective use of command and control methods is to break governments' monopoly of enforcement power, and to encourage citizen groups and individuals to play a greater part. Hence the greater attention paid by the EU in recent years to so-called 'soft laws' in the environmental context, including public rights of access to environmental information, eco-audit and now, civil liability. An enhanced civil liability system can empower public interest groups and individuals with rights to commence proceedings, where governments are unable, or have failed, to act. Its purpose is not to tighten up on enforcement of command and control, but to reshape traditional legal instruments such as injunctions and other judicial orders to prevent environmental damage from occurring, and to secure the restoration of the environment when damage has occurred.

But to meet these objectives, the system needs to be enhanced. One of the most significant drawbacks of conventional systems is that they provide no protection for the unowned environment. Legal systems generally have rules which allow individuals to seek protection from a court against the possibility of harm being caused to them or to their property, and which allow an injured plaintiff to recover damages from the defendant who causes such damage. But such a system confers protection on environmental goods only to the extent that they are in private ownership; thus the extent to which they protect the broader environment may depend upon how widely property rights are defined in any given jurisdiction. For example, in the UK, river fishermen (anglers) may acquire a property right to fish; and where they have such a fishing right, they have similar rights to those of owners of land adjoining the river and are entitled to sue in respect of any river pollution which harms that right.[1] That is not to say that private property in such cases necessarily serves the public interest. An owner's interests may be bought out by the polluter; or the injured party's loss may be purely economic, capable of being remedied without the environment being cleaned up.[2]

However, where there is no private ownership, the environment is a free good: no individual has the capacity to commence proceedings against another individual who exploits it or damages it. States generally find a way through this dilemma by creating special rights of action by the state – in some cases under a constitutional theory that deems all such environmental goods, including groundwater and lakes, to be in the ownership of the state itself. This may allow them to recover clean-up costs and other restoration expenses. But a state monopoly on such civil proceedings is potentially subject to the same problems as enforcement under command and control systems, not least in cases where the state itself is a major polluter.

There are other special problems that arise in applying established principles of civil liability to the special case of environmental damage. Take, for example, the problems of long-term impairment of the environment through the gradual discharge of contaminants that lead eventually to pollution. The pollution of groundwater as a result of badly managed landfill sites, or leaking underground storage tanks, is a familiar example. Civil liability systems are used to responding to instances of accidental damage, but perform less well in investigating the causes of damage that may have taken 20 or more years to occur, where rules of limitation may inhibit the commencement of proceedings, where industrial practices and scientific knowledge may have changed significantly since the time the steps were first taken that gave rise to the damage, and where contemporary knowledge of the facts is limited because the parties who were originally responsible no longer have any link with the land. Time lapse also affects questions of proof, increasing the burden upon a plaintiff to prove that it was this defendant who caused the damage complained of (causation), and also, under a fault-based system, that he was at fault by the standards of the era in which he was acting. Conventional causation

---

1   The leading British case on this point is *Pride of Derby and Derbyshire Angling Association* v *British Celanese* [1953] Ch 149.
2   See, for example, *Cambridge Water Co Ltd* v *Eastern Counties Leather plc* [1994] 1 All ER 53, where the plaintiffs claimed that groundwater used by them for supplies of drinking water to the public had been contaminated by the defendants. Their claim was not, however, for the costs of cleaning up the supply, but for shifting of their abstraction facility to a new location where the contamination had not reached.

and liability rules are also notably difficult to apply where the cause of the damage is the conduct of many actors contributing over time (such as domestic consumers of coal, or diesel vehicles discharging particulates); and where the damage comes about as a result of a 'cocktail' effect of a chemical combination of substances, each discharged separately and each perhaps harmless in itself.

Of course, an enhanced liability system is not a universal panacea for improvement in environmental standards. Indeed, by focusing on repair and restoration, rather than prevention, there is a risk that civil liability concentrates on the wrong thing, by being *ex post* in effect and hence focusing on remedying damage rather than preventing it. However, the risk of *ex post* liability will clearly have an *ex ante* effect on decisions taken by firms in relation to levels of precaution against causing environmental damage.[3] The greatest risk in relying too heavily upon an enhanced civil liability system is that, in practice, its strength is wholly dependent upon the defendant's solvency, and it thus requires underwriting of the risk through insurance or other form of collective risk management. Moreover, there is the risk that liability can in practice be avoided by clever corporate or property transactions which insulate the true defendant from primary liability.

II THE EUROPEAN COMMISSION'S GREEN PAPER

A clear commitment to establishing a new environmental liability system was included in the fifth environmental action programme, *Towards Sustainability*,[4] which undertakes that

> ... an integrated Community approach to environmental liability will be established. ... Liability will be an essential tool of last resort to punish despoilation of the environment. In addition – and in line with the objective of prevention at source – it will provide a very clear economic incentive for management and control of risk of pollution and waste.[5]

Moreover, Member States have separately committed themselves[6] to the implementation of the Rio Declaration, Principle 13 of which requires states to develop domestic law on liability for environmental damage.

---

3 Although it cannot, *ex hypothesi*, have that effect in relation to damage that has already been done, and a retrospective system therefore requires special justification, to which we shall return.

4 *A European Community Programme of Policy and Action in Relation to the Environment and Sustainable Development*, COM(92) 23 final, Vol II, p.68.

5 Note also the request of the Joint Transport and Environment Council of 25 January 1993 for an 'examination of the feasibility of developing a system of penalties and civil liability for pollution of the environment', noted in the Green Paper at para. 1.0.

6 Lisbon Environmental Council, February 1993.

However, the Commission has experienced great difficulty in carrying forward its programme. The first significant step was the publication in 1993 of the *Green Paper on Remedying Environmental Damage*,[7] but this was more a consultative than a decision-making paper. It rehearsed the problems without suggesting how they might be resolved.

There appears to be broad agreement as to the competence of the EU to enact legislation relating to civil liability for environmental damage,[8] and the Commission is clearly correct in identifying a wide variation, in both substantive content and procedure, between the existing liability systems in force in Member States. An illustrative list is given in the Green Paper at Annex I. Notable examples of recent trends in national legislation include the German liability law of 1990, with its special provisions for proof of causality; and the Netherlands law with its broad rights to commence proceedings.

However, substituting a uniform European system for the existing national variety means that decisions have to be reached on the following main components:

1   the definition of environmental damage;
2   the setting of the liability threshold;
3   proof of causation;
4   retrospectivity;
5   who may sue?;
6   who may be sued?;
7   what remedies should be available, and
8   how can liability be underwritten?

We shall now examine each issue in turn.

III   THE MAIN COMPONENTS OF A UNIFORM LIABILITY SYSTEM

1   The definition of environmental damage

Any extension of liability to the unowned environment requires a definition of what 'damage' would render a defendant liable. This concept is difficult enough in a conventional liability context, especially in relation to 'environmental' damage to personal health, upon which the epidemiological evidence of heightened risk

---

7   7099/93; COM(93)47 final; Communication from the Commission to the Council and European Parliament and the Economic and Social Committee, *Green Paper on Remedying Environmental Damage*.
8   For a detailed analysis of the legislative alternatives, see G Betlem, Environmental Liability, in *Towards a European Civil Code*, Dirdrecht: Martinus Nijhoff, 1994.

may be insufficiently convincing to satisfy a court that damage has occurred. It is usually more straightforward in relation to property damage, because there is a market against which the plaintiff's loss can be measured: the property is damaged if its market value is diminished, and that decrease is the measure of the damage.

But with damage to the unowned environment, no individual plaintiff's interests have been injured. Many states already enable a state agency to take preventive measures to forestall environmental damage, and to restore the environment where damage has occurred, and to recover the costs from those responsible. In this case, the test of whether or not damage has occurred, or was threatened, rests with the agency, and the court may be restricted simply to reviewing whether the sum the agency seeks to recover from the defendant is reasonable.[9] Many still see this type of arrangement as providing the most efficient use of resources, because it allows a balance to be drawn between the extent of the damage and the cost of its repair. But, against this, is its susceptibility to political interference and inefficiency.

But if the state's enforcement monopoly is lifted, then the question falls to be determined directly by a court. A court must therefore have some criterion or test to guide it, and there is an initial choice between attempting to provide specific objective thresholds for uniform application throughout the EU, or providing a more general test, like that of 'significant damage', and allowing the courts to develop specific principles on a case-by-case basis. There are obvious weaknesses with both approaches. Pure environmental damage is incapable of precise definition in the abstract, and even in the specific context of its function within an environmental liability system it begs a number of questions. It does not equate simply, for example, with notions such as contamination or pollution, which may be shortlived phenomena from which the affected environment will quickly recover. The notions of 'damage' and 'repair' imply something that is longer-lasting, requiring positive steps to be taken to restore things so far as possible to their former state. Damage may arise in a particularly sensitive environment as a result of a spillage which in another environment would not have caused damage at all. As the *Braer* disaster demonstrated, the capacity of the local environment to dilute and disperse pollution may be highly dependent upon prevailing local climatic conditions following the incident.[10] None of these complex variables, nor their interaction, is likely to be fully captured by a set of *a priori* definitions. Yet, on the other hand, simply to leave the issue open to case-by-case interpretation would be to undermine, rather than promote, the harmonization objective of the legislation.

Fundamental to this debate, though implicit rather than explicit, is the relationship between damage and clean-up costs. In two major international conventions,

---

9 See, for example, the UK's Water Resources Act 1991, s.161 (recovery by the National Rivers Authority of clean-up costs incurred by them, from any person causing or knowingly permitting polluting matter to enter controlled waters).

10 See further *The Environmental Impact of the Wreck of the Braer*, Scottish Office, 1994.

environmental damage is defined primarily as an economic concept including (1) damage caused to man; and (2) the cost of 'reasonable' measures taken to repair environmental damage. Under both the 1992 Protocol to the International Convention on Civil Liability for Oil Pollution Damage[11] and the Council of Europe Convention[12] (the Lugano Convention), the court is left not only to determine whether there has been some 'impairment of the environment' (which in the case of the Lugano Convention is further qualified by an exemption for liability in respect of damage 'caused by pollution at tolerable levels under local relevant circumstances'[13]) but also with determining the economic balance denoted by the test of reasonableness: whether, for example, the plaintiff will be, or was, justified in spending a relatively large sum in rectifying comparatively minor environmental impairment.

2   The setting of the liability threshold

The appropriate threshold of conduct for the imposition of liability lies at the heart of the Commission's Green Paper. The primary issue is whether liability should depend upon proof that the defendant was at fault (such as negligence in handling substances known to be likely to cause environmental damage), or should be strict (in other words, that it should follow automatically from proof that the defendants' acts or omissions caused the environmental damage complained of). There are strong arguments for heightening the tests in environmental cases, certainly those

---

11 The International Convention on Civil Liability for Oil Pollution Damage, as amended by the 1992 Protocol (Cm 2657), Art 2, defines 'environmental damage' as extending to 'loss or damage caused outside the ship by contamination resulting from the escape or discharge of oil wherever such escape or discharge may occur, provided that compensation for impairment of the environment other than loss of profit from such impairment shall be limited to costs of reasonable measures of reinstatement actually undertaken or to be undertaken'.

12 Convention on Civil Liability for Damage Resulting from Activities Dangerous to the Environment (Lugano, 21 June 1993), which defines 'damage' as meaning: (a) loss of life or personal injury; (b) loss of or damage to property other than to the installation itself or property held under the control of the operator, at the site of the dangerous activity; (c) loss of or damage by impairment of the environment in so far as this is not considered to be damage within the meaning of subparagraphs a or b above provided that compensation for impairment of the environment, other than for loss of profit from such impairment, shall be limited to the costs of measures of reinstatement actually undertaken or to be undertaken, to the extent that the loss or damage referred to in subparagraphs a to c of this paragraph arises out of or results from the hazardous properties of the dangerous substances, genetically modified organisms or micro-organisms or arises or results from waste.

13 Lugano Convention, Art. 8d.

where firms choose to employ hazardous substances or processes in their operations. Strict liability is gradually becoming the standard in national environmental legislation, and it has prevailed at international level for many years in relation to radioactive substances. But these arguments need to be strong enough to overcome a natural reluctance to hold defendants liable where the cause of the environmental damage was not their fault. It is often the case that only the defendant has the information upon which an adequate assessment of culpability can be made, and therefore national environmental liability systems have, in practice, tended to impose notionally strict liability, but then to establish defences which, if a defendant can satisfy the burden of proof, will allow him to avoid liability.[14] It is rare in practice for liability to be truly strict.

The common defences can be classified into four main groups:

a)   force majeure;
b)   'state of the art' and development risks;
c)   regulatory compliance;
d)   third-party intervention.

a)   Force majeure

This defence is generally poorly defined, and it is important to ensure that it is confined to acts that were unforeseeable and irresistible.[15]

b)   'State of the art' and development risk

A 'state of the art' defence was included in the EU's product liability Directive.[16] It allows a defendant to show that the state of scientific and technical knowledge at the time of the product's supply was not such that a producer might be expected to discover the defect complained of. It is not obvious that such a defence should apply to environmental liability, particularly where the defendant has control of an inherently hazardous product or process. It runs close to converting strict liability into a fault-based system under another name. Moreover there is a danger of pro-

---

14   A parallel approach is that of the English common law, exemplified by the *Cambridge Water Company* case, where the defendants would have been held strictly liable for the escape of chemicals from their land, even though they had exercised all due care to prevent it from occurring, if they could reasonably have foreseen that the seepage of the chemicals could have caused the environmental damage complained of.

15   See, for example, the exemption under the Lugano Convention, Art. 8 for damage which the defendant proves 'was caused by an act of war, hostilities, civil war, insurrection or a natural phenomenon of an exceptional, inevitable and irresistible character'.

16   85/374/EEC.

viding industry with a disincentive to study the effect of its products, for fear of liability arising from the time that some risk of environmental liability became identified.

c)   Regulatory compliance

One common defence is to allow the defendant to show that he did nothing that was not in accord with the operating permits granted to him by the state. The arguments for allowing this defence were well summarized in the Green Paper:

> ... if the operator has fully disclosed all relevant data for evaluation by the permitting authority and complies with the standards set in the permit, there may be reasons for holding the public authority – and ultimately the taxpayer – responsible for ensuing damage. It would provide the operator with an incentive for full disclosure and compliance with the permit, so as to avoid liability. It would provide the Government authority with an incentive to make responsible decisions, including setting precise and clear restrictions in permits.[17]

However, all this assumes a rather more perfect system of command and control than commonly exists: there are areas of environmental protection where regulation is poor or even non-existent, and even in well regulated areas permits are often not fully comprehensive in their prohibitions. To allow a defence of regulatory compliance in such circumstances would be to grant immunity by default. In the longer term, it might simply induce regulators to reduce emission limits to unnecessarily low, and economically inefficient, levels in order to avoid future liability themselves.

d)   Third-party intervention

In theory, it is right that a firm should not be held liable for acts committed entirely by another person. But, in practice, responsibility is often obscure. For example, firms should take adequate precaution to prevent third parties from tampering with their plant. French courts have taken a very narrow approach to this defence, and restricted it to damage caused 'solely' by the acts of a third party, which makes it practically impossible to prove. A more flexible approach would be to allow apportionment of liability, but under either model it should not be possible for an operator to escape liability unless he has taken all possible precautions to prevent third party interference.

---

17   Para. 2.1.5(ii).

3   Proof of causation

Another issue to be reviewed is that of causation. It arises separately from the strictness of the liability imposed. Whether a defendant has acted negligently or not, it must still be proven that his acts or defaults actually caused the damage complained of. Here there is often a heavy burden. The defendant often has exclusive knowledge of what actually occurred on the site, including the vital links in the chain of causation. There is therefore the question of whether the causation rules should be amended so as to reverse this burden of proof, once the plaintiff has crossed at least an initial threshold.

In some contexts, use has been made of so-called irrebuttable presumptions, such as the Japanese law on damage to health from environmental accidents; and the French law on nuclear installations, under which the government is empowered to establish a list of illnesses deemed to be caused by the incident. It has not yet been used in practice. These measures are simply too strong for anything but exceptional cases. Greater flexibility, however, is given by the use of rebuttable presumptions: these allow the burden of proof to be reversed once the plaintiff passes an initial threshold, such as the proximity to an installation deemed to have a propensity to cause damage of the sort alleged. The German Environmental Liability Law provides an example.[18] It shifts the burden of proof by raising special liability presumptions in relation to processes assumed to have the propensity to cause particular types of damage. This model has yet to be tested, and there is a risk that such a mechanical plant-related approach will give rise to technical litigation that narrows the ability of the court to apply a broader view.

One approach which leans in the same direction is to indicate to the court that it is dealing with a situation where certainties are difficult to establish, and that it would therefore be appropriate to look for a lower standard of proof of environmental causality than in other civil suits. The EU's Draft Waste Directive[19] proposed such an approach and the Lugano Convention provides a similar model under which the court is required to 'take due account of the increased danger of causing such damage inherent in the dangerous activity'.[20]

---

18 The text of the law is accessible in English in G. Winter (ed.), *German Environmental Law. Basic Texts and Introduction*, Dordrecht: Martinus Nijhoff, 1994.

19 Civil liability for damage caused by waste (amended proposal 28 June 1991; OJ C192/6, 23 July 1991).

20 Ibid., Art. 10.

4 Retrospectivity

There is a widespread presumption in European states against retrospectivity in legislation. It is reflected in the Commission's earlier draft Directive on Civil Liability for Damage to the Environment Caused by Waste, which specifically excluded retrospective effect, as does the German Liability Law of 1990. The Danish Supreme Court has ruled that the legislature could not retrospectively introduce stricter forms of liability, and that the applicable standards had therefore to be those prevailing at the time the activities complained of were carried out; and the English House of Lords has declined to allow any doctrine of retrospective liability to develop in the common law.[21] Nonetheless, the US Superfund scheme has notoriously imposed liability which is not only retrospective but unlimited in point of time. The Commission's Green Paper prefers not to address the issue directly. Instead it points to technical defects with a retrospective system:

> ... civil liability may not, however, provide a way to recover the costs of restoring such damage. Sometimes the damage is from so far back in time that no liable party is identifiable. Sometimes the party can be identified but is not liable, because liability was not established when the damage occurred. Or the party may be identifiable, liable, but insolvent.[22]

There are serious problems both of practice and principle in introducing a crudely retrospective system. Certainly, historic pollution cannot simply be left wholly to a civil liability system because even a widely cast net of liability is unlikely to be able to raise all the funding necessary. Not surprisingly, insurance is not available for historic pollution: insurers will not provide cover in respect of damage that has already occurred, and although indemnity may still be available under the more general cover that was written in the 1960s and 1970s before environmental liabilities were understood (so-called 'insurance archaeology'), this is only on an extremely limited and largely fortuitous basis.

Moreover, a national clean-up programme needs to proceed on the basis of environmental priorities, rather than focus exclusively on sites where liability is clear and there are solvent defendants. If the right to sue were extended to third parties, then any attempt to make the most efficient use of available resources in terms of environmental priorities would be doomed. It must still be for the State to set priorities and standards and, where necessary, to intervene and actually carry out remedial works.

For historic pollution, therefore, the central question is that of raising funds in order to meet a state-directed clean-up programme. This implies establishing a

---

21 *Cambridge Water Co Ltd* v *Eastern Counties Leather plc* [1994] 1 All ER 53, at 77–78.
22 *Green Paper on Remedying Environmental Damage, op.cit.*

balanced system of private and public sector contribution. The case for the public sector bearing part of the cost is both practical (in the sense that private liability rules will not provide all of it) and justifiable as reflecting the economic benefit of past pollution that were distributed to society as a whole in the form of cheaper goods and lower taxes. It also reflects the broad spectrum of firms' blameworthiness in relation to historic pollution. If a firm could have foreseen that its activities would harm the environment, there is not necessarily any injustice in holding them liable today for remedying any damage actually caused, even if the range of liability is now widened to allow the recovery of costs for restoring the unowned environment. Indeed, several Member States already have legislation to that end.[23] There are difficulties in avoiding retrospectivity altogether, simply because of the time lag between the incident causing the damage and the discovery of the damage itself. Moreover, culpability may change over time, such as where the defendant has become aware of damage being caused by his past acts but has failed to take the necessary action to contain it.

In any event, policy for dealing with historic pollution of land needs special attention. Landowners have an economic stake in the clean-up – which suggests that at the very least they should not simply benefit from the expenditure of public money on their clean-up – but they may or may not be culpable in respect of the contamination themselves, and hence may or may not be required to meet clean-up costs. A viable approach to cleaning-up of land also needs to be designed in the context of other economic instruments, such as land use laws which could be deployed so as to focus redevelopment opportunities on the affected sites as a means of raising land values and making remedial works more economic. This would allow state aid to be applied selectively as a means of pump priming, with a view to enhancing demand for the site. State aid is also needed for 'orphan sites' where no private contribution will be forthcoming.

5   Who may sue?

An extension of the rights of citizens to commence proceedings for damage to the unowned environment is fundamental to any extension of liability rules. On this, the Commission's Green Paper comments:[24]

---

23 See, for example, in the UK, the Water Resources Act 1991, s.161, which allows the National Rivers Authority to recover clean-up costs from any person causing or allowing pollution to enter controlled waters; and the Environmental Protection Act 1990, s.61 (not yet in force) which will allow a waste regulation authority to undertake remedial action to prevent pollution from a closed landfill, and to recover the costs from the present owner of the land.

24 Para 2.1.9.

In a civil liability case, the right to sue is normally given only to the party with a legal interest in recovering compensation. Where damage occurs to property that is not owned, no injured party with the right to bring a legal action can be identified. With no legal or natural person to sue on behalf of the environment, the costs of restoring environmental damage cannot be recovered via civil liability. There exists several different approaches to the question of access to justice for environmental matters among the Member States.

However, there are serious policy difficulties in determining which remedies it is appropriate to allow individual citizens and interest groups to pursue. Environmental citizen suits have proved an important enforcement tool in the USA under such legislation as the Clean Air and Clean Water Acts, but this has been primarily in the context of supplementing regulation rather than civil liability. So too with judicial review, where there is a general trend towards more lenient rules of standing, which in itself helps to overcome some of the state's monopoly power over enforcement. The Lugano Convention would confer rights on environmental organizations to seek prohibition, prevention and restoration orders; and there has been a landmark decision of the Dutch Supreme Court[25] which held that environmental protection organizations were entitled to seek injunctions in tort relating to harmful effects on the interest they were promoting, without having to establish any additional interest over and above that of a member of the public.

Nevertheless, other European states are still some way short of this position. Many have extended rights of action for judicial review in order to enable citizens to challenge actions and omissions by regulators without having to show any special interest in the subject matter over and above that of the population at large.[26] Courts are able to recognize the particular position of well funded and specialized interest groups who have special expertise which will expedite proceedings and allow them to be conducted at a more focused way than they might be if they were brought by an individual plaintiff.

Attempts to extend rights further, however, have not surprisingly met with stiff resistance from industrial interests which fear that legal actions might be used to harass them or that they will lack the negotiating capacity which they might expect with a regulatory agency. In fact, much depends upon the nature of the action. The justification for a third-party action in tort can be found in a doctrine of public custodianship of the unowned environment. There are obvious cases where a voluntary group should be able to recover their reasonable costs following an envi-

---

25 *De Nieuwe Meer*, 27 June 1986; followed in the Kaunders case, Supreme Court, 18 December 1992.

26 A recent example is *R v Her Majesty's Inspectorate of Pollution and the Ministry of Agriculture, Fisheries and Food, ex parte Greenpeace Ltd* (Otton J., 29 September 1993).

ronmental incident, such as when they have instituted an immediate response for dealing with estuarine birdlife affected by a chemical or oil spill. There may, of course, be instances of competition between different interveners: between different voluntary groups, or with rescue efforts mounted by the polluters, by regulatory authorities or by individual landowners. Again, if voluntary groups were to be entitled to sue for injunctive orders, their intervention might well conflict with, or duplicate, action being taken by a regulatory body so that it may be necessary to require prior notice to be given to that body and to limit third-party action to cases where the regulatory body are unable, or unwilling, to use their own powers.

6   Who may be sued?

Much debate under this heading relates to the necessity of focusing liability. The person primarily liable under a civil liability system must be the person who had actual operational control of the facility or activity concerned at the time the damage was caused. This approach gives maximum recognition of the 'polluter pays' principle. However, responsibility may also rest with others who contributed to the acts which caused the environmental damage, or who had the power to prevent it. Hence it is necessary to examine how widely that group should be defined, and also the basis upon which liability should be apportioned between the liable parties. From a plaintiff's point of view, joint and several liability has the great advantage of allowing a recovery action to be focused on one or two key (and sufficiently solvent) players, rather than having to untangle a complex skein of responsibility. Joint and several liability exists already to some extent in most national legal systems, at least where the parties have acted together, or have each had the capacity to influence each other's conduct.

Moreover, in relation to the contamination of land, it is necessary to have regard to the position of the current owner of the site, who is the person with the greatest current capital interest in it, and the person who will benefit from any contribution to its clean-up. Once a system of liability becomes crystallized, it will be reflected in conveyancing techniques (such as requiring a careful environmental site audit prior to land acquisition) and in land prices, to reflect the risks assumed by the purchaser.

The position of lenders is of particular interest under all of these mechanisms. In order to protect its security, a lender may become involved in the management of the firm – for example by having a directorship or by insisting upon certain management practices. Where this gives the lender capacity to control the firm's operations, it also confers an inference of culpability if the firm then damages the environment. Or the lender may have only the conventional security of being able to force the sale of the land. In some jurisdictions, enforcement of the security involves the lender or his agent taking physical control of the land for the purposes of selling it. Hence there is a prospect of the lender being cast in the role of owner, even if only for a brief period. The critical importance of these relationships lies in the nature of the apportionment of liability. If each is responsible only to the extent that each can be shown to have contributed to the environmental damage, there may be little problem with lender liability. However, an alternative approach is to make each party jointly and severally liable with all other parties as this has been the case under the US Superfund legislation. This means that one party may be sued for the whole damage and is left to recover contributions from the other parties. Where that party is a lender – perhaps a large financial institution – it is convenient for the plaintiff to focus all action on that party in pursuit of so-called 'deep pocket' liability, even if the lender has had only a relatively brief period of control over the land.

Some arguments relating to joint and several liability were reviewed briefly in the Commission's Green Paper:

> Under joint and several liability, each party is liable for the entire amount, but may often proceed in turn to seek contribution from other liable parties. This can cause several problems, including congestion in the courts. Inequity results if the injured party sues the party with the most financial assets first, instead of the party who caused the most damage. This is known as the 'deep pocket' effect. Joint and several liability may also lead to 'forum shopping', if parties are from different countries and one country's laws are more favourable to the injured party.
>
> As liable parties sort out among themselves how the costs of compensation should be shared, litigation becomes complex. This can make civil liability a compensation mechanism with extremely high transaction costs. A way to alleviate such problems is to allocate responsibility in advance by designating the order in which potentially liable parties should be sued, or by the channelling of liability.[27]

There is a difficult balance to be struck here. Banks have no wish to be identified as an easy 'deep pocket' for environmental liability purposes nor to assume the role of environmental policemen. This raises the risk of their withdrawing from the financing of future high technology development. Indeed, there is some evi-

---

27 Para 2.1.4. See also the formula adopted by the Lugano Convention, which prescribes a system of joint and several liability only in relation to: (1) an incident consisting of a continuous occurrence; and (2) an incident consisting of a series of occurrences having the same origin; but in both cases an operator who can prove that the occurrence at the time when he was exercising control of the dangerous activity caused only a part of the damage is liable for that part only (Art. 6.2 and 6.3). Thus it is a joint and several system, but with a capacity for a defendant to restrict his exposure to that damage which he can prove was the result of his activities.

dence of this having occurred already in the current state of uncertainty about what a future European environmental liability system might contain. Unless it is coupled to an actual culpability test, the channelling liability along the lines suggested in the Green Paper would do nothing more than postpone 'deep pocket' liability to a position of residual rather than primary exposure, yet still rely upon 'deep pockets' for residual compensation. It would also encourage the use of corporate structures to minimize exposure to liability in an undesirable way, such as through the deployment of 'one-site' companies, which could probably only be effectively overcome by reaching right into the corporate web and extending personal liability to directors, managers, and associated companies and parent companies, independently from the direct liability on the responsible company itself.

There is also a risk that joint and several liability will punish the more efficient and more profitable companies (who tend to have higher environmental standards) by shifting to them liability for environmental damage caused by less efficient or law-abiding companies (the 'cowboys') who lack the financial capacity to meet their own liabilities.

7   What remedies should be available?

The nature of the suit to be brought is also important. A civil liability system implies the need for legal actions for:

1   the prevention of environmental damage;
2   the repair of environmental damage that has occurred;
3   the provision of other environmental goods in substitution for repair which cannot be carried out because the damage is irreversible.

Not all are appropriate to action by third parties, and the third item remains controversial. Without it, irremediable environmental damage (such as the extinction of a species, or the destruction of fauna) remains outside a liability system, and there is no incentive in civil liability terms (though the criminal law may provide an answer) for firms whose activities may cause such damage to internalize their external effects. There are, of course, complex valuation problems in assessing what measure of damages a firm should pay for environmental destruction over and above the costs of carrying out repairs, such as clean-up costs.

8   How can liability be underwritten?

Some form of underwriting of liabilities is essential if a civil liability system were to work in practice. The problems of extended time scales, and the risk of insolvency of polluting firms mean that there is a high risk that, at the time the damage comes to remedied, there will be nobody capable of meeting the liability. The two principal mechanisms currently under consideration are insurance and joint compensation funds.

Current uncertainties about liability render it difficult for insurers to assess risk accurately, and the European market for environmental insurance seems to be currently in a similar state to that for product liability some 30 years ago. As it becomes easier to quantify risk, so the range of insurance products available in the market is likely to grow. At present, and for the foreseeable future, only 'claims made' cover is likely to be available (although this raises the problem of determining when the relevant 'damage' occurred). Even once it becomes easier to evaluate risk with greater certainty, future cover is likely to be very limited, because insurers have been alarmed by the recent propensity of courts, particularly in the USA, to spell wide-ranging cover out of policies that had never been written with environmental liabilities in mind.

One way to ensure that potential liabilities are adequately underwritten, and that risk is spread widely across the industrial sector, would be to insist upon mandatory environmental insurance. However, this carries severe disadvantages. Insurers are either obliged to provide cover to all, with only limited selectivity as to risks, or they become surrogate regulators, refusing cover or raising premiums to those whose activities – in the eyes of the insurers, but not necessarily the state's regulators – carry high risks and who are thereby forced out of business. Under mandatory insurance the insurers assume responsibility for setting the standards, and operators who succeed in obtaining cover may in practice be relieved from responsibility for taking all necessary measures for preventing environmental damage.

An alternative to conventional insurance cover is the use of mutual funding within particular industrial sectors, and the Commission's Green Paper sets some store by these joint compensation mechanisms:

> First, the ability to act quickly may be essential in some instances of environmental damage. In contrast to civil liability, which requires a lengthy legal process before obtaining compensation, joint compensation schemes can gather funds in advance. Financing could thus be readily available for emergency remedial action or to reimburse early restoration work. Moreover, the burden of damage may be more readily shouldered by collective rather than individual action. Finally, if the cost of cleaning up a particular incident is high, it may not be possible to recover all the costs from a liable party with limited financial resources. A joint compensation system would help provide the additional resources needed for carrying out the restoration.[28]

---

28 Para 3.0.

The Green Paper then goes on to note certain problems with such systems, and also to comment upon international experience. A joint compensation scheme will work best where conventional insurance will also work best. The advantage is that decisions about targeting clean-up funds are uncoupled from whether blame can be attributed against a particular polluter: in place of a court apportioning liability there can be a panel to prioritize funding.

There has been some experience of environmental liability associations, and the use of environmental liability financing funds, particularly in Germany, and an analysis of these by Dr Scherer[29] concludes that the financing fund model provides the greatest potential for environmental liability. One example is the North-Rhein Westphalian licensing model, which has established a licensing requirement for the disposal of hazardous waste under which special fees are charged that are then used to finance the clean-up of historically contaminated sites. It is an 'association' model, comprising the participating enterprises and the cities, counties and communes of the area. The fund applies 70 per cent of the monies received from these fees to cleaning up historically polluted sites and takes emergency measures to deal with those sites only where the measures would otherwise have to be taken by the government in lieu of the responsible party, or where the responsible party cannot be identified or is insolvent. The communes and the counties must also contribute to the costs of the remedial works, and there is a right of recourse against the landowner if the land value is enhanced by the works. Work is undertaken in accordance with a five-year plan, which is subject to approval by the State Ministry of the Environment.

Different models operate in the State of Hesse, which is based to a large extent upon voluntary cooperation between industry, state government and the communes, and also in the states of Baden-Wurttemberg, Rhineland-Palatinate, Bavaria, and Lower Saxony. But all have adopted a compensation scheme approach, though subject to different rules as to their structure, access to funds and decision-making on the application of the funds. A notable feature is that liability to contribute is mainly based upon the amount of hazardous wastes currently generated by the industry concerned, or by particular sectors, and this is a very loose notion of causation. However, the potential inequity of taxing today's producers for the pollution of yesterday's producers is mitigated to a certain extent by sharing liability with communes and regional governments, and by involving industry sectors in the decision-making process.

---

29 Joachim Scherer, Joint compensation schemes, (paper prepared for European Commission seminars on environmental liability, under contract no. B4-3040-348-93), Frankfurt: Baker & Mackenzie/Döser Amereller Noack, December 1993.

Dr Scherer argues that the various features of a joint compensation fund could readily be the subject of harmonization under European law, with the objective of establishing a legal framework for regionally organized, regionally financed and regionally operating funds for the financing of the exploration and decontamination of historically contaminated sites. But he leaves open the question of whether the time is yet ripe for the creation of a Europe-wide compensation fund, or even for a European framework for national compensation funds.

IV CONCLUSIONS

The environment does not fare well under existing national schemes for civil liability. Protection for the unowned environment is limited; and protection for the owned environment is measured in terms of its owner's economic loss rather than the cost of restoring the environment itself. An enhanced liability system can address some of these problems but will not, of itself, ensure that environmental damage does not occur nor that finance will always be available to restore the environment when damage does occur. It has limited applicability to historic pollution, and there are great legal complexities in extending existing systems, especially in attempting to establish a common system through different European states with their widely differing legal traditions in relation to liability rules and procedures.

Yet the case for broadening existing national liability systems is powerful, and this chapter has reviewed the issues that arise from the debates in the context of the European Union's former commitment to legislation in this sphere.

15 Self-regulation by Industry

Eckard Rehbinder

Table of Contents

I INTRODUCTION

1 The need for self-regulation

In implementing its objectives, modern environmental law primarily employs regulatory strategies (command and control regulation). Environmental law has covered industrial societies with a dense network of laws, regulations and administrative rules that prohibit certain activities, lay down requirements for other types of activities, make the exercise of such activities conditional on the fulfilment of certain prerequisites – the granting of a permit or prior notification – and subject prohibited activities to criminal and administrative sanctions. Moreover, increasing recourse to planning of environmental quality amounts to the establishment of a public management system for natural resources that allots scarce absorption capacities to particular polluters according to selection criteria ranging from the principle of priority to equal and fair apportionment. Apart from the tradition of police law which is the source of modern environmental law, this pattern of regulation has been favoured for various reasons. One reason is that administrative regulation is deemed to be effective – that is, to ensure that the environmental quality goals are met. Another reason is that it provides for participation of the public, transparency of agency decisions and political accountability of administrators; hence, administrative regulation embodies a democratic element.

However, in recent years this pattern of command and control regulation has been criticized increasingly on the grounds that it is inefficient because it neglects individual costs of pollution control and prevention, hampers innovation, and, due to implementation and enforcement deficits that are inherent in this type of regulation, does even not achieve its environmental objectives. Therefore, a certain tendency towards deregulation of environmental policy has emerged, although administrative regulation still is clearly dominant. The primary means of deregulation offered by critics of administrative regulation are economic instruments such as charges, 'bubbles' and tradeable permits. Indeed, in some countries – especially in the USA and Germany, and with respect to charges also in France, the Netherlands and recently Belgium, – the first steps towards greater use of economic instruments have already been taken.[1]

Another response to existing or presumed deficits of command and control regulation is self-regulation by industry.[2] However, self-regulation also responds to weaknesses of economic instruments. Contrary to common understanding, economic instruments, as discussed in recent years, are instruments of an interventionist environmental policy which requires the setting of concrete environmental protection or precaution targets; they can only react to pressures exerted by a particular environmental problem and, hence, require that such a problem already exists or is being perceived as such. They are not a suitable, or at least not a comprehensive, means to a 'proactive' environmental policy which aims at an environmentally friendly societal structure but, since it is not able to formulate precise environmental quality targets, has to rely on mere guidance as to the general di-

---

1 See Chapter 13 by Gyula Bándi in this volume.
2 For an alternative approach, namely interactive government and network decision-making, see Chapter 12 by Pieter Glasbergen in this volume.

rection of intended change.[3] The need for proactive environmental policy lies in the enormous complexity of modern environmental policy. Widespread scientific uncertainty about the existence and extent of risks, the complexity of potential adverse impacts of environmental policy measures on industry and the labour market, the danger of shifting the problem from one environmental medium to another, the need to achieve structural change of the economy as well as change in the society's value system, all these factors render conventional means–ends rationality almost obsolete and require proactive environmental policy. Economic instruments are not capable of steering the behaviour of potential polluters, especially process and product innovation in an environmentally friendly direction. The mere knowledge of potential polluters that, in the case of later environmental problems, the state could intervene with regulatory or economic instruments is not a sufficient incentive for considering the environmental perspective early at the stage of process and product development.

Self-regulation is a possible response to deficiencies both of administrative regulation and economic instruments. At first glance, this seems paradoxical. There seems to be no reason why entrepreneurs who cannot be made to behave in an environmentally friendly way by means of administrative regulation or economic instruments should be willing to demonstrate such desirable behaviour through voluntary self-regulation. The answer is simple. Since 'pure' – that is, strictly voluntary – self-regulation can hardly be expected because it runs counter to the interests of the relevant actors and is contrary to the logic of a market economy, the state exercises a certain degree of pressure on the resolution of existing or anticipated environmental problems by self-regulation.

Environmental self-regulation occurs either in the 'shadow' of possible administrative or economic regulation – that is, under the threat of the state adopting such regulation – or as a result of institutional or organizational arrangements set by the state. 'Pure' self-regulation is extremely rare. With this method the state normally attempts to direct entrepreneurs' behaviour by setting environmental policy targets and/or creates an informational or organizational framework that is designed to promote their environmentally friendly behaviour. It is hoped then that, in the course of their activities, especially process or product innovation, they themselves then consider the environmental consequences of their intended activity, which may include excessive material and energy consumption, the generation

---

3 For the notion of proactive environmental policy see Volker von Prittwitz, Gefahrenabwehr – Vorsorge – Ökologisierung. Drei Idealtypen präventiver Umweltpolitik, in Udo Simonis (ed.), *Präventive Umweltpolitik*, Frankfurt/New York: Campus, 1988, pp. 49–64; Timothy O'Riordan, Anticipatory Environmental Policy, in ibid., pp. 65–76; Georges Fülgraff, Jochen Reiche, Proaktive Umweltpolitik, in Wolfgang Schenkel, Peter-Christof Storm (eds), *Umwelt, Politik, Technik, Recht, Festschrift von Lersner*, Berlin: E. Schmidt-Verlag, 1990, pp. 103–114.

of emissions and waste, hazard to man or the environment and becoming unrecyclable waste at the end of its useful life. Instead of the state giving orders or applying monetary pressure, it relies on incited consensus, information (disclosure) and organization. In emphasizing the (necessary) framework conditions that make environmental self-regulation possible, rather than the resulting act of self-regulation, these can be described as 'soft' instruments of environmental policy.[4]

The need for state involvement in the process of self-regulation has important implications for its use as an instrument of environmental policy. Self-regulation supplements administrative and economic regulation in that it aims to achieve policy objectives that are beyond the reach of, or cannot effectively be achieved by, administrative or economic regulation. It assumes the existence of a sophisticated environmental policy, a high level of baseline regulation and an adequate organization of the environmental administrative structure. Where these prerequisites are not met, recourse to self-regulation would be quite dangerous.

The presence of the state in the process of self-regulation also raises the question as to how self-regulation and administrative regulation may be delimited. A clear-cut answer is not possible. The decisive factor would seem to be the degree of industry's self-responsibility in devising environmental quality objects and means for implementing them. This means that not all contractual techniques of environmental policy are equivalent to self-regulation. Where the state is dominant – for example, where agencies clearly negotiate against the background of existing law and can be trusted to comply with an administrative order that could be made under that law – one should not speak of self-regulation. This is particularly true of environmental compliance agreements which, in order to reach a flexible, less costly and sometimes more comprehensive improvement of environmental quality in the neighbourhood of a facility, are often concluded between operators of facilities and the competent agency in lieu of administrative acts. Such agreements may be, and frequently are, the basis for 'bubble' or offset agreements and then are a constituent part of economic instruments. In any case, insofar as the operator does not go beyond what he is generally legally required to do, the self-regulatory element is slight.

Self-regulation can avoid frictions in the economic process and thereby efficiency and innovation losses normally associated with administrative regulation and also, to a certain extent, with economic instruments. The price paid for this advantage is that environmental policy objectives may be accomplished to a lesser degree or with lesser certainty; this loss of accuracy of goal achievement is a possible, maybe probable, although not necessary, result of voluntariness. Therefore, self-regulation as a rule cannot – or at least should not – be used for the prevention

---

4 See Werner Rengeling, *Das Kooperationsprinzip im Umweltrecht*, Köln: Heymanns-Verlag, 1988, pp.3–14.

of clearly unacceptable risk, but, rather, in those areas where risks that are below the level of unacceptability should be further reduced as a precaution. However, given the difficulty in delimiting these two types of risk, this only is a rule of thumb. Where self-regulation is used for tackling clearly unacceptable risk, which is arguably acceptable with respect to binding environmental agreements that remove the need for agency intervention, the agency would seem to be obliged to closely monitor the environmental results of self-regulation and reserve to itself the right of immediate intervention if the environmental targets are not or no longer met.

2   Types of self-regulation

Consensus, information, and organization are the characteristic elements of self-regulation. Although there is a certain degree of overlap, one can coordinate particular types of self-regulation to these elements:

1   *Consensus*: environmental agreements (contracts and covenants), normalization, codes of conduct;
2   Information: eco-audits, eco-balances, product life cycle analysis, emission release information, classification and labelling of dangerous substances, product safety data sheets, eco-labelling;
3   Organization: environmental officers and directors, obligation to establish an environmental management system or obligation to develop an environmental protection concept within the firm.

It should be noted that eco-audit and product life cycle analysis bear a strong organizational element and can lead to organizational innovation; moreover they can also be used as strictly internal 'accounting' instruments of self-regulation.

Apart from the characteristic features indicated above that relate to the object of the relevant instrument, one can classify instruments of self-regulation according to the degree of state intervention or, conversely, self-responsibility with respect to the environmental policy targets to be pursued and/or the institutional framework. The intensity of self-regulation is the product of both features (see figure next page).

Classification of Instruments of Self-regulation

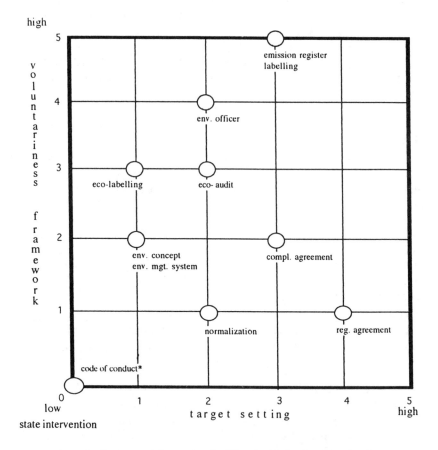

*same classification: eco-balance and product life cycle analysis as long as purely voluntary.

II CONSENSUS-ORIENTED INSTRUMENTS

1 General remarks

Throughout developed environmental legal systems there is a certain trend towards the use of contractual techniques of environmental policy, although the extent to which states resort to such techniques is quite varied. These variations can be explained by the different degree of legalization of a given society as well as its basic value orientation. In the USA with its highly legalistic command and control regulation, the emphasis on legal accountability of administrators, the extensive judicial protection of diffuse interests and the adversarial value system of society, there is less room for contractual instruments of environmental policy than in European countries where formal rule-of-law thinking plays a somewhat less prominent role and the political decision-making process is either more technocratic or more consensus-oriented.[5]

However, in most states that have used contractual techniques, there is widespread mistrust against the trend towards contractualization – or even 'commodification' – of environmental policy-making and implementation of environmental laws, especially from a legal point of view but also from the perspective of effectiveness of environmental policy.[6] The critics' main argument is that 'bartering rationality' tends to be quite different from regulatory decision-making rationality in that it neglects (procedurally fair and sound) fact-finding, preserves or even promotes inequality, concentrates on divisible and monetarizable goods,

---

5 For differences in policy styles between the USA and Europe see David Vogel, *National Styles of Regulating Environmental Policy in Great Britain and the United States*, London/Ithaca: Cornell University Press, 1986; Jeremy Richardson (ed.), *Policy Styles in Western Europe*, London: Allen & Unwin, 1982.

6 See, for example, Rengeling, *op.cit.*, pp. 160–5; Alfred Rest, The Integration of Environmental Covenants and Contracts into the Public Law System, in van Dunné (ed.), *Environmental Contracts and Covenants: New Instruments for a Realistic Environmental Policy?*, Lelystad: Vermande, 1993, pp. 225–30; Gerd Winter, Bartering Rationality in Regulation, *Law and Society Review*, **19**, 1985, pp.219–50; Harry Edwards, Alternative Dispute Resolution: Panacea or Anathema, *Harvard Law Review*, **99**, 1986, pp.668–84; Michel Paques, Les conventions sectorielles en matière d'environnement du point de vue de droit public, in Hubert Bocken, Ives Traest (eds), *Milieubeleidsovereenkomsten*, Brussels: Story Scientia, 1991, pp. 55–89; Ellen Basse, The Contract Model – The Merits of a Voluntary Approach, *Environmental Liability*, **2**, 1994, pp. 74, at 81–82; François Ost, L'auto-organisation écologique des entreprises: un jeu sans conflits et sans règles?, *Revue interdisciplinaire d'études juridiques*, **28**, 1992, pp. 147, at 160–162.

favours private over public values, presents the danger of capture of agencies by industry, excludes the general public from participating in the decision-making process, reduces legal protection of indirectly affected persons and prevents structural reform. In addition, there is a danger of lessening of the level of environmental protection. Not all of these points are valid for all kinds of agreement of course, but a detailed analysis of this is beyond the scope of this chapter.

The extent to which environmental agreements can be fitted into the relevant legal system raises rather complex and often highly technical legal questions that vary between countries and also between types of agreement, but, with the possible exception of Japan the legality of such agreement is accepted nowhere.[7] Denmark has made the unique attempt at formally integrating consensual techniques at the level of target setting and implementation into its legal order. Articles 10 and 11 of the Environmental Protection Act provide for formal authority for the conclusion of such agreements, their binding force, the parties and other persons to be bound, the sanctions in case of violations as well as procedural rules; in particular, environmental organizations have an opportunity to comment on the draft agreement.[8] This resolves a number of controversial legal issues in the debate. However, practice seems to indicate that industry continues to prefer informal agreements which, in turn, raises the question whether 'formalization of informality' is not so contradictory that it amounts to the quadrature of the circle.

The primary problem of evaluation of contractual techniques is the development of an adequate system of criteria. In my view, the point of reference cannot be an idealized configuration of traditional regulation but, rather, the configuration that would have existed if, in a realistic perspective, normal administrative procedures had been followed. In other words, it is not appropriate to compare a realistic contractual configuration with an idealized regulatory one. Seen in this perspective, many of the objections voiced against environmental agreements are less convincing if it cannot be shown that, under the circumstances of the particular case, regulation would have rendered a better result. For example, regulatory agreements, (agreements that are substituted for regulation) often have an experi-

---

7 This is even true in the Netherlands where environmental agreements are generally accepted; see, for example, Peter van Buuren, Environmental Covenants: Possibilities and Impossibilities, in Jan van Dunné (ed.), *op.cit.*, pp. 49–55.

8 See Basse, *op.cit.*, pp. 79–84: idem, Environmental Contracts: A New Instrument to be used in the Danish Regulation of Environmental Law, in van Dunné (ed.), *op.cit.*, pp. 197–224; Jesper Jörgensen, Legislation on 'Eco-Contracts' in Denmark, in van Dunné (ed.), *op.cit.*, pp. 73–85. Both authors reprint the relevant sections of the Danish Environmental Protection Act. In the Belgian region of Flanders, a legal regulation on environmental agreements has been proposed in the framework of codification of environmental law; see Hubert Bocken, Covenants in Belgian Environmental Law – Remarks on the Draft Decree on Environmental Covenants, in van Dunné, *op.cit.*, pp. 57–71.

mental function in that they test the potential of future regulation which, due to the complexity of circumstances, is presently not yet feasible. Given the normally broad political discretion enjoyed by the government in deciding whether to regulate and in what way, such a temporary recourse to regulation should not offend even a fierce adherent to the rule of law. As for the concern about narrowing the consideration of affected interests, this argument assumes that conventional regulation and implementation would, as a matter of course, fully consider the interests of persons living far away, persons not interested in environmental protection, future generations and so on, which may or may not be the case. However, it is true that there might be a better chance for such consideration, if broad public participation is allowed, although this can also have the reverse effect of completely blocking the reaching of a decision. Furthermore, legal protection of indirectly affected persons remains a problem, although this can be solved by an adjustment of traditional models of judicial review which is oriented at administrative orders to the contractual configuration.[9] Finally, widespread recourse to negotiation may mask a need for reforming the regulatory system. Seen from a systemic point of view, therefore, contractual techniques amount to curing mere symptoms. However, it is questionable whether, in view of the structural conservativism of modern social systems, it would be responsible – and realistic – to wait for the aggravation of conflicts and an ultimate collapse of regulation.

2   Environmental agreements

In quite a number of countries, environmental agreements are being used as a means of accomplishing a concerted reduction of pollution. These agreements may be legally binding on the parties (environmental contracts), but they may also – and in practice normally are – non-binding 'gentlemen's agreements' (environmental covenants). On the side of industry, industrial associations rather than their members often conclude the agreement which raises some questions of representation and loyalty and further diminishes the *de facto* binding effect of the agreement.

---

9 See Michael Kloepfer, Zu den neuen umweltrechtlichen Handlungsformen des Staates, *Juristenzeitung*, 1991, pp. 737, at 743; Richard Stewart, Environmental Contracts and Covenants: A United States Perspective, in van Dunné, *op.cit.*, pp. 143–4; Basse, *op.cit.*, pp. 81–2.

a)   Types of agreements

Two main types of agreements can be distinguished: regulatory and implementation (compliance) agreements.

Regulatory agreements   These are concluded by industry and/or distributors with or without formal participation of the state and are normally substituted for generic regulation in the form of formal environmental policy targets, prohibitions, emission or waste reduction obligations, environmental standards, adjustment schedules or permit requirements. Sometimes, as in Germany under the Waste Disposal Act, the state may be empowered to promote the conclusion of such agreements by setting environmental quality targets.[10] Even if this is not the case, the state exercises an important influence on the conclusion and contents of such agreements by target-setting. Since industry concludes regulatory agreements in order to avoid direct state intervention, the threat of such intervention is used as a means of achieving consensus. Often, the state is a formal party to the agreement.

Implementation (compliance) agreements   These concern the application of environmental laws, regulations and rules in a particular case, for example in siting conflicts for new facilities or where an existing source must adjust to new requirements.

It should be noted that the distinction between regulatory and compliance agreements is not clear-cut. Especially where a regulatory agreement requires for its implementation a behaviour which, in the framework of command and control regulation, is ordered by administrative acts (for example, agreements for the reduction of emissions at existing sources), regulatory agreements do not always leave the implementation of the agreed-upon objectives to the members of the contracting industrial association, but may devise, or at least provide for, the determination of company implementation plans or contracts and even their translation into permit requirements.[11] Such hierarchical agreements are both regulatory *and* compliance agreements. The same is true where a regulatory agreement contains a scheme for the granting of a subsidy in case the firms implement the agreement.

---

10   Para. 14 Waste Disposal Act of 1986, OJ 1986 I, p. 1410; the new Waste Management Act of 1994, OJ 1994 I, p. 2705 maintains this provision in its para. 25.
11   See Jit Peters, Voluntary Agreements between Government and Industry, The Basic Metal Covenant as an Example, in van Dunné (ed.), *op.cit.*, pp. 19–31; Jan van den Broek, Covenant and Permit in the Dutch Target Group Consultation, in ibid., pp. 33–43; a summary of the Dutch Basic Metal Covenant is reprinted in ibid., pp. 285–308.

b) Regulatory agreements

Regulatory agreements have quite frequently been concluded by industry in some Western countries such as the Netherlands, Germany, France, Japan, Belgium and Denmark, especially in the fields of reduction of effluents by existing sources, reduction of toxic emissions, prevention and recycling of waste, and phasing out of hazardous substances and export of pesticides. The environmental effects of these agreements are mixed. Since such agreements normally are simple 'gentlemen's agreements' and are not legally binding on the affected enterprises and, moreover, it is not always possible to reach the participation of the whole industry, meeting the self-established targets already poses major problems.

The Netherlands probably has the most extensive experience with regulatory agreements.[12] Since 1985 about 25 agreements have been concluded. Many of these concern branches of industry that have been designated as priority target groups for implementing environmental quality objectives laid down in the Dutch environmental programmes. Apart from socio-cultural factors, the general success of these agreements can often be related to their broad scope. The agreements also comprise the stage of individual implementation at company level, including provision for translation of the company implementation plan into permit requirements. To this extent, the Dutch regulatory agreement is a hybrid between a regulatory and compliance agreement, but also between consensual and regulatory technique. By contrast, in Germany, where the firms normally do not assume concrete individual commitments for implementing the agreement, the majority of environmental agreements concluded so far have ultimately failed.[13] Although there are also examples of successful agreements, such as the early phasing out of CFCs and the imposition of export restrictions for pesticides. In France, most of the agreements have been quite successful.[14] This is particularly true of the early

---

12 See above note 11.
13 See Günter Hartkopf, Eberhard Bohne, *Umweltpolitik*, vol. 1, Opladen: Westdeutscher Verlag, 1983, pp. 451–60; Der Rat von Sachverständigen für Umweltfragen, Sondergutachten September 1990, *Abfallwirtschaft*, Stuttgart: Metzler-Poeschel, 1991, No. 803–806; Bundesverband der Deutschen Industrie, *Freiwillige Kooperationslösungen im Umweltschutz*, Köln, February 1992; Christl Illig, *Das Vorsorgeprinzip im Abfallrecht*, Berlin: E. Schmidt-Verlag, 1992, pp. 205–6; Michael Kohlhaas, Barbara Praetorius, *Selbstverpflichtungen der Industrie zur CO_2-Reduktion*, Berlin: Duncker & Humblot, 1994.
14 See Tierry Lavoux, Expériences françaises relatives à l'usage de contrats de branche en matière de protection de l'environnement, in Bocken, Traest, *op.cit.*, pp. 103–9; Michel Prieur, *Droit de l'environnement*, (2nd edn), Paris: Dalloz, 1991, pp. 116–9; Pierre Lascoumes, Les contrats de branche et d'entreprise en matière de protection de l'environnement en France, in A. Morand (ed.), *L'état propulsif*, Paris: Publisud, 1991, pp. 221–35.

branch agreements for the adjustment of existing facilities concluded between the state and industrial associations that set a framework for the granting of subsidies, but also for the later branch programmes that were not associated with subsidies. On the other hand, agreements concluded at the end of the 1970s and beginning of the 1980s that provided for voluntary measures of energy-saving and recycling of beverage containers as well as wastepaper and board, although not failures, did not meet the envisaged guidance. In Japan administrative guidance (gyosei shido) formulated by the competent authorities, the Environmental Agency or MITI, the competent agency for trade and industry, normally is based on long negotiation between the state and industry.[15] In this sense one can say that administrative guidance is just the legal form of regulatory quasi-agreements. Examples are recommendations with respect to emissions from the computer industry, recycling of industrial wastes, and environmental impact assessment.

In principle, regulatory agreements are capable of contributing to the implementation of a precautionary environmental policy. Certainly, they often have the disadvantage that the state must pay in terms of a reduction in the desirable level of environmental protection, but this may be offset by the advantage that a prompt solution of the problem is possible. Furthermore, due to their acceptance by the most directly affected firms, there may be fewer enforcement problems, although, admittedly, this would require participation of all the affected members of the relevant branch of industry which is not always ensured since small and medium-sized firms are frequently underrepresented in industrial associations.

There are a number of prerequisites for the environmental success of regulatory agreements that substantially limit their applicability, although these factors are not absolute, but are relative and not necessarily cumulative: industry and distributors must not anticipate considerable disadvantages (costs, competitive disadvantages, loss of turnover) as a consequence of the agreement; there must be a certain homogeneity on the part of the affected industry; there must be a fairly uniform public attitude about the assessment of the environmental problem to be solved by so placing industry under pressure; and the agency must have a considerable threat potential in that, if there is a lack of consensus about, or compliance with, the agreement, the adoption of a more disadvantageous administrative regulation might be anticipated.[16] As with the Netherlands, France and Japan, the sociocultural environment – in particular the consensus-orientation of the political cli-

15   See, for example, Michio Hashimoto, Administrative Guidance in Environmental Policy: Some Important Cases, in Sigeto Tsuru, Helmut Weidner (eds), *Environmental Policy in Japan*, Berlin: Sigma, 1989, pp. 252–60; Hiroshi Shiono, *Administrative Sciences*, **48**, 1982, pp. 239–46; Yoichi Ohashi, Verwaltungsvorschriften und informales Verwaltungshandeln, *Verwaltungsarchiv*, **82**, 1991, pp. 220–45.
16 Cf. P. Winsemius, Environmental Contracts and Covenants: New Instruments for A Realistic Environmental Policy?, in van Dunné, *op.cit.*, pp. 5–15.

mate and/or the existence of close educational and professional links between administrators and company managers – promotes the conclusion of, and compliance with, regulatory agreements.

Regulatory agreements may also be concluded with the participation of environmental interests. While the agreements concluded in Europe are pure self-commitments by industry, in the USA we find a type of regulatory quasi-agreement between the regulated industry and environmental groups whose purpose is not to substitute an agreement for administrative regulation but, rather, prepare the development of programmes and regulations – especially the adoption of environmental programmes or standards – by agreement between the two real parties in interest.[17] It is presumed that the competent agency will then seriously consider the mutual understanding and eventually transpose it into a published proposal on administrative rules. Sometimes the reaching of consensus is promoted by taking recourse to mediation. In 1990 the Administrative Procedure Act was amended so as to formally provide for such a procedure in administrative rule-making. This technique of regulatory quasi-agreement must be seen against the background of the US system of highly formalized, adversarial participation in administrative rule-making which almost invariably ends up in litigation instituted by either party in interest. Regulatory negotiation and mediation are used as means of breaking up the frequent impasses that are associated with this type of participation.

So far, there are few practical examples of negotiated rule-making, and experience does not seem to be generally positive.[18] Reasons for its limited success include the difficulty in involving all parties that could challenge the legality of the resulting regulation, differences of principle or the high degree of politicization of the issue.

c) Implementation agreements

Implementation agreements are more diverse. They play a prominent role in the USA and Japan, but there are also some examples in Germany.

---

17 Philip Harter, Negotiating Regulations: A Cure for the Malaise?, *Georgetown Law Journal*, **71**, 1982 pp. 1–117; idem, The Role of Courts in Regulatory Negotiation, *Columbia Journal of Environmental Law*, **11**, 1986, pp. 51–72; Lawrence Susskind, Gerard MacMahon, The Theory and Practice of Negotiated Rulemaking, *Yale Journal of Regulation*, **3**, 1985, pp. 133–65; Susan Rose-Ackerman, Consensus versus Incentives: A Sceptical Look at Regulatory Negotiation, *Duke Law Journal*, **43**, 1994, pp. 1206–20.
18 Stewart, in van Dunné, *op.cit.*, pp. 148–50; but see Lawrence Susskind, Jeffrey Cruikshank, *Breaking the Impasse – Consensual Approaches to Resolving Public Disputes*, New York: Basic Books, 1987, pp. 230–2.

The US 'model' of implementation agreement is unique in that the agreement is often an institutionalized part of the permitting process, containing prescribed substantive law elements such as the option for more stringent standards and compensation of the municipality for the sacrifice in accommodating a facility.[19] In view of the growing resistance of local communities against the siting of new waste deposit and incineration facilities, in the 1980s some states introduced in to state decision-making mandatory negotiation procedures on new or significantly modified waste disposal facilities. Other states created optional procedures. Under the former law, the conclusion of a siting contract between the operator and the municipality that must contain agreements as to the construction, design and operation of the facility, as well as compensation to the local community, is a mandatory prerequisite for an affirmative decision by the state authorities on a siting application.

The contract is negotiated by a local negotiation committee in which the local community is represented. Quite far-reaching provisions for public information are designed to remove information desequilibria. Furthermore, to prevent a veto by the municipality, the relevant laws prescribe conflict resolution mechanisms – sometimes in the form of mediation; in all cases in the form of arbitration. Finally, the relevant laws provide for the participation and compensation of strongly affected neighbouring municipalities.

Despite all these attempts of the legislature to make institutionalized negotiations on siting conflicts attractive, the success of the relevant laws has been mixed.[20] In Massachusetts, the procedure apparently has not extensively promoted the siting of new waste disposal facilities, mainly because neither the authorities nor the affected municipalities have ever been willing to run through the administrative process in such a way that the state of negotiation could be reached at all. By contrast, in Wisconsin, quite a number of siting contracts are concluded every year. The differences between the two states may be explained by differences in population density and ensuing 'sacrifice' situations, but by also different attitudes towards the problem of toxic waste.

It should be noted that this mixed record of institutionalized negotiation between polluters and affected local communities on politically highly sensitive sit-

---

19 See Gail Bingham, Daniel Miller, Prospects for Resolving Hazardous Waste Siting Disputes Through Negotiation, *Natural Resources Lawyer*, **17**, 1984, p. 473–489; Joan Gardner, Massachusetts Siting Act and Experience To Date, in Wolfgang Hoffmann-Riem, Eberhard Schmidt-Assmann (eds), *Konfliktbewältigung durch Verhandlungen I*, Baden-Baden: Nomos, 1990, pp. 205–13; Bernd Holznagel, Negotiation and Mediation: The Newest Approach to Hazardous Waste Facility Siting, *Boston College Environmental Affairs Law Review*, **13**, 1986, pp. 329–78; idem, *Konfliktlösung durch Verhandlungen*, Baden-Baden: Nomos, 1990, pp. 149–52, 167–9.

20 See, in particular, Gardner (1990), *op.cit.*, Holznagel (1986), *op.cit.*

ing conflicts cannot be generalized in relation to other negotiation on less politically sensitive issues. Indeed, there are, albeit isolated, cases of 'good neighbour agreements' in which plant operators have committed themselves to environmental groups and local communities to substantially reduce toxic emissions.

In Japan, implementation agreements in which operators of polluting facilities commit themselves to prefectures and/or municipalities to comply with requirements for the control of pollution or improvement of nature and landscape that go beyond legal requirements are an important element of environmental policy.[21] The number of existing agreements is now about 40,000, the number of new agreements ranging between 1,500 and 2,600 per year. While municipalities often consider themselves as representatives of local communities, there are also numerous cases of direct citizen participation in environmental agreements. Roughly speaking, in about 20 per cent of all agreements there is a degree of formal local community participation, either as sole party, co-party or observer. Where local communities are the sole parties, they often have carried their point of view through with the plant operator in opposition to the prefecture or municipality, or they have made a direct agreement with the municipality in its capacity as operator of a polluting facility.

Implementation agreements in Japan act as a highly effective local or regional counterweight against weak or inappropriate central regulation, including slow reaction to new problems or the new scientific or technical knowledge. Although, clearly, the agreements do not comprehensively supplant central regulation, they are the most important source of improvements of environmental conditions in urban agglomerations and set forth the controlling requirements, at least for major polluters, even outside these areas.

The political acceptance of implementation agreements is high. In principle, even industry accepts implementation agreements as a major instrument of Japanese environmental policy. There are various factors that motivate industry to conclude such agreements. The most important of these factors are: material advantages, especially access to municipal land; administrative pressures; interest in establishing an ongoing relationship with the administration; social pressures from local communities; social responsibility; and consensus orientation. It is im-

---

21 See Julian Gresser, Koichiro Fujikura, Akio Morishima, *Environmental Law in Japan*, Cambridge/Mass./London: MIT Press, 1981, pp. 248–9, 346; Geoffrey Leane, Environmental Contracts – A Lesson in Democracy from the Japanese, *University of British Columbia Law Review*, **25**, 1991, pp. 361–85; Eckard Rehbinder, Ecological Contracts: Agreements between Polluters and Local Communities, in Gunter Teubner, Lindsay Farmer, Declan Murphy (eds), *Environmental Law and Ecological Responsibility*, London: John Wiley, 1994, pp. 145, at 151–155; Kazuo Yamaouchi, Kiyuharo Otsubo, Agreements on Pollution Prevention, in Tsuru & Weidner, *op.cit.*, pp. 221–45.

possible to generalize to what extent these factors account for the conclusion of agreements.

Irrespective of their contents, implementation agreements between polluters and local communities have one main purpose, namely to overcome acceptance conflicts between a state agency, an author of an infrastructure project or an operator of a private facility on the one hand, and local communities that may be represented by municipalities or selected or self-appointed representatives, on the other. Seen in this perspective, the phenomenon of implementation agreement reflects, and responds to, the crisis of traditional participation as a means of securing acceptance by potentially adversely affected parties. Arguably, negotiation leads to a broader information input – a participation that accompanies the whole process - the removal of asymmetries of influence and cooperative, problem-solving behaviour.

Beyond this more procedural aspect, implementation agreements have a substantive content. They lead to a 'fine tuning' of law considering the particular case, the real parties, the diverging interests and the real power balance.[22] They couple topics and actors which are separated by too narrow or rigid formal law but are inseparable politically. Normally, such agreements provide for some kind of compensation for disadvantages incurred as a result of an administrative decision such as stiffening of standards, improvement of the environment at some other place, preservation of the status quo for the future, other kind of physical compensation or even monetary compensation. There are no substantive criteria for the evaluation of the time horizon, the subject and the kind of compensation granted to adversely affected parties. However, one may say that compensation constitutes an element of an adequate distribution of burdens and advantages between the author of a project or the operator of a facility and the group(s) of adversely affected persons. Although there may be limits to highly complex coupling of different matters, the compensatory element of implementation agreements should not be denigrated as simple 'commodification'.

3   Normalization (standardization)

In many Western European countries – in contrast to the USA – normalization by private technical institutions plays a great role as an instrument of neo-corporatist self-regulation.[23] Normalization serves to implement the many broad statutory

---

22 Holznagel (1990), *Konfliktlösung, op.cit.*, pp. 259–69.
23 See Peter Marburger, Thomas Gebhard, Gesellschaftliche Umweltnormierungen, in Alfred   Endres,   Peter   Marburger,   *Umweltschutz   durch   gesellschaftliche Selbststeuerung*, Bonn: Economica, 1993, pp. 1–48; Volker Eichener, Helmut Voelz-

terms contained in environmental laws, such as 'unacceptable' or 'unreasonable risk', 'precaution against risk', 'best available technology', 'state of science and technology'. The task of implementing these key terms is not merely technical/scientific, although it requires a high degree of technical and scientific knowledge; rather it involves political value judgements that, in principle, should be made by politically legitimized authorities. However, because of the complexity of standard-setting, the competent agencies, instead of preparing or setting forth their own environmental standards, often rely on norms laid down by private institutions, either by way of incorporation, formal reference or by applying these norms as expression of expert opinion. Independent of the legal effect of private norms that may vary from statute to statute and country to country, their practical importance has been great.

In the harmonization programme of the European Community of 1985,[24] the Commission laid down the principle that Community regulation in the field of products should be limited to setting forth basic requirements for the protection of human health, the environment and safety, while the implementation of these requirements should be left to European normalization institutions.

Although the European Union has met with considerable difficulties in implementing environmental Directives that call for the setting of Union standards, in contrast to consumer protection the 'new approach' to product harmonization has as yet played no particular role in environment-related regulation. The only exception is the Building Products Directive.[25] Arguably, the reason for this reluctance is that environmental standard-setting is so highly politicized that it cannot be left to private normalization, even if controlled by the Union's organs. In the light of the proposal on integrated pollution control and prevention (IPPC Directive),[26] the tendency has been more to leave standard-setting to member states rather than to European normalization institutions.

Normalization by private technical institutions has some clear advantages over regulation. First, the expertise, the practical experience, the different fact configurations and interests of all directly affected persons enter into the private norm. Compared to administrative regulation, there is more flexibility for adjusting private norms to scientific and technical progress. Since persons directly affected can participate in the norm-setting process, acceptance and compliance is promoted, while necessary deviations from a norm are possible, thereby not unduly hampering innovations.

---

kow, *Umweltinteressen in der verbandlichen Techniksteuerung*, Duisburg: waz-Dr., 1991, pp. 47–62.
24 OJ 1985 No. C 136 p. 1.
25 OJ 1989 No. L 40 p. 12; OJ 1994 No. L 365 p. 10.
26 OJ 1993 No. C 311 p. 16.

Conversely, deficiencies of normalization are undeniable. As yet, the environmental perspective has not played an important role in the process of normalization. Despite the formal openness of the norm-setting process, a balanced representation of all interests affected, including environmental interests, is not ensured; there is a dominance of big industry and the science and technology establishment. Finally, the compromise character of many norms may be at odds with the mandate of the law to be implemented. For these reasons, critics of traditional normalization have demanded procedural and organizational safeguards for the conformity of normalization with the relevant statutory mandate, its objectivity, and balanced interest representation.[27]

In principle all this is also true of European normalization. Here, additional negative factors are the mediatization of interests brought about by the composition of the European normalization institutions – only membership organizations are represented – and the doubtful conformity of the 'new approach' with Article 155 of the EC Treaty.

Normalization may also aim at concretizing requirements of good environmental management. In this case, it is a mere ramification of organizational techniques of self-regulation.

4 Codes of conduct

In recent years, both national and international industrial associations have increasingly adopted guidelines for the environmentally responsible behaviour of their members or membership organizations (for example, the ICC Business Charter for Sustainable Development, the Chemical Industry Programme on Responsible Care, the Japanese Industrial Federation Environmental Guidelines).[28] These recommendations reflect industry's awareness of its environmental responsibility and will have a certain effect on the transformation process that is currently taking place in industry vis-à-vis their approach to environmental regulation. However, quantifiable effects can hardly be expected.

Sometimes, as in the case of the Nitrate Directive of the European Community,[29] environmental laws expressly refer to codes of conduct for concretizing vague statutory terms. Here the code of conduct is close to normalization.

---

27 See, for example, Michael Kloepfer, Eckard Rehbinder, Eberhard Schmidt-Assmann, Philip Kunig, *Umweltgesetzbuch – Allgemeiner Teil*, (2nd edn), Berlin: Erich Schmidt Verlag, 1991, pp. 460–84.

28 See Georg Winter, *Das umweltbewußte Unternehmen*, (5th edn), Munich: C.H. Beck, 1993, pp. 390–415, 440–70.

29 OJ 1991 No. L 375 p. 1 (Art. 4).

III   SELF-REGULATION THROUGH ENVIRONMENTAL INFORMA-TION

1   General remarks

There are a number of environmental information techniques that may, and often will, function as incentives to polluters to carry out voluntary measures for environmental improvement, especially for early consideration of environmental risks in process and product innovation. However, it should be noted that the term 'voluntary' is used in this connection in a rather broad sense. Insofar as the provision of environmental information as such is not voluntary but is imposed by administrative regulation, environmental information is used as a soft instrument to incite – through the pressure of public opinion or isolated court action by neighbours or associations so informed – an environmentally-friendly behaviour which the state is unable or unwilling to prescribe in detail. The pillory effect of public information about high toxic substances releases, unsatisfactory environmental performance found in the course of an eco-audit or an eco-balance, or a negative result of a product life cycle analysis is a calculated element of information strategies of soft environmental regulation.

This does not mean that such information incentives to environmentally-friendly behaviour should be considered as illegitimate or even constitutionally doubtful. In the field of traditional economic disclosure, the negative effects of poor balance sheets on the image of the relevant firm are accepted without question because public control of economic performance is considered as an important incentive for good economic behaviour. In principle, the same is true of the environmental performance, although the lack of a common 'currency' for describing environmental 'value' suggests some caution in mandating the publication of negative information, especially negative product information.

2   Eco-audits and eco-balances

Relying on US and Dutch experience with purely voluntary types of eco-audit, the EC Regulation on Environmental Management and Environmental Audit[30] pro-

---

30   Regulation No. 1836/93, OJ 1993 No. L 168 p. 1; see Dieter Sellner, Jörn Schnutenhaus, Umweltmanagement und Umweltbetriebsprüfung ("Umwelt-Audit"), *Neue Zeitschrift für Verwaltungsrecht*, 1993, pp. 928–34; generally on environmental audits see Terrel Hunt, Timothy Wilkins, Environmental Audits and Enforcement Policy, *Harvard Environmental Law Review*, **16**, 1992, pp. 365–427; C. Ledgerwood, E. Street, R. Therival, *The Environmental Audit and Business Strategy*, London: Pitman, 1992.

vides for the most comprehensive system of environmental accounting that exists
to date. It aims at introducing a procedure whereby the environmental performance of a firm, limited to a particular site, is regularly audited. Participation in the
system is voluntary. However, the participants in the system are subjected to mandatory publicity. Agency intervention is limited to setting the framework conditions of the system, which must be further detailed by normalization.

The regulation requires the development of an environmental management
system within the firm which includes both substantive targets and an appropriate
environmental organization and whose aim is continuously to improve the firm's
environmental performance. The environmental performance of the participating
firms must be audited by an accredited auditor, and the firm must make a public
statement as to the results of the audit. The basic criterion whereby to measure
environmental performance and its improvement is compliance with the applicable legal and administrative rules. However, beyond that, the firms must strive to
meet the requirements of *best available technology* (BAT). Although this standard
is not very demanding – by definition it entails an important economic qualification, while many states today prescribe a more demanding technological standard
such as the most recent state of technology or maximum available control technology – the initiation of a mechanism towards environmental improvement is the
very conceptual idea underlying the eco-audit system. On the other hand, the possible danger that the eco-audit could be misused as an instrument of mere promotion of the environmental image of the firm cannot be ruled out.

The object of an eco-audit is the entire environmental performance of the firm,
albeit one limited to a particular site, including its product innovation, material
and energy consumption and waste problems. It is expected – and experience so
far with voluntary schemes seems to confirm this – that the audit will enable the
management to obtain a clearer idea about the relevant environmental problems of
the firm and assess the effectiveness of the environmental management. This may
promote innovation, both at the management and organizational and the 'output'
level. However, the system has a certain bias towards facility-related environmental problems, environmental management and organization as such, and the
use of technology. This is also evidenced by the current discussion as to whether
firms that are testified to have a positive environmental performance should be
released from mandatory monitoring requirements. It is doubtful whether the system will generate sufficient incentives for considering environmental problems at
the initial stage of product innovation.

It has been proposed to replace or at least supplement the eco-audit by eco-
balances which would comprise the total environmental impacts and the resource

and energy consumption (material flows) of an enterprise.[31] However appealing such a holistic concept may be, due to the enormous methodological problems of data collection, determination of indicators, delimitation of the relevant system, aggregation and evaluation as yet unresolved, it is premature to consider the introduction of such a system. The existing methodological problems also justify the strategy of voluntary participation in the eco-audit for which the EU has opted. As long as there are no reasonable conventions about evaluation criteria, it would not be responsible to compel enterprises to adhere to the system. Rather, one should trust in the inherent dynamics of a voluntary system and the bandwagon effect that the voluntary adherence of a number of firms will have on other firms.

3   Product life cycle analysis

Product life cycle analysis is a procedure whereby one tries to account for all environmental impacts and resource and energy consumption of a particular product from cradle to grave – that is, from raw materials extraction and energy generation via production, marketing and consumption to waste disposal.[32] In this analysis one can, for example, compare different packaging materials, such as glass, aluminum, paper and various plastics, or different kinds of further use of these materials after primary use, such as re-use (returnable containers), recycling, incineration and deposit.

Compared to other methods of risk assessment, product life cycle analysis constitutes a fundamental innovation in that it tries to overcome the traditional segmentation of risk assessment into several unrelated stages and assesses a product on the basis of all environmental impacts and resource and energy consumption attributed to it during its whole life cycle. It is thus closer to the circular flow of materials in the real world. Product life cycle analysis can be an instrument of purely internal accounting which facilitates a firm's internal decisions as to new products in the framework of environmentally-friendly management. It can also be used as an instrument of public information as to the firm's product-related performance. Finally, it can function as a constituent part of an authorization or screening procedure for new substances or products; in the latter case, it is no longer an instrument of self-regulation.

---

31 See Frieder Rubik, Thomas Baumgartner, *Evaluation of Eco-Balances*, Luxemburg: European Communities, 1992; Stephan Ahbe, Arthur Braunschweig, Ruedi Müller-Wenk, *Methodik für Ökobilanzen auf der Basis ökologischer Optimierung*, Bern: BUWAL, 1990.

32 See Umweltbundesamt, *Ökobilanzen für Produkte*, Berlin, 1992; furthermore the authors cited note 30 above.

Although there are examples of voluntary product life cycle analyses in practice, this method does not yet play a major role as an instrument either of pure or of information-supported self-regulation. There are various reasons that explain this lag of practice behind theory.

Product life cycle analysis is fraught with the negative image of societal needs analysis which many of its adherents demand. However, it would also be useful if limited to environmental protection and the saving of natural resources as such. The real problem is that product life cycle analysis raises the same kind of unresolved methodological problems as eco-balancing. For example, the comparison of different beneficial and adverse effects of competing products (for example, water pollution in the case of returnable bottles versus air pollution associated with incineration of one-way containers) is methodologically difficult and permits possible misuse as a simple marketing device. The delimitation of the 'system' – that is, the determination as to how far the analysis should be extended – raises complex problems as well as unresolved questions as to the aggregation and quantification of impacts. This calls for some regulatory framework for this type of analysis. However, arguably, the methodological development has not yet proceeded far enough to allow the setting of such a framework, and premature state intervention might hamper the ongoing learning process within industry with respect to product life cycle analysis.

4   Hazardous substances emission information and classification and labelling of hazardous products

A conceptually more modest and methodologically much simpler, but more effective information strategy is to require operators of facilities that emit hazardous substances to monitor their emissions and regularly report to the public on the nature and extent of such emissions. Likewise, the producers can be obliged to classify their products into prescribed risk categories and label them accordingly and to provide safety data sheets that accompany the product. The most prominent example of such an emission-oriented information obligation is presented by the US Emergency Prevention and Community Right to Know Act of 1986,[33] although similar information obligations also exist in Japan, albeit mostly based on voluntary agreements.[34] Under US law, facilities within certain industrial catego-

---

33   42 USC paras 11001–11050 (1986); see Michael Baram, Risk Communication Law and Implementation Issues in the United States and the European Community, in Michael Baram, Daniel Partan, *Corporate Disclosure of Environmental Risks*, Salem/N.H.: Butterworth, 1990, pp. 65, at 77–86.

34   See Helmut Weidner, *Umweltberichterstattung in Japan*, Berlin: Sigma, 1987, pp. 65–128.

ries must make annual reports of emissions, differentiated according to the recipient environmental media, for each toxic chemical used above a threshold limit. Likewise, reports about the material and waste stream are prescribed. Finally, notification about extremely hazardous substances is required. This information is regularly published in an identifying form (toxic release inventory) and is also available at public libraries. The regular publication of the data has resulted in both internal and external pressures on firms to reduce emissions and the use of toxic chemicals, including agreements with the US Environmental Protection Agency, though sometimes only after strong public campaign, the threat of regulatory action or even the institution of private citizen law suits.[35]

This points to some important limitations of a purely information-based strategy of self-regulation. One cannot expect that all members of a branch of industry that has a high toxic chemicals flow will voluntarily curtail this flow and the ensuing emissions. To the extent that the unwilling firms, as a result of disclosure of their data, are exposed to massive public pressure, the limits of what is tolerable under the rule of law may soon be reached.

Another technique of self-regulation through public information about potential hazards presented by an activity is the classification and labelling of dangerous substances and preparations and the obligation to supply safety data sheets to accompany such products. The legislation for the control of hazardous substances, for example the EC Directive on Dangerous Substances,[36] often entrusts the producer with this task, although it sets forth quite a rigid framework for the generation of the necessary data (testing obligations) as well as the method of classification and the kind of information that must be contained in the safety data sheet. Normally, self-regulation only is preliminary; it is required until the competent agency itself has an opportunity to undertake its own risk assessment and act accordingly. Labelling and related requirements may have a preventive effect in that they deter the producer from placing particularly hazardous substances on the market.

5 Eco-labelling

Eco-labelling is an advertising technique whereby the producer tries to increase sales by advertising the environmentally-friendly properties of his product. In or-

---

35 See, for example, Sanford Lewis, The Right to Know About Toxic Hazards and Related Trends Towards Environmental Democracy in the United States, in Betty Gebers, Jerzy Jendroska (eds), *Environmental Control of Chemical Substances and Products*, Frankfurt-am-Main: Lang, 1994, p. 143.

36 Directive 92/32/EEC, OJ 1992 No. L 154 p. 1.

der to avoid misleading advertisement, some national laws, as well as the EC Eco-Label Regulation,[37] provide for an organized procedure for granting the label. Indirectly, the availability of the label will prompt environmentally-friendly product innovation. Conversely, there is also a certain danger of misleading consumers.[38] This is evident if the label only relates to the particular environmental properties of the product, rather than its overall environmental-friendliness and the necessary trade-offs to be made in respect of suitability and safety. By contrast, if, as the EC Eco-Labelling Regulation provides, the grant of the label is based on a comprehensive assessment of all the environmental impacts of the product, ranging from the preproduction stage (energy and raw materials consumption) to waste disposal, and a reduction of product quality and safety is prohibited, the consumer receives condensed or filtered information. This raises the question of why the consumer might not be directly informed about the environmental properties of products. Furthermore, unless the grant of the label is frequently revised, product innovation can be hampered.

IV   SELF-REGULATION THROUGH ORGANIZATION OF THE FIRM

1   General remarks

While the instruments of self-regulation discussed so far concern the firm's external relationships, either in the form of horizontal coordination as in the case of regulatory agreements, or in the form of vertical coordination or communication as in the case of implementation agreements and environmental information techniques, there is also room for purely internal instruments of self-regulation. For both voluntary compliance with existing legal or administrative requirements or the further-reaching target of environmentally-friendly management, an appropriate management system which includes both the formal organization of the firm (structural organization) and institutional arrangements for relevant activities within the firm (process organization) is an indispensable prerequisite for achieving these objectives.

In a market economy the determination of the firm's organization is, in principle, within the discretion of the entrepreneur, since organization is a response to the challenges of the firm's competitive environment. However, by imposing upon the firm particular organizational arrangements, the state may try to create frame-

---

37 Regulation No. 880/92, OJ 1992 No. L 99 p. 1.
38 Gerhard Roller, Der "Blaue Engel" und die "Europäische Blume", *Europäische Zeitschrift für Wirtschaftsrecht*, 1992, pp. 499–505; Ost (1992), *op.cit.*, pp. 172–3; James Salzman, *Environmental Labelling in OECD Countries*, Paris: OECD, 1991.

work conditions for self-regulation in the form of voluntary compliance and environmentally-friendly management.[39]

In an international perspective there are some countries that have widely used this organizational approach to self-regulation and others which prefer recourse to consensus- and information-based self-regulation. Although this is highly speculative, it may be suspected that the degree of market orientation and the power of public opinion play an important role here.

The problem with organizational intervention for promoting self-regulation is that it may cause overregulation that impairs the firm's organizational flexibility. The firm's organization is a highly sensitive area in which the state should not intervene without cogent reasons and, if it does, only in a considerate manner. However, so far, mandatory organizational requirements only set forth an organizational framework within which the entrepreneur has a wide margin of autonomous decision, or else they only reflect rules of good corporate governance that are generally accepted.

2   Environmental officers and directors

Apparently independently from one another, in the 1970s Germany and Japan both introduced the institution of an environmental officer (Japan also of an environmental controller) to be nominated by operators of polluting facilities whose emissions or wastes reach certain thresholds or which otherwise undertake hazardous activities.[40] In the USA, under some laws, the nomination of an environ-

---

39 See Eckard Rehbinder, Reflexive Law and Practice – The Corporate Officer for Environmental Protection as An Example, in Günter Teubner, Alberto Febbrajo, *State and Economy as Autopoietic Systems, European Yearbook in the Sociology of Law*, 1991–1992, pp. 579–608; idem, Umweltschutz und technische Sicherheit im Unternehmen aus juristischer Sicht, in *Umweltschutz und technische Sicherheit im Unternehmen*, Heidelberg: R.v.Deckers Verlag, 1993, pp. 29–68; Christopher Stone, Public Interest Representation: Economic and Social Policy Inside the Enterprise, in Klaus Hopt, Gunter Teubner (eds), *Corporate Governance and Directors' Liabilities*, Berlin: De Gruyter, 1985, pp. 122–46; Leonie Breunung, Joachim Nooke, Environmental Officers: A Viable Concept for Ecological Management?, in Gunter Teubner, Lindsay Farmer, Declan Murphy (eds), *Environmental Law and Ecological Responsibility*, London: John Wiley, 1994, pp. 267–97.

40 For Germany see Eckard Rehbinder, Andere Organe der Unternehmensverfassung, *Zeitschrift für Unternehmens- und Gesellschaftsrecht*, 1989, pp. 305–68; for Japan see Law concerning the nomination of environmental officers in certain facilities, Law No. 107 of 1971.

mental officer can be imposed ad hoc as a reaction to widespread violations of the relevant legal and administrative requirements.[41]

The relevant laws conceive the environmental officer as an organ of entrepreneurial self-responsibility, not as an internal watchdog in the service of the state. In Germany the officer has no competence to give directions to the personnel; rather, he is an independent adviser of the management. He or she has four functions: supervision, participation in process and product innovation; communication within the firm; and, to a certain extent, also representation of the firm to the authorities. The environmental officer must be heard before decisions on both important investments and the introduction of new processes and products. By contrast, the Japanese environmental officer is accorded the competence to give directions; he is a member of the upper management. While his functions are similar to the German counterpart, his representative function is more highly developed and his tasks concentrate on the technical operation of the plant.

In Germany the assessment of the environmental officer's effectiveness is controversial; this is especially true of his innovative function.[42] Although the hopes that the institutionalization of an 'environmental conscience' within the firm would incite significant efforts towards voluntary environmental protection have not been entirely fulfilled, the environmental officer is a well established part of environmental self-regulation in Germany. One reason for the deficiencies in his innovative function seems to be that, due to his normally low position in the enterprise hierarchy, he is excluded from strategic decisions. It has been concluded from this that the firm should, in addition, nominate a responsible director within the board of management who would concentrate responsibility for environmental protection and safety in one and the same holder of a management function.[43] Although, due to the fact that environmental tasks within the firm cross the boundaries of the normal functional elements of enterprise organization, such a model is not without problems, it should be seriously considered. The German legislature has gone some way in this direction in providing that operators of cer-

---

41 See Stone (1985), *op.cit.*, pp. 127–33.
42 See Rehbinder, *European Yearbook, op.cit.*, pp. 595–9; idem, *Umweltschutz und technische Sicherheit, op.cit.*, pp. 344–54.
43 Kloepfer *et al.* (1991), *op.cit.*, pp. 377–80, 384–5, 388; Rehbinder, *Unternehmen und technische Sicherheit, op.cit.*, pp. 46–53; for criticism, see K.H. Ladeur, Management of Environmental Risk by Proceduralization of the Enterprise – Proceduralization of the Enterprise by Proceduralization of Environmental Law, in Teubner, *op.cit.*, pp. 299, 316–29; Blecher, Environmental Officers: Management in an Ecological-Quality-Organization, in Teubner, *op.cit.*, pp. 237–61.

tain facilities must inform the competent authority as to which senior management person is responsible for environmental protection.[44]

In Japan, probably due to the higher ranking in the firm's hierarchy and his/her more limited tasks, the effectiveness of the environmental officer has been judged more favourably than in Germany. There has been a considerable improvement in communication with the agencies, and an important contribution to environmental innovation within firm firms.[45]

3 Functional organization

The Eco-Audit Regulation[46] requires the participating firms to establish an environmental management system and an appropriate environmental organization as a prerequisite for improving their substantive environmental performance; it is one of the tasks of the auditor also to check the firm's achievements in this respect. In some countries, such as the UK, normalization institutions have made great efforts to recommend models of environmental management and organization mainly to promote compliance with existing regulations and avoid civil liability.[47] Another, more interventionist, approach is used in Germany where certain plant operators must notify to the authority the environmental organization of the plant insofar as necessary for fulfilling their substantive obligations – namely to prevent danger to health and the environment and to take precautionary measures according to the state of the art.[48] It is doubtful to what extent the authority, after having received a notification, has a right of intervention. Since the law does not, and cannot, prescribe a particular organizational model, the plant operator in principle has a wide margin of discretion. It is only in extreme cases of evidently inadequate organization that the authority will be able to intervene.

This points to a certain weakness of this kind of incited self-regulation. In a market economy, the law can hardly prescribe organizational optimization, the more so since, in view of the variety and dynamics of types of business organization existing and developing in the real world, general criteria are difficult to establish. Thus, the obligations of plant operators in this respect are practically reduced to 'organizational common sense'. However, this does not exclude a further-

---

44 Para. 52a (1) Federal Immission Protection Act of 1974, as amended in 1990, OJ 1990 I p. 880; see Rehbinder, *Umweltschutz und technische Sicherheit, op.cit.*, pp. 39–46.
45 OECD, Environmental Performance Review: Japan, Paris: OECD, 1993, p. 104.
46 see note 29 above.
47 British Standard 7750 'Specification for environmental management systems'.
48 Para. 52a (2) Federal Immission Protection Act, note 46 above; see Gerhard Feldhaus, Umweltschutzsichernde Betriebsorganisation, *Neue Zeitschrift für Verwaltungsrecht*, 1991, pp. 927–35.

reaching effect as an incentive for optimization. The very existence of a notification obligation will cause plant operators to review the existing environmental organization and consider possible changes with a view to improving it. In other words, the notification obligation may initiate a learning process within the firm. Nevertheless, in this respect, the concept underlying the Eco-Audit Regulation, as well as the British standardization concept, may be superior.

4   Process-oriented obligations

Rather than trying to influence the firm's organizational structure, some laws intervene in its process organization in order to incite environmentally-friendly behaviour in key areas of environmental policy. Process intervention may also be additional to a structural one. For example, as provided in some states in the USA and also by the new German Waste Management Act, certain plant operators may be required to set forth concepts for the reduction of toxic emissions or the prevention of toxic waste.[49] Such requirements compel plant operators to develop a medium- and long-term policy of their own which sets concrete targets and strategies for implementing them. Since they have to report on the setting and the achievement of the targets to the authority, either regularly or on request, they are entangled in an ongoing discussion with the authority. While maintaining self-responsibility on the side of the firm and self-restraint on that of the authority, it is hoped that this will lead to cooperative learning towards environmentally friendly behaviour. Other examples of process-oriented techniques of self-regulation are documentation obligations as to the consideration of environmental problems at the stage of product development or obligations to undertake research and development for the solution of a particular environmental problem.

It is difficult to assess the effectiveness of these techniques. Due to their novelty, empirical evidence still is missing. The relevant obligations are more concrete than those of the more global eco-audit programme (in its substantive performance-related aspects) and their impact on the firm's behaviour may therefore be stronger.

---

49 Massachusetts Toxic Use Reduction Act of 1989; see Massachusetts Toxic Use Reduction Institute, *Toxic Chemical Management in Massachusetts*, Lowell/Mass., 1993; Para. 19 Waste Management Act of 1994, see note 10 above.

V SOME CONCLUDING REMARKS

Self-regulation, be it purely voluntary or incited by soft instruments, is not a panacea of modern, precautionary or proactive environmental law and policy. On the one hand, self-regulation in its various forms is capable of supplementing or filling gaps left by traditional command and control regulation as well as economic instruments, especially where concrete goals cannot yet be formulated or the complexity of the effects caused by using these instruments is prohibitive. On the other hand, with the mere appeal to self-responsibility the state accepts less, or at least less accurate, implementation of environmental policy objectives. While one may postulate that proactive environmental policy within the firm is necessary for the long-term survival of the market economy, the short-term constraints exerted by the very laws of the market economy are an important countervailing factor. Also, given the great variety of instruments of self-regulation, it must be admitted that a systematic approach to using these instruments is still missing. Uncoordinated use of several instruments side by side, or together with economic instruments can cause undesirable overlap and even overregulation. Self-regulation is still in its experimental phase.

FURTHER READINGS:

1   Ellen Basse, The Contract Model – The Merits of a Voluntary Approach, *Environmental Liability*, **2,** 1994, p. 74–84.
2   Eckard Rehbinder, Ecological Contracts: Agreements between Polluters and Local Communities, in Gunter Teubner, Lindsay Farmer, Declan Murphy (eds), *Environmental Law and Ecological Responsibility: The Concept and Practice of Ecological Self-Organization*, London: John Wiley, 1994, p. 145 at 151–155.
3   Christopher Stone, Public Interest Representation: Economic and Social Policy Inside the Enterprise, in Klaus Hopt, Gunter Teubner (eds), *Corporate Governance and Directors' Liabilities*, Berlin: De Gruyter, 1985, p. 122–146.
4   Jan van Dunné (ed.), *Environmental Contracts and Covenants: New Instruments for a Realistic Environmental Policy?*, Lelystad: Vermande, 1993.
5   Gerd Winter, Bartering Rationality in Regulation, *Law and Society Review,* **19,** 1985, pp. 219–250.

Part IV
The European Community
Framework

16 The Development of EC Environmental Law

Jan Jans

Table of Contents

I THE FIRST PHASE

The development of European environmental law can be split into a number of phases. The first phase started with the entry into force of the original version of the EEC Treaty on 1 January 1958 and continued up to 1972. This was the period during which the Community institutions paid no specific attention to the development of an environment policy. Only incidentally were decisions taken which, in retrospect, could perhaps be regarded as environmental measures, such as in 1967 Directive 67/548 Relating to the Classification, Packaging and Labelling of Dangerous Preparations, and the 1970 Directive 70/157 Relating to the Permissible Sound Level and the Exhaust System of Motor Vehicles. Although these were primarily measures taken with a view to the attainment of the common market, environmental considerations undoubtedly played a part.

II THE SECOND PHASE

In fact the true starting signal for the development of a European environment policy was only given in 1972 when a summit meeting of the heads of state or governments of the Member States of the EEC declared that economic expansion, which is not an end in itself, must as a priority help to attenuate the disparities in living conditions. It must emerge in an improved quality as well as an improved standard of living. Special attention should be paid to non-material values and wealth and to the protection of the environment so that progress shall serve mankind. The heads of state and government stressed the value of a Community environment policy.[1] They therefore requested the Community institutions to draw up an action programme with a precise schedule before 31 July 1973. This Declaration marked the beginning of the second phase, which lasted until the entry into force of the Single European Act on 1 July 1987.

In the Declaration of the Council of the European Communities and of the representatives of the Governments of the Member States meeting in the Council of 22 November 1973 on the programme of action of the European Communities on the environment, we read:

> Whereas in particular, in accordance with Article 2 of the Treaty, the task of the European Economic Community is to promote throughout the Community a harmonious development of economic activities and a continuous and balanced expansion, which cannot be imagined in the absence of an effective campaign to combat pollution and nuisance or of an improvement in the quality of life and the protection of the environment.

Although the term 'environmental protection' was not as such to be found in the objectives enumerated in Articles 2 and 3 of the EEC Treaty in those days, this Declaration did in effect mean that, by an 'extensive' interpretation of 'economic expansion', which is expressly included as an aim in Article 2, environmental protection could become the subject of Community decision-making. Henceforth economic expansion was to be regarded not only in quantitative terms, but also qualitatively. Despite the Declaration, the issue of the extent of the competence of the EEC to effect a comprehensive environment policy remained a matter of controversy. Nevertheless, many tens of Directives and regulations have been adopted on almost every conceivable aspect of environment policy since 1971. One feature of this second phase was that policy which was specifically presented as Community environment policy was developed on the basis of a treaty which had no specific environmental slant.

In this second phase, decision-making in respect of European environment policy was based primarily on Articles 100 and 235 of the EEC Treaty. Examples of environmental measures dating from this period that were based exclusively on Article 100 are:

- Directive 85/210 concerning the lead content of petrol;
- Directive 73/404 relating to detergents;
- Directive 78/1015 on the permissible sound level and exhaust system of motor cycles.

Article 100 could be used where differences in national environmental laws had a detrimental effect on the common market. This practice was confirmed by the

---

[1]   Bulletin EG 1972, no. 10.

Court of Justice in Case 92/79, in a decision in which the validity of Directive 75/716 relating to the maximum sulphur content of liquid fuels was raised. In the words of the Court:

> It is by no means ruled out that provisions on the environment may be based upon Article 100 of the Treaty. Provisions which are made necessary by considerations relating to the environment and health may be a burden upon undertakings to which they apply and if there is no harmonization of national provisions on the matter, competition may be appreciably distorted.

Most of the Community's environmental decisions which date from the period before the Single European Act are based on both Article 100 and Article 235. Important examples include:

- Directive 76/464 on pollution caused by certain dangerous substances discharged into the aquatic environment of the Community;
- Directive 84/360 on the combating of air pollution from industrial plants;
- Directive 82/501 on the major accident hazards of certain industrial plants; and
- Directive 78/319 on toxic and dangerous waste.

In practice it was apparent that there was a clear need for an additional legal basis besides Article 100 in the field of environmental protection. After all, the objectives of Article 100, namely the prevention, elimination and avoidance of distortion of competition, placed constraints on the use that could be made of that Article as a legal basis for environment policy. On the principle that the Community's powers extend only to what has been conferred by the Treaty, Article 100 cannot be employed where other, or more far-reaching, environmental measures have to be taken than are necessary for the proper functioning of the common market. Article 3(h) of the Treaty also provides that the approximation of laws is only possible 'to the extent required for the proper functioning of the common market.'

To provide for this lacuna the Council would generally invoke Article 235. This article can be used 'if action by the Community should prove necessary to attain, in the course of the operation of the common market, one of the objectives of the Community and this Treaty has not provided the necessary powers'. It has already been noted that, by extensive interpretation of Article 2 of the Treaty, environmental protection was considered an objective of the Community.

This was confirmed by the Court of Justice in 1985[2] in a case concerning the validity of a Directive on the disposal of waste oils. It was contended that provisions imposing a system of permits on undertakings which disposed of waste oils and a system of zones within which such undertakings had to operate were incom-

---

2 Case 240/483 (the ADBHU case).

patible with the principle of the free movement of goods. The Directive in question was based on both Article 100 and Article 235. This joint legal basis was justified in the preamble to the Directive as follows. On the one hand it was pointed out that any disparity between the provisions on the disposal of waste oils in the various Member States could create unequal conditions of competition, thus necessitating the use of Article 100 as the legal basis for approximation. On the other hand the Council felt it necessary to accompany this approximation of laws by wider regulations so that one of the aims of the Community – protection of the environment – could be achieved. For this purpose it invoked Article 235 as an additional legal basis. The Court held as follows:

> In the first place it should be observed that the principle of freedom of trade is not to be viewed in absolute terms but is subject to certain limits justified by the objectives of general interest pursued by the Community provided that the rights in question are not substantively impaired. There is no reason to conclude that the directive has exceeded those limits. The directive must be seen in the perspective of environmental protection, which is one of the Community's essential objectives.

The Court continued:

> It follows from the foregoing that the measures prescribed by the directive do not create barriers to intra-Community trade, and that is in so far as such measures, in particular the requirement that permits must be obtained in advance, have a restrictive effect on the freedom of trade and of competion, they must nevertheless neither be discriminatory nor go beyond the inevitable restrictions which are justified by the pursuit of the objective of environmental protection, which is in the general interest. That being so, Articles 5 and 6 cannot be regarded as incompatible with the fundamental principles of Community law mentioned above.

The significance of this decision was that the Court had for the first time recognized 'environmental protection' as one of the Community's essential objectives. This meant that Article 235 could be used not only as a supplementary legal basis to Article 100, but could itself form the legal basis for Community environment policy.

An example of a Directive based solely on Article 235 is Directive 79/409 on the conservation of wild birds. Nevertheless, only a few measures have been based solely on Article 235, for example, Directive 82/884 on a limit value for lead in the air, Recommendation 81/972 concerning the re-use of paper and the use of recycled paper, and Decision 82/795 on the consolidation of precautionary measures concerning chlorofluorocarbons in the environment.

III THE THIRD PHASE

The third phase in the development of the Community's environment policy commenced on 1 July 1987, the date when the changes to the EEC Treaty brought about by the Single European Act came into force, and continued until the date the Treaty on European Union ('Maastricht') entered into force. Although the case law of the Court of Justice had specifically dealt with environmental protection before then, this phase was notable because for the first time the objectives of the Community's environment policy were enshrined in the Treaty. The inclusion in the Treaty of provisions designed specifically to protect the environment, for example Articles 130r, 130s, 130t, 100a(3) and 100a(4), confirmed the Community's task in developing a Community environment policy. The Treaty incorporated specific powers aimed at the protection of the environment. In accordance with the principle of subsidiarity, these powers were only to be exercised if the Community's environmental objectives could be attained better at Community level than at the level of the individual Member States.[3]

In view of these express environmental powers, it is not surprising that Article 235 is now hardly ever invoked as a legal basis for environmental measures. Articles 100a and 130r–t make this unnecessary. Only in exceptional cases are environmental measures still based on Article 235, such as Directive 93/76 to limit carbon dioxide emissions by improving energy efficiency.

IV THE FOURTH PHASE

The fourth, and current, phase of European environmental law starts with the entry into force on 1 November 1993 of the Treaty on European Union – in other words, the post-Maastricht phase. For the first time the term 'environment' is actually referred to in the key Articles 2 and 3 of the Treaty, which set out the objectives and activities of the Union. Article 2 now refers to 'the promotion, throughout the Union, of a harmonious and balanced development of economic activities, sustainable and non-inflationary growth respecting the environment', while Article 3(k) states that one of the activities for attaining this is 'a policy in the sphere of the environment'.

The formulation 'sustainable growth' in Article 2 can be criticized as being a departure from the more usual formulation 'sustainable development'. From the point of view of environmental protection, the concept of 'sustainable growth' seems marginally weaker than that of 'sustainable development'. However, it seems unlikely that this will have significant legal consequences. 'Sustainability'

---

[3] Art. 130r(4), EEC Treaty.

is referred to in other of the Treaty's articles. Article B of the Treaty on European Union, for example, states that one of the Union's objectives is 'to promote economic and social progress, which is balanced and sustainable'. As far as it goes, 'sustainable progress' would seem to allow slightly more room for policy on the environment than 'sustainable growth'. Another occurrence is in Article 130u(1) of the EEC Treaty, which states that, in the sphere of development cooperation, Community policy shall foster 'the sustainable economic and social development of the developing countries'. Thus the term 'sustainable development' is in fact used here. Finally, in the Declaration on Assessment of the Environmental Impact of Community Measures, in the Final Act of the Treaty,

> The Conference notes that the Commission undertakes its proposals, and that the Member States undertake in implementing those proposals, to take full account of their environmental impact and of the principle of sustainable growth.

Be that as it may, the incorporation of an environmental objective can certainly be said to be of great political significance. We jurists will simply have to learn to live with this slightly unusual formulation.

The fourth phase is also distinct in that, for the first time, decisions under the Title on the Environment can now be taken by a qualified majority. The 'normal' decision-making procedure is the cooperation procedure set out in Article 189c of the Treaty. Another striking change as a result of Maastricht is the status given to the action programmes on the environment (Article 130s(3)). The increased powers of the European Parliament in the adoption of these programmes should also be noted. From now on these programmes will have to be adopted under what is known as the 'co-decision' procedure, referred to in Article 189b, which means the European Parliament can exercise a veto.

17 Objectives and Principles of EC Environmental Law

Jan Jans

Table of Contents

I THE OBJECTIVES

The objectives to be pursued by the Community policy on the environment are formulated in the first paragraph of Article 130r of the EC Treaty. They are:

- preserving, protecting and improving the quality of the environment;
- protecting human health;
- prudent and rational utilization of natural resources;
- promoting measures at international level to deal with regional or world-wide environmental problems.

1   Preserving, protecting and improving the quality of the environment

The first objective formulated in Article 130r is fairly general and indeterminate. The term 'environment' is given no further definition. On the one hand this is an advantage in that the objective is sufficiently flexible to be adapted to new developments and new needs for protection. On the other hand, it is impossible to determine with absolute certainty from the Treaty itself what might, under Community law, be understood by a Community environment policy. The following problems of interpretation present themselves in connection with the uncertain scope of these environmental objectives.

Does the objective also include protection of nature and landscape values? Having regard to the Habitat Directive, I would suggest that it does. The first consideration of the preamble to this directive states that the preservation, protection and improvement of the quality of the environment, 'including the conservation of natural habitats and of wild fauna and flora, are an essential objective of general interest pursued by the Community, as stated in Article 130r of the Treaty'.

Not only measures which result directly in the improvement of the environment fall under this objective, but also those which result in the improvement of the environment in a more indirect fashion fall within its scope. In the preamble to Directive 90/313 on the freedom of access to information on the environment, the Council states that access to information on the environment held by public authorities 'will improve environmental protection'. More generally, it is.arguable that decision-making in respect of the non-substantive or procedural aspects of environmental legislation, such as issues of legal protection, authorization procedures and even measures concerning the administrative organization of the environment sector, is also within its compass. Eco-audit Regulation 1836/93 also clearly falls within the sphere of this objective.

In the pre-Maastricht period, the territorial limitation or otherwise of the Community's environmental objective was a matter for discussion. In other words, can the Community act not so much to protect its 'own' environment, but to preserve the environment outside the Community, to address global and regional environmental problems, or even the environment of other states? This problem of interpretation has largely been resolved. Now the fourth objective of Article 130r explicitly includes 'promoting measures at international level to deal with regional or worldwide environmental problems'. This objective will be discussed in slightly more detail below.

An entirely different matter is the question whether the Community is entitled to concern itself with local and regional environmental problems. As Article 130r does not contain any such restriction, this must be regarded as a possibility. Of course, the principle of subsidiarity would have to be taken into consideration here, which might require restraint in this respect. Article 2(3) of the Habitat Directive is relevant in this context. Protective measures taken pursuant to this Directive must explicitly take account of 'regional and local characteristics.'

The final problem of interpretation I wish to discuss concerns the formulation 'preserving, protecting and improving'. This is also broadly and flexibly worded. It affords possibilities to take environmental measures of a preservative, curative, repressive, precautionary and active nature. There is no question of a restriction to a certain type of measure. A reference to preserving, protecting and improving the quality of the environment can, for example, be found in the preamble to Directive 93/12 on the sulphur content of certain liquid fuels.

2 Protecting human health

The most important question of interpretation in respect of this objective is whether 'protecting human health' is a wider concept than protecting public health. The answer must be that it is. Protection of public health indicates measures required to protect the collective health interests of people in a given society. However, the wording of Article 130r makes action possible even when it is not so much a collective interest that is at stake as the interest of certain individuals or groups in society. Of course the principle of subsidiarity must be taken into account in such cases.

It should be noted that the distinction between the two concepts has become blurred in the decisions of the Court of Justice as, for example, in the Fumicot case,[1] where the applicability of Article 36 to measures restricting the importation of plant protection products was at issue. Article 36 does in fact talk of the protection of health and life of humans, animals or plants, and not of 'public health'. However, in its judgement (at para. 13) the Court equates the two concepts:

> In that respect, it is not disputed that the national rules in question are intended to protect public health and that they therefore come within the exception provided for in Article 36.

A second problem of interpretation concerns the fact that the Article only refers to human health. Does this therefore mean that the protection of flora and fauna must be regarded as lying outside the scope of the objective? On the other hand it has been shown above that the protection of flora and fauna may be included within the first objective mentioned in Article 130r. The restriction of the second objective to the protection of human health does not therefore seem essential.

---

[1] Case 272/80.

A reference to this objective can, for example, be found in Directive 92/3 (Euratom) on the supervision and control of shipments of radioactive waste between Member States and into and out of the Community.

3   Prudent and rational utilization of natural resources

The inclusion of this objective in the Treaty at the time of the Single European Act was accompanied by the following declaration in the Final Act:

> The Conference confirms that the Community's activities in the sphere of the environment may not interfere with national policies regarding the exploitation of energy resources.

In the literature only limited value is attached to this declaration – first because in legal terms such declarations derogate but little from the express text of a treaty and, second because it refers only to the exploitation and not the use of energy resources. One practical example where this declaration did have some legal effect is Article 6 of Directive 88/609 on emissions from large combustion plants. This provides that Member States may authorize plants to exceed the normal emission limit values contained in the Directive, if 'major difficulties connected with the nature of the lignite so require and provided that lignite is an essential source of fuel for the plants'

What precisely should be understood by 'natural resources' is not entirely clear. From an international law point of view, Principle 2 of the Declaration of the United Nations Conference on the Human Environment (the Stockholm Declaration) may offer some assistance. Here natural resources are taken to mean: 'natural resources of the earth including the air, water, land, flora and fauna and especially representative samples of natural ecosystems...'. The following natural resources are referred to in the literature: wood, minerals, water, oil, gas and chemical substances. Sevenster mentions the following policy items which might give some indication as to what might fall under the management of natural resources: nature conservation, soil protection, waste disposal (encouraging re-use), policy on urban areas, coastal areas and mountaineous areas, disaster policy, water management, an environmentally friendly agricultural policy and energy-saving.[2]

On the basis of the above it can be concluded that this objective also has a wide scope. References to this objective can be found in Directive 91/676 on nitrates (protection of living resources), in Directive 93/76 to limit carbon dioxide emissions by improving energy efficiency (rational use of oil products, natural gas and

---

[2]   H.G. Sevenster, *Milieubeleid en Gemeenschapsrecht*. Leiden: Dissertatie RU, 1992, p.100.

solid fuels) and in Directive 92/42 on efficiency requirements for new oil- and gas-fired hot-water boilers. This directive explicitly refers to a prudent and rational utilization of natural resources.

4   Promoting measures at international level to deal with regional or world-wide environmental problems

As has already been mentioned, at the time of the Single European Act the question to what extent the environmental objectives of the Community were limited in a territorial sense was a matter of discussion. An important part of European environment policy is not concerned primarily with protecting the Union's own environment, but also the environment outside the Union. The following are examples of this:

- Regulation 2455/92 concerning the export and import of certain dangerous chemicals, in which the preamble states that measures are necessary for the protection of man and the environment in both the Community and third countries;
- Regulation 3254/91 prohibiting the introduction of pelts;
- Regulation 348/81 concerning the protection of whales;
- Directive 89/370 concerning the importation of skins of seal pups;
- the measures concerning the export of waste to countries outside the EC;
- Regulation 3626/82 on the implementation in the Community of the Convention on international trade in endangered species of wild fauna and flora (CITES).

In addition the Union is a party to several multilateral conventions which have an extraterritorial objective, such as the 1985 Vienna Convention for the protection of the ozone layer and the 1987 Montreal Protocol, the 1989 Basel Convention on the control of transboundary movements of waste, the 1992 Framework Convention on Climate Change and the 1992 Convention on Biological Diversity.

The question of the territorial limitation of the Community's environmental competence has hardly been considered by legal writers. While the Single European Act applied, if any mention was made of the subject at all it went no further than the bald statement that, in view of the fact that the objectives in Article 130r are not restricted in a territorial sense, the Community is competent to engage in extraterritorial protection of the environment. However, this statement and this interpretation of Article 130r do little justice to the fact that extraterritorial protection may, under certain circumstances, clash with legitimate claims to jurisdiction on the part of third states and thus give rise to conflicts.

The Community could easily be told to mind its own business. Or, put in legal terms: the Community could be said to be interfering with matters falling within the domestic jurisdiction of a sovereign state. An interpretation of Article 130r which would put the Community in breach of its international law obligations must therefore be rejected. In other words, if Article 130r leaves room for extra-territorial action, this must in any event be interpreted in conformity with international law.

In the present, post-Maastricht version of the Treaty, it has at any rate become clear that Article 130r does in principle allow room for extraterritorial environmental objectives. By the inclusion of 'promoting measures at international level to deal with regional or worldwide environmental problems', existing practice has been confirmed and given the status of treaty law.

Nevertheless, this phrase is still unclear in several respects. For example, is it intended to exclude unilateral measures? A large part of the Community's present extraterritorial environment policy has in fact been created by means of such measures.

Nor is it clear whether, by referring only to 'regional or worldwide' problems, action to protect the environment of only one or a few third states is excluded. Take, for example, a prohibition of imports of tropical hardwood that has not been sustainably produced. It is highly debatable whether this would amount to a regional or worldwide environmental problem. In general, this kind of case will involve specific consequences for the environment in one state or a number of states.

For the time being I would like to argue in favour of not interpreting Article 130r too narrowly. Nor would I wish to exclude, a priori, unilateral environmental measures or environmental measures directed at protecting the environment in only one state or a few states, even though the problem of the international law constraints is at its most pronounced in this very case.

II   THE PRINCIPLES OF EUROPEAN ENVIRONMENT POLICY

Article 130r(2) sets out the principles on which European environment policy is based. These are:

- preserving, protecting and improving the quality of the environment;
- protecting human health;
- prudent and rational utilization of natural resources;
- promoting measures at international level to deal with regional or worldwide environmental problems.

1   High level of protection

Article 100a(3) of the Single European Act (SEA) provides that the Commission, in its internal market proposals in the field of environmental protection will take as a base a high level of protection. This proposal was criticized as being directed only at the Commission and that the Council, as the ultimate decision-making body, can depart from the Commission's proposals. It is also doubtful to what extent the prescription in the Article is open to review by the courts. Suppose the Council were to take its decision in conformity with the Commission's proposal. Could it then be argued before the courts that the decision was invalid because it did not take as a base a high level of protection? It seems hardly conceivable.

Another objection to Article 100a(3) was the fact that the principle of a high level of protection was only mentioned in the context of the establishment of the internal market and not in the Treaty's specific title on the environment. 'Maastricht' changed this, and the principle now goes even further than Article 100a(3). Article 130r(2) of the Maastricht Treaty does not refer to proposals from the Commission, but to the 'Community', in other words, including the Council. Nevertheless there still seems to be no question of its being legally enforceable. Community policy 'shall aim' at a high level of protection 'taking into account the diversity of situations in the various regions of the Community'. In fact this addition is totally unnecessary, as a similar formulation was also included in Article 130r(3), second indent. It is now stated twice.

2   The precautionary principle

A new feature of the Treaty is that the Community's environment policy is based on the precautionary principle which has its roots in what is described in German environmental law as the *Vorsorgeprinzip*. This means that, if there is a strong suspicion that a certain activity may have environmentally harmful consequences, it is better to act 'before it is too late' rather than wait until scientific evidence is available which incontrovertibly shows the causal connection.

In this context it has rightly been pointed out the consequences of this principle for the interpretation of the first sentence of Article 130r(3), which provides that in preparing its policy on the environment, the Community shall take account of 'available scientific and technical data'.[3] While the SEA applied, this could easily have been used by the Community as a ground for not acting until there was absolute proof of the causes of certain undesirable environmental effects. Such an interpretation would now be at odds with the precautionary principle. It could even

---

[3]   Ibid., p. 407.

have the opposite effect: tentative and indicative scientific data might now well be sufficient ground on which to take measures to protect the environment.

3   The prevention principle

The principle of preventive action was included in the Treaty by the SEA. Put simply, 'prevention is better than cure'. The prevention principle allows action to be taken to protect the environment at an early stage. It is no longer primarily a question of repairing damage after it has occurred. Instead the principle calls for measures to be taken to prevent damage in the first place. The prevention principle must not be confused with the precautionary principle. The latter is more far-reaching (see above).

A strong focus on the prevention principle was made in the Third Environmental Action Programme .[4] Prevention rather than cure was the central element of this programme. According to the programme the following conditions must be met *inter alia*, if the prevention principle is to have full effect:

- The requisite knowledge and information must be improved and made readily available to decision-makers and all interested parties, including the public. See for instance Council Directive 90/313 on the Freedom of Access to Information on the Environment.
- Procedures for judgement must be formulated and introduced, which will ensure that the appropriate facts are considered early in the decision-making processes relating to any activity likely significantly to affect the environment. In this respect the EIA Directive should be mentioned. The preamble to the Environmental Impact Assessment Directive (85/337), referring to the first three Environmental Action Programmes, states 'that the best environment policy consists in preventing the creation of pollution or nuisances at source, rather than subsequently trying to counteract their effects'. For the same reason account should be taken of the consequences of planning and decision-making processes for the environment at as early a stage as possible. Environmental impact assessment is an excellent example of an instrument in which the principle of prevention plays a vital role.
- The implementation of adopted measures must be monitored to ensure their correct application and their adaptation if circumstances or new knowledge should so require. In this respect one could point at provisions in Directives concerning the adaptation of technical standards to technical and scientific progress (for instance Article 13 of the Sewage Sludge Directive 86/278). Another example is Directive 80/68 on the protection of groundwater. This Directive imposes extensive monitoring and survey requirements on Mem-

---

4   OJ 1983, C 46/1.

ber States. Before the competent authorities may grant an authorization to discharge substances, a detailed investigation of the effects on the environment must have been carried out.

4   The source principle

According to the source principle, environmental damage should preferably be prevented at source, rather than by using 'end-of-pipe technology'. This principle also implies a preference for emission standards rather than environmental quality standards, especially to deal with water and air pollution. This preference becomes abundantly clear if we examine the Community's water quality legislation. Article 6(1) of Directive 76/464 on pollution of the aquatic environment provides for threshold values which emissions standards must not exceed for substances on the black list. A Member State can, however, opt to observe quality objectives rather than emission thresholds, but only where the Member State can prove to the Commission that the quality objectives are being maintained throughout the area affected by the discharges. Here water-quality objectives are clearly a 'second-best' solution. This is even clearer in the TiO2 Directive (92/112). Here too the threshold values laid down in the Directive will normally apply. Alternatively, under Article 8(1), Member States may choose to make use of quality objectives. However, this does require the permission of the Commission.

The principle was given an unexpected extension in Case C-2/90,[5] where the Court of Justice applied it in determining to what extent Walloon measures restricting imports of foreign waste were discriminatory. The Court held that the principle means that every region, municipality or other local authority must take those measures necessary to ensure the reception, processing and removal of its own waste. The waste must be disposed of as close as possible to the place of production in order to limit its transport as far as possible. Consequently the Court held that, in view of the differences between the waste produced at various locations and the connection with the place of its production, the Walloon restrictions could not be considered discriminatory. In this case the source principle was thus equated with what is known as the 'proximity principle' in the law on waste.

5   The 'polluter pays' principle

Community action is based on the 'polluter pays' principle. This principle was one of the cornerstones of Community environment policy even before it was incorpo-

---

[5]   *Walloon waste*, not yet reported. Reprinted in L. Krämer, *EC Environmental Law*, London: Sweet and Maxwell, 1993, p. 71.

rated into the Treaty. It was referred to as a principle of Community environment policy in the First Action Programme on the Environment.

The 'polluter pays' principle is set out in a Communication from the Commission to the Council in 1975 regarding cost allocation and action by public authorities on environmental matters. According to the resolution on the Fourth Environmental Action Programme, the 1975 communication is still the guiding principle for policy in that respect. The communication is not as such binding. The Council has, however, recommended that Member States conform to the principles contained in the communication. Both the communication and the recommendation were prompted by the consideration that the costs connected with the protection of the environment against pollution should be allocated according to the same principles throughout the Community, on the one hand to avoid distortions of competition affecting trade, which would be incompatible with the proper functioning of the common market, and on the other, to further the aims set out in the First Action Programme on the Environment.

This programme is based on the principle that charging polluters the costs of action to combat the pollution they cause will encourage them to reduce that pollution and endeavour to find less polluting products or technologies. This would enable a more rational use to be made of scarce environmental resources. Apart from the use of charges, the principle can also be implemented by imposing environmental standards. Companies which are required to observe environmental standards will have to make various investments in their production process if they are to comply with the statutory standards. Setting standards in this way also helps ensure that the polluter bears the cost of pollution.

The Community must therefore ensure, especially by laying down standards and environmental charges, that persons who are responsible for pollution in fact bear the cost. In other words environmental protection should not in principle depend on policies which rely on grants of aid and place the burden of combating pollution on the Community.

The 'polluter pays' principle is of particular relevance with respect to new Community guidelines on state aid for environmental protection.[6] According to the Commission the application of the EC Treaty rules on State aid (Articles 92-94) must reflect the role economic instruments can play in environmental policy. This means taking account of a broader range of financial measures in this area. Aid control and environmental policy must, in the Commission's view, also support one another in ensuring stricter application of the polluter pays principle.

In secondary EU legislation several references to the 'polluter pays' principle can be found. Article 15 of the Waste Directive 75/442 states that, in accordance with the 'polluter pays' principle, the cost of disposing of waste must be borne by:

---

[6]   OJ 1994, C 72/3.

- the holder who has waste handled by a waste collector or by an undertaking authorized to carry out waste disposal activities; or
- the previous holders or the producer of the product from which the waste came.

Article 14 of the Waste Oils Directive 75/439 provides that indemnities may be granted to collection and/or disposal undertakings for services rendered. These indemnities may be financed by a charge imposed on products which, after use, are transformed into waste oils, or on waste oils. The financing of indemnities must be in accordance with the 'polluter pays' principle (Article 15). According to the Court of Justice in the ADBHU Case,[7] provisions like these do not conflict with the Treaty rules on state aid.

6   The integration principle

Perhaps the most important of all the principles mentioned in Article 130r(2) is the integration principle: 'Environmental protection requirements must be integrated into the definition and implementation of other Community policies.' This refers to what is known as 'external' integration – in other words, the integration of environmental objectives in other policy sectors.[8]

   The Maastricht version of the integration principle differs from the version under the SEA. There it was provided that 'Environmental protection requirements shall be a component of the Community's other policies'. The Maastricht version is clearly stronger, as is the explicit reference to both 'definition' and 'implementation'. The addition of 'other Community policies' also makes it clear that the operation of the principle is not confined to Part Three of the Treaty, entitled 'Community Policies', but extends to the entire Treaty.

   The first question which presents itself is what precisely has to be integrated. The Treaty refers to 'environmental protection requirements'. What should this be taken to mean? Certainly it would seem to include the objectives of Article 130r(1). It also seems likely that it includes the other principles referred to in Article 130r(2), such as the precautionary principle and the principle that preventive action should be taken. And, finally, integration of the policy aspects referred to in Article 130r(3) should not *a priori* be excluded, although it is true that the Treaty does not state that these aspects have to be integrated, but only that they should be taken into account. This wide interpretation of the integration principle in effect leads to a general obligation on the Community institutions to reach an integrated

---

[7]   Case 240/83, ECR 1975, 531.
[8]   See further Chapter 1 by R. Macrory in this volume.

and balanced assessment of all the relevant environmental aspects when adopting other policy. The Declaration on Assessment of the Environmental Impact of Community measures in the Final Act of the Treaty on European Union provides support for this interpretation. It states:

> The Conference notes that the Commission undertakes in its proposals, and that the Member States undertake in implementing those proposals, to take full account of their environmental impact and of the principle of sustainable growth.

The next problem concerns the question whether the integration principle implies that the Community's environment policy has been given some measure of priority over other of the Community's policy areas. All the more so because the integration principle is only to be found in the field of environment policy. Probably it has not, at least if by priority it is meant that, in the event of a conflict with other policy areas, the Community's environment policy has a certain added value from a legal point of view. The text of the Treaty does not support such a conclusion. The integration principle is designed to ensure that protection of the environment is at least taken into consideration, even when commercial policy is involved or when other decisions are being taken, for example in the fields of agriculture, transport,[9] development aid, regional policy and so on, and which has to be worked out in more detail in those areas. However, the manner in which potential conflicts between protection of the environment and, for example, the functioning of the internal market should be resolved cannot be inferred from the integration principle as such. I would advocate that such conflicts be resolved against the background of the body of case law established by the Court of Justice in respect of the principle of proportionality. If Community legislation for the protection of the environment, which the Court has already designated one of the essential objectives of the Community in the ADBHU case, results in restrictions of trade, this is regarded as permissible as long as the measures are not discriminatory and do not entail restrictions that go beyond what is strictly necessary for the protection of the environment. The principle of proportionality may also prove a useful guide in relation to other areas of policy in which conflicts flowing from the integration principle are involved.

At the same time it should be noted that when interpreting Article 39 of the EC Treaty, in the context of the Community's agricultural policy, the Court also has to weigh various objectives against each other. The institutions of the EC have wide discretionary powers when harmonizing policy in relation to the various objectives contained in Article 39 (increasing productivity, ensuring a fair standard

---

[9]   Case C-17/90, *Pinaud Wieger*, ECR 1991, I-5253; Regulation 1738/93, Art. 7(1); Case C-195/90, *Commission* v. *Germany*, not yet reported.

of living for the agricultural community, stabilizing markets, assuring the stability of supplies and ensuring supplies reach consumers at reasonable prices). One or more of these objectives may (temporarily) be given priority, as long as the policy does not become so focused on a single objective that the attainment of other objectives is made impossible. This approach could also be employed in respect of the environment. It would then be arguable that, if a given objective could adequately be achieved in a variety of ways, the integration principle would entail a choice for the least environmentally harmful.

Having addressed the question of the priority of the Community's environment policy, the problem of the legal enforceability of the integration principle looms large. I would like to make the following comments on this point. The Court's decisions clearly show that the contention that the integration principle is of no value whatever is not correct. For example, the principle fulfils an important function in the choice of the proper legal basis of environmental measures. In the first Chernobyl case,[10] at issue was whether Regulation 3955/87 on the conditions governing imports of agricultural products originating in third countries following the accident at the Chernobyl power station was rightly based on Article 113 rather than Article 130s. The Court held that the provision contained in the second sentence of Article 130r(2), 'which reflects the principle whereby all Community measures must satisfy the requirements of environmental protection, implies that a Community measure cannot be part of Community action on environmental matters merely because it takes account of those requirements'. In the TiO^2 case,[11] the Court confirmed this, stating: 'That principle implies that a Community measure cannot be covered by Article 130s merely because it also pursues objectives of environmental protection.'

A second legal consequence of the integration principle, closely connected with the above, is the following. The principle broadens the objectives of the other powers laid down in the Treaty and thus limits the role of the 'attributed powers' doctrine in environmental policy. The Chernobyl case and the TiO^2 case demonstrate that 'environmental objectives' can be pursued in the context of the Community's common commercial policy and its internal market policy. Without the integration principle, it is debatable to what extent environmental objectives, for example in connection with the approximation of laws for the attainment of the internal market, could be taken into account by the Council. It was not without reason that most Community environmental measures in the period prior to the SEA were based on a combination of Articles 100 and 235. The powers of approximation are limited in Article 3(h) 'to the extent required for the proper functioning of the common market'. And because the requirements of a properly functioning com-

---

[10] Case C- 62/88, ECR 1990, I-1527.
[11] Case C-300/89, ECR 1991, I-2867.

mon market were not always and automatically synonymous with the requirements of environmental protection, it was necessary to invoke the additional legal basis supplied by Article 235. The integration principle makes such artificial devices unnecessary. Not only does it extend the objectives of the internal market policy and the common commercial policy, but environmental objectives can also be taken into account in other policy areas without the attributed powers doctrine interfering. Thus in the *Pinaud Wieger* case[12] the Court held that the achievement of freedom to provide services in the transport sector can only be attained in an orderly fashion in the context of a common transport policy 'which takes into consideration the economic, social and ecological problems'.[13]

In this respect two fields should be noted where the role of the integration principle could potentially be very important. First, the principle seems to imply that the impact on the environment can be taken into account when the Commission is considering whether or not to grant an exemption under Article 85(3) to the prohibitions on restrictive agreements contained in Article 85(1). Another example is the Commission's practice of granting aid under Article 92(3). It can now take the environmental consequences of national grants of aid into account when deciding whether or not to approve such aid.[14]

A third aspect which is important when evaluating the legal status of the integration principle is whether the legitimacy of actions of the Council and Commission can be reviewed by the Court in the light of the principle. Can the validity of a Directive or regulation, for example in the field of transport or agriculture, be questioned on the grounds that the decision has infringed the environmental objectives of the Treaty? In other words, the question as to the legal enforceability of the principle is in fact a question as to the legal significance of the objectives, principles and other aspects referred to in Article 130r(1), (2) and (3). It has already been noted that the present version of the principle has been formulated more forcefully ('must be integrated') than under the SEA. In principle the review of Community measures in the light of the environmental objectives should therefore be regarded as possible. Indeed, in its decision in the first Chernobyl case, the Court speaks in just such strong terms ('must satisfy the requirements of environmental protection'). However, it should be borne in mind that the institutions have wide discretionary powers as to how they shape the environment policy, whereby they will have to balance the relative importance of the environmental objectives and other Community objectives. Only in very exceptional cases will a measure be susceptible to annulment (or be declared invalid) because certain environmental objectives seem not to have been taken sufficiently into account. Another factor

---

[12]   See note 9 above.
[13]   See also Case 195/90 cited in note 9 above
[14]   See the new EU guidelines on state aid for environmental protection, OJ 1994, C 72/3.

that will probably also have to be taken into account is that the degree to which measures are open to judicial review may differ depending on whether the objectives of Article 130r(1), the principles of Article 130r(2) or the policy aspects of Article 130r(3) are involved. As far as the latter are concerned, the Treaty states that the Community shall 'take account of' these aspects, which is not the same as observing them. Besides this, Article 130r(2) states that the Community shall 'aim' at a high level of protection. The conclusion must surely be that the application of the integration principle is amenable to judicial review, but that the extent of that review is limited and may differ from one case to the next.

The following two cases are relevant in this respect.[15] First, the Irish environmental protection organization An Taisce has invoked Article 173 against a decision by the Commission not to suspend or withdraw the allocation of Community structural funds for financing a visitors centre in a nature reserve in Mullaghmore. Article 7 of Regulation 2052/88 provides that measures financed by the Community's financial instruments must be in keeping with, *inter alia*, Community policy on environmental protection. This Article is one of the rare applications of the integration principle in Community secondary legislation. The Court however did not decide on the matter, because the action for annulment was declared inadmissable. The appeal procedure is currently pending at the Court of Justice. The other case, *Greenpeace* v. *Commission*, is similar and concerns the Commission's financing of two power stations on the Canary Islands. Here, too, an action has been brought for annulment, *inter alia* because of infringement of the integration principle.

A final question I would like to discuss in connection with this principle is that of the possible consequences for Member States. In principle, in view of the fact that the text of the Treaty expressly refers to 'Community policy', the integration principle should have no direct legal consequences for the Member States. Of course, there will be indirect effects, in the sense that the Council and the Commission will observe the principle in their legal acts, which are often addressed to the Member States and, because these are often integrated regulations and Directives, the Member States will also be required to observe a certain degree of integration.

On the other hand, it seems unlikely that the Member States will be bound by the environmental objectives and principles of the Treaty in areas that have not been harmonized, other than by the general obligation contained in Article 5. National environmental laws cannot be reviewed directly in the light of Article 130r(2) of the Treaty.[16]

---

[15]   Case C-461/93, *An Taisce* v. *Commission* and Case T-585/93, *Greenpeace* v. *Commission*.

[16]   See Case C-379/92, Peralta, ECR 1994, I-3453 at paras 55-59.

7   The safeguard clause

This clause is clearly of a different order from the above principles. It is debatable whether its place in the Treaty, next to the 'true' principles, is well chosen. The second paragraph of Article 130r(2) provides that a Directive or regulation may include a safeguard clause allowing Member States to take measures to protect the environment in cases of urgency. In practice there are many examples of this kind of safeguard clause, actually embodied in the Community measure in question. For example, Article 11 of Directive 91/414 concerning the placing of plant protection products on the market provides that, where a Member State has valid reasons to consider that a product which is authorized under the Directive constitutes a risk to human or animal health or the environment, it may provisionally restrict or prohibit the use and/or sale of that product on its territory. Another example is Article 31 of Directive 67/548, as amended by Directive 92/32, relating to the classification, packaging and labelling of dangerous preparations, which states:

> ...where in the light of new information, a Member State has justifiable reasons to consider that a substance, which has been accepted as satisfying the requirements of the Directive, nevertheless constitutes a danger for man or the environment, by reason of classification, packaging or labelling which is no longer appropriate, it may temporarily reclassify or, if necessary, prohibit the placing on the market of the substance or subject it to special conditions in its territory.

Here, too, the directive provides for an extensive monitoring and control procedure.

The question is to what extent the safeguard clause provided for in Article 130r(2) is really necessary, bearing in mind Article 130t. Under Article 130t Member States are entitled to take more stringent protective measures than those adopted pursuant to Article 130s. A safeguard clause under Article 130r(2) would, in my view, only be relevant if measures implementing 'total harmonization' could be based on Article 130s, notwithstanding the provisions of Article 130t. Only this interpretation would prevent Member States from taking more stringent protective measures under Article 130t in particular cases.

Use of a safeguard clause is allowed for 'non-economic environmental reasons'. This too is strange. After all, many environmental Directives already contain safeguard clauses designed to protect interests other than environmental interests – for example, Articles 9 and 10 of Directive 80/778 relating to the quality of water intended for human consumption, which provide that Member States may adopt lower standards than provided for in the Directive in order to take account of such situations as the nature and structure of the ground, or exceptional meteorological conditions. The minimum quality standards contained in the Directive may also be exceeded in the event of 'emergencies'. The present text of Article 130r(2) might suggest that this type of safeguard – not after all for 'environmental reasons' – is no longer possible. This would be extremely unfortunate. It would prevent Member States from acting in emergencies to protect wider interests of a higher order than environmental interests.[17]

A similar clause can also be found in Article 100a(5), although that refers to 'one or more of the non-economic reasons referred to in Article 36'. This does offer a possibility to exceed minimum environmental standards, if this should be necessary in connection with, for example, public health. It should also be noted that a safeguard clause within the framework of Article 100a(5) has a much more important function than one within the framework of Article 130s. Harmonization for internal market purposes will often be attained by means of 'total harmonization'. In that case the powers of Member States to take measures to protect the environment are limited to the margins allowed by the Directive in question. Thus the legal basis for action by the Member States must be created in the Directive itself. The Plant Protection Directive and the Dangerous Preparations Directive referred to above are examples of total harmonization. Here, creating a safeguard certainly does have a function. This need will be much less for measures based on Article 130s, which will generally implement 'minimum harmonization'.

III   THE POLICY ASPECTS TO BE TAKEN INTO ACCOUNT

According to Article 130r(3) the Community shall, in preparing its policy on the environment, take account of:

- available scientific and technical data;
- environmental conditions in the various regions of the Community;
- the potential benefits and costs of action or lack of action;
- the economic and social development of the Community as a whole and the balanced development of its regions.

By comparison with the formulation of the integration principle ('must be integrated'), the language of the third paragraph is much less forceful. Account shall be taken of the policy aspects referred to in it. The Treaty does not therefore prescribe observance of these criteria in all cases. It is true that inclusion of these policy aspects does not imply that the Community's environmental objectives are, in a legal sense, subordinate to them. However, in practice, Member States will no

---

17   See, for example, the Court's decision in the Leybucht case, C-57/89, ECR 1991, I-883, where the Court assumed that protection of the coast against flooding is just such an interest.

doubt seize on them as an excuse to delay environmental policies that do not suit them.

1   Available scientific and technical data

It is said that the function of this criterion under the SEA was to ensure that the Community would only act when sufficient scientific data was available to prove that a given activity or product – for example, CFCs in aerosols – would have a harmful effect on the environment (in this case, depletion of the ozone layer). As has already been shown in the discussion of the precautionary principle, a different interpretation would now seem more appropriate. Indeed, all kinds of provisional, indicative and tentative scientific data may now be sufficient to require protective measures and action by the Community.

2   Environmental conditions in the various regions of the Community

Application of this criterion entails a differentiated environmental policy based on the quality of the environment in a given region. This might give rise to the assumption that there is a preference for environmental quality objectives rather than emission limits. After all, the quality of the receiving environment would then determine the extent of emission of pollutants. However, in section III.4 below, two Directives containing measures to prevent water pollution are discussed. Member States were able to opt for a system of water-quality objectives as an alternative for emission limits. There it was concluded that, from the point of view of the source principle, emission standards were preferred over environmental quality standards. However, where regional differences in environmental quality are at stake, the opposite might apply. It is up to the Council to consider in more depth the relative merits of these different aspects.

On the other hand the criterion could also be applied differently. Additional protective measures might well be called for precisely in order to conserve those areas in which the environmental quality is high. See, for example, the air quality Directives of the 1980s. These Directives enable Member States to lay down more stringent air quality standards than those set out in the Directives, for zones which in the view of the Member State require special protection from an environmental point of view.

3   The potential benefit and costs of action or lack of action

This criterion requires that the potential costs and benefits of action are assessed. Besides producing benefits for the environment, environmental action by the Community entails costs for the Member States in the sense of legislation, administrative organization, enforcement and the like, and for private actors, such as industrial plants which cause pollution and manufacturers and importers of goods and products which are harmful to the environment. Viewed in this way, the criterion could be seen as prompting application of the principle of proportionality, and thus adding little to what has already been provided in the third paragraph of Article 3b of the Treaty.

An example of how the Council applies this criterion in practice can be found in Article 4 of Directive 84/360 on the combating of air pollution from industrial plants. An authorization may only be issued when the competent authority is satisfied that 'all appropriate preventive measures against air pollution have been taken, including application of the best available technology, provided that the application of such measures does not entail excessive costs'.

4   The economic and social development of the Community as a whole and the balanced development of its regions

In fact this aspect is an elaboration of the more general principle contained in Article 7c of the Treaty. Differentiated environmental policies may be adopted, whether or not on a temporary basis, depending on the economic and social development of certain regions. This opens the possibility of a 'multi-speed' environmental policy. An example of such a multi-speed policy is given by Directive 88/609 on the limitation of emissions of certain pollutants into the air from large combustion plants. Article 5 provides that Spain is temporarily entitled to apply less stringent emission standards than those normally laid down by the Directive. This is explained in the preamble to the Directive by pointing out that Spain considers it needs a particularly high amount of new generating capacity to allow for its energy and industrial growth.

Apart from giving certain Member States the power to derogate from Community standards, the element of economic and social development can also be translated in terms of financial support by the Community for those Member States which find it difficult to meet the standards required by a Directive. An example of this is Directive 92/43 on natural habitats. Article 8 provides for a system of co-financing where measures to protect priority natural habitats and priority species would result in excessive financial burdens for some Member States.

Another example is provided by Article 130s(5). If the Council adopts an environmental measure based on Article 130s(1) which involves disproportionately high costs for the public authorities of a Member State, the Council can lay down appropriate provisions in the form of temporary derogations and/or financial support from the Community's Cohesion Fund (Article 130d).

18 The Elaboration of EC Environmental Legislation

Ludwig Krämer

Table of Contents

I INTRODUCTION

Community environmental regulation[1] has a number of specific features additional to general characteristics of Community standard setting. Community legislation is marked in particular by the fact that the decision-making procedure is significantly different from that in a nation-state. Community institutions do not have a general competence; there is no Community-wide public opinion which influences the law-making process; Regulations are adopted behind closed doors, without public participation; the rules generally address Member States and not individu-

---

[1] The following chapter uses the notion of law-making, legislation, rules, standards and so on in a non-technical way.

als;[2] implementation and enforcement is normally done at Member State level; Community rules are largely ignored. All these characteristics also apply to environmental regulations adopted at Community level; however, the following specifics must be borne in mind which particularly concern environmental regulation:

1   European Community environmental policy and regulation have developed since about 1970 without an express legal basis in the EEC Treaty. Only in 1987 was a Treaty amendment introduced to provide such a legal basis for environmental action.

2   Environmental law and policy inside the Community - and in most of its Member States - has developed only over the last 25 years. Little legal and political know-how for environmental legislation was available. Thus, methods, tools and instruments for policy design and implementation had first to be invented and tested.

3   If environmental policy is defined as a coherent, consistent set of measures in order to reach a progressive improvement of the environment, it seems as if only a minority of Member States have such an environmental policy at national level. This differs from sector to sector, such as industrial, agricultural, regional, transport or energy policy.

4   Community environmental regulation has been made, despite a permanent shortage of staff and financial resources. This situation, which is not especially different from the conditions under which environmental administrations in the individual Member States, make environmental proposals difficult to defend inside administrations which are not always open to environmental problems.

5   Public participation in environmental matters is particularly weak at Community level. Non-governmental organizations are few in number, short of staff and money and have great difficulty in getting access to information and to the decision-making machinery. Environmental lobbying is in its infancy.

II   ENVIRONMENTAL ACTION PROGRAMMES

Under the present EC Treaty it is the Commission which has a monopoly over formal proposals for regulation made to the Council. The European Parliament, the Council or private pressure groups are certainly able to make suggestions for drafting environmental Directives or Regulations, or, in the case of the Council,

---

2   Environmental law at Community level normally takes the form of Directives. Regulations are adopted, where Community rules also concern international aspects and, more recently, where the achievement of the internal market requires greater uniformity.

place in a piece of this or that Community secondary legislation the requirement to make a proposal for another piece of legislation. In legal terms, however, the Commission is not bound by such requests, but determines according to its own responsibility, if and what kind of proposal it will submit to the Council.

Since the original EC Treaty contained no mention of the environment, the Commission thought it appropriate, when it first addressed environmental problems in a communication to the Council, to announce the elaboration of an environmental action programme. This First Action Programme was submitted to the Council in March 1972. In October 1972 the heads of state and government of the European Community expressly called for such an action programme, and it was adopted in 1973.[3] In 1977, 1983, 1987 and 1993 new action programmes were adopted.[4]

The Commission's proposal, the opinions of the European Parliament and Economic and Social Committee on it and the text which is finally adopted, are published. The environmental action programme contains a number of actions which are to be elaborated during the lifetime of the programme. The announcement of a specific Directive or a Regulation is rather the exception. Usually, the action programme states that the Commission will make 'appropriate proposals' or something similar, or even uses a more general wording. It is therefore impossible to trace all the different proposals for environmental Directives or Regulations in the different action programmes. These programmes thus set the general context for objectives and priorities within which specific actions may be announced and submitted, but also allow proposals which have not been specifically announced to be submitted to the Council.

The resolution adopting the First Programme contained a commitment by the Council to decide on proposals from the Commission 'within nine months'. However, the additional words 'if possible' allow more latitude and, in practice, hardly any proposals were adopted by the Council within nine months after submission; indeed several proposals have not been adopted at all. This example demonstrates the political nature of the action programmes and the proposals for regulations contained therein.

In a way the environmental action programmes are completed by the annual working programmes which the Commission publishes at the beginning of each calendar year. These working programmes which cover the whole activity of the

---

[3] First Action programme 22 November 1973; OJ 1973, No. C 112/1.
[4] Second Action programme 22 November 1973; OJ 1977, No. C 132/1; Third Action programme 17 May 1983; OJ 1983, No. C 46/1. Fourth Action programme 19 October 1987; OJ 1987, No. C 328/1. Fifth Action programme 1 February 1993; OJ 1993, No. C 138/1.

Commission, have been published in the Official Journal of the EC[5] since 1993. They are relatively precise and give indications of the Commission's actual activities, although the indication that the proposals would be submitted during the calendar year is not to be seen as a legal commitment, but rather as an indication of good intentions.

Action programmes and annual programmes are elaborated within the Commission's administration and, in particular, in the environmental department of the Commission. This applies also to political speeches, statements or other forms of communication which contain amendments to any of the planned environmental Directives. Suggestions relating to draft Regulations also come from the European Parliament via its many resolutions on environmental policy; from national governments which intend to regulate at national level a problem which could better or best be tackled at Community level; from non-governmental organizations, interest groups, individuals, journalists, researchers and so on.

It is obvious that the inclusion of an environmental Directive in an action programme or annual working programme does not automatically and in all circumstances mean that it will actually ever appear. The concrete decision to start work on a specific Directive is a political-administrative decision taken by the member of the Commission in charge of the Environment and the Director-General for the environment. This decision is also influenced by the availability of staff, other priorities, available data on the subject, pressure from outside, activities in Member States, technical assistance and so on.

III   THE DRAFTING OF A PROPOSAL FOR A DIRECTIVE

Once a decision to start work on a Directive is taken, a first draft of a text is prepared. These texts are prepared by the technical units, that is a 'water' Directive is prepared by officials working in the water unit, not by a central 'drafting' unit. Frequently the first draft of a Directive is accompanied by, or even preceded by, a general discussion paper which outlines the problem, the strategy to follow, available data and so on. For the preparation of the text, the available data will be assembled. Usually, the subject matter will have been the object of one or several studies made for the Commission to examine the scientific, technical, economic and/or legal aspects of the problem. At this stage consultation with outside bodies is unusual, but discussions with experts, lobbyists or other persons who are interested in the subject matter are not excluded.

---

[5]   See Legislative Work Programme 1993, OJ 1993 no. C 125, p. 1; 1193, OJ 1994, no. C 60, p. 1.

Consultations with Member States at an administrative level generally start with a first draft for a Directive, which is frequently accompanied by background documents which explain the approach chosen, indicate the options and raise other matters that might be of interest. Practice varies as to whether at this stage of the drafting a consensus is sought with other departments inside the Commission before a text is sent to the outside.

Bilateral discussions with Member States - which would take place in the different capitals rather than in Brussels - are exceptional and never take place with all national administrations, although occasionally such bilateral discussions with officials from particularly 'important' Member States might take place at this early stage, in order to consult on the approach to be taken or the strategy to be adopted.

All draft proposals for environmental Directives are the subject of multilateral discussions between the Commission's administrations and the Member States. These meetings take place in Brussels by invitation of the Commission, which chairs them. Officials from other departments of the Commission participate in the meetings. The invitation is addressed to the Permanent Representation of Member States within the European Community and asks them to designate 'experts' to attend the meeting. The experts need not come from the administration or even the environmental administration. The idea for retaining this formula was originally that national 'experts' should not represent the Member State, but should be chosen because of their experience in the matter. They would therefore be able to express an independent view and thus assist the Commission in preparing a proposal. In practice, the majority of all those who attend are government officials, the 'independent expert' element thus having been lost almost completely.

As environmental law is often technical and often has few existing national rules to take into consideration, only one or two of such multilateral meetings of experts are usually needed to reach a consensus. In areas where more general problems are touched upon, discussions inside the Commission and with Member State experts may take a long time. Thus, while the Commission administration drafted 23 texts for a proposal on environmental impact assessment[6] before the text could become an official proposal for a Directive and be sent to the Council, the Directive on liquid beverage containers[7] had almost as many drafts in the preliminary stage alone.

Parallel to the meeting with government experts, discussions with organizations from trade and industry and environmental organizations take place. No systematic consultation is organized, although the Commission's administration

---

[6]   Directive 85/337; OJ 1985, No. L 175/40.
[7]   Directive 85/339; OJ 1985, No. L 176/18.

favours consultation with European organizations rather than with national organizations or even with individual companies. The sheer number of professional organizations guarantees them a greater frequency of consultation, compared to environmental organizations, which are underrepresented in Brussels and lack resources, know-how and expertise in successful lobbying. Hearings rarely take place.

At the end of the consultation process a draft text emerges which the environmental administration takes back into the Commission in order to start the formal adoption phase. The text is sent to all interested departments - and in all cases also to the Legal Service - with the request for approval.

Divergent positions are discussed and compromises reached. The revised text then goes into the approval procedure of the Commission itself. At this stage remaining differences between the administrations are settled, as well as disagreement - mostly of more strategic or political nature - among the 17 members of the Commission itself. It may happen that a text is not capable of being approved by the Commission, though this is rather unusual in environmental matters.

The approved text becomes an official Commission proposal for a Directive. The proposal itself is published in the *Official Journal of the European Communities*; the explanatory memorandum, which is not an integrated part of the proposal, is made available to the public in the form of an official document. The text of the proposal is drafted in the nine working languages, whereas the explanatory memorandum is usually produced in only three languages. The draft proposal's quality is largely left to the discretion of the Commission, as is its manner of presentation. Both aspects need some explanation.

Prior to 1993 the environmental chapter in the EC Treaty, Articles 130r to 130t, did not contain a specific mandate for the Commission to present proposals which offer a high level of protection. It is true that a number of clauses in this chapter, read together, led to the conclusion that the Treaty intended an efficient environmental policy to be conceived, elaborated and pursued at Community level. However, this did not mean that any proposal from the Commission could be attacked on grounds that it did not offer a sufficient high level of protection.

In contrast, under Article 100a, which is part of the rules aiming at the completion of the internal market, the Commission's environmental proposals were to be based on a high level of protection. Proposals under Article 100a were adopted by majority decision of the Council under the cooperation procedure with the European Parliament. Under the rules of this procedure an opinion[8] of the Parliament which is concurrent with the Commission's proposal, or amended proposal, can only be overturned by the Council by unanimous decision. This meant in

---

[8]   See Article 189 c of the EC Treaty.

practice that where the Parliament is interested in a high level of environmental protection it must have a right to challenge the quality of the Commission's proposal based on Article 100a. Otherwise, a Commission proposal with a low level of protection may be adopted by the Council with a majority decision even where the Parliament had asked for a higher level of protection.

Since the end of 1993, when the Maastricht Treaty entered into force, Article 130r(2) has requested the EU environmental policy to aim at a high level of protection, whilst simultaneously taking care of regional diversities. This requirement refers to the 'policy', not to the individual measure. At the same time, the increased renationalization of policies in general seems to lead more to environmental framework legislative measures, which might allow for a high level of protection should a Member State so wish, but which would not impose this. It will be seen in future to what extent measures of a high level of protection will be adopted at EU level.

It is entirely up to the Commission whether it wishes to present proposals on a specific sector or whether it wishes to be more general. A current Commission proposal deals with liability for damage caused by waste. The Commission could have presented either a proposal concerning liability for the transport of waste, or liability for damage caused by dangerous waste only, or it could have drafted a general proposal on liability for damage caused to the environment.

IV   PARLIAMENT AND ECOSOC

The proposal is transmitted to the Council which passes the text to the European Parliament and the Economic and Social Committee (ECOSOC) which both give their opinion on the texts. These opinions are prepared in committees for the environment under the responsibility of a *rapporteur* who is selected from the members of the Committee. Commission officials attend committee meetings, answer questions and explain reasons for the options taken. Their attitude is marked by the necessity to 'defend', if possible, the proposal adopted by the Commission.

There is no standard practice for how the *rapporteurs* assemble the necessary knowhow to prepare their report which is the basis of the opinion to be adopted. It is carried out mostly by means of informal contacts take place, often with persons or groups which are politically close to the *rapporteur's* political party; formal written consultations with groups or public hearings in the Parliament are exceptional and almost never take place in ECOSOC.

The draft report is discussed in the Environmental Committee of the Parliament, together with detailed suggestions for amendments to be made to the proposal from the Commission and the draft for the resolution of the Parliament. The

Committee then reports to Parliament's plenary session where, again, amendments to the proposal and to the final resolution may be introduced on which the final vote takes place. The amendments which the Parliament suggests to the Commission's proposal and the final resolution are published in the *Official Journal of the European Communities*. The Committee's report is not published, but is available from the European Parliament.

Since 1979 when the Parliament became elected by general election there has been agreement between the Commission and the Parliament that the Commission will take on board amendments suggested by the Parliament wherever possible. Obviously, such a vague clause - which raises difficulties in practice - does not satisfy the Parliament which is of the opinion that all amendments to proposals should be accepted by the Commission. The European Parliament uses procedural means - delays or refusals to vote - in order to compel the Commission to accept its amendments, as well as extensive discussions and negotiations between the *rapporteur* and the Commission's administration or the chairman of the Environmental Committee and the member of the Commission who is in charge of environmental matters.

Since the end of 1993 the Parliament has been able to formally ask the Commission to submit any appropriate proposal on a matter which it finds of importance (Article 138b(2) EC Treaty). While this possibility is not legally binding on the Commission, it will certainly have a considerable political weight, since the Parliament is the only EC institution which is elected by general elections.

To date, however, the Commission still has the exclusive right to initiate legislative proposals which implies the right to decide if and to what extent it will present an amendment of its proposal to the Council.

The European Parliament's attitude to environmental proposals made by the Commission can be summarized as follows:

1   On general questions of the environment or on horizontal legislation, the European Parliament constantly urges the Commission and the Council to go further in their proposals and to better protect the environment. (I am not aware of a single proposal from the Commission where Parliament was of the opinion that it would be too ambitious, too protective or too far-reaching.)

2   Proposals which are of a more technical nature are only exceptionally challenged as to the approach chosen by the Commission. Normally, the approach is accepted. The amendments suggested by the Parliament concern the need for more, 'better', protection of the environment.

3   The European Parliament constantly pleads for more progressive and efficient environmental legislation at Community level. Also, it seeks more transparency of environmental measures, better access to information, and greater participation of environmental organizations in the decision-making process.

4   The European Parliament is also gradually managing to introduce environmental considerations into amendments to proposals for legislation in agricultural and regional matters, the internal market and other policies. In Parliament, the 'greening' of regulation - the integration of environmental considerations into other policies - is more advanced than within the Commission or the Council. This affects the very important role played by the Environmental Committee within the European Parliament; indeed in terms of the number of its members as well as the number of its resolutions and so on transmitted to the Parliament's plenary, the Environmental Committee is one of the biggest, most active and most influential committees of the European Parliament.

ECOSOC's activity resembles that of the European Parliament, although the drive for better environmental proposals is much weaker. This might be due to the fact that only one member of the present ECOSOC expressly indicates his alliance to an environmental group.

The Commission's proposal is first discussed in a working group on the basis of a report made by an appointed *rapporteur*. Commission officials participate in that discussion. The approved report and the draft opinion are submitted to the Environmental Section and finally to the ECOSOC plenary session which votes only on the opinion. It seems to be ECOSOC's policy to look for an opinion which is capable of being agreed upon by all members. Large majorities in the final vote are therefore the rule. ECOSOC's opinion is published in the *Official Journal*. The report from the sections is not published, but available from ECOSOC.

V   DISCUSSION IN THE COUNCIL

At Council level, the Commission's proposal for a Directive is first examined by a working group composed of civil servants from the Member States, in some cases assisted by officials from the Member States' Permanent Representation within the Union. Generally, the same officials act in these working parties that attended, as experts, the meetings organized by the Commission to prepare the proposal.

The working parties are set up in order to prepare the decision by the Council of Ministers. Since the Council meets under relatively specific headings (Agricultural Council, Transport Council, Environmental Council, and so on) a proposal which has been prepared by the environmental department in the Commission usually goes to an environment working group in Council, although this was not easily achieved in the 1970s when Community environmental policy was in its infancy.

The working group may start examining the Commission's proposal without waiting for the opinion from the European Parliament and ECOSOC. Whether this is actually done depends on the working groups' work load. The determining factor, however, is whether the Member State which has the presidency in the Council actually wishes to proceed with the proposal. Whereas some proposals are immediately taken up by the working group, others are hardly looked at.

The working group is chaired by a representative from the Member State which has the presidency in Council. It starts with a general discussion and then goes through the text Article by Article. The Commission participant in these discussions explains the proposal and tries to defend the text which was submitted. After having revised the proposal, listed objections to it and noted alternatives for drafting, the chairman of the working group sends the text to the committee of permanent representatives (COREPER). He may also do so when he wishes to receive political instructions on questions which the working group feels unable to solve. The report sent to COREPER contains the new text accompanied by remarks or declarations by national delegations, reservations or suggested compromise solutions.

COREPER meets once a week and deals with practically all questions. In environmental matters COREPER tries to concentrate discussion on Commission proposals in one or several meetings which take place in preparation for Council meetings on environmental matters. An environmental proposal is discussed and then it is either sent back to the working group with further instructions or it is sent to the Council for decision or guidance. COREPER prepares the Council agenda, deciding - in close liaison with the presidency, the Council Secretariat and the Commission - what is put on the Council's agenda. The final decision on the contents of the agenda lies, however, with the presidency.

At present, the Environmental Council meets four to six times a year - in other words two to three times under each presidency which rotates every six months among Member States. One or two of the meetings are informal where no decisions are taken, but one or more basic environmental questions are discussed. The Council has the task of removing the last objections of one or several Member States, discussing compromises and, if possible, adopting the proposal. If this is not possible, the proposal is sent back to COREPER for further discussion.

The Council proceedings are confidential. Interpretations of adopted texts are often buried in unpublished minutes. Although the European Court of Justice has ruled that such declarations in Council minutes have no legal value, their political importance is nevertheless considerable, in particular where the Commission has also joined in such a declaration.

An environmental proposal may only be adopted by the Council when the Parliament and ECOSOC have given their opinion. However it may happen - and it seems to be more frequent in recent years - that all substantial work in the Council's working group, at COREPER and Council level is finished before Parliament has given its opinion. In such cases the Council does not adopt the proposal but simply approves it, waiting for Parliament's opinion. When this opinion is given, the proposal is again put on the agenda of the Council and formally adopted.

The European Parliament regularly requests to be consulted a second time when the Council intends to deviate significantly from the Commission's proposal, which was the basis for the Parliament's discussion. Until now, the Council has only proceeded to such a second consultation of the Parliament where the Council changed the legal basis of an environmental proposal; indeed, under Articles 100a and the co-decision procedure fixed in that Article, the Parliament must be consulted twice, once on the Commission's proposal and once on the common position which the Council has reached. Where the Council changes the legal basis to Article 130s, the Parliament's rights are affected, since Article 130s only asks for one consultation. In such cases the Council will consult the Parliament a second time.

This practice seems legally suspect, since the legislative rights of the European Parliament under the cooperation procedure go further than just being consulted twice. The Council does not seem to have the right to change the legislative procedure within the procedure. It is hoped that the European Court will soon clarify this matter. The European Parliament has been trying for several years to introduce a conciliation procedure in cases where the Council deviates significantly from the Parliament's opinion.

The Maastricht Treaty introduced a co-decision procedure between the European Parliament and Council, amongst others for measures to be adopted by virtue of Article 100a and for environmental action programmes (Article 130s (3)). The co-decision procedure, the details of which are fixed in Article 189b of the EC Treaty, is, procedurally, a cooperation procedure. After the first consultation of the Parliament, the Council fixes a common position which is published. Parliament reconsiders this common position. If it agrees, the legislative measure is adopted jointly by Parliament and Council and published. Where Parliament suggests amendments which the Council accepts, the measure is also approved. Where the Parliament suggests amendments which the Council does not approve or where the Parliament rejects the common position, a conciliation procedure is started between Parliament and Council at which the Commission participates. The compromise text of the conciliation committee must be approved both by Parliament and Council. Parliament has always the possibility to reject a text by an absolute majority of its members.

The procedure is currently undergoing its efficiency test.

VI   SOME OBSERVATIONS ON SPECIFIC DIRECTIVES

In the following, a number of Directives will be examined more closely in order to comment on the legislative process.[9]

1   Directive 76/160 on the quality of bathing water

• Commission proposal	07/02/1975, OJ 1975, No. C 67/1
• Parliament's opinion	13/05/1975, OJ 1975, No. C 128/13
• ECOSOC's opinion	24/09/1975, OJ 1975, No. C 286/5
• Council Directive	08/12/1975, OJ 1976, No. L 31/1

The First Action Programme gave no clear indication that the Commission would draft a proposal in this sector. The decisive point of departure was probably a French notification on a draft circular which fixed parameters for fresh water.

The Commission proposal covered fresh and sea waters where bathing was authorized or tolerated. As regards quality criteria the proposal distinguished between sea water and fresh water; the quality requirements for fresh water were more stringent. The proposal set a minimum frequency of sampling and stated that bathing waters were to comply with the Directive's requirements within eight years, underlining the importance of clean-up measures. It also provided for an adaptation of the Directive's requirements to allow for technical progress.

The European Parliament gave its opinion within three months, ECOSOC within five. Neither opinion questioned the Commission's general approach. The Council adopted the Directive ten months after its submission. The Council deleted the differentiations between fresh and sea bathing waters, thereby opting for the less stringent requirements in the Commission's proposal. The compliance date was extended to ten years, but the reference to the necessity of clean-up measures was deleted. Furthermore, Member States were allowed to provide, under specific conditions, longer delays for compliance. The Council added a requirement for regular reporting to the Commission on the quality of bathing waters and for the publication of a Community report.

The main problems with the implementation of the Directive were the difficulties in getting Member States to provide for the supervision of all bathing waters which fell under the Directive, to inform the public of the quality of bathing wa-

---

[9] There is little systematic information available on the elaboration of environmental Directives. Some useful information is given by N. Haigh, *E.E.C. Environmental Policy and Britain*, (2nd edn), London: Longmans, 1989; S. Johnson, G. Corcelle, *L'autre Europe 'verte': la politique communautaire de l'environnement*, Paris/Brussels, 1987.

ters and in particular to undertake the necessary clean-up measures. The fixing of quality objectives as such did not lead to improvement measures. In its first report on the state of the environment the Commission described the commitment of the Member States to respect the quality requirements of the Directive as onerous, drawing attention to the enormous investments which were necessary. It is obvious that in a number of Member States these investments have not been made. Generally the quality of bathing waters is still not up to the standards required.

2   Directive 76/464 on discharges of polluting substances into waters

- Commission proposal   22/10/1974, OJ 1975, No. C. 12/4
- Parliament's opinion   08/01/1975, OJ 1975, No. C 5/62
- ECOSOC's opinion   15/05/1975, OJ 1975, No. C 108/76
- Council Directive   04/05/1976, OJ 1976, No. L 129/23

The Commission made a proposal for a decision with the aim to reduce emissions of dangerous substances into the water, based on the principle of emission limits. This proposal was made at the request of Belgium and was subsequent to ongoing work under international water conventions.[10] The Council was unable to agree to this approach because the UK preferred quality objectives and was not prepared to accept Community-wide emission standards. The final compromise in the Directive allowed Member States to opt for this or that approach. This also influenced later Directives on discharge of polluting substances into the water and the discrepancy between the UK approach and that of the rest of the Union has not yet been resolved. It is probably the cause of the very serious delay in the conception and implementation of efficient measures to combat water pollution by dangerous substances. In 1988 a Council resolution suggested a dual legislative approach in order to improve the situation, but this resolution has not yet led to new legislative initiatives.

3   Directive 80/68 on the protection of groundwater

- Commission proposal   27/01/1978, OJ 1978, No. C 37/3
- Parliament's opinion   11/12/1978, OJ 1978, No. C 296/35
- ECOSOC's opinion   20/06/1978, OJ 1978, No. C 283/39
- Commission amendment   30/12/1978, OJ 1979, No. C 27/2

---

10   See Haigh (1987), *op.cit.* p. 72.

- Council Directive   17/12/1978, OJ 1980, No. L 20/43

The Directive was drafted using as a model Directive 76/464 on the pollution of waters by certain dangerous substances, which had proposed that a separate Directive on groundwater protection be elaborated.

The Commission's proposal was considerably refined by the Parliament's amendments, which the Commission accepted. In particular, a ban of all direct or indirect discharges of List I or List II substances into groundwater that was used for drinking water purposes was introduced. The Council accepted this general ban only for List I substances and even there provided for exceptions, at the same time making the wording of the Directive more ambiguous.

Artificial recharges of groundwater were also introduced at the Parliament's request, and this was accepted both by the Commission and the Council. The Council also provided for very detailed specifications as regards authorizations for discharges into groundwater, limited authorization in time, fixed the principle of monitoring obligations for Member States, required an inventory of authorizations to be set up, and even introduced a clause on the Directive's application to existing waste landfills - although this Article has not been applied in practice by the Member States.

Overall, the structure of the Commission proposal was not changed substantially during the law-making process. There seems to have been the conviction that the legislative approach chosen by Directive 76/464 ensured the satisfactory control of pollution.

4   Directive 80/778 on the quality of drinking water

- Commission proposal   31/07/1975, OJ 1975, No. C 214/2
- Parliament's opinion   09/02/1976, OJ 1976, No. C 28/27
- ECOSOC's opinion   12/06/1976, OJ 1976, No. C 131/13
- Council Directive   15/07/1980, OJ 1980, No. L 229/11

The initiative inside the Commission for this Directive came from the Health Protection Department which tried to incorporate into Community legislation drinking water standards recommended by the World Health Organization.

The Commission's proposal was based on Article 100, which provides for greater conformity of rules. The Council discussed the proposal for more than five years, in 52 meetings of working groups, before it adopted the proposal on the basis of Articles 100 and 235.[11]

The structure and general outline of the Directive remained largely unchanged during the legislative procedure. The European Parliament had asked in particular for a revision of permitted concentrations at least every five years; in preparation for that, a report was to be made by each Member State at those intervals. This request was not taken up by the Council and the control of implementation of this Directive is particularly difficult since the Commission does not possess enough data on the situation in Member States.

Furthermore, the Council introduced a number of changes to the maximum authorized concentrations of undesirable substances in drinking water, which slightly lowered the standards with regard to the Commission's proposal, introduced a specific temporary derogation clause in cases of catastrophe, introduced an obligation that full compliance with the Directive should be achieved five years after the adoption of the Directive, allowed a prolongation of this delay in exceptional cases and under certain conditions and considerably reduced the frequency of sampling for drinking water.

5 Directive 82/501 on the major accident hazards of certain industrial activities

- Commission proposal   19/07/1979, OJ 1979, No. C 212/4
- Parliament's opinion   19/06/1980, OJ 1980, No. C 175/49
- ECOSOC's opinion   21/07/1980, OJ 1980, No. C 182/25
- Council Directive   24/06/1982, OJ 1982, No. L 230/1

The Commission's proposal was initiated in the aftermath of the serious industrial accident which had occurred in Seveso in 1976 and where a proportion of the adjacent population had to be evacuated. Other serious accidents had occurred earlier in other parts of the Community without any reaction from the Commission; it might have been the insistence of the Italian commissioner in charge of the environment that this accident instigated legislative initiatives.

The model for drafting accident prevention rules was partly taken from the nuclear energy legislation and also from the safety at work legislation. Since most of the Member States agreed in principle with the need to prevent accidents, the core of the Directive was not really disputed. Discussions focused in particular on whether environmental accidents should be included - they eventually remained

---

[11] See also P. Kromarek, *Die Trinkwasserrichtlinie der E.G. und die Nitratwerte*, Bonn: Institut für Europäische Umweltpolitik, 1986.

included - what kind of information the manufacturer would have to give to the supervising authorities and, in particular, what kind of information should be released in the case of installations with a 'transnational' risk. France was afraid that any solution might have an adverse impact on its nuclear installations, some of which are situated near national borders, and delayed the adoption of the Directive. The compromise formula adopted after long discussion introduced an obligation to inform only the neighbouring Member State, but not the citizens.

It might be worthwhile to note that, in 1988, a major amendment was introduced to the Directive which included references to the storage of dangerous substances and which was triggered by an accident near Basel in Switzerland in 1986.

6   Directive 85/337 on the environmental impact of certain public and private projects

- Commission proposal   16/06/1980, OJ 1980, No. C 169/14
- Parliament's opinion   18/02/1982, OJ 1982, No. C 66/78
- ECOSOC's opinion   29+30/04/1981, OJ 1981, No. C 185/8
- Commission amendment   01/04/1982, OJ 1982, No. C 110/5
- Council Directive   27/06/1985, OJ 1985, No. L 175/40

The Commission had suggested a list of 35 types of project for which an environmental impact assessment should always take place. Forty-five other types of project should undergo such an assessment where their characteristics so required. In order to specify this clause Member States were to fix thresholds below which no impact assessment or simplified assessments were required. The proposal also required the operator to submit reasonable alternatives for the project.

The European Parliament slightly increased the number of projects for which an impact assessment should be mandatory and asked for an assessment also to be required for decisions not to proceed with a specific project.

The Council reduced to nine the number of types of project for which a mandatory assessment was required and even created the possibility for ad hoc exemptions to be decided by Member States. Furthermore, the question on when a project in Annex II would have to undergo an environment impact assessment was answered in an extremely unclear wording which led, at a later stage, to numerous legal disputes between the Commission and Member States.

The Commission suggested a number of detailed studies and data which the developer of a project should submit. Again the Parliament increased the requirements and the Council considerably reduced them submitting these requirements largely to a case-by-case decision.

In general it seems no exaggeration to stress that the Council tried to retain as much discretion as possible for the national administration to decide whether an environmental impact assessment should be made. The general setting of the Directive was already fixed by the Commission's proposal which the Council changed only very little and where also the Parliament did not have much to contribute.

7 Directive 88/609 on air emissions from large combustion installations

• Commission proposal	19/12/1983, OJ 1984, No. 49/1
• Parliament's opinion	16/11/1984, OJ 1984, No. C337/438
	+14/6/1985, OJ 1985, No. C175/297
• ECOSOC's opinion	21/11/1984, OJ 1985, No. C 76/6
• Council Directive	24/11/1988, OJ 1986, No. L 336/1

The initiative for this Directive came from the European Council after the discussion in 1983 on acid rain and '*Waldsterben*' which had caused great concern in West-Germany and also in some other Member States. The proposal following West-German initiatives was for legislation on large combustion plants. The Commission's proposal provided for the entry into force of the Directive by 1 January 1986. The final date in the Directive was 30 June 1990. The European Parliament had already severely criticized the Council and some Member States for their attitude as regards the Commission proposal.

The Commission had suggested that national programmes should have until the end of 1995 to reduce emissions from combustion plants with a capacity of more than 50 megawatt for sulphur dioxide by 60 per cent, black smoke by 40 per cent and nitrogen oxides by 40 per cent as compared to 1980 levels . The Council supported reductions of sulphur dioxide and nitrogen oxides but not of black smoke for existing installations and set delays until 1988 (NO_x) and 2003 (SO_2). Different reduction quantities were fixed for each member state. Greece, Ireland and Portugal were allowed to increase their emissions from existing installations. The repartition of emissions among the different installations existing within a Member State was left to the Member States' discretion.

The Council fixed emission threshold values also for new installations which were differentiated according to the size of the installations providing for special rules in the case of national solid fuels and giving special permission to Spain to authorize more polluting combustion plants until the year 1999.

The Directive, which has only recently come into effect, requires a very tight supervision system. It is the first time that an environmental Directive has provided for a differentiated approach for each Member State and for a concept of global national reduction ('bubble' concept). Both aspects were developed during the Council discussions.

8   Directives 90/219 and 90/220 on genetically modified organisms

- Commission proposal   16/05/1988, OJ 1988, No. C 198/ 19
- Parliament's opinion   24/05/1989, OJ 1989, No. C 158/122
- ECOSOC's opinion   08/11/1988, OJ 1989, No. C 23/ 45
                             14/03/1990, OJ 1990, No. C 96/ 87
- Commission amendments   23/08/1989, OJ 1989, No. C 246/5+6
- Council Directive   23/04/1990, OJ 1990, No. L 117/1+15

The Commission submitted two proposals, one on the contained use and the other on the deliberate release of genetically modified organisms. Both proposals were based on Article 100a. Despite the fact that the procedure of legislative cooperation applied which required a double consultation of the Parliament, it took less than two years to get both Directives adopted. The Council based the Directive on contained use on Article 130s.

The structure and content of the two Directives were not changed considerably. The Council drafted several Articles in a more precise way including for instance the stipulation that the written agreement of the competent authority should be a condition for the deliberate release of genetically modified organisms.

Both the Parliament and ECOSOC had suggested a provision to inform the concerned public prior to a deliberate release of genetically modified organisms. The Council did not take up this proposal but limited the authorization procedure to a discussion between the developer and the competent authorities.

VII   CONCLUSION

This brief outline of some environmental Directives does not give the full picture of how environmental regulation is prepared. The following tentative conclusions therefore constitute a first attempt to provide an answer. With this proviso, the following observations can be made:

1   Regulation is very strongly influenced by the Commission which has the monopoly on legislative intitiatives. It is exceptional that a Commission proposal is significantly amended during the legislative process. It is the Commission which selects the topics for regulation, decides on the shape and frequently on the content of Directives, fixes priorities and changes orientations.

2   The European Parliament is more or less limited to a consultative role. Even in areas where the Parliament has, since 1987, had a function as cooperator in the regulatory process (Article 100a - environmental legislation, with a bearing on the completion of the internal market) the Parliament has only once managed to impose its political will on the Community, namely in the case of standards for car emissions where an alliance of Parliament and Commission succeeded in obtaining better environmental standards adopted by the Council.

It remains to be seen whether the new provisions in the Maastricht Treaty on the European Union, which provide, as a rule, for majority decisions under Article 130s (legislative cooperation with the Parliament) and, as regards environmental action programmes, legislative co-decisions (Council and Parliament), will increase the Parliament's influence.

3   The Council is a regulatory body. However, despite the frequent meetings at ministerial level the Council has not developed much of a political vision for the environment. Its approach to legislative measures follows that of the Commission which is, for historic and other reasons, not always consistent.

4   The discrepancy between Member States as regards environmental awareness and, at the same time, the need for (until now) unanimous decisions in the Council is sometimes obscured by the adoption of Regulations which transpose the problem to the stage of enforcement. Examples such as the elaboration of reports on implementation, the drafting and enforcement of clean-up programmes and the continuous adaptation to technological progress show, in practice, enormous divergencies between Member States, despite Union-wide regulation. This phenomenon is to be found in all sectors, be it the implementation of drinking water standards (water); the best available technology not entailing excessive costs (air); waste elimination without risk to man and the environment (waste); accident prevention schemes for industrial installations (chemicals) or the designation and protection of habitats (nature).

5   The Commission, particularly at the start of its environmental acitivity, frequently lets itself be inspired by legislative initiatives in a particular Member State. This phenomenon has increased since Germany adopted a rather 'green' policy at national level. Air pollution Directives and Directives on biotechnology and packaging are recent examples. The model of national legislation as a forerunner to Community legislation is likely to play an important role in future, in particular in view of the completion of the internal market.

6   Participation at Commission level remains informal. This privileges the representations made by vested interests; environmental organizations have little

access to the Commission's activities, mainly due to lack of staff and resources and organizational problems.

7   There seems to be resistance to fixing precise and stringent pollution reduction standards which directly affect private business.

8   Assessing the Community's legislative procedure in the environmental sector gives a distorted impression if it is not compared to regulation in the Member States. Indeed, all Member States rely heavily on the administration's capacity to legislate in environmental matters. Article 3b of the EC-Treaty is a reminder that, in the environmental sector also, one has always to consider what would happen in the absence of Community legislation. If it is true that only a minority of Member States has a real national environmental policy, regulation at Community level, imperfect as it is, is much better for the environment than the making of environmental regulations only at national level.

9   The temptation to compare environmental regulation at Community level and in the United States must be strongly resisted. The situation is so very different that such comparison, which is rather fashionable, can only be misleading. The European integration process is unique; it has its difficulties and weaknesses and the legislative procedure is certainly capable of being improved. However, if one is looking for a model of environmental law-making among sovereign nation states to offer to other parts of the world, the European Community model is much more capable of being exported than the US model.

10   Attempts for improvement should therefore concentrate on phenomena which are appropriate to the Community environmental system. Legislation on access to environmental information would be an example; others could be systematic hearings at the level of the Commission and Parliament. ECOSOC could meet more representatives from the environmental associations. Generally, a greater transparency in the law-making process is urgently needed.

19 The Competences for EC Environmental Law

Jan Jans

I GENERAL REMARKS ON THE ENVIRONMENTAL POWERS OF THE EC

1 The principle of attribution and the exercise of Community environmental powers

Establishing the legal basis of a proposed Community measure on the environment is important for at least three reasons. In the first place because, under Community law, the Community's institutions do not have the unlimited powers of the national legislatures to take whatever measures they please. The institutions' powers extend only to what has been expressly conferred by Treaty. As provided in Article 3b of the EC Treaty: 'The Community shall act within the limits of the powers conferred upon it by this Treaty and of the objectives assigned to it therein.' Even in Community law, acting without competence results in invalid decisions.

Second, deciding the legal basis is relevant for the decision-making procedure to be followed when adopting a particular environmental measure. In the text below we shall see that Community law provides for various decision-making procedures in respect of environmental measures. Some decisions have to be taken unanimously, others by a qualified majority and yet others using the 'cooperation procedure' or the 'co-decision procedure'. The role played by the various participants in the decision-making process (Commission, European Parliament and Council), and thus their means of influencing the Community's environment policy, is different under each of these procedures.

Third, the choice of legal basis affects the extent to which Member States are entitled to adopt more stringent environmental measures than those on which agreement has been reached within the Community.

2   The principles of subsidiarity and proportionality in the exercise of the Community's environmental competence

a)   Subsidiarity

The second paragraph of Article 3b of the EC Treaty refers to the principle of subsidiarity in general terms:

> In areas which do not fall within its exclusive competence, the Community shall take action, in accordance with the principle of subsidiarity, only if and in so far as the objectives of the proposed action cannot be sufficiently achieved by the Member States and can therefore, by reason of the scale or effects of the proposed action, be better achieved by the Community.

The principle thus contains both a negative criterion (not sufficiently achieved by the Member States) and a positive one (better achieved by the Community) by which to judge acts by the Community. Since Maastricht, the Commission's proposals for Community legislation have indicated to what extent Community action is necessary in the light of the subsidiarity principle.

At the 1992 Edinburgh European Council, several guidelines were adopted to further clarify this concept. For example does the matter involve cross-border problems which cannot be dealt with satisfactorily by the action of the individual

Member States? In view of the territorial limitations of many government powers, unilateral action by Member States is clearly less effective than concerted action where the source of pollution is situated abroad. This would, for example, apply to action to restrict all kinds of transfrontier environmental pollution of a regional (water and air pollution) or global nature(depletion of the ozone layer, greenhouse effect resulting from carbon dioxide emissions, maintenance of biodiversity), or to the protection of wild fauna and flora. As early as 1987 the Court held that Directive 79/409 on the conservation of wild birds is based on the assumption that the protection of wild birds is 'typically a transfrontier environment problem entailing common responsibilities for the Member States'.[1] Directive 92/43 on the conservation of natural habitats also stipulates that it is necessary to take measures at Community level to conserve threatened habitats and species, as these form part of the Community's natural heritage and the threats to them are often of a trans-boundary nature. Further reference can be made to Directive 91/676 on pollution caused by nitrates from agricultural sources. Its preamble states that action at Community level is necessary because pollution of water due to nitrates on one Member State can influence waters in other Member States. Other examples of Directives in which the preamble refers to possible transfrontier effects are Directive 90/219 on genetically modified micro-organisms and Directive 89/369 on the incineration of municipal waste. In general, therefore, action by the Community on transfrontier environmental matters would seem to pass the test of subsidiarity.

Another important element of the application of the subsidiarity principle is whether action by the Member States alone, or inaction by the Community, would result in infringement of the provisions of the Treaty, such as to ensure competition, to avoid trade restrictions and to strengthen economic and social cohesion. A national, product-oriented environment policy would soon result in restrictions on imports and exports of certain environmentally-harmful goods and products. A strict environmental quality policy, or stringent anti-emission Regulations would not improve the competitive position of national industries compared with those abroad. There is no reason why the principle of subsidiarity should result in the Community pursuing too tame an environmental policy in such a case.

Finally, the Council – in this respect the most important legislative institution – must be convinced that action at Community level, by reason of the scale and the effects of the proposed action, will clearly be more beneficial than action at a purely national level. And it is precisely in cases of transfrontier environmental issues, a product-oriented environment policy or an environmental quality policy and stringent anti-emission measures that Community action can produce significant benefits of scale. If the environmental legislation that the Community has produced up to now were reviewed in the light of the above requirements of the

---

[1] Case 247/85, *Commission* v. *Belgium*, ECR 1987, 3029.

principle of subsidiarity, I very much doubt whether a single environmental Directive or Regulation would fail to pass the test.

b) Proportionality

The third paragraph of Article 3b continues: 'Any action by the Community shall not go beyond what is necessary to achieve the objectives of this Treaty.' This is a statement of the principle of proportionality. Here too the European Council has provided several guidelines. All charges, both for the Community and for the national governments must be kept to a minimum and be proportionate to the proposed objective. The Community must choose measures which leave the greatest degree of freedom for national decisions, and the national legal system should be respected. As much use as possible should be made of minimum standards, whereby Member States are free to lay down stricter national standards. Use of the Directive is to be preferred over the use of the Regulation, and the framework Directive is to be preferred over detailed measures. Non-binding instruments such as Recommendations should be used wherever possible, as well as voluntary codes of conduct.

Examples of such voluntary codes can already be found in various of the Community's environmental acts. Article 4 of Directive 91/676 on pollution caused by nitrates provides that the Member States must establish codes of good agricultural practice, to be implemented by farmers on a voluntary basis. The purpose of these codes is to reduce the pollution of water caused by nitrates from agricultural sources. Another example is Regulation 880/92. This Regulation, which introduces a Community eco-label award scheme, operates on a wholly voluntary basis. Where a product meets the applicable environmental criteria, the Community eco-label may be used. What is unusual here is that the various interest groups (industry, retailers, environmental organizations and so on) must be consulted for the purpose of defining the criteria that should apply. In the same vein is the 'Eco-audit' Regulation (1836/93) which aims to stimulate industry's own sense of responsibility for the environment by introducing a scheme of eco-management and eco-auditing. Participation in this scheme is not compulsory either: companies are encouraged to participate on a voluntary basis.

The Community's environment policy can also be said to comply with the guidelines in terms of its use of the Directive. From the start it has been customary to use the Directive for Community action in the field of the environment. Regulations have been used in only a few exceptional cases, chiefly in those sectors where a more uniform regime is necessary – for example to implement international agreements or to regulate international trade. Examples are Regulations 3626/82 on international trade in endangered species of wild fauna and flora, 348/81 on imports of whales and other cetacean products, and 259/93 on the export of hazardous waste. These all regulate the trade in certain goods or products with third countries. A more or less uniform Regulation is required at the external frontier of the Community in order to avoid deflections of trade. In these cases a Regulation is a more appropriate instrument than a Directive, because of its direct applicability. However, Regulations are used not only to regulate international trade. They are also used when it is necessary to grant certain rights directly to manufacturers, importers or even particular companies, or impose obligations on them. A good example of this is Regulation 793/93 on the evaluation and control of the risks of existing substances. This requires certain manufacturers and importers to submit information on potentially hazardous substances. The preamble states that a Regulation is the appropriate legal instrument, as it imposes directly on manufacturers and importers precise requirements to be implemented at the same time and in the same manner throughout the Community. The element of uniformity and identical application of rules throughout the Community was also the primary reason to opt to use this instrument for the measures on the Community eco-label and eco-management and audit schemes (Regulations 880/92 and 1836/93).

As far as the preference for 'minimum harmonization' expressed in the guidelines is concerned, minimum standards have regularly been utilized in Community environmental law. The principle is even stated in so many words in the EC Treaty itself, in Article 130t. In the vast majority of European environmental laws – for example the measures to combat water and air pollution – the Member States are empowered to introduce more stringent measures for their own territory. On the other hand, minimum standards are used less frequently in Community legislation on product standards. Perhaps the guidelines will change this, though in view of the impact product standards may have on the free movement of goods, the objectives of harmonization may stand in the way of the option of minimum harmonization. After all, it will then often be impossible to guarantee the free movement of goods, at least if the Member State of importation were also allowed to apply its stricter product standard laws to the product imported.

Finally it should be noted that the phenomenon of 'framework legislation' can already be found in European environmental law, for example, in Directive 76/464 on pollution caused by certain dangerous substances discharged into the aquatic environment of the Community and Directive 91/156 on waste.

II ARTICLE 130S

'Maastricht' has not made decision-making in the context of the Title on the Environment any easier. By my count, Article 130s provides for four different decision-making procedures.

1   Cooperation of Parliament and Council majority

The standard procedure is the cooperation procedure, as regulated in Article 189c. This features two references to the European Parliament. An essential element of this procedure is that the Council can vote by a qualified majority on a Commission proposal if it intends to accept the amendments to the Council's common position which have been formulated by the European Parliament and adopted by the Commission. On the other hand, the Council must take decisions unanimously if the European Parliament rejects the Council's common position or if the Council wishes to amend the re-examined proposal of the Commission. Article 130s(1) states that the Council, acting in accordance with the cooperation procedure, shall decide what action is to be taken by the Community 'in order to achieve the objectives referred to in Article 130r'.

2   Consultation of Parliament and Council unanimity or majority

Para.2 of Article 130s states that by way of derogation from this procedure, and without prejudice to the provisions of Article 100a, the Council, acting unanimously on a proposal from the Commission and after consulting the European Parliament and ECOSOC, shall adopt:

- provisions primarily of a fiscal nature;
- measures concerning town and country planning, land use with the exception of waste management and measures of a general nature, and management of water resources;
- measures significantly affecting a Member State's choice between different energy sources and the general structure of its energy supply.

The interpretation and application of para.2 can be expected to generate considerable problems. These include the following.

First, it should be noted that the term *fiscal nature* probably refers only to tax measures and not to all decision-making relating to financial instruments. In this sense the term must be interpreted narrowly. Where the provisions contemplated are indeed primarily of a fiscal nature, a Council measure should be based on Article 130s(2). It is not clear how this accords with Article 99 of the Maastricht Treaty, which regulates the Council's power of harmonization in respect of turnover taxes, excise duties and other forms of indirect taxation. Apparently Article 130s(2) does not apply without prejudice to the provisions of Article 99. For that to have been the case, Article 99 would have had to have been specifically excluded in the same way as Article 100a. This would mean that environmental measures primarily of a fiscal nature relating to the harmonization of turnover taxes, excise duties and other forms of indirect taxation would have to be based on Article 130s(2) and not on Article 99. The specific rule of Article 130s(2) would then have to be regarded as taking precedence over the general rule contained in Article 99.

An important question is therefore: when is an environmental provision primarily of a fiscal nature? Are the objectives of the intended policy relevant in answering this question, or are the instruments of policy more important? Or are perhaps both relevant?

The answer to this question is important even though the decision-making procedure provided for in Article 130s(2) is no different from that in Article 99. Both require unanimity. However, an important difference remains as to the legal consequences Article 130t attaches to decisions adopted pursuant to Article 130s. In any case, the legal basis is also important for the Council to be able to use its power under para.2 of Article 130s(2) to define which matters may be decided by qualified majority.

The drafters of the Treaty text were probably contemplating provisions such as the Commission proposal to introduce a tax on carbon dioxide emissions. This proposal is intended to achieve the harmonized introduction of a specific tax in the Member States, based on carbon-dioxide emissions and the calorific value of several fuels. The Commission regards a harmonized approach as necessary, on the one hand to ensure the free movement of the fuels subject to the tax and to prevent distortions of competition, and on the other to promote a rational use of energy. This is thus a measure of a fiscal nature designed to achieve certain environmental objectives. The present formulation of Article 130s(2) could thus be interpreted in such a way that measures which concern the harmonization of national taxes, but which ultimately aim to attain environmental objectives, could only be taken unanimously.

Another problem with the interpretation of Article 130s(2) is that it is not clear what should be understood by the addition of the word *primarily*. Probably the term can be regarded purely as a contrast with 'incidentally'. This does not mean that unanimity is therefore immediately required to adopt an environmental measure which incidentally provides for a limited measure of tax harmonization. When an environmental measure has only incidental fiscal effects, the primary decision-making rule contained in Article 130s(1) applies.

The exceptions referred to in the second sentence of Article 130s(2) are also problematic. Measures concerning town and country planning are also exempted from the cooperation procedure. But is there then any power at all to pursue an independent town and country planning policy under the title on the environment? This does not follow from the objectives of Article 130r(1). Nor will a comprehensive Community competence in the field of town and country planning be found elsewhere in the Treaty. But if such a power does not fall within the scope of Article 130r there is no need to except it. The question which then arises is, of course, whether it was the intention that any measure which has consequences for the physical layout of the territory of a Member State, and in that sense 'concerns' town and country planning, should be taken unanimously. That would mean that any area-related environmental policy would have to be adopted unanimously, whether within the framework of the protection of flora and fauna (Wild Birds and Habitat Directives), water quality policy (designation of fishing and swimming areas) or the combating of air pollution (zoning in connection with air quality policy). And what about measures in connection with environmental impact assessment? Equally, the rule of unanimous decision-making in respect of land use is ambiguous. Would it, for example, cover an amendment of Directive 86/278 concerning the protection of the environment and, in particular, of the soil when sewage sludge is used in agriculture? The text in no way makes this clear.

However, an exception is made to the requirement of unanimity for waste management and measures of a general nature. In these cases the normal procedure contained in Article 130s(1) applies again. This means that a Directive concerning the landfill of waste or other measures designed to protect the soil against environmental hazards caused by waste would in any event fall within the scope of application of Article 130s(1).

It is not apparent from the text what is to be understood by *measures of a general nature*. In the first place it could be asked whether the exception to the requirement of unanimity for 'measures of a general nature' only refers to the category of land use, or whether it also applies to measures concerning town and country planning. If the latter were the case, and the text does seem to indicate this, this would mean that general measures regulating town and country planning and land use are not covered by the requirement of unanimity laid down in Article 130s(2). However it is still not clear how this interpretation accords with the remarks made above about area-related environmental policy.

In the Dutch text of the Treaty, the word 'quantitative' has been added to the exception *management of water resources*. This would imply that only measures concerning the quantity of water are covered by the exception. The English text refers simply to *management of water resources*, the French to *la gestion des ressources hydrauliques* and the German to *der Bewirtschaftung der Wasserressourcen* – in other words without the addition of 'quantitative'. In view of these differences, it is not clear to what extent measures of water quality management should be excepted from the normal decision-making procedure. This would be an unfortunate development and would detract from the principle that water quality policy has traditionally been one of the core areas of European environment policy. A restrictive interpretation of the exception 'management of water resources' would therefore seem reasonable.

The third element of the paragraph is problematic in respect of the interpretation of the phrase *significantly affecting the choice between energy sources*. Sevenster rightly refers to the example of the carbon dioxide tax.[2] Does such a tax significantly affect the choice between various sources of energy or not? Or is it a measure primarily of a fiscal nature? Or is it one involving the harmonization of indirect taxes?

Another example is given by Directive 88/609 on the limitation of emissions of certain pollutants into the air from large combustion plants. This Directive sets emission limit values for power stations. The requirements are so stringent that those Member States in which brown coal is used for power production faced serious difficulties. The Directive authorizes such Member States to exceed the limit values under certain circumstances. The question which arises here is whether or not this Directive 'significantly affects' a Member State's choice between the various sources of energy.

These questions demonstrate that the interpretation of this category of measures, to which the requirement of unanimity ought to apply, will necessarily give rise to problems in practice.

The second subparagraph of Article 130s(2) states that the Council may, acting unanimously, define on which of the matters discussed above decisions are to be taken by a qualified majority. This is thus the third decision-making procedure contained in the Article. Article 7 of Regulation 594/91 on substances that deplete the ozone layer offers a practical example from the period of the SEA. In that Article the Council is charged with laying down rules with respect to the importation into the Community of products manufactured with CFCs or halons, but not themselves containing these substances. According to the provision the Council is to act by a qualified majority.

3   Co-decision of Parliament

The fourth decision-making procedure, referred to in Article 130s(3) is the so-called co-decision procedure. As with the cooperation procedure, the European Parliament is twice consulted on the measure proposed. However, an important difference lies in the Parliament's power ultimately to prevent the adoption of a proposal. This procedure applies to the adoption of what the Treaty calls 'general action programmes setting out priority objectives to be attained'.

According to para.3, these action programmes are to be adopted 'in other areas'. But what other areas are in fact contemplated? Other areas than those re-

---

[2] H.G. Sevenster, *Milieubeleid en Gemeenschapsrecht*, Leiden: Dissertatie RU, 1992, pp. 412–3.

ferred to in paras 1 and 2 of the Article? This seems unlikely, as it would imply that action programmes are adopted for those environmental sectors which are not covered by paras 1 and 2. But if that were so, it would be hard to conceive of any example of an action programme that could still be adopted. The second subparagraph of para.3, which refers to the measures necessary for the implementation of the programmes which are to be adopted under the terms of paras 1 and 2, also makes it clear that this cannot be the right interpretation. We shall have to assume that the drafters of the Treaty were in error here, and the phrase 'in other areas' should perhaps be regarded as never having been written. It will therefore be assumed below that action programmes on the environment, which are adopted under the co-decision procedure, may cover the whole environmental spectrum.

However, it would seem that only priority objectives can be set in these action programmes and that they cannot give rise to direct legal consequences for the Member States. This interpretation is supported by para.2 of Article 130s(3). Measures which are necessary for the implementation of these programmes must be based on paras 1 or 2 of Article 130s, depending on the subject matter. Obligations for Member States could then only be imposed by adopting the necessary measures of implementation (Directives and Regulations).

III   ARTICLE 100A

Article 100a of the Maastricht Treaty provides that the Council shall, acting in accordance with the co-decision procedure, adopt the measures 'for the approximation of the provisions laid down by law, Regulation or administrative action in Member States which have as their objective the establishment and functioning of the internal market'.

It will be clear that many measures which can be characterized as environmental measures may also have a significant impact on the establishment of the internal market. This is recognized in the Treaty. The provisions of Article 100a(3), by which the Commission, in its proposals on, *inter alia*, environmental protection, will take as a base a high level of protection, indicates that at any rate certain environmental measures fall within the scope of Article 100a.

Thus it could be said that the harmonization of the conditions under which certain environmentally harmful products are placed on the market is important for attaining the free movement of goods. After all, as long as the product standard laws continue to differ in the various Member States, there can be no question of the free movement of environmentally hazardous goods. Harmonization of the conditions under which such products are allowed to be placed on the market and/or used will thus often fall within the scope of Article 100a.

However, many other environmental measures may relate very directly to the functioning of the internal market such as, for example, emission standards and environmental quality standards. Emission threshold values regulate the maximum permitted level of emissions of a given environmentally harmful substance, and consequently affect the investments companies have to make and their competitive positions. If a Member State adopts more stringent emission threshold values than is usual in other Member States, its own industry is, at least to some extent, put at a competitive disadvantage.

Similar comments could be made in respect of environmental quality standards (air/water/radiation) and legislation for the prevention and management of waste. Harmonization of emission threshold values and environmental quality objectives has a levelling effect on conditions of competition and thus on the proper operation of the internal market.

Differences in non-substantive or procedural requirements – for example, environmental impact assessment, environmental statements, openness, access to the courts and so on – may also produce distortion of competition. Here, too, to a greater or lesser extent, internal market considerations play a part.

In the past many authors have assumed a limited interpretation of the concept 'internal market'. In view of the definition in Article 7a of the Treaty – an area without internal frontiers in which the free movement of goods, persons, services and capital is ensured – it was doubtful whether distortions of competition caused by differences in national emission or environmental quality standards would still fall within the scope of the abolition of the internal frontiers. It now appears that this doubt was misplaced. In the *TiO$_2$* case,[3] the European Court of Justice, referring to its decision in Case 92/79 observed:

Action intended to approximate national rules concerning production conditions in a given industrial sector with the aim of eliminating distortions of competition in that sector is conducive to the attainment of the internal market and thus falls within the scope of Article 100 A, a provision which is particularly appropriate to the attainment of the internal market.

The Court held that the content of Directive 89/428 on the reduction of pollution caused by waste from the titanium dioxide industry fell within the scope of Article 100a. The Directive contains rules prohibiting or requiring the reduction of the discharge of waste and lays down timetables for the implementation of the various provisions. An unusual feature of this case was of course that the Directive applied to a specific industry. The Court referred to this in its judgement.

The question which now arises is to what extent environmental measures which have a more diffuse effect on the competitive position of companies can in princi-

---

[3]   Case C-300/89, ECR 1991, I-2867.

ple fall within the scope of the Article. In its decision in Case C-155/91[4] on the validity of Directive 91/156 on waste, the Court does acknowledge that the obligation contained in Article 4 of that Directive – under which Member States are required to take the necessary measures to ensure that waste is recovered or disposed of without endangering human health and without harming the environment – can have a certain harmonizing effect, so that 'les charges des opérateurs économiques soient désormais largement équivalentes dans tous les Etats membres'. However, the mere fact that the internal market is concerned ('est concerné') is insufficient to cause Article 100a to apply. It therefore seems that this case can be used to show that a measure does not have to be a harmonization measure within the meaning of Article 100a, if the effect of attaining market integration is only incidental.

Case C-155/91 involved environmental legislation relating to a large group of companies. But even with legislation on the harmonization of product standards the question may arise whether, and if so when, the effect on the internal market is only incidental. In the second Chernobyl case,[5] the validity of Regulation 3954/87 was discussed. This Regulation lays down maximum permitted levels of radioactive contamination of foodstuffs and feedingstuffs. Products with too high a level of contamination may not be placed on the market. The European Parliament contended that, in view of the prohibition on marketing, it was an internal market measure which should therefore have been based on Article 100a. The Court, however, concluded that the Regulation, according to its objectives and its content, was designed to protect the general public against the dangers of foodstuffs which have been contaminated with radioactivity. It held that the prohibition of marketing

> ...is only one condition for the effectiveness of the application of the maximum permitted levels. The Regulation therefore has only the incidental effect of harmonizing the conditions for the free movement of goods within the Community inasmuch as, by means of the adoption of uniform protective measures, it avoids the need for trade in foodstuffs and feedingstuffs which have undergone radioactive contamination to be made the subject of unilateral national measures.

The Court held that, as a result, the measure falls outside the scope of Article 100a. This shows that not every harmonization of national product standards necessarily falls within the scope of the Article. If the effect on the internal market is no more than a logical consequence of a particular environmental measure, it can be argued that the measure should not be based on Article 100a. This might par-

---

[4] Not yet reported.
[5] Case C-70/88, ECR 1991, I-4529.

ticularly be the case for Community environmental measures which oblige the Member States to prohibit certain environmentally harmful products, but, like Regulation 3954/87, do not contain a 'free movement clause' and thus do not prevent the Member States imposing more stringent standards. It might be said of this type of environmental Directive that they are protective measures according to their objectives and their content and that the effect on the internal market should only be regarded as an incidental consequence.

It is reasonable to conclude that the scope of Article 100a is, in principle, more than sufficient to serve as a basis for measures approximating national laws on product standards and for environmental measures which remove distortions of competition in a particular industry. However, in neither case is its scope unlimited. For more general environmental measures, which have a diffuse, rather than a specific, effect on the competitive position of companies, it can be concluded from the case law that, when the effects are of an incidental nature, the measure falls outside the scope of Article 100a. The Article's scope of application is also limited in respect of the harmonization of product standards. Here, too, the term 'incidental' is important.

In view of the wide scope of Article 100a in principle, and the equally wide powers of the Council under Article 130s, all kinds of problems of demarcation arise. Examples of environmental measures the Council has based on Article 100a are:

- Directive 90/220 on the deliberate release into the environment of genetically modified organisms;
- Directive 91/157 on batteries and accumulators containing certain dangerous substances;
- Directive 92/112 on procedures for harmonizing the programmes for the reduction and eventual elimination of pollution caused by waste from the titanium dioxide industry;
- Regulation 793/93 on the evaluation and control of the risks of existing substances;
- Directive 93/12 relating to the sulphur content of certain liquid fuels.

These are certainly measures in which the preamble states that Community action is needed – on the one hand, because the laws in force in the Member States may constitute a barrier to trade or result in unfair conditions of competition and, on the other, because measures are necessary from the perspective of protecting the environment.

IV   OTHER INCIDENTAL LEGAL BASES FOR THE COMMUNITY'S ENVIRONMENT POLICY

1   The provisions on the common agricultural policy

Under Article 39 of the EC Treaty the objectives of the common agricultural policy (*CAP*) are: to increase agricultural productivity; to ensure a fair standard of living for the agricultural community; to stabilize markets; to assure the availability of supplies; and to ensure that supplies reach consumers at reasonable prices.

Environmental considerations have played a part (even if only in part) in many measures which have been adopted, within the context of the policy as, for example, in Directive 75/268 on mountain and hill farming in certain less favoured areas, which created the possibility of giving aid for conservation of the countryside.

Important measures which have been taken in this context are:

- Regulation 2078/92 on agricultural production methods compatible with the requirements of the protection of the environment and the maintenance of the countryside;
- Regulation 2083/92 on organic production of agricultural products and indications referring thereto on agricultural products and foodstuffs;
- Directive 91/414 concerning the placing of plant protection products on the market; Regulations 1613/89 and 1614/89 on protection of the Community forests (against air pollution and fire).

2   The provisions on the common transport policy

The second sector in which the Treaty refers to a common policy is transport. In the same way as with agriculture, environmental considerations play a part in transport policy. Council measures on transport, based at least partly on Articles 74 and 84 of the Treaty, and where environmental considerations figure are:

- Directive 92/6 on the installation and use of speed devices for certain categories of motor vehicles within the Community;
- Directive 92/55 on the approximation of the laws of the Member States relating to roadworthiness tests for motor vehicles and their trailers (exhaust emissions);
- Directives 80/51, 83/206, 89/629 on the limitation of noise emissions from subsonic aircraft;
- Directive 93/75 concerning minimum requirements for vessels bound for or leaving Community ports and carrying dangerous or polluted goods.

3 Harmonization of indirect taxes under Article 99

These days a great deal is said about making more frequent use of market-oriented instruments for the pursuit of environmental policy.[6] Financial instruments should be used to attain certain environmental objectives. One of the means at the disposal of the Member States is indirect taxation. According to Article 95 of the Treaty Member States may use environmental criteria to justify tax differentiation. Put briefly, the Treaty allows the possibility of taxing products that cause more environmental pollution than those that cause less. However, it will be clear that, if Member States introduce varying differentiations based on environmental considerations, this will have a negative impact on the operation of the internal market. Thus Article 99 offers the Council a legal basis on which to adopt provisions for the harmonization of legislation concerning turnover taxes, excise duties and other forms of indirect taxation. The more popular the national authorities find the use of financial instruments to protect the environment, the more frequently the Council will be required to use its powers under Article 99.

It should be noted that Article 99 does not provide a basis for a truly 'European' environmental tax in the sense of an environmental tax introduced by the Community and for the Community. The only basis for such a tax is to be found in Article 130s(2), and would in any case require an 'extensive' interpretation of the provision.

Up to now Article 99 has played only a minor role in the field of the environment. The Commission has, for example, based its proposal for a Directive introducing a tax on carbon dioxide emissions and energy on Articles 99 and 130s. One of the considerations stated in the preamble is that a number of Member States have already introduced or are planning to introduce taxes on carbon dioxide emissions and the use of energy, and that a harmonized approach is therefore needed to ensure the functioning of the internal market.

4 The provisions on research and technological development

Articles 130f–p provide for powers in the field of research and technological development. The Community's objective is to strengthen the scientific and technological bases of Community industry and to encourage it to become more competitive at international level, while promoting all the research activities deemed necessary by virtue of other Chapters of the Treaty.

---

[6] See the related Chapters 13 and 15 by G. Bándi and E. Rehbinder respectively, in this volume.

Examples of environmental research programmes that were instituted under the SEA are the following:

- the biotechnology programme (Decision 92/218);
- the JOULE programme (Decision 89/236);
- the STEP and EPOCH programmes (Decision 89/625);
- Decision 91/354 adopting a specific research and technological development programme in the field of the environment (1990–1994).

5   Articles 30, 31 and 32 of the Euratom Treaty

The most significant environmentally relevant legal bases outside the EC Treaty are to be found in the Euratom Treaty. Chapter 3 of Title II of that Treaty in particular deserves mention here. Health and Safety Articles 30–39 require that basic standards be laid down for the protection of the health of workers and the general public against the dangers arising from ionizing radiation. According to Article 30 the expression 'basic standards' means:

- maximum permissible doses compatible with adequate safety;
- maximum permissible levels of exposure and contamination;
- the fundamental principles governing the health surveillance of workers.

The Council has based various decisions on Articles 31 and 32 for the purpose of attaining these objectives. These decisions relate to radiation from permanent plants, radioactive products, cross-border transport of radioactive waste and products contaminated with radiation. The case law shows that if the Council's measures, according to their objectives and their content, are designed to protect the general public and workers against the dangers of radioactivity, they will fall within the scope of application of Article 31. In the second Chernobyl case[7] the European Parliament tried to restrict the scope of Article 31 to measures concerning protection against 'primary' radiation – in other words, radiation released directly from a nuclear plant or resulting from the handling of fissile materials. In the view of the European Parliament, Article 31 did not relate to so-called 'secondary' radiation – that is, radiation emanating from contaminated products and other incidental consequences of primary radiation. The Court rejected this restricted interpretation:

> There is no support in the relevant legislation for that restrictive interpretation which cannot therefore be accepted. The indications are rather that the purpose

---

[7]   Case C-70/88, ECR 1991, I-4529.

of the Articles referred to is to ensure the consistent and effective protection of the health of the general public against the dangers arising from ionizing radiations, whatever their source and whatever the categories of persons exposed to such radiations.

The only real restriction on the scope of application of the Article is to be found in its objectives. Advocate General Van Gerven properly concluded that Article 31 cannot be used as a legal basis for the adoption of measures relating to the establishment and functioning of the internal market. Thus the question arises to what extent measures of the Council, based exclusively on Article 31, may contain provisions which limit the freedom of Member States to enact more stringent measures than those actually provided for in the measures in question.

6   Article 37 of the Euratom Treaty and other Euratom provisions

Under Article 37 of the Euratom Treaty, each Member State is required to provide the Commission with such general data relating to any plan for the disposal of radioactive waste in whatever form, as will make it possible to determine whether the implementation of that plan is liable to result in the radioactive contamination of the water, soil or airspace of another Member State. In Recommendation 82/181 the Commission indicated what information the Member States were supposed to supply to the Commission. After consulting experts, the Commission is to give its opinion to the Member State, particularly in respect of possible transboundary consequences. Over the years the Commission has given its opinion in some dozen cases under Article 37.

In the *Cattenom* case,[8] the Court of Justice ruled on the interpretation of Article 37. This case concerned the question of whether a Member State has to supply the Commission with the relevant data before or after the issue of authorization by the national authorities. The Court held:

> ... it must be acknowledged that, where a Member State makes the disposal of radioactive waste subject to authorization, the Commission's opinion must, in order to be rendered fully effective, be brought to the notice of that state before the issue of any such authorization.

> If a decision has already been adopted, it becomes more difficult to take account of an unfavourable Commission opinion, which would oblige the public authority to repudiate the action of departments or bodies which inspired that decision. Furthermore, it is possible that, in certain Member States, an authorization for the disposal of radioactive waste might confer rights upon the person

---

8   Case C-187/87, ECR 1988, 5013.

to whom it it was granted and could not easily be withdrawn. Finally, knowledge of the Commission's opinion may be use for the purpose of enabling any person concerned to assess the merits of a possible legal action against the decision granting authorization.

All the foregoing lead to the view that the Commission's opinion has no real chance of being examined in detail and of having any effective influence on the attitude of the State concerned unless it is issued before the adoption of any decision definitively authorizing disposal, which a fortiori implies that the opinion must be sought before such authorization is granted.

Article 34 gives the Commission a power more far-reaching than the right to give an opinion contained in Article 37. Where 'particularly dangerous experiments' are involved, which are liable to affect the territories of other Member States, the assent of the Commission is required. If no such consequences are to be expected, the Commission only has a right to deliver an opinion. These days, where the peaceful use of nuclear energy will not easily be regarded as a 'particularly dangerous experiment', Article 34 has hardly any practical significance.

V   PROBLEMS OF DEMARCATION: THE RELATIONSHIP BETWEEN ARTICLES 100A AND 130S OF THE EC TREATY

1   The situation under the Single European Act

From the above it is clear that a great deal of European environmental law has a dual objective: the protection of the environment and the proper functioning of the internal or common market. This dual objective was the reason that the vast majority of Community environmental legislation was based on both Article 100 and Article 235 of the Treaty. This practice was in conformity with the Court's view in the TiO_2 case:

... where an institution's power is based on two provisions of the Treaty, it is bound to adopt the relevant measures on the basis of the two relevant provisions.[9]

This dual legal basis presented no problems in the environment sector, because the decision-making procedures involved were virtually the same.

However, following the entry into force of the SEA, continuation of the practice of using a dual legal basis did present problems. The procedures contained in Article 100a – the cooperation procedure and a qualified majority – and Article 130s

---

[9]   Case C-300/89, ECR 1991, I-2867.

– unanimity – were different. And, by virtue of Articles 100a(4) and 130t the legal consequences of decision-making were not the same either. As a result a single legal basis was employed in practice, either Article 100a or Article 130s. It has even been the case that an issue which could, on substantive grounds, appropriately have been dealt with in a single Directive, was split over two separate Directives – namely Directives 90/219 and 90/220 on genetically modified organisms (GMOs). The 'commercial' aspects of the use of GMOs are regulated in a Directive based on Article 100a, while the safety and environmental aspects are contained in one based on Article 130s.

As to the question of when Article 100a is the appropriate legal basis and when it is Article 130s, the Court has attempted to supply the answer in two cases, the TiO$_2$ case and Case C-155/91. In the TiO$_2$ case the Court held that Directive 89/428 had wrongly been based on Article 130s rather than Article 100a. The Court had to reach a decision as to which of the two provisions of the Treaty should be used. It offers three considerations:

1   The integration principle set out in Article 130r(2) provides that environmental protection requirements shall be a component of the Community's other policies. That principle implies that a Community measure cannot be covered by Article 130s merely because it also pursues objectives of environmental protection;

2   The Directive aims to eliminate distortions of competition in the titanium dioxide industry. Thus the Directive is conducive to the attainment of the internal market and falls within the scope of Article 100a;

3   Article 100 A (3) requires the Commission, in its proposals for internal market measures, to take as a base a high level of protection in matters of environmental protection. That provision thus expressly indicates that the objectives of environmental protection referred to in Article 130 R may be effectively pursued by means of harmonizing measures adopted on the basis of Article 100 A.

The second consideration seems the least convincing, because although it shows that the Directive falls within the scope of Article 100a, it does not show that Article 100a should therefore be used. The Directive also falls within the scope of Article 130s. That is precisely the problem. The other two arguments, the integration principle and the principle of a high level of protection, are more convincing. They are systematic arguments which indicate that the Treaty assumes that measures designed to attain the internal market and protect the environment will be based on Article 100a. Only in this interpretation do both principles have a purpose. The principle of a high level of protection contained in Article 100a(3) is unnecessary if environmental measures are always going to be based on Article

130s. The same applies to the integration principle, at least in so far as it relates to internal market measures.

Because of this case law, many legal writers have drawn the conclusion that the bulk of Community environment policy should be based on Article 100a. The only function of Article 130s is said to be in the field of the protection of flora, fauna and nature. After all, the vast majority of Community environmental legislation relates both to the protection of the environment and the elimination of barriers to the internal market.

It was thus not surprising, in the light of the TiO_2 case, that the Commission disputed the validity of Directive 91/156 amending Directive 75/442, the 'old' Directive on waste, in Case C-155/91. The Directive was based on Article 130s, although the Commission argued that Article 100a was the proper legal basis. However, to many people's surprise, the Court held that the Directive was properly based on Article 130s. Above it was noted that the TiO_2 Directive concerned, in-dissociably, a dual objective. In the case of the Directive on waste, the Court found the situation to be different. Here there was no question of indissociably linked objectives, but of the primary objective ('objet principal', para. 20 of the judge-ment) of protection of the environment, while the effects on the internal market and the conditions of competition were regarded as incidental and accessory (paras 18 and 20). In a case like this, the legal basis should depend on the primary objec-tive.

The question which then arises is, of course, when does a Community measure have indissociably linked objectives, as in the TiO_2 case, and when does it pri-marily have the protection of the environment as its objective, as in Case C-155/91?

The central element in both decisions is that the choice of the legal basis for a Community measure must depend on objective factors which are amenable to ju-dicial review. In other words, the Council is not free to choose the legal basis of the proposed measure. The proper legal basis flows, as it were, from the aim and the content of the proposed measure. However, from the way the Court determines the aim and content of a measure, it is evident that to some extent Community lawmakers are indeed able to influence the choice of legal basis.

In Case C-155/91 the primary aim of Directive 91/156, protecting the environ-ment, was determined by the Court on the grounds of the provisions contained in the fourth, sixth, seventh and ninth recitals of the Directive's preamble. These expressly encompassed environmental protection. It is true that the fifth recital concerned the better functioning of the internal market, but this 'only' led the Court to conclude that this was an incidental or secondary objective. It could be contended that, by placing such a one-sided emphasis on the objectives formulated by the Council in the preamble to the Directive, the Court has more or less given the Council a licence to determine for itself the legal basis of a measure. As long as the Council mentions sufficiently frequently that the objective of a measure is the protection of the environment and that there are either no effects on the internal market or that such effects are of only incidental significance, it would seem able to use Article 130s as a legal basis. This means that there can hardly be any question of the objective factors referred to above.

As far as determining the content of a measure is concerned, the Court appears primarily to examine the concrete obligations referred to in the Directive. In the TiO_2 case the Court deduced from the content of the Directive – it prohibits, or requires the reduction of, the discharge of waste – that it was concerned both with the protection of the environment and the harmonization of conditions of competition. In Case C-155/91 the Court deduced from the content of the Directive on waste – it requires the prevention of the production of waste, the disposal of waste without risk to human health or the environment, the setting up of an integrated and adequate network of disposal installations – that its primary object was the protection of the environment. The harmonizing effects on the conditions of competition were in this case found to be incidental and accessory.

It is still curious that harmonization of the conditions under which waste from the titanium dioxide industry is processed does appear to have an effect on the internal market, but that harmonization of the conditions under which other waste is processed must be regarded primarily as environmental protection. Perhaps the explanation is that the TiO_2 Directive affected a specific industry and that the effect of the cost of disposal on the production costs could therefore be precisely demonstrated. By contrast, the Directive on waste is a more diffuse piece of legislation applying to the whole of industry.

What impact do these decisions have on the rest of the Community's environment policy? First, it should be remembered that, as has already been noted several times, almost every Community environmental measure aims to bring about both the protection of the environment and the attainment of the internal market. What the cases discussed above show is that the question which then arises is whether the objectives are indissociably linked, or whether they are primary or incidental objectives. It is hard to say in advance whether they will be regarded as the one or the other. Determining the validity of legislation adopted under the SEA therefore remains a matter of some uncertainty from a legal point of view.

The decision in Case C-155/91 has clouded the legal situation even in respect of harmonization of environmental product policy, a field in which legal writers had thus far unquestioningly assumed that this could be implemented on the basis of Article 100a. Could measures only be based on Article 100a if they are intended to attain fully liberalized free movement of goods? This interpretation is supported by paras 11–15 of the judgement in Case-155/91. On the other hand the practice of environmental product harmonization also provides the best examples of indissociably linked protective and internal market objectives: on the one hand imposing environmental conditions on a product, on the other often containing a 'free movement clause' stating that if the products comply with the requirements of the legislation Member States may not impose further restrictions. See, for example, para. 22 of the judgement in Case 278/85. Under the SEA, such harmonization measures would have had to be based on Article 100a.

However, if measures designed to harmonize product standards do not contain a 'free movement clause' and if there is no question of full harmonization, the situation may be different. It follows from the Court's decision in the second Chernobyl case[10] that in such cases there is a situation in which the effects on the internal market must be regarded as incidental. In this case the Court held that the primary objective of a Regulation laying down maximum permitted doses of radiation with which agricultural products may be placed on the market (which did not contain a free movement clause) was protection of the general public, and that any effects on the internal market were only incidental. The Regulation was therefore correctly based on Article 31 of the Euratom Treaty and not on Article 100a of the EEC Treaty. In view of the fact that Article 31 of the Euratom Treaty has a similar 'protective objective' to that of Article 130s of the EEC Treaty, it would seem that the Court's approach could be extended to cover the demarcation of Articles 100a and 130s. Harmonization of environmental product standards which does not extend to full harmonization, perhaps because there is no 'free movement clause', would then have to be based on Article 130s.

In summary the conclusion can be drawn that, at the time of the SEA, the demarcation of Articles 100a and 130s seemed clear in theory, but that it has in practice led to considerable legal uncertainty as to the validity of a great deal of Community legislation enacted during that period.

2   The present legal situation

The question is to what extent the conclusions that have been drawn above are still relevant today. This question is particularly relevant because both Articles 100a and 130s have undergone significant changes. Nonetheless, the decision-making procedures laid down in the two Articles still differ. It might therefore be assumed that the problems of demarcation have remained essentially unchanged and that the decisions in the TiO_2 case and Case C-155/91 not only still apply, but will still be followed. This conclusion is too simple. It must be remembered that in the $TiO2$ case the Court was forced to choose between Article 100a and Article 130s, because the two procedures were incompatible. The sole fact that decision-making

---

[10]   Case C-70/88, ECR 1991, I-4529.

procedures differ does not automatically mean that a choice has to be made. There are examples of Court of Justice decisions where different procedures flowing from different Articles have been combined. For example, in *Commission* v. *Council*[11] the Court held that the procedures of Article 28 (then requiring unanimity) and Article 113 (qualified majority) together constituted an appropriate legal basis. It has also allowed the combination of the procedures of Article 128 (absolute majority) and Article 235 (unanimity). Where different decision-making procedures are combined, the modalities of the two procedures are cumulative. In fact this means that the 'tougher' of the two procedures should be adopted, plus any additional modalities of the 'easier' procedure.

In the light of the above it must be examined to what extent the four different decision-making procedures contained in Article 130s are either incompatible or cumulatively applicable with the co-decision procedure laid down by Article 100a.

Article 130s(1) provides for the cooperation procedure and thus differs from Article 100a, which requires the co-decision procedure. However, the differences do not seem to be such that the two procedures could not be applied cumulatively. By comparison with the cooperation procedure, the co-decision procedure basically contains two additional elements: the role of the conciliation committee and the veto of the European Parliament. These two elements can, in my view, be applied cumulatively with the cooperation procedure.

Article 130s(2) requires unanimity in the Council. This seems incompatible with the co-decision procedure. After all, the co-decision procedure can be viewed as a cooperation procedure with a number of additional features including, significantly the veto of the European Parliament. If the Court decides, as it did in the TiO$_2$ case, that the cooperation procedure cannot be combined with a procedure requiring unanimity, this must apply *a fortiori* to the co-decision procedure. The principle laid down in the TiO$_2$ case is therefore fully applicable here. Measures which fall within the scope of Article 130s(2) and which, in addition to an environmental objective, also concern, indissociably, an internal market objective will thus have to be based solely on Article 100a.

In the light of Case C-155/91, measures which fall within the scope of Article 130s(2) and which only incidentally concern the internal market should be based solely on Article 130s(2). Demarcation from Article 100a is not in itself a problem in relation to decision-making based on the second subparagraph of Article 130s(2), because this only provides for a form of self-delegation. The second subparagraph can therefore only function in those policy areas in which the framework decision has been based on Article 130s(2). As has just been noted, these will be environmental measures which in principle fall within the scope of Article 130s(2) and only incidentally relate to the internal market.

---

[11]   Case C-165/87, ECR 1988, 5545.

As far as the adoption of action programmes is concerned, there are no problems of demarcation. Both action programmes based on Article 130s(3) and 'the measures' referred to in Article 100a are adopted using the co-decision procedure. Where necessary Article 100a can therefore be invoked in addition to Article 130s(3). No particular problems are anticipated in practice.

FURTHER READING ON EC ENVIRONMENTAL LAW

Baldock, D. and Beafoy, G., *The Integration of Environmental Protection: Requirements into the Definition and Implementation of other EC Policies*, London: Institute for European Environmental Policy, 1992.
Brinkhorst, L.J., *Subsidiariteit en Milieu in de Europese Gemeenschap*, Leiden: Oratie RU, 1992.
Jarass, H.D. and Neumann, L.F., *Umweltschutz und Europäische Gemeinschaften*, Berlin, 1992.
Jans, J., *Europees Milieurecht in Nederland*, (2nd edn), Groningen: Woltersboek, 1994.
Krämer, L., *Focus on EEC Environmental Law*, London: Sweet and Maxwell, 1992.
Krämer, L., *European Environmental Law Casebook*, London: Sweet and Maxwell, 1993.
Krämer, L., *EC Treaty and Environmental Protection*, (2nd edn), London: Sweet and Maxwell, 1995.
Rehbinder, E. and Stewart, R., *Environmental Protection Policy*, Berlin: de Gruyter, 1985.
Rengeling, H.-W. (ed.), *Umweltschutz und andere Politiken der EG*, Köln, 1993.
Sevenster, H.G., *Milieubeleid en Gemeenschapsrecht*, Leiden: Dissertatie RU, 1992.
Verhoeve, B., Bennet, G. and Wilkinson, D., *Maastricht and the Environment*, Arnhem, 1992.

20 Transboundary Transfers of Dangerous Goods

Gretta Goldenman

Table of Contents

I INTRODUCTION

International trade can lead to significant economic and political benefits, including more jobs and improved standards of living.[1] But commercial exchanges across national borders can also bring counterpart environmental problems. The opening of a country's borders so that its industries and consumers can benefit from the larger global marketplace can make control of risks accompanying certain products and materials difficult. International trade rules aimed at removing barriers to trade can impede a country's efforts to achieve the level of environmental or consumer protection it desires within its own territory.

---

1 Indeed, the free movement of goods is one of the four freedoms that has led to the economic success of the European Union. Article 30 of the Treaty of Rome prohibits Member States from setting quantitative restrictions and all measures having equivalent effect on imports. The other three 'freedoms' enshrined in the Treaty of Rome are the free movement of capital (Art. 67), the free movement of workers (Art. 48), and the freedom of establishment (Art. 52).

Problems also arise when countries seek to raise the level of environmental and consumer protection by, *inter alia*, setting in place stringent environmental regulations. Regulations requiring the safe disposal of industrial wastes have led to a rise in the global trade of such wastes as companies seek to reduce costs by exporting waste for cheaper disposal elsewhere. The highly developed environmental regulatory systems of the advanced industrialized countries have been blamed for the relocation of some high-risk manufacturing facilities to countries with less developed environmental regulations. Moreover, a new generation of environmental laws aimed at addressing the environmental impact of a product throughout its life cycle are under scrutiny as possible trade barriers against products coming from countries with lower environmental standards.

Setting in place laws which strike the right balance between free trade and environmental protection is difficult. A country's national laws on these issues can reflect deep societal values which may not be shared by countries that have different goals. Even within the relatively limited arena of the European Union, conflicts between the principle of free circulation of goods and national preferences for higher levels of environmental protection are not easily solved.

This chapter reviews some of the international efforts to control the environmental impacts of transboundary trade, taking the Member States of the EC as a reference point. It provides an overview of the debate over the relationship between trade and the environment, and some of the various international, regional and national bodies involved in the debate. It takes a closer look at the history of international controls over traffic in hazardous goods. It then surveys the EC's laws which control (a) the circulation of goods within and into the single market, and (b) the export of hazards to third countries. Finally, it considers the significance of the EC's laws, and of the international debate over environmental controls and the free circulation of goods, for the countries of Central and Eastern Europe which aspire to eventual EC membership.

II   ENVIRONMENTAL PROTECTION VERSUS FREE MOVEMENT OF GOODS: A MULTI-LEVELLED DEBATE

The debate over the relationship between trade and the environment, including controls over international traffic in hazardous goods, is taking place on multiple levels – internationally, within regional organizations such as the European Union, and nationally. International efforts to address environment-related problems arising from transborder trade first focused on the development of a common set of rules to cover the transboundary transport of dangerous goods, for example, the *Recommendations* of the United Nations Committee of Experts on the Transport of Dangerous Goods (the so-called Orange Book). Other UN- affiliated efforts to control international traffic in hazards have emanated from the World Health Organization (WHO), the Food and Agriculture Organization (FAO), the International Labor Organization (ILO), and the United Nations Environment Programme (UNEP). The Organization for Economic Cooperation and Development (OECD) has also been an important international forum for international cooperation on controls over dangerous goods.

In recent years, provisions allowing for trade sanctions as a means of enforcing compliance have been included in some 20 international environmental agreements. Among the more well known are those in the Montreal Protocol on Substances that Deplete the Ozone Layer ('Montreal Protocol')[2] and the Basel Convention on the Control of Transboundary Movements of Hazardous Wastes ('Basel Convention').[3] Such trade provisions, especially if they discriminate against countries that are not Parties to the agreement, may be incompatible with general rules of international trade.

Internationally, the issue came to the fore during the Uruguay Round of the General Agreement on Tariffs and Trade (GATT). GATT is aimed at lowering national tariffs on raw materials and manufactured goods.[4] It also provides a forum for trade disputes between GATT parties. Although GATT permits a country to restrict imports if 'necessary to protect human, animal or plant life or health', such restrictions are not allowed if they constitute 'unjustifiable' discrimination against foreign competitors.

In 1991 a panel of GATT trade arbitrators ruled that the embargo provisions of a US law protecting marine mammals were an unfair barrier to trade.[5] The panel held that 'extraterritorial' enforcement of a country's own laws was not recognized under international law. It also held that laws regulating the *process* by which a product is harvested or produced were harmful to free trade because they could be used to discriminate against foreign companies.

The ensuing debate led to international agreement to set up a permanent trade and environment committee within the new World Trade Organization established

---

2 Cf. Art. 4: 'Control of Trade with Non-parties' of the 1987 Montreal Protocol, and Article 1.O of the London Amendments to the Montreal Protocol amending Article 4.

3 Cf. Art. 4: 'General Obligations' of the 1989 Basel Convention prohibiting Parties, *inter alia*, from exporting hazardous wastes to a non-Party or importing such wastes from a non-Party.

4 GATT is the major multilateral agreement on international trade. More than 100 countries have signed GATT. Since GATT was first agreed in 1948, the average tariff has been reduced from 40 to 5 per cent. The Uruguay Rounds, concluded in 1994, focused on expanding GATT to cover more goods and, for the first time, services. Non-tariff barriers to trade were also considered.

5 The US Marine Mammal Protection Act banned the sale of tuna in the USA from countries where more dolphins were killed by fishermen than allowed under US standards.

by the Uruguay Round, to consider the relationship between international trade rules and environmental controls. Environment-related provisions are included in the Uruguay Round. Technical regulations adopted by parties to GATT, including environmental standards and measures, must 'not be more trade-restrictive than necessary to fulfil a legitimate objective.'[6] In addition, the Uruguay Round requires all national standard-setting bodies of GATT Parties to base national standards on international norms. Exceptions to international standards must be supported by 'available scientific and technical information'. Environmental advocates fear that these provisions could be used to subordinate national environmental concerns to the push to remove technical barriers to trade.

The heart of the debate is the inherent conflict between free trade and environmental protection. Free trade stands for the unrestricted exchange of commerce across national borders.[7] Environmental protection laws seek to prevent harm to the environment by restricting certain practices and products. Free trade does not require the elimination of product standards or environmental rules. It does, however, require that those rules not be designed or administered in a way that unfairly discriminates against the industries of other countries.

Free trade advocates point out that advanced environmental standards could cause companies from countries without the technology or expertise to meet those standards to lose market access into those countries maintaining high environmental standards. In order to maintain open business competition, they would harmonize environmental regulations. Environmental protection advocates worry that a liberalized (that is, deregulated) free trade system will reduce existing environmental protection laws to the lowest common denominator and dictate the content of national or even local laws in such diverse areas as forest harvesting, energy use, toxic chemicals and food safety. They are also concerned about suggestions that the trade sanction provisions in international environmental treaties should be subject to GATT Council approval.

---

6 Art. 2.1, 'Agreement on Technical Barriers to Trade' in Annex 1A: Multilateral Agreement on Trade in Goods, Marrakesh Agreement Establishing the World Trade Organization. Protection of human health or the environment is considered a legitimate objective.

7 A fundamental precept of free trade is the economic principle of comparative advantage. Under this principle, each country should specialize in those goods it produces most efficiently and trade with other countries for the goods they produce most efficiently. The principle of comparative advantage holds that such specialization enhances the overall level of economic activity in all trading countries.

III INTERNATIONAL ENVIRONMENTAL LAW AND TRANSBOUND-ARY TRANSFERS

International environment-related legal rules concerning transboundary commerce have focused on two areas: promotion of the free circulation of goods by harmonization of product standards, and protection of human health and the environment by establishing controls over materials and products considered to pose particular risks.

1 Promotion of trade by harmonization of product standards

National health, sanitary and safety standards have long been recognized as potential impediments to trade. Environment-related product standards – for example, pesticide residue standards for food products or motor vehicle emission standards – can also pose non-tariff trade barriers if imported products do not meet national requirements.

A long-standing effort to develop harmonized international standards, and thereby facilitate trade, centres on food standards. The Codex Alimentarius Commission – a joint effort of the WHO and FAO based in Geneva – works towards global harmonization of food standards, including international standards for pesticide residues on foods for human consumption. The OECD, through its Chemicals Programme, is also working on harmonization of environment-related product standards.

A recent development in national environmental policies is posing new challenges to international efforts to harmonize product standards. The use of product life cycle assessment (LCA) to characterize products by their impact on the environment over their entire life cycle (from production to disposal) is reaching beyond more traditional environmental concerns to come into more direct conflict with international trade rules. Specific examples of LCA-oriented policies are eco-labelling schemes, packaging waste rules, and recycling programmes.

Eco-labelling schemes are intended to encourage the marketing of more environmentally friendly products. They are usually granted on the basis of criteria relating to the ecological impacts of a particular product type during its life cycle. The trade concern is that eco-labelling can discriminate against products on the basis of the environmental impact of their method of production, and therefore may be used by one country to impose its environmental standards on another.

LCA-oriented policies can be enforced when products stay inside the country of production, but pose difficulties when products are traded across national borders. How competing products are produced is not considered relevant under current

346 European Environmental Law

trade rules since the exporting (not the importing) country is polluted in the process. How products are disposed of is considered more of a problem for the importing nation.

In an effort to address some of these issues, the International Standards Organization (ISO) has convened several working groups to develop international standards for, *inter alia*, eco-labelling schemes and LCA. The World Trade Organization's committee on trade and environment has also made the compatibility of environmental requirements for products with the WTO's trade goals a priority item on its upcoming work programme.[8]

International harmonization of such standards would minimize their use as covert trade barriers. It would also reduce the high costs of designing, producing, and selling products meeting divergent standards of fragmented markets. The problem with international harmonization is that countries differ in their preferences and capacities to assimilate environmental impacts. An internationally uniform standard would be too high for some countries, and too low for others. Moreover, once international standards are established, changes to those standards may be difficult to achieve – even if new environmental evidence becomes available.

2 Protection of the environment by controls over exports of hazards

Transboundary transfers of useful hazardous materials and technologies can bring significant economic benefits. However, if the hazards are not controlled – for example, if operators lack safety training or access to protective equipment – the risks to human health and the environment can outweigh the reputed benefits. The pesticide poisoning rates of lesser developed countries, for instance, have been estimated as 13 times higher than the rates found in industrialized countries.[9] The export of banned pesticides to countries with less developed regulatory controls has been cited as one of the reasons for this disproportionate impact.

Efforts to control transboundary transfers of hazardous materials and products have often become bogged down in debates over who should bear primary responsibility for such controls – the exporting country, the importing country, or the private parties selling, buying or transporting the materials and goods. Exporting countries have been accused of using a 'double standard' if they allow hazardous materials subject to domestic bans or restrictions to be exported. Exporting countries have countered that restrictions on such exports would constitute an unac-

---

8 Williams, Eco-labelling tops agenda for new group, *Financial Times*, 13 July 1994.
9 See Weir, Schapiro, *Circle of Poison: Pesticides and People in a Hungry World*, 1981.

ceptable infringement of other countries' sovereign right to make their own decisions about what activities and materials to allow within their own territories.

From an environmental protection point of view, the hazard that makes a material too risky for uncontrolled use in its country of origin can also pose unacceptable risks in the country of destination. Moreover, many lesser developed countries lack the resources to keep unwanted goods and materials from crossing their borders, let alone control the marketing and use of those materials.

The general consensus today is that responsibility for risks posed by hazards in international trade should be shared. Primary management responsibility should lie with the importing country – for example, decisions concerning whether certain materials should be allowed to enter the country and regulatory controls to deal with the risks posed by the hazardous materials allowed into its market. The exporting state, on the other hand, is responsible for stopping a pending export if the importing state decides it does not want the hazard to enter its territory.

The first international controls over hazards were restricted to exchanges of information or non-binding guidelines. Exchanges of information and procedures of notification are intended to provide importing states with sufficient information about the hazards coming into their territories, so that they can adequately manage those hazards. An important international mechanism in this regard is the International Registry of Potentially Toxic Chemicals ('IRPTC'), established in the 1970s by UNEP. Since its founding, the Geneva-based IRPTC has served as a repository of information and advice on hazardous chemicals and on the implementation of policies and regulations to control those hazards.

In 1984, the OECD adopted the 'Guiding Principles on Information Exchange Related to Export of Banned or Severely Restricted Chemicals'. The 'Guiding Principles' called for voluntary once-only notifications (a) whenever a government took action to control a chemical, and (b) the first time a banned or severely restricted chemical was about to be exported. Information on why the chemical was banned or restricted was supplied only if requested by the importing country.

The same year the United Nations Environmental Programme (UNEP) adopted a 'Provisional Notification Scheme for Banned or Severely Restricted Chemicals'. UNEP's scheme went beyond the OECD's Principles by providing for 'mandatory information exchange' whenever a government had taken a control action with regard to a particular chemical. At a minimum, such notifications were to identify the chemical, summarize the control action taken, and describe the reasons for the action. Notifications of exports were to include an 'intent-to-export' declaration and a copy of the original notification concerning the control action.

In 1985 the FAO adopted the International Code of Conduct on the Distribution and Use of Pesticides. Like UNEP's scheme, the Code is voluntary. Its original provisions on exports were similar to the OECD's principles and UNEP's scheme

– exporting governments were to notify importing governments about control actions taken and about pending exports.

An important debate during the development of these schemes centred on whether importing countries were to receive export notifications prior to the hazard's export, and if the governments of importing countries should be able to decide whether or not they wanted the hazard to enter their territory. These concepts came to be known as 'prior informed consent' ('PIC'). Under the principle of PIC, an exporting country should prevent the export of banned or severely restricted materials unless the importing country's government has (i) been fully informed of the reasons for the ban or restriction, and (ii) has positively consented to the import of the controlled pesticide.

Notification prior to transfer of the hazard is important if authorities in the importing country are to assess the country's capacity to control risks related to the hazard, and then take a decision as to whether to allow the hazard into their territory. An importing country's capacity to control risks would depend, *inter alia*, on local legal requirements, the administrative capacity of authorities to implement and to enforce compliance with those requirements, the technological capacity to take necessary risk-reduction measures, availability of trained workers and of safety equipment, and the power of workers to demand safe working conditions.

In 1987, extensive pressure from developing countries and environmental advocates compelled both UNEP's Governing Council and the FAO Conference to agree to incorporation of the concept of PIC into the 'London Guidelines for the Exchange of Information on Chemicals in International Trade'[10] and the FAO Code of Conduct.

After years of intergovernmental consultations, schemes for implementing PIC are taking shape. It has been agreed, for instance, that a substance will be considered 'banned or severely restricted' if it has been subject to restrictive controls in at least five countries. The European Union's legislation establishing a scheme of PIC for exports of controlled substances from the EC are discussed later.

The principle of PIC is also an integral part of the 1989 Basel Convention on the control of transboundary movements of hazardous wastes and their disposal. The Basel Convention represents a further development of international law in this area in that it obliges exporting countries to refuse permission for exports of certain wastes unless there is assurance that the wastes will be treated or disposed of in an 'environmentally sound' manner in the recipient country. Moreover, if the wastes are not in fact treated or disposed of in an 'environmentally sound' manner, the exporting country is obliged to bring the waste back to its own territory and arrange for its safe disposal.

---

10 The 'London Guidelines' replaced UNEP's earlier 'Provisional Scheme'.

IV EC CONTROLS OVER TRANSBOUNDARY TRANSFERS

The international efforts to address hazards in international trade and other trade-related environmental concerns have depended on voluntary actions and the building of multilateral consensus. Apart from the Basel Convention on shipments of waste, no international convention covers the international trade of hazardous substances and products. In contrast, the European Union has been able to enact legislation in this area binding even on dissenting Member States.[11] Because of its ability to take collective action, some international commitments have been set into legislation more quickly than would have occurred if the Member States had acted individually. On some transboundary issues, such as phase-outs of ozone-depleting chemicals, the EC has stepped out in front of international efforts.

The EC, however, is dependent on the Member States for enforcement of its legislative measures. Actual implementation of EC laws remains a significant problem in a number of Member States. Moreover, tension between environmental protection and trade also occurs within the EC itself. Member States with a preference for higher levels of environmental protection come into frequent conflict with Member States having different goals.

This section considers the EC's regulatory controls in two areas: environment-related controls over goods and materials circulated within the single market, including imports; and controls over hazards having transboundary impacts. Then it looks at the various legislative mechanisms built into EC laws for maintaining harmonization and for adapting existing laws to take account of new developments on the national level.

1 Environment-related product standards for goods marketed within or imported into the EC

Much of the EC's product-related legislation was originally motivated by the need to harmonize divergent national product standards and thereby facilitate the free circulation of goods placed on the Single Market. Products which do not meet the EC's standards are prohibited from being marketed within the EC.

The first environment-related EC legislation – Directive 67/548 on the classification, packaging and labelling of dangerous substances[12] – established a harmo-

---

11 Legislation enacted on the basis of Art. 100A of the EC Treaty – that is, for harmonization of Member State laws so as to achieve the common market, requires only a qualified majority of Member States in favour of the measure.

12 Council Directive 67/548 of 27 June 1967 on approximation of laws, regulations and administrative provisions relating to the classification, labelling and packaging of dan-

nized system of classification of hazardous chemicals according to categories of hazards, and then set specific labelling and packaging requirements for these categories. A 1988 Directive[13] brought dangerous preparations, defined as mixtures and solutions of two or more chemical substances, under the same classification and labelling requirements. A dangerous substance or preparation that meets the requirements of Directive 67/548 with regard to classification, packaging and labelling can be marketed throughout the EC. Exports of dangerous substances or preparations from the EC are also subject to Directive 67/548's labelling and packaging requirements.

The need to harmonize national standards also led to Union-wide controls over motor vehicle emissions. A 1970 Directive[14] prescribing threshold values for certain gaseous emissions from petrol engines was followed by a 1972 Directive setting limits for emissions from diesel engines.[15] The threshold values set in these Directives have been made progressively more stringent through subsequent legislation.[16]

Framework legislation for harmonizing restrictions on the marketing and use of specific dangerous chemicals was enacted by the EC in 1976.[17] These controls are based on negative lists of banned or restricted chemicals. Chemicals and products

---

gerous substances, OJ L196, 16 August 1967, at 1, *as amended.* Directive 67/548 has been amended and adapted to technological progress more than 25 times since its enactment. The 'Sixth Amendment' established pre-market testing and notification requirements for all new chemicals placed on the EC market after 1981. The 1993 'Seventh Amendment' introduced the principle of risk assessment for guiding the EC's decisions in identifying, assessing, and then controlling the risk posed to humans and the environment by chemical substances.

13   Council Directive 88/379 of 7 June 1988 on the approximation of the laws, regulations and administrative provisions of the Member States relating to the classification, packaging and labelling of dangerous preparations, OJ L187, 15 July 1988, at 14, *as amended.*

14   Council Directive 70/220 of 20 March 1970 on the approximation of the laws of the Member States relating to measures to be taken against air pollution by gases from the engines of motor vehicles, OJ L76, 6 April 1970, at 1; *as last amended* by Council Directive 91/441 of 26 June 1991, OJ L242, 30 August 1991, at 1.

15   Council Directive 72/306 of 2 August 1972, OJ L190, 20 August 1972, at 1, *as amended.*

16   For example, Council Directive 91/441 of 26 June 1991, OJ L242, 30 August 1991, at 1, sets exhaust emission thresholds for both petrol and diesel cars, and requires in effect that all new petrol-engined cars marketed within the EC will be equipped with three-way catalysts.

17   Council Directive 76/769 of 27 July 1976 on the approximation of the laws regulations and administrative provisions of the Member States relating to restriction on the marketing and use of certain dangerous substances and preparations, OJ L262, 27 September 1976, at 201, *as amended.*

regulated under this legislation include PCBs, PCTs, monomer vinyl chloride, asbestos, benzene, PCP, and lead carbons and lead sulphate in paint. A 1979 Directive harmonizes bans and restrictions over the marketing and use of agricultural pesticides containing certain hazardous chemicals.[18]

EC legislation aimed at harmonization is required to take as a base a high level of environmental protection. However, some Member States with strong environmental traditions may already have national legislation setting even higher levels. In such a case, Article 100a(4) of the EC Treaty permits a Member State to apply differing national provisions if they can be justified on grounds of major need, or protection of the environment. The Member State must notify the European Commission about the differing provisions, and then the Commission must confirm that the provisions are not a means of arbitrary discrimination or a disguised restriction on trade.

Commission approval for stricter national measures than those provided in EC legislation is not always an easy hurdle.[19] For one thing, the Commission interprets Article 100a(4) as requiring that the national measure must be in place before the harmonizing measure is adopted at the EC level. And, even if the Commission agrees to the stricter measure, the measure may be attacked by other Member States as a barrier to trade. For example, in the first part of 1994, the European Court of Justice (ECJ) overturned the Commission's approval of Germany's total ban on the production and use of pentachlorophenol (PCP), on procedural grounds. The ECJ ruled that the Commission had not adequately documented why Germany's situation merited stricter controls than provided under EC law. The Commission has since submitted new documentation affirming Germany's PCP ban on grounds of special national circumstances.

From a trade point of view, environment-related exceptions to the EC's harmonized schemes do create barriers to trade. In the *Danish Bottles* case, the ECJ recognized that environmental protection concerns could legitimately limit the application of Article 30 of the EC Treaty.[20] It ruled, however, that such measures had to be *proportionate* – that is, be the least restrictive to the free movement of goods – and *non-discriminatory* – that is, apply equally to domestic and imported goods.

---

18 Council Directive 79/117 prohibiting the placing on the market and use of plant protection products containing certain active substances.

19 See, for a broader discussion of this point, Chapter 19 on EC competences by J. Jans in this volume.

20 In the *Danish Bottles* case, the ECJ found Denmark's requirement for a deposit and return scheme for beer and soft drink bottles to be proportionate to the aim of protecting the environment, but held that the requirement for prior approval of bottles was disproportionate to the environmental aim. *Commission* v. *Denmark*, Case 302/86, ECR 1988, 4607.

In recent years the EC has utilized a new legal mechanism for harmonization of controls over chemicals. The 1991 Directive on plant protection products[21] sets in place a system of authorization for agricultural pesticides based on the principle of 'mutual recognition'. Instead of a negative list, the 1991 Directive provides for a 'positive list' of active ingredients. Once an active ingredient is placed on this 'positive list', it will be authorized for 10 years, unless new information dictates an earlier review.[22]

Products containing one or more active ingredients listed on the 'positive list' can be authorized by any Member State upon application by the manufacturer or importer. One Member State's authorization of a pesticide product will lead to authorization by any other Member State to which application is made. A product authorized in this way can be produced, distributed and used freely in all the Member States.[23]

If a Member State wishes to restrict the product, it must utilize an opposition procedure requiring it to justify with objective arguments why the product is un-suitable for use in its territory. In particular, it must show that its 'agricultural, plant health and environmental (including climate) conditions' differ from the conditions found in the authorizing country, such that the product would have an unacceptable effect on human or animal health, or on the environment within its territory. This can be a difficult burden of proof.[24] Member States, such as Den-

---

21 Council Directive 91/414 concerning the placing of plant protection products on the market. OJ L230, 19 August 1991, at 1, *as amended.*

22 In order to get a new active ingredient listed in this 'positive list', an applicant is re-quired to submit to any one member State (i) a set of health and environmental data for that active ingredient and (ii) a dossier for at least one product containing the active substance. The Member State carries out an evaluation of the dossiers and submits the evaluation to the Commission and to the other Member States, with a recommendation to include or not include the active ingredient in the positive list. Producers and im-porters of substances used for plant protection will be able to cooperate by pooling their data and thereby avoid duplication of substance testing and of applications for authorization.

23 Council Directive 94/43 of 27 July 1994 establishing Annex VI to Directive 91/414 (OJ L227, 1 September 1994, at 31) sets out 'unifom principles' for Member States to use in the evaluation and authorization of plant protection products. The Directive allows for the conditional approval of pesticides for five years even if its concentration in groundwater is likely to exceed EC standards for pesticides in drinking water. Pesti-cides given this conditional approval will not be permitted to circulate freely in the re-mainder of the European Union.

24 In order to assure equivalent standards for Member State assessment of safety and en-vironmental data for active ingredients and products, the European Union recently adopted a Directive setting 'uniform principles'. Council Directive 94/43/EC of 27 July 1994 establishing Annex VI to Directive 91/414 concerning the placing of plant pro-tection products on the market, OJ L227, 1 September 1994, at 31.

mark and the Netherlands, with pesticide use reduction programmes, are concerned that the Plant Products Directive may no longer allow them to ban a pesticide on the basis that less hazardous products are available, if the pesticide has received EC approval.

A draft 'Biocides Directive' covering non-agricultural pesticides,[25] such as disinfectants and preservatives, would also be based on the principle of mutual recognition and establish a 'positive list' of authorized biocidal active ingredients. The draft Biocides Directive contains a provision that would permit authorization to be refused if another less harmful product or pest control technique is available. The product would have to be equally effective, and not pose 'significant economic and practical disadvantages to the user'. If this provision remains in the draft proposal as it goes through the EC legislative process, Member States will have a means to substitute less harmful products in the place of biocides they consider to be overly hazardous.

The conflict between concern for the free movement of goods and the desire for higher national standards has come to the fore in the debate over the proposal for an Union-wide Directive on packaging and packaging waste.[26] The Packaging Directive establishes specific objectives for the collection and recovery of packaging waste and for recycling of packaging waste output. Packaging which does not respect 'essential requirements' – including minimization of packaging volume and weight, and design allowing re-use and recovery – is denied access to the EC's market.

The Packaging Directive was approved despite the opposition of Germany, the Netherlands and Denmark. These Member States opposed the objectives set in the proposal for collection, recovery and recycling of packaging waste, on the grounds that these objectives are too low (the three countries had already achieved the objectives in their own national packaging waste programmes), and in order to preserve their rights under Article 100a(4) of the EC Treaty to have stricter standards.

Even before the Packaging Directive had been adopted, the European Commission decided to initiate legal proceedings against Germany over its 1991 law on packaging waste. The high refill and recycling quotas set by Germany's law, and its ban on incineration of packaging waste, are not the main point of contention, although it is generally agreed these constitute barriers to trade. The issue is whether Germany's unilateral measures were justifiable on environmental grounds under the EC Treaty. In these proceedings, the Commission alleged that large quantities of waste exported from Germany because of lack of domestic recycling

---

25 Proposal for a Council Directive concerning the placing of biocidal products on the market as of 17 July 1993, OJ C239, 3 September 1993, at 3.

26 OJ L365, 1994, p.10.

capacity undermined other countries' own collection schemes. It argued that, while Germany may have protected its own environment, its unilateral approach harmed the environments of other Member States. If the Court accepts the Commission's argument, Member States wishing to set in place more stringent national standards will have to justify their national measures in relation to the environment of the EC as a whole.

Recent EC environmental initiatives taking a product life-cycle assessment approach ('LCA') to environmental protection are also engendering controversy about the relationship between environmental protection and trade. One such initiative is the EC's voluntary eco-labelling scheme,[27] which provides a way to reward companies for products determined to have a reduced environmental impact in comparison to other products in a particular product category. Criteria for eco-label awards must be based on an LCA.[28]

A debate that took place over criteria for detergents illustrates some of the difficulties in using LCA to derive objective criteria. The European detergent industry criticized early proposals for placing too much emphasis on water pollution impacts and insufficient attention to raw material consumption. Some non-EC chemical producers suspected the process of being misused to give EC-produced chemicals used in detergents an unfair competitive advantage over imported chemicals. A similar crisis was sparked by the criteria for tissue paper products. Many European paper producers opposed the criteria as being 'unscientific', because the criteria favoured recycled paper over paper from sustainable tree plantations. Non-EC producers accused the process of criteria selection of lack of transparency and of improperly favouring European commercial interests.

The process of setting eco-label criteria is clearly designed to discriminate, but against products having a more harmful impact on the environment, not against imported goods as such. If legal challenges are brought against eco-labelling criteria for specific product groups, such criteria will survive only if they can be shown to be justifiable on environmental grounds and can withstand the Danish Bottles tests of proportionality and non-discrimination against imported goods.

---

27 Council Regulation 880/92 of 23 March 1992 on a Community eco-label award scheme, OJ L99, 11 April 1992, at 1.

28 Five stages in a product's life are to be considered: (i) pre-production, (ii) production, (iii) distribution (including packaging), (iv) utilization, and (v) disposal. For each stage, the analysis is to consider waste relevance, soil pollution and degradation, water contamination, air contamination, noise, consumption of energy, consumption of natural resources and effects on eco-systems.

2 Controls over hazardous exports and hazards having transboundary impacts

The need to control the environmental impacts of exports of hazards from the European Union has presented a somewhat different challenge to EC law-makers than the product standards discussed above, since the environment requiring protection lies outside the European Union. The task has been to avoid a double standard of exporting hazards not permitted within the EC, while respecting the right of third countries to determine their own preferred levels of environmental protection.

The first step taken by the EC to control the export and import of certain hazardous substances was to establish a basic notification scheme for exports and imports of dangerous substances.[29] The 1988 legislation applied to some 21 chemicals banned or severely restricted within the EC. It followed the OECD's 'Guiding Principles' in requiring an export notification form to be sent at the time of the first export of a banned or restricted chemical to a particular importing country.

A 1992 regulation on the export and import of certain dangerous chemicals[30] continues the notification procedures established under the 1988 legislation. More significantly, it makes the UNEP/FAO 'prior informed consent' (PIC) scheme mandatory for those chemicals subject to the PIC procedure, listed in Annex II of the Regulation.[31] It also imposes the same packaging and labelling requirements on exports of hazardous chemicals as apply within the EC.

In order to comply with Regulation 2455/92, an exporter wishing to export a dangerous chemical from the EC must check whether the chemical is listed in one of the regulation's Annexes. The 24 chemicals and chemical groups listed in Annex I are subject to the regulation's notification procedure.[32] If the product has never been exported from the EC to the country of destination, the exporter must inform his national authorities about the intended export at least 30 days before intended shipping date. In turn, the national authorities must notify the government of the importing country at least 15 days before the shipment is dispatched.

If the chemical is listed in Annex II, it is subject to the PIC procedure. If the country of destination has decided to ban or control the chemical, that decision

---

29 Council Regulation 1734/88 of 16 June 1988 concerning export from and import into the Community of certain dangerous chemicals, OJ L155, 22 June 1988, at 2.

30 Council Regulation 2455/92 of 23 July 1992 concerning export from and import into the Community of certain dangerous chemicals, OJ L251, 29 August 1992, at 13.

31 In 1985, the Netherlands became the first exporting country to enact legislation providing for a voluntary system of PIC for banned or restricted chemicals.

32 A proposal to amend Annex I of Regulation 2455/92 to bring the number of chemicals and chemical groups listed to 39 was expected to be adopted before the end of 1994. See Council Position 19/94 of 8 June 1994, OJ C213, 3 August 1994, at 1.

must be respected. If the country of destination has not yet taken an import decision, then a 'status quo' principle must be applied. The export may not proceed
unless the chemical is registered in the country of destination, or previous imports
have been accepted.

As of January 1994, only six chemicals – aldrin, dieldrin, DDT, dinoseb,
fluoroacetamide, and HCH – had been included in Annex II. Out of the 20 countries listed in Annex II as having made import decisions about the six chemicals,
no Central or Eastern European countries were to be found. Since more than 115
countries reportedly participate in the UNEP/FAO's PIC scheme, the EC's implementation of PIC is far from complete.

Controls over transborder shipments of hazardous waste were initiated by a
1984 Directive[33] regulating the shipment of waste within, to and from the EC.
Before hazardous waste could be exported from the EC, the holder of the waste
had to notify – and receive an acknowledgement from – the country of destination.
The acknowledgement had to be indicated on the consignment note.

The 1984 Directive was repealed on 6 May 1994, when Regulation 259/93 on
the supervision and control of shipments of waste within, into and out of the
European Community[34] came into effect. Regulation 259/93 implements the Basel
Convention. In providing for bans on exports of waste from or imports to the EC,
and for the possibility of a general prohibition on shipments between Member
States of waste for disposal, the regulation clearly places environmental protection
considerations ahead of free trade.

Article 4(3)(a)(i) of the Regulation states:

> In order to implement the principles of proximity, priority for recovery and self
> sufficiency at Community and national levels ... Member States may take
> measures in accordance with the Treaty to prohibit generally or partially or to
> object systematically to shipments of waste.

Member States may not, however, ban imports of hazardous waste from other
Member States that produce such waste in quantities too small to enable cost-
effective operation of specialized disposal facilities.

The extent to which a transboundary shipment of waste comes under the scope
of the Regulation depends on the country of destination, the type of waste, and
whether the waste is headed for final disposal or for a recovery operation.[35] Since

---

33 Council Directive 84/631 of 6 December 1984 on the supervision and control within
   the European Community of the transfrontier shipment of hazardous waste, OJ L326,
   13 December 1984, at 31, *as amended.*
34 Council Regulation 259/93 of 1 February 1993, OJ L30, 6 February 1993, at 1.
35 The Regulation covers: (i) transfers of waste for disposal or recovery between EC
   Member States; (ii) exports of waste for disposal outside the EC (prohibited except to
   EFTA countries); (iii) exports of waste for recovery operations outside the EC

exports of waste from the EC are generally banned unless the waste is destined for a recovery operation, the distinction between disposal and recovery – and the types of waste which are recoverable – is important. Three different categories of recoverable waste are listed in the Regulation's Annexes – 'green list', 'amber list' and 'red list' of wastes.[36] In every case, the shipment of waste must be destined for recovery operations within a facility which operates according to the applicable laws of the importing country; in other words, the recovery operation must be carried out in an environmentally sound manner.

'Green list' wastes are considered those wastes which should not normally present a risk to the environment if properly recovered in the country of destination. They are generally excluded from the Regulation's system of controls.[37] Wastes on the 'amber' and 'red lists' are deemed to present a greater risk to the environment. They cannot be shipped for recovery unless the entity who proposes to ship the waste has notified the importing country's competent authority about the pending shipment. In the case of 'red list' wastes for recovery and wastes for recovery not yet assigned to one of the three categories, the consent of the 'competent authorities concerned' must be provided in writing prior to the commencement of the shipment.

The regulation contains a 'take-back' requirement. The company that shipped the waste may be required to bring it back to the country of dispatch if the shipment cannot be 'completed', that is, disposed of or recovered in accordance with the terms to which the importing country has consented, or in an 'alternative and environmentally sound manner'. Repatriation is also obligatory if the shipment is deemed 'illegal traffic',[38] if the shipper was responsible for the illegal traffic,[39] or

---

(prohibited except to Parties to Basel, countries having bilateral arrangements with the EC or Member States, and countries subject to the OECD Decision); (iv) imports of waste into the EC for disposal or recovery (prohibited except from EFTA countries, Parties to Basel, or countries having bilateral arrangements with the EC or Member States); and (v) waste in transit from outside and through the EC for disposal or recovery outside the EC.

36   These categories correspond to the categories of waste for recovery set down in the OECD Decision of 30 March 1992 on the control of transborder movements of wastes destined for recovery operations (the 'OECD Decision').

37   The importing country must first confirm in writing that it will accept 'green list' waste without such controls. In any case, certain 'green list' wastes may be controlled as if they were 'amber list' or 'red list' wastes, if they exhibit certain hazardous characteristics. Such wastes are to be listed in Annex II(a) in accordance with a specified committee procedure.

38   'Illegal traffic' is defined to include shipments of waste which did not comply with the notification, consent, consignment note, or other requirements of the regulation; or for which consent was obtained through misinterpretation, lies or fraud; or which resulted in 'disposal or recovery in contravention of Community or international rules'.

if the waste in question cannot be otherwise disposed of or recovered in an environmentally sound manner. The shipper's (and exporting country's) obligation to take the waste back does not end until the person to whom the waste was shipped for disposal or recovery provides a certificate of disposal or a certificate of recovery.

Shippers of waste have complained about the complexity of the scheme, and the confusion that accompanied efforts to implement its requirements. The variety of official responses to the EC's scheme indicates the complexities of keeping track of what types of wastes exported from the EC would be permitted to enter Central and Eastern European (CEE) countries:[40]

Estonia, Slovenia	All 'green list' wastes accepted if destined for facilities operating under applicable domestic laws.
Albania	Importation of all 'green list' wastes prohibited except for certain specified categories.
Czech Republic	All types of waste accepted, but subject to the 'red list' procedure.
Poland	All types of waste accepted subject to the 'amber list' procedure, but wastes from agro-food industries exempted from controls.
Bulgaria, Croatia, Hungary, Lithuania, Romania, Slovakia	All types of 'green list' wastes subject to additional controls, but additional measures to be taken not specified.

Since Regulation 259/93 only came into effect in May 1994, it is too early to gauge its impact on shipments of waste to, from and within the EC. The Regulation's provision permitting Member States to establish general prohibitions against imports of waste from other Member States is already under legal attack by shippers of waste who had previously shipped German waste to France for treatment.[41]

39　If the person or undertaking to whom the waste is shipped for recovery or disposal was responsible for the illegality of the waste shipment, the importing country is responsible for ensuring that the waste in question is disposed of in an environmentally sound manner.

40　Before the regulation came into effect, the Commission requested that third countries confirm in writing whether they would accept 'green list' waste without further control procedures or whether such waste would be subject to the control procedures for 'amber list' or 'red list' wastes. A 6 May 1994 Commission notification listed the responses received to date.

41　*Buralux SA, Satrod SA and Ourry SA* v. *Council of EC*, Case C-145/93.

In a 1992 case, the ECJ partially upheld a ban on imports of waste because of EC laws promoting the disposal of waste close to its source. In the *Walloon Waste Import Ban* case,[42] the ECJ assessed the discriminatory character of a Decree prohibiting the storage, tipping or dumping of waste from a foreign country or from other national regions. It held that the ban was not discriminatory, in light of the EC's principles of self-sufficiency and proximity which promoted the disposal of waste as close to its source as possible. Because EC legislation for waste disposal was only general in nature, the Court did not find a breach of EC law with regard to non-hazardous waste. However, EC legislation concerning hazardous waste was much more detailed and established a comprehensive system of control.[43] The ECJ therefore found that the Walloon region did not have the right to impose a general ban on imports of hazardous waste.

Given that Regulation 259/93 now sets in place a specific and comprehensive Union-wide regime for all transboundary shipments of waste, the rights of Member States and their regions to take unilateral measures concerning waste imports will require further clarification by the ECJ.

3   Mechanisms for ongoing harmonization and adaptation

The EC's institutions utilize a number of mechanisms to minimize barriers to the free movement of goods and to adapt existing legislation, and these can affect both EC and national environmental protection initiatives. The European Commission's legal action against Germany's packaging regulation discussed earlier is just one example.

Another way for the EC to keep national regulatory initiatives from affecting the common market is provided by the 1983 Standstill Directive.[44] The Standstill Directive requires a Member State to inform the European Commission if it intends to adopt a new technical regulation or national standard which may affect the free movement of goods.[45] The Member State must stay its legislative proce-

---

42 *Commission* v. *Belgium*, Case C-2/90 (1992).
43 Council Directive 84/631 of 6 December 1984 on the supervision and control within the European Community of the transborder shipment of hazardous waste, OJ L326, 13 December 1984, at 31, *as amended*.
44 Council Directive 83/189 of 28 March 1983 laying down a procedure of information in the field of technical standards and regulations, OJ L109, 26 April 1983, at 8, *as amended* by Council Directive 88/182 of 22 March 1988, OJ L81, 26 January 1988, at 75.
45 Technical regulations are mandatory requirements for a product. They can cover the characteristics required of a product such as quality, performance, safety or dimensions;

dure (the 'standstill') for at least three months after the notification, to allow the European Commission and the other Member States time to assess the draft technical regulation's potential impact on the functioning of the single market. After the three month standstill period has elapsed, the Member State may proceed to adopt the technical regulation unless objections were raised on the basis of impediment to free movement of goods, or if the European Commission has adopted or intends to adopt, a technical regulation to harmonize at Community level.

In its original form, the Standstill Directive only covered technical regulations and standards related to the product as it was placed on the market. A 1994 Amending Directive also includes a notification duty for technical requirements related to a product's life cycle, taking particular account of consumer and environmental protection.[46]

Another means used by the EC to eliminate technical barriers to trade is the EC's so-called *new approach* – that is the setting of certain essential requirements for products, and then establishing European standards for those requirements.[47] Products manufactured according to those standards are presumed to conform to the essential requirements and may circulate freely throughout the EC.[48] Conversely, products not conforming to the essential requirements will not be permitted on the common market.

CEN, the EC's standardization body, is currently developing a number of environmental norms, including a European standard for the EC's 'eco-audit scheme'. The essential requirements for packaging foreseen by the proposed Packaging Directive will also be developed by CEN.

The Standstill Directive discussed earlier also covers national standard-setting efforts. National standardization bodies intending to adopt new standards must notify the European Commission and all other national standardization bodies, which may comment on the proposed standards. If a European standard is under preparation by CEN, national standardization bodies may not take any action

---

and the characteristics applicable to the product such as terminology, symbols, testing and test methods, packaging, marking or labelling.

46 Directive 94/10 of the European Parliament and the Council of 23 March 1994 materially amending for the second time Directive 83/189, OJ L100, 19 April 1994, at 30.

47 Standards are technical specifications laying down characteristics for a product which have been approved by a recognized standardization body. Each EC Member State has one or two recognized standardization bodies. The European standardization bodies are CEN (Comité Européen de Normalisation), CENELEC (Comité Européen de Normalisation Electrotechnique) and ETSI (European Telecommunications Standards Institute).

48 To date, the EC has adopted Directives containing essential requirements for the following products: pressure vessels, toys, construction products, machine safety, personal protective equipment, certain weighing instruments, medical devices, heating equipment, gas appliances, explosives for civil use.

which could prejudice the harmonization intended to be achieved by the European standard. CEN works in close cooperation with the ISO in order to minimize those differences between EC and international standards that could have an impact on trade.

In addition to these harmonizing mechanisms, the EC has devised a standard consultative procedure to permit existing EC legislation to be adapted for better implementation. A 1987 Council decision (the 'Comitology decision')[49] sets forth three different decision-making procedures which can be used by the Commission to carry out its implementation function. The procedure utilizes committees comprising Member States' representatives and chaired by a Commission representative.

The committee procedures enable Member States to monitor the Commission's work and to advise on decisions. They are typically used for adaptations of annexes to technical progress. For example, the 'regulatory committee' procedure provided under Article 28 of Directive 67/548 was used to amend Annex II to Council Regulation 2455/92 concerning the export and import of certain dangerous chemicals, to specify the chemicals covered by the PIC procedure.[50]

The above mechanisms for adjusting EC legislation and for balancing the interests of the Member States against the EC as a whole are imperfect. Application of the Standstill Directive slows down or even stops national regulatory initiatives, while the 'new approach' and the comitology procedures are frequently charged with a lack of transparency. For non-EC countries engaged in trade with the EC, the EC's balancing act between a high level of environmental protection and harmonization in the interests of free trade can be especially difficult to decipher.

---

49 Council decision 87/373 of 13 July 987 laying down the procedures for the exercise of implementing powers conferred on the Commission, OJ L177, 18 July 1987, at 33. The Comitology decision provides for three types of consultative committees to advise and cooperate with the Commission on the implementation of EC legislation: (1) advisory committees; (2) management committees; (3) regulatory committees. It also stipulates the legislative procedures followed in each instance for implementing measures proposed by the Commission into EC law.

50 The procedure specified by the Comitology decision for decisions to be taken by 'regulatory committees' is as follows: the Commission is required to submit a draft of 'the measures to be taken' to the committee and to set a time period for the committee to deliver its opinion. If the committee approves the proposed measures by a qualified majority, the Commission adopts the measures. If the committee does not agree with the proposal, the Commission submits the proposal to the Council of Ministers. The Council can adopt or reject the proposed measures on the basis of a qualified majority. If it cannot reach a qualified majority decision within three months the Commission can adopt the measures.

V   SIGNIFICANCE OF EC LAWS ON TRANSBOUNDARY TRANSFERS FOR CENTRAL AND EASTERN EUROPEAN COUNTRIES

The countries of Central and Eastern Europe (CEE) are also affected by the EC's laws relating to trade and the environment. CEE exporters wishing to develop new markets in Western Europe must comply with the EC's product standards. Moreover, they must also take account of the development of LCA and eco-labelling as devices for marketing consumer goods. If they are to carve out a share of Western Europe's highly competitive markets, CEE manufacturers must consider the environmental impact of the products themselves, and of the manufacturing processes used in their production.

On the other hand, CEE countries remain vulnerable to exports of hazardous products and materials from the EC. Despite the EC's laws controlling transboundary shipments of waste, illegal shipments of hazardous wastes have continued to enter the CEE border states from the EC. Poland has had to establish special border patrols and on-the-spot laboratory facilities to analyse the contents of shipments seeking to enter the country by truck and by train, and to turn back rejected products and materials.

The problem of unwanted exports, as explained earlier, must be a shared responsibility. The EC and its Member States are responsible for enforcing existing laws governing exports of hazardous chemicals and of wastes in general, and that responsibility includes making existing laws more effective. On the other hand, CEE countries are responsible for setting in place effective environmental regulatory structures that are capable of addressing the problem of unwanted imports. In that regard, a minimal step would be to take decisions concerning the import of those chemicals subject to the PIC procedure under Regulation 2455/92.

The prospect of integration with the EC will hopefully accelerate the development of CEE regulatory structures for environmental protection.[51] The EC and its Member States took significant steps in this direction by reaching Association Agreements in 1993 and 1994 with Poland, Hungary, Czech Republic and Slovakia.[52] These Association Agreements are aimed at, *inter alia*, promotion of the expansion of trade and harmonious economic relations between the parties. They are also intended to provide an appropriate framework for gradual integration into the EC, including economic integration.

---

51   See the Chapter 23 on options for Central and Eastern European states by L. Krämer in this volume.

52   For example, Council decision on the Conclusion of the Europe Agreement establishing an association between the European Communities and their Member States, of the one part, and the Republic of Poland, of the other part, OJ L348, at 2.

The Agreement with Poland, for example, states that the major precondition for Poland's economic integration into the Community is the approximation of that country's existing and future legislation to that of the Community.[53] The Article addressing environmental protection mentions a number of issues where cooperation is a priority, including (but not limited to):

- classification and safe handling of chemicals;
- waste reduction, recycling and safe disposal;
- implementation of the Basel Convention.

Harmonization in these areas will take considerable effort since the regulatory gaps between CEE countries and the EC are significant. For example, the system of classification, hazard symbols and other controls over hazardous chemicals used in the former Soviet bloc countries varied significantly from the EC's system under Directive 67/548, including the scientific basis and the testing methodology related to the classification criteria.

For CEE governments working on harmonizing existing legislation with that of the EC, it will be vital to know not only what requirements have already been set in place, but what is now being drafted and deliberated in consultative committees and in the EC's standardization bodies. Participation will be important, if CEE decisionmakers are to have any say in EC law-making concerning the balance between trade and environmental protection.

Participation in the EC's consultative committees and working groups has not been open to non-Member State experts in the past. However, the fact that CEE ministers of environment were included in the October 1994 Council of Environment Ministers could augur a new era of increased transparency in EC regulatory decision-making.

---

53 Ibid., Art. 68.

Part V
Central and Eastern Europe in Search of a Fitting Model

21 Drafting New Environmental Law in Poland: Radical Change or Merely Reform?

Jerzy Jendroska

Table of Contents

I INTRODUCTION

The shift towards democracy and a free market economy that has taken place in former Soviet bloc countries since 1989 was expected to be followed by radical changes in their environmental policies. The common opinion was that, to this end, the appropriate institutional framework would have to be built from scratch, because these countries were believed to have no environmental regulatory programme at all, or, at best, to have some environmental legislation that was, however, neither enforceable nor actually enforced.

The process of transition was considered a great opportunity for the Central and Eastern European nations to introduce environmental policy based on the concept of sustainable development. The governments of the region have been urged by forces both inside and outside their societies to adopt legislation that would foster the development of an ecologically sound economy. According to the radical view, these countries were hoped to 'leapfrog' the West ecologically. To this end, new legislation was anticipated to employ the most advanced and progressive legal instruments developed in the West.

However, not all the countries in Central and Eastern Europe have managed to adopt entirely new environmental legislation . Poland does not belong to those in the forefront in this respect and perhaps will be the last country to have a comprehensive set of brand new environmental laws. Introduction of new environmental legislation turned out to be a very slow process and, indeed, this process might be better described by the term 'reforming' than by radical changes. This represents a retreat from the position taken at the outset because at the beginning of transition, Poland, like its neighbours, anticipated radical changes in the institutional framework of environmental protection.

This chapter aims to clarify some basic features of Polish environmental law and the dilemmas faced by the law-makers and policy-makers when redesigning it. It seems therefore to be worthwhile first to highlight some of the factors that provoked the initial enthusiasm for radical reform and then to identify other reasons why this attitude was replaced by a cautious policy of reforming and amending existing legislation rather than adopting entirely new schemes. Bearing in mind that changes in the institutional framework of environmental protection have never been treated, at least in Poland, as a value in themselves but rather as a means to an end, this chapter also examines whether the lack of radical legislative reform has prevented Poland from adopting and implementing any reasonable and effective environmental policy. A brief account of the experience that might be drawn from legislative reform in Poland is offered at the conclusion of the chapter.

II   THE COMMUNIST LEGACY: INSTITUTIONAL FRAMEWORK OF ENVIRONMENTAL PROTECTION PRIOR TO 1989

1   Historical setting

Despite widespread opinion to the contrary the environmental problems of communist governments were not caused by the absence of environmental legislation. This is especially true in the case of Poland which, prior to 1989, had already developed quite an extensive institutional framework of environmental protection.[1] The origins of modern environmental legislation in Poland can be traced back to the Nature Protection Act of 1935 and the Water Act of 1922, which is considered an early example of pollution control legislation.

The two most important pieces of environmental legislation from the communist period are: the Nature Conservation Act of 1949 and Environmental Protection Act of 1980. In contrast to the piecemeal media-related approach applied until quite recently in most countries and preceding the famous US National Environmental Policy Act (NEPA) of 1969, the 1949 Act addressed environmental problems in a comprehensive way, proclaimed environmental protection among the national policy goals, and established a special central agency responsible for monitoring compliance with this policy. In addition, the Act introduced a special action-forcing mechanism which functionally corresponds to 'strategic' environmental impact assessment (EIA). The reason why NEPA, incorporating these three elements, became well known and acknowledged worldwide as a pattern to be followed, while the Polish 1949 Act remains forgotten, is that NEPA was introduced into a political system that allowed the three elements work effectively.

Although circumstances prevented the wider practical implementation of the provisions of the 1949 Act, these provisions gave a basis for further legislation. In

---

[1]   Cf. W. Radecki, J. Rotko, *Entwicklung des Natur- und Umweltschutzrechts in Mittel- und Osteuropa*, Baden-Baden: Nomos, 1991.

1980 Poland adopted the Environmental Protection Act (EPA) which not only provided basic principles for overall environmental policy but also attempted to regulate most pollution issues. The EPA 1980 was meant to be a step towards an 'environmental code', an idea recently widely recognized in many Western countries including the USA, where the traditional media-based approach driven by the powerful interests within the legislative branch produces a maze of statutes and regulatory powers.

2   Overview of the institutional framework

a)   Constitutional basis

By 1976 environmental issues had been introduced into the constitution in the form of both policy guidelines and citizens' rights. The 1976 Amendments included two environmental provisions: Article 12, para 2: 'The Polish People's Republic ensures the protection and rational management of the environment'; and Article 71: 'Citizens of the Polish People's Republic have the right to enjoy the values of the natural environment and the duty to protect it.'

b)   Pollution control scheme

The EPA 1980 attempted to regulate most of the issues of pollution – namely, controls over air and soil pollution, noise and vibration, and waste disposal . As for water pollution, the Act supplemented the Water Act 1974. Both the water and air pollution controls were based on ambient quality standards and emission threshold values set individually to meet nationwide ambient standards. Each of the 49 voivodship's governors[2] were given the discretion to set the emission thresholds for permits (for water and air emissions) issued in the given voivodship.

c)   Economic instruments

Poland was one of the first countries to apply the 'Polluter Pays Principle' (PPP) in a way that employs financial incentives to make reductions in pollution and the use of resources. Unlike in many Western countries, in Poland such incentives have never been limited to fees for the issue of permits and performing inspections, but have always included a form of 'polluters pay' (note the plural) which

---

[2]   Voivodship is the intermediate administrative level between the local authorities and the central government.

emphasizes the preventive role of economic incentives rather than retroactive and individual responsibility of polluters for abatement or clean-up. Poland introduced the first pollution charges in 1974 and by the 1980s charges were applied to the whole panoply of natural resources. Per-unit charges were mandated for air pollution emissions, waste storage, water diversion and consumption, waste water discharges, use of agricultural land for non-agricultural purposes, and the felling of trees and bushes.

The charges, as well as non-compliance fines, were channelled to special funds earmarked for various purposes (environmental protection , water management and so on). The 1987 Amendment to the EPA created a system in which 50 per cent of the money derived from pollution charges was left with the governors to be allocated, through their 'voivodship funds', to those environmental investments most significant to their particular voivodship, while the rest was transferred to Warsaw into the National Fund for Environmental Protection and Water Management and allocated to investments most significant to the country as a whole. Both the National Fund and *voivodship* funds are separate from the general state budget. The money must be spent each year on sponsoring environmental investments.

d) Public participation

Polish environmental legislation appears to have been quite progressive in the 1980s with respect to the broad participation and litigation rights granted to ecological *NGOs*. These rights included, for example, the right to file an exclusively public interest civil lawsuit.

e) Administrative arrangements

In the 1960s a central agency already existed, exclusively responsible for both air and water pollution control. In 1972 Poland, following the model of the UK Department of the Environment, attempted to create an environmental 'super-department'. The Ministry for Administration, Local Management and Environmental Protection was responsible for local administration and municipal services as well as for the whole array of environmentally relevant issues, including land use planning, pollution control and water management. The idea of solving the problem of coordinating the government's various environmental responsibilities through the creation of a 'super-department' ultimately failed and was replaced by the concept of a single-mission regulatory agency – the Office of Environmental Protection and Water Management. Established in 1983, this Office was partly modelled on the US Environmental Protection Agency, although it retained some economic tasks, such as water management for example. In 1987 the Office was elevated to fully-fledged Cabinet-status and was re named the Ministry of Environmental Protection, Natural Resources and Forestry in 1989.

f) Infrastructure

The 1980s witnessed the emergence of a basic infrastructure for developing a successful environmental policy. This included the growth of ecological awareness, the birth of an independent ecological movement and the development of professional expertise.

An opinion poll conducted in 1983 showed a deep ecological concern throughout Poland environmental problems were indicated as the third most important threat facing the country. An independent ecological movement seems to be the one outcome of the liberalization period of 1980–81 which was the least affected by Martial Law between 1981 and 1983. In the late 1980s ecological NGOs began to flourish rapidly, and quite a number of them were granted legality (such as, for example, the most renowned and respected Polish Ecological Club). The creation, in 1986, of another independent NGO, the Polish Environmental Law Association, witnessed the emergence of another important factor: environmental lawyers. By the early 1970s there were established two environmental law centres: in Warsaw (with Warsaw University) and in Wroclaw (with the Polish Academy of Sciences), each employing a couple of academics dealing exclusively with environmental law (which again, and not only by Eastern European standards, was quite unusual for that time). By the mid 1980s the number of lawyers dealing with environmental law was estimated to be about 50 in universities, private practice and public administration and 30–40 in industry (in-house lawyers mainly involved in voluntary environmental damage compensation schemes and environmental liability litigation).

All the factors mentioned above have created a certain infrastructure for the country enabling it to face the challenge of adapting environmental legislation to the needs of democratic society and market economy.

III   DEFICIENCIES OF THE OLD FRAMEWORK

1   Overall assessment

By the 1980s Poland's environmental problems had already been fairly well identified and widely publicized. As a result, Poland was often considered the most polluted country in the world and became something of a symbol of environmental disruption. The disastrous ecological situation was attributed mainly to the deficiencies in the institutional framework of environmental protection. Literally thousands of experts researching in various 'environmental' fields heavily criticized the government's environmental record and, furthermore, accused it of failing to have any comprehensive environmental policy whatsoever. There are two characteristic features of this critical assessment: a focus on details and tenous links between legal and non-legal analysis.

Even the most ardent critics tended to take a 'hard look' only at particular issues within the area of their expertise rather than attempt rather to question generally the entire regulatory programme. Therefore, despite the numerous shortcomings on the level of the 'specific', the legislation 'in general' was considered excellent. Only a few experts – mainly lawyers – demonstrated that the internal inconsistencies, lack of judicial precision, shortage of procedural rules, and surplus of 'ends' over 'means' were the features that prevented the law from being an effective instrument of environmental policy. Engineers and scientists thought of law in terms of its 'beauty' rather than of its effectiveness. They considered the law merely as a declaration of intentions to be achieved by applicable administrative arrangements and policy measures and therefore seemed quite satisfied with a legislation that included nice ideas, consequently focusing their attention on influencing governmental policy. As a result, it was long believed that the pricipal reason for the country's poor environmental performance was a 'bad' administration failing to implement 'good' substantive laws.

The revolutionary mood that seized the country when the communist government fell also addressed environmental protection and reversed this approach to environmental legislation. It is difficult to assess whether the call for radical change now taken up by almost everyone was commonly accepted because of the opinion that the entire institutional framework created by the *'ancien regime'* was insufficient and failed to prevent serious deterioration of the environment or because of the feeling that environmental law, having been created by communist government, was designed for a centrally planned economy and was therefore unworkable in a democratic society and free market economy.

The failures and deficiencies of the institutional framework were seen not only in the context of domestic experience but, above all, in the context of the most advanced Western solutions – particularly the US ones. One of the most important goals was to keep up with 'Western legal standards': new environmental law was expected to follow the most recent trends in environmental policy and to employ all the sophisticated legal instruments to achieve these goals. Among these were: public participation in environmental decision-making and freedom of environmental information, which both coincided very well with the general goal of the transition: democratization. Like democratization, also decentralization and economization were both the goals of transition in general and of environmental legislation. In addition the 'juridicization' of environmental law, favoured by many lawyers, corresponded to the 'rule of law' principle that had recently officially been proclaimed as constitutional principle. Rather specific in this context was another goal, 'ecologization', which tentatively was supposed to mean the introduction of the concept of sustainable development into the country's entire economy, but in practice meant efforts to replace the traditional 'anthropocentric' approach of environmental legislation and attempts to address 'global' issues (such as ozone depletion, global warming and so on).

The above mentioned goals were clearly set for new environmental legislation. However, underlying all these goals was the assumption that new law should first of all be effective and should rapidly improve the quality of the environment.

2   Major challenges

A new institutional framework was supposed to cure all the problems the system had either addressed insufficiently (for example, significant gaps in waste control schemes) or failed to address at all (for example, completely non-existent environmental control over chemicals). The 'shopping list' for new legislation was quite long but a few of the most vigorously debated issues might suffice to give an impression of expectations with respect to new legislation.

a)   Enforcement

Polish environmental law was notorious for its lack of enforcement and, at the time, both foreign and domestic sources considered this to be the main problem. There were, however, various opinions as to the reasons and possible cure for this problem. One of the questions was whether the old law, as in the case of many other laws inherited from the communist era, was inherently unenforceable and therefore could not, by definition, be enforced under any circumstances. This radical view was not commonly shared, and proposals for changes focused on either redesigning administrative arrangements for monitoring compliance and enforcement, or strengthening citizens' enforcement.

The environmental regulatory scheme made a governor (the *voivoda* – the head of regional governmental administration) responsible for both granting permits and enforcement. Since the primary task of governors was to satisfy central government with their records in fulfilling socio-economic plans, it was unlikely they would take any serious action to enforce environmental laws. Therefore the best remedy seemed to be to establish a strong 'environmental watchdog' – a central agency free of any economic or management tasks and responsible only for monitoring compliance and enforcement.

The proposal regarding citizens' enforcement was based on the assumption that effective environmental enforcement depends on the number of lawsuits, including citizens' suits, brought to courts. Since in Poland this number, as compared with the USA, was very small, much attention was paid, especially by foreign observers, to draft provisions related to enforcement actions in the courts, especially those providing citizens with the right to file an exclusively public interest lawsuit in the civil courts (the so-called '*actio popularis*').

b) Outdated nature conservation law

The above mentioned Nature Conservation Act of 1949, though quite progressive for the 1940s, had become outdated by the 1970s and did not reflect the progress in scientific and legal concepts concerning nature protection. Since then there had been a number of drafts aimed at replacing the 1949 Act, and dealing with problems in a more up-to-date way. For various reasons, however, none of these drafts was accepted and the 1949 Act remained in force until 1989 without amendment.

c) Lack of effective pollution control instruments

The air and water pollution control schemes based on ambient quality standards turned out to be insufficient, principally because of the weak link between the ambient standards and individual permits. The law required polluters to apply for permits in which individual standards were to be set. When issuing individual emission threshold values in permits authorities were bound to observe ambient quality values, which themselves were not binding on polluters. Lack of BAT or BATNEEC criteria[3] and broad discretionary powers in issuing permits resulted in inconsistencies in setting individual standards which, bearing in mind the inconsistency between administrative and ecological boundaries, made it extremely difficult to achieve the ambient standards, and in fact hindered any effective pollution control policy.

The proposed remedy for the above problems included the introduction of special water authorities and a water management scheme based on catchment areas, as well as a proposal to employ a technology-based approach in granting air pollution permits.

---

[3] Best available technology or best available technology not entailing excessive cost; see for the difference between the environmental quality and the technology-related approaches Chapter 3 on substantive criteria by G. Winter in this volume.

d)   Insufficient public involvement

Despite quite elaborate participation and litigation rights real public involvement in environmental decision-making was very modest. The reasons for this, apart from lack of judicial precision and the shortage of specific procedural provisions in the relevant laws, might be attributed to two basic features of the entire legislation – lack of access to governmental information, and a preference for collective over individual participation.

By the early 1980s the 'environmental community' in Poland had realized that access to information is a prerequisite for any meaningful participation in decision-making. Access to governmental information outside the area of pending proceedings did not exist as a separate legal issue: there was neither a general citizens' right of access nor any right-to-know law. The lack of any procedural rules in this respect, and a presumption in favour of secrecy well rooted in Poland's bureaucratic tradition, resulted in governmental reluctance to release any specific information regarding the quality of the environment, let alone information about individual polluters.

Another sign of governmental aversion to accountability was the reluctance to grant individuals any meaningful participation rights. Broad participation rights could not be granted to the general public which was not the subject of control, but could be granted to ecological associations as these were supposed to be. Since, in principle, there was no room in a communist country for independent organizations no one expected these rights to create any 'nuisance' for the government. Indeed, even the establishment of some independent ecological associations, which had legal status, did not much change the scope of participation and litigation rights employed to influence decision-making. Both independent and 'controlled' associations preferred less adversarial and less demanding (in terms of legal requirements) informal methods of influencing the government.

This tendency towards association rights in preference to individual participation rights was widely criticized, and many experts considered that the introduction of broad individual rights would be the best way of strengthening public participation in environmental protection. The proposed rights encompassed not only rights to be heard (via public hearings to be introduced to the process of granting environmental permissions), but also rights to monitor compliance and enforce the law by imposing administrative sanctions (via the institution of Public Guardians of the Environment) or taking enforcement actions in civil courts (via *'actio populus'*).

New law was also expected to provide almost unlimited access to environmental information and documents held by either administrative agencies ('freedom of information') or private business ('right to know').

e) Inefficient economic instruments

The rates of pollution charges and non-compliance fines were considered too low to be effective incentives to reduce pollution. The way in which they were imposed sometimes rendered them counterproductive since the scheme allowed no differentiation between those who made some effort to reduce pollution (through investment in clean technologies or pollution abatement devices) and those who did nothing to improve their environmental performance. Granting subsidies from environmental funds did not encourage polluters to make effective use of the funding available for environmental purposes.

Self-financing of pollution control was supposed to be the basic principle of the environmental policy. New legislation was generally expected to create a framework that would rely on market forces to prevent and combat pollution and would make economic instruments equally as important as those of command and control. This encompassed not only the creation of an effective pollution charges scheme, but also the provision of guarantees of independence for off-budget environmental funds, and the introduction of a whole array of instruments to supplement state subsidies: special soft-loans, reduced taxes, preferential duties for pollution control devices and so on. The worldwide debate on emission trading, stimulated by draft laws in the USA which led to the Clean Air Act Amendments in 1990, was echoed in Poland with the proposal to employ this idea in its air pollution scheme.

IV   TOWARDS A NEW INSTITUTIONAL FRAMEWORK

1   The Protocol of the Ecology Subgroup at the Round Table

The Round Table Talks held in Spring 1989 between the communist government and the democratic opposition laid foundations for the transition process, including principles for a new environmental policy. The Protocol of the Ecology Subgroup consisted of 28 goals adopted as a programme of temporary action to be realized in 1989–90. These goals included recommendations for new economic, legal and administrative instruments as well as obligations to take immediate action (for example, closure of certain dangerous facilities, and programmes to rescue certain endangered areas) .

The Protocol can be treated as an officially approved 'shopping list' for new legislation. It covers almost all the issues mentioned above as being the main deficiencies of the old framework and sets forth deadlines to achieve each goal. Goal no. 10 required a comprehensive reform of the environmental legislation to be accomplished by the end of 1990 (that is within less than 2 years). To achieve this a special legislative task force, the Environmental Law Reform Commission ('Codification Commission'), was to be appointed.

2   The Environmental Law Reform Commission

The Commission was appointed in summer 1989 and consisted ultimately of about 70 experts in the broad range of environmental issues, representing mainly academia, various governmental agencies and ecological associations. The Commission initially debated in regular plenary sessions, but the burden of work shifted later to working groups. It spent much of its time debating the need for a comprehensive 'omnibus' environmental Act and, in particular, whether nature conservation issues should be associated with pollution control issues and included in this comprehensive Act. The final product was a draft comprehensive environmental protection Act, produced in 1991 and deriving from four consecutive working versions each subjected to a notice and comment procedure. Consequently, this final draft, having already been watered down by compromise, hardly satisfied anyone. For this reason as well as others the government pressed ahead with 'sectoral' laws rather than wait further for an agreed comprehensive environmental act.

The new legislative policy was officially proclaimed in the White Paper on the National Environmental Policy, which was prepared by the government and approved by the parliament in form of a resolution in May 1991. The concept of sustainable development lies at the heart of this new agenda. The White Paper set out the basic principles of the new policy and priorities in environmental protection. It also provided the tools which are to be used to reach its goals, indicating a whole set of new environmental laws to be adopted.

3   Development of Legislation

Since 1989 environmental legislation has been subjected to many changes. The changes have been introduced gradually and in a variety of forms – by adopting new laws, amending old laws or issuing new regulations under old laws. The changes have not always addressed all problems adequately nor have they set up a new comprehensive institutional framework: nevertheless the old framework seems to have been significantly redesigned at least in relation to nature conservation, pollution control, economic instruments, environmental impact assessment and enforcement.

a) Nature conservation

The long-awaited Nature Conservation Act 1991 replaced the outdated 1949 Act. The main goal of the 1991 Act is to provide sufficient legal basis for the Protection of Living Natural Resources Strategy based on the World Conservation Strategy. To this end the Act seeks to implement some scientific concepts (such as biodiversity or ecosystems) into the legal norms.

The Act supplements the existing four legal methods of nature conservation (national parks, nature reserves, natural monuments and species protection) with several new ones. It provides now for two new forms of protected areas – landscape parks and protected landscape areas – and also establishes new forms of special purpose protection, namely documented sites of geological curiosities, ecologically useful sites and landscape reserves. The Act also provides for some general duties concerning the protection of wildlife and its habitats, and migration routes. The Act establishes a system of nature conservation authorities and provides them with broad powers. The general rule is that in protected areas (now covering about 18 per cent of the country's total area, and ultimately to be extended to 30 per cent) no development or economic activity may be carried out unless approved by the relevant nature conservation authority (that is, directors of national parks or *voivodes* acting through their nature conservation officers).

Although the 1991 Act is poorly drafted from a legal point of view and is not always properly implemented, nature conservation seems to be the one area where all the legislative goals have essentially been achieved, and the legislation meets almost all the requirements set forth by the relevant EU Directives.

b) Pollution control

Changes in the pollution control scheme have been less spectacular, but are nevertheless quite significant. First, new regulations have gradually introduced generally applicable emission standards to air and water pollution schemes. In the case of air pollution a technology forcing approach is applied which, by setting a timetable for stricter standards coming into force in future, aims to give industry time to adjust its technology to new requirements. As to water pollution, a first step towards a new water management system based on catchment areas has been made: the 1990 regulations established seven regional Water Management Boards which are granted broad powers under the new Water Act.

Quite an interesting development has taken place in relation to the waste control scheme. A new Act which is expected to introduce an entirely new scheme is still being drafted, but consecutive amendments to the EPA 1980 have radically changed the approach to the transborder shipment of waste. In 1989 a total ban was introduced, which was lifted in 1993 to be replaced with the more flexible approach and supplemented with a set of rules that implement Basel Convention requirements.

c)   *Economic instruments*

The 1993 Amendment to the EPA 1980 completed the process of separating environmental funds from the state budget which started in 1989. The 1993 Amendment established a three-tier system of environmental funds: the National Fund for Environmental Protection and Water Management, voivodship funds and local funds. Both the national Fund and voivodship funds are 'arms length' legal entities reporting to independent Boards and entitled to operate their own capital which basically derives from their share of pollution charges and non-compliance fines.

In order to increase the funds available the National Fund has established its own bank, the Bank for Environmental Protection, which invests the Fund's capital on a commercial basis. The Fund's recent policy has been to provide polluters with preferential credits rather than with subsidies for environmental investments.

It is worth mentioning that, meanwhile, the rates of pollution charges and non-compliance fines have grown substantially and now are among the highest in the world (for example, to release a tonne of sulphur dioxide costs about US$ 84, and to release a tonne of a carcinogenic pollutant, such as asbestos may cost as much as US$ 40,000).

d)   *Environmental impact assessment*

In 1990 significant progress was made to the environmental impact assessment (EIA) scheme which had been operational at least since the Land Use Planning Act of 1984 which made EIAs obligatory for projects 'especially harmful for the environment and human health', by regulations issued in 1985 which listed categories of such projects.

New regulations in 1990 gave a new impetus to the EIA scheme by providing detailed requirements as to the content of EIAs and establishing a special EIA agency, the EIA Commission, following on the Dutch model. The new Land Use Act of 1994 brought further progress through the introduction of a kind of 'Strategic' EIA which is required in relation to land use plans, and by authorizing the Environment Minister to establish two lists of categories of projects subjected to EIA procedures (intended to follow respectively Annex 1 and Annex 2 projects of the EC Directive 85/337).

e) Enforcement

In 1991 an attempt was made to remedy deficiencies in enforcement by strengthening the role of the State Environmental Protection Inspectorate, which was originally established by the EPA 1980 as the central agency responsible for monitoring compliance. It was, however, a 'watchdog without teeth'. The State Environmental Protection Inspectorate Act of 1991 hands over to the agency enforcement powers previously allocated to governors and sufficient status and resources to cope with this new task.

The Inspectorate is directly responsible to the Environment Minister and acts through the Chief Environmental Protection Inspector and environmental inspectors who are the chiefs of its branches at the voivodship level. Inspectors have the power to impose non-compliance fines, to halt activity which is endangering the environment, and to ban the sale and import of raw materials and other products which fail to meet Polish environmental standards. In addition the Inspectorate is responsible for running the nationwide environmental data base system. Inspectors are entitled to recover the costs of inspecting facilities (for example, costs of sampling) if the inspection results in a finding of non-compliance.

V HOPES MEET REALITY: CREEPING REFORM REPLACES RADICAL CHANGE

1 Neither easy nor quick

By 1991 it had become clear that initial hopes of completing the entire restructuring of the environmental institutional framework within two to three years were over-optimistic. The reasons for giving up the idea of radical change cannot be attributed only to the lack of political will to make these changes or to the fact that environmental protection is not a priority of the transformation process. There are also merits to the existing system.

Existing environmental legislation seems to be not only quite a developed machinery in itself but is also so closely interconnected with the entire legal system that the available human resources (though quite significant by Eastern European standards) could not reasonably be expected to thoroughly revise it within a relatively short period of time. Moreover, the drafters encountered many problems and had to employ different approaches in order to solve the several legislative dilemmas they faced.

2   Problems encountered

a)   Coordination

The transition period, with its historic task to establish a completely new economic and political system might be considered an excellent opportunity to introduce the most progressive concepts regarding environmental policy and law. Indeed, the transition period has meant a certain bias towards progressive thinking and radical changes which, as a general political approach, allows much more room for policy-makers and law-makers than any stable system can offer. The stable, well established system, regardless of whether or not it is democratic, is by nature much more conservative and therefore less likely to accept any radical change or even reform. On the other hand such a system offers a firm framework, which is a huge advantage because new schemes cannot be developed in a vacuum. Even the most radical changes over particular issues, in order to be operational, must somehow be related to the overall institutional framework. In this respect, contrary to the expectations of many, the transition period is not a paradise for policy-makers and law-makers. In fact, from the technical side, policy-making and legal drafting becomes a nightmare when, in a relatively short period, all policies are reoriented and all laws are redesigned.

The collapse of the communist regime caught the democratic opposition by surprise. Unlike the opposition in democratic systems, the opposition in Poland was in no position to prepare any comprehensive and detailed programme of changes before it actually took power. Bearing in mind insufficient access to information, the opposition's lack of experience in government and its internal political diversity, and the huge task to be accomplished, such a comprehensive programme could not be reasonably expected.

New laws and policies related to all matters of public policy were being developed in myriads of legislative committees and task forces. Since different provisions in a single legislative programme must be at least compatible, the results of their work were changes in the entire administrative framework. These changes, especially decentralization, have had their ups and downs and are still far from being completed. The latter concerns such important issues as: the restructuring of central government; the reorganization of regional governmental administration towards bigger provinces covering entire geographical areas; and the establishment of a second tier of local self-government. Lack of any progress in relation to these issues still hinders serious discussion over the introduction of neccessary changes to environmental administration.

b) Insufficient knowledge

The ambitious goals with which law-makers have been presented were adopted without due regard to the question as to whether the environmental infrastructure had sufficient background knowledge concerning the issues to be addressed. In fact, much of the expertise available turned out to be irrelevant , mainly because years of insufficient access to international information and exchange of experience had resulted in a lack of a broad perspective in drafting environmental laws. Very few Polish experts had anything more than just a rough idea about the 'Western' laws and ecological concepts which were supposed to provide guidance for environmental policy and law in Poland. Even fewer people knew, and only in relation to certain issues, how to achieve the goals set out.

Much of the initial impetus for legal drafting was based on analysis and research carried out by independent experts who had previously unsuccessfully approached the government with their ideas in the 1980s. Shortly after 1989 it had become clear, however, that the range of issues to be addressed by new legislation was much broader than the number of 'shelved' drafts or concepts inherited from the past. The problem was that, with the exception of those shelved issues , there was hardly any issue in relation to which background studies allowed the development of a comprehensive scheme within a fixed period of time. Among those issues which required further studies there were well identified problems, such as shortcomings in the pollution control scheme, which had been thoroughly assessed in reaction to the domestic situation, but required studies concerning the solutions applied in other countries in order to propose any meaningful remedies. There were also issues, such as environmental control over chemicals, which had only recently been identified as a problem which required the investigation of not only foreign solutions but also the domestic situation. In the case of access to environmental information, another quite recently identified problem, much background work on the domestic situation and foreign solutions was available, but a comprehensive scheme seemed to require changes in other laws.

c) New issues

The law-makers encountered new additional problems arising from the transition period itself – namely, deregulation, privatization and marketization.
Deregulation   The most hotly debated environmental problem attributable to deregulation shortly after the 1988 liberalization of economic activity was caused by removing barriers to foreign trade in order to establish market conditions. Before 1988 only a few state-owned companies were authorized to carry out foreign trade and their licences listed the categories of goods or materials they were authorized to trade. Since waste was not listed in any authorization there was no problem

with the transborder shipment of waste. No one could anticipate however, that the side-effect of liberalizing foreign trade would be a flow of sometimes extremely hazardous waste. In effect the abolished foreign trade authorization scheme had provided efficient control over the shipment of waste, even though it had not been designed for this purpose.

Privatization   Industrial privatization introduced to Poland a range of issues related to environmental liability in property transfers. These questions were neither considered while starting to draft new environmental legislation nor identified in privatization legislation. Therefore the Polish government was surprised when environmental issues were raised by prospective investors. Two ad hoc remedies were applied to overcome these shortcomings:

1   The Privatization Ministry created a joint task force with the Environment Ministry to deal with environmental issues in privatization.
2   Western advisors were employed by the Privatization Ministry to provide expertise necessary in negotiating environmental liability issues in sale deals with foreign investors. Both remedies appeared to be very successful, and no doubt will contribute much to the development of a scheme to deal with contaminated land, which is a somewhat neglected issue in environmental legislation.

Marketization   Introduction of the free market made the economic system show greater respect for consumers. Restructuring of the economy and a shift from producing investments goods to consumer goods resulted in significant changes in waste management. The problem was not only the unprecedented increase in the total volume of waste, but also a change in its nature: it was now mostly household waste. The old waste control scheme seemed inadequate to deal with both challenges as it was focused on industrial waste disposal.

d)   Legal tradition

Public participation seems to be the sole issue where, despite having a comprehensive draft scheme that included most of the advanced Western solutions in this respect, no progress whatsoever has been reached as yet. The reasons for this seem to lie deeper than in the natural bias of bureaucrats against any public involvement in their business.

Public participation and access to governmental information have both established themselves as necessary elements of any contemporary environmental regulatory programme. Both of these instruments reflect the concept of 'open' government which is alien to Poland's legal culture. Poland's administrative system is based on the German, Austrian and Russian traditions, each notorious for secrecy and aversion to public involvement. Administrative procedure in Poland is based on traditional nineteenth-century German concept and assumes a basic dichotomy: on the one hand administrative authority represents the public interest while, on the other, a party to the procedure represents his own individual interest. Consequently, the model favours 'cabinet' proceedings where only experts are invited to participate. Consequently, it is not easy to introduce public participation rights for any environmental decision-making procedure in Poland.

This is especially the case in respect of the public hearing, which has its origin in a system where participation is treated as an individual right, and proceedings have adversarial character with the administrative authority acting as a judge. Nonetheless the conceptual reason which makes Poland's authorities so reluctant to have public hearings is not this, but rather a disregard of the layman and an aversion to additional duties. This attitude is equally reinforced by a general misconception concerning public participation. Many governmental officials tend to understand public participation only in its most radical form, according to which granting participation rights in decision- and rule-making procedures requires that citizens' comments are binding.

3   Legislative policy dilemmas

Drafting the legislation involved a number of dilemmas that had to be solved one way or another. Some of these are discussed below, without any attempt to grade their importance.

a)   *Judicial precision versus common understanding*

There is a long tradition in Poland of a strong sense of individual rights and a disregard for law, which can be traced back at least to the sixteenth century. The traditional disregard for law has been reinforced by communist rule. In case of environmental law this general attitude coincided well with the tradition, commonly held to be typical in Europe, of treating environmental matters as a 'technical' rather than a 'legal' issue. Since environmental law in Poland has traditionally been drafted, implemented and even enforced by non-lawyers, neither administration nor industry felt bound by the law but treated it more as a 'guidance'.

The dilemma was whether to draft the new laws in precise legal jargon and risk having them misread or even neglected by the administration, or to support the discredited tradition of drafting imprecise, incoherent laws even if the main policy goals are implemented.

A strong pressure to make laws very short, laconic and simple was confronted with a pressure to regulate precisely all matters already at the statutory level. The latter arose from criticism of the abusive practice of giving too much regulatory power to the administration (through delegated powers), which reflected a distrust of administration inherited from the communist era (the so called 'them and us' approach, which assumed fundamental a conflict of interests between the government and citizens). This approach dictated a policy of granting fewer discretionary powers, which in turn was confronted with a call for more flexible policy, enabling different approaches towards those polluters who made efforts to improve their environmental performance and towards those who did not .

b)   Enforceability versus progressive policy

Many problems were caused by the contradictory character of some of the goals set out for the new legislation. Old legislation was criticized in respect of both lax standards and unenforceability. New legislation was expected to be more ecologically progressive (by establishing, for example, stringent quality standards) as well as to be fully enforceable. Since achieving both goals in the given circumstances seemed impossible, the law-makers usually preferred the law to be enforceable.

c)   Ideal solutions versus reality

One of the biggest dilemmas in drafting was whether to follow the previous approach and focus on drafting nice-looking, comprehensive and modern law that could be proudly presented or to focus on drafting a law that would be less 'fancy' but operational. The latter approach required much attention to be given to the capacity of the administration and its ability to handle its tasks, to the economic situation of polluters, and to the compatibility of environmental law with the entire institutional framework. This approach also assumed making use of pre-existing institutions and procedures for new purposes instead of creating new ones.

d)   Decentralization versus effectiveness

The trend towards decentralization was confronted with the necessity of having environmental programmes administered by well qualified professionals, unlikely to be found in small communities in the country.

e)   Environmental code versus sectoral laws

Perhaps the most hotly debated, though not the most important, issue was the question whether to create an 'omnibus' code-like environmental law or to proceed with the 'sectoral' laws as soon as they were ready. The biggest disadvantage of the first solution was that it required well advanced conceptions of the necessary changes required in respect of all the issues and the fact that a single controversial issue might prevent the draft law from being adopted.

4 Approaches employed

Law-makers in Poland employed a very cautious approach to new instruments and institutions. Efforts to balance what was necessary with what might be ideal sought to avoid establishing new requirements that either the industry would not be able to meet, or the administration was incapable of administering. Some proposals for an ambitious chemical control scheme, otherwise badly needed, have not been fully adopted for this reason. Also postponed were proposals for legislation which in the current situation might be either practically unenforceable (such as stringent standards) or even counterproductive (such as the introduction of BAT or BATNEEC criteria). However, the redesign of the pollution control schemes towards technology-based standards began by the gradual introduction of generally applicable emission standards. Another reason for slowing down the process of reform was the necessity of building a professional infrastructure (the approach successfully employed in the EIA scheme which was built up gradually) or of gaining some experience through pilot projects (as in the case of emissions trading).

5 Mistakes

Many of the mistakes that were made when drafting a new environmental framework originated from an incorrect overall assessment of the old framework. First, it was much more efficient than it was believed to be; the problem was an ineffective economy. The critical assessment was based on two false assumptions:

1   It was compared to modern Western environmental legislation, whereas because of the state of technology, it should have been compared with the legislation existing in the West in the 1950s and 1960s at the latest.
2   It was assessed taking into account only the body of law called 'environmental law' while a lot of control functions were provided by other instruments (compare the already mentioned example of the control of transborder shipment of waste).

So much time was spent prescribing a cure for the 'old' problems that new problems were overlooked. One example is in the area of the debate over decentralization. The State Inspectorate for Environmental Protection was given enforcement powers because of the reluctance of governors, being primarily responsible for the state-owned economy in the region, to introduce enforcement actions against companies subordinated to them. These links were broken with the privatization process, leaving no other important justification for separating licensing from monitoring compliance and enforcement. Attention should be given instead to making a reasonable distinction between simple and dangerous technologies in order to define activities best subjected to either local or central environmental licensing, monitoring, and enforcement.

The government was preoccupied with searching for a remedy to problems that could be solved by alternative methods. For example much (unsuccessful) effort was devoted to strengthening public participation through establishing individual rights, while a more practical remedy would have been to change the restrictive association law and introduce Polish NGOs into the international fundraising system. As a result, functionally, Poland has a situation similar to that in the USA, in that, in both countries, it is mainly the ecological NGOs that take advantage of existing participation rights. The situations differ legally only : in the USA individual participation rights are used by NGOs; in Poland NGOs make use of rights which were specifically created for associations.

It was assumed that privatization would automatically improve compliance and that particularly breaking the official economic link between agencies and the regulated community would make enforcement in respect of private companies easier. In fact, however, the situation turned out to be quite the reverse. State owned firms could not ostensibly neglect laws because of the communist party's effective control, while private companies did not bother with environmental requirements, because inefficient monitoring and enforcement schemes were not supplemented by any 'establishment' control. The US experience of citizens enforcement via civil courts seemed attractive, but the hopes placed in the civil lawsuit as a means of improved enforcement were based on a misunderstanding as it failed to take into account at least two differences between the USA (where this instrument was invented) and Poland. First, the supervision of administrative decisions in Poland is channelled through administrative courts, which are a separate and independent branch of the judiciary, and, moreover, the administrative courts offer cheaper options for citizens seeking court protection, when compared with the civil courts, where, unlike in the USA, there is no *pro bono* practice and there is a rule that the losing party bears the winner's litigation costs and counsel fees.

VI CONCLUSIONS

1 Does it work?

It is difficult to judge whether a radical reform of environmental law, formulated by acts of parliament, would have served environmental performance better than the cautious reform made through regulations. It is possible, however, to monitor whether or not the cautious path has a success. This is a considerable test for the kind of critical opinion which accuses Poland not only of failing to introduce radical changes to environmental legislation but also of generally missing its opportunity to reorient the fallacious economic policy of the communist regime, with a consequent failure to make any progress in the economy's environmental performance.

All accessible data seem to show something different. A significant drop in the pollution level since 1989 has been observed, which to a large extent should be attributed to the process of restructuring the economy, particularly the shut-downs of outdated, energy-consuming and heavily polluting heavy industrial plants. Yet, without doubt, the new environmental policy must also have contributed to this improvement. It must be remembered that in terms of environmental expenditures, Poland has recently reached the level of 1 per cent of GDP which, in relative terms, corresponds to what is currently spent in the OECD countries and corresponds in absolute terms to the per capita level spent by these countries when they began their environmental recovery programmes.

2 Lessons learned

Poland definitely has not undergone a radical reform of environmental law. The experience of the past five years shows that it neither could, nor should, have done this. It is a cliché to say that legislative reform requires expertise and time. Initial hopes that Poland might 'leapfrog the West' were overoptimistic. A comprehensive, modern environmental system requires a certain infrastructure: knowledge, technology, administration, economy. They must all be developed hand in hand.

Environmental legislation, in order to work effectively, must fit the existing legal tradition and be properly integrated in the entire institutional framework. Therefore, as the Polish experience shows, foreign assistance is the most effective not with respect to the drafting of laws, but rather through providing the lawmakers with all the necessary information available in more advanced systems concerning a given issue. Taking advantage of foreign experience is crucial, provided this does not imply the literal adaptation of certain provisions, but rather the creation of the functional equivalents of certain foreign institutions adapted to local needs. Before so doing, it is worthwhile establishing what role a given institution plays in the foreign environmental system, to identify the reasons why it works effectively and finally to assess those conditions under which its domestic equivalent might work as effectively.

Prior to 1989, Poland was fortunate enough to have quite a developed environmental protection framework. This has gradually been changed as a result of extensive self-analysis aimed at answering the following questions: what instruments were designed to fit only the old system, what instruments worked in the old system and would they be working in a new system, what instruments did not work in the old system and would they be working in the new system, and what new instruments are needed to make this system work effectively?

All these gradual changes significantly redesigned the entire scheme, developed infrastructure and provided sufficient background knowledge as well as procedures to start adjusting Poland's environmental law to EC requirements.

22 Environmental Law Reform in Central and Eastern Europe: the Case of Hungary

Gyula Bándi

Table of Contents

I CENTRAL AND EASTERN EUROPEAN ENVIRONMENTAL PROBLEMS

Central and Eastern European societies have entered the transition period with acute political, economic and environmental problems. Accumulated debts weigh heavily on both the present and the future – namely, several billion dollars of debt owed to the international financial system, as well as an almost indeterminable degree of ecological damage. According to some expert estimates annual environmental damages amount to 8–15 per cent of GDP (according to bolder estimates damages caused by vehicular traffic alone amount to 5–7 per cent of GDP); according to other expert estimates, it is very likely that the cost of the accumulated environmental damage to the region will be larger than the foreign debt.

Mistreatment of the environment in Central and Eastern Europe has had serious effects on human health. For example, in the most polluted part of the former Czechoslovakia, life expectancy is reported to be five years less than in less polluted areas of the two present countries. Environment-related health problems in Hungary are estimated to account for 13 per cent of health and welfare expenditures.

Productivity of natural resources also has declined. In former Czechoslovakia, 54 per cent of agricultural land is considered endangered, and 30 per cent of Hungary's agricultural land is estimated to be at risk. In Poland, eliminating food production in the most highly degraded regions is a top priority and the availability of water for home and industrial purposes can no longer be taken for granted in heavily polluted areas.

Environmental resources and biodiversity have also suffered. Eighty-two per cent of Poland's forests show some kind of damage; respectively, 73 per cent of the former Czechoslovakia and 36 per cent of Hungary's forests have incurred significant damage. The impact on flora and fauna has been particularly grave.

Some of the main causes of concern include:

- very high air pollution levels, primarily associated with coal-burning and metallurgy;
- high sulphur dioxide emissions per dollar GNP in CEE countries relative to OECD countries;
- severe pollution of rivers, lakes and groundwater supplies;
- inadequate water treatment facilities for municipalities and industrial facilities;
- uncontrolled mining operations and environmentally-insensitive agricultural practices;
- inadequate waste treatment;
- weak or non-existent arrangements for treating municipal, industrial and hazardous wastes and poor information on the location, volume and toxicity of previously dumped wastes;
- nuclear safety as a major source of uncertainty.

The economic and political conditions prevailing in Hungary until 1990 were basically determined by the country's membership of both Comecon and the Warsaw Pact. The economic and social institutions of the past, the previous dominance of Comecon relations and the undesirable consequences of Hungary's isolation from Western countries still overshadow economic development.

As a result of the features of the previous economic system,[1] the Hungarian economy had been tackling the major inefficiencies which had existed for many decades. Such inefficiencies were reflected in high energy consumption, the material intensity of production, low capital efficiency as well as in a series of balance of payments deficits.

The communist economic reform in 1968 and the subsequent attempts at economic renewal failed. The 1968 reform undoubtedly changed the framework of the existing economic system but did not eliminate the traditional model of an over-centralized planned economy subordinated to political targets. It also failed to change the political institutions and property relations. Although central management became less rigid, the state's dominance remained decisive: specifically it was paternalistic toward company activity. Capital refund considerations were neglected; no real market was created, and the economy remained isolated from the world market.

The level of environmental degradation in Hungary is dramatic, although not unlike that in the West prior to the 1970s. The soil is acidifying, the waters and air are more polluted than ever, and most groundwater is not suitable for human consumption. Although a comprehensive risk analysis has not been undertaken in Hungary, the results of various studies indicate that the three most important environmental problems are air pollution, water pollution and hazardous waste contamination. Notwithstanding some improvements, the Hungarian environment is deteriorating quickly, and such degradation is not going to slow down: air quality, for example, may not improve substantially, even with regulation, because pollution from increased traffic and heating could offset any improvements.

The current state of Hungary's environment can be traced to economic, legal and political factors. In Hungary's centralized economic structure – if we add other reasons to the aforementioned problems of economic management – the polluter was typically the same entity as the enforcer – the state – whose self-interest perpetuated artificial economic development. This artificial economic system never rewarded energy efficiency, conservation of raw materials or pollution prevention. Political interests and the acquisition of political power undermined sound environmental and economic management. Environmental protection was not a high priority, and little money was spent on collecting environmental data. Environmental protection agencies faced the impossible task of making decisions with little or no information.

---

[1] A system wherein the economy was subordinated to a hierarchical state power structure; there was politicization of economic targets; limited assertion of economic interests; centralized economic management taking and redistributing the largest shares of income; highly limited independence of companies; and a pseudo-market occupying the place of a real market.

Hungary's environmental plight also has roots in its legal and political system. The state focused on technical issues, rather than regulation and enforcement. As a result, monitoring, largely conducted by industry with poor equipment and very little regulatory oversight, produced little useful information. Such enforcement and implementation that existed tended to focus on sanctioning those who polluted rather than on preventing the pollution. The imposed penalties were rarely sufficient to provide an incentive to curb pollution.

Perhaps most importantly, there was no public participation in the decision-making process. The role of civil law and the courts was very limited. Citizens could neither influence a decision before it was made, nor could they challenge the decision ex post facto. Even when citizen intervention was permitted, non-governmental organizations were too weak to support successful public involvement.

Organizational weaknesses also limited Hungary's ability to protect the environment. The central environmental agency is much weaker than the economic ministries, both in terms of power and resources. Spheres of authority are poorly defined and are rapidly changing. This unclear division of power creates uncertainty and hesitation, not only for the environmental agencies, but also for the regulated community.

II CENTRAL AND EASTERN EUROPE IN TRANSITION

If we examine the state of environment in modern Hungary then – being a little cynical – the slightly positive changes are more or less due to the economic difficulties affecting a number of polluting facilities. Here we can mention three different examples of these unintended kinds of environmentally-friendly change:

1   The use of chemicals in agriculture is lower than ever before as a result of the great rise of chemical prices due to the cancellation of state subsidies to chemical industry.
2   A number of polluting facilities have been shut down or have diminished their production due to the lack of financial resources.
3   One of the biggest polluters, the military, has drastically reduced its activity, as well as the production of military industries.

1 Background variables

Before going into the specifics of environmental protection in Hungary, it is useful to examine some of the background issues in order to get a more detailed view of the current situation. The following is a list of opportinities for, and difficulties of, environmental protection deriving from these background issues.

a) Political structure

After a long history of the one-party system the fundamentals of policy-making have radically changed in most of the Central and Eastern Europe (CEE), and the states have opened their closed shop to issues and debates introduced by international multi-party systems.

Opportunities   In developing a multi-party system, there is a better opportunity to emphasize environmental interests. Hence, most of the new government programmes cover environmental issues from the outset. Taking international commitments seriously implies that those conventions which are favourable gain influence over CEE policy.

Difficulties   The relationship between economic and environmental priorities in policy-making greatly favours economic interests.

A concrete environmental policy and strategy – going beyond a mere set of statements – is lacking both in national or regional policy and also on the party-policy level. As a result, environmental protection in the regulatory arena has always been, and in most cases still is, mere 'show-business'. It declares a concern for protection but does not create a real set of political, economic and legal requirements.

The transition process has resulted in numerous political, social and economic problems especially related to social security and unemployment concerns. These run against the interests of environmental protection.

b) Economic structure

While the main source of environmental problems is economic development, the same economic development can also provide the only effective opportunity for environmental protection.

Opportunities   For the most part, the state is no longer both the potential polluter and the responsible controlling administration. This gives a greater opportunity to enforce environmental requirements.

The market economy and consumer policy, taken together, may have a self-monitoring and regulating effect (for example in the prices of raw materials and energy).

There is a greater probability that an environmentally-friendly (or energy-saving, recycling and so on) industry and services will be developed as a response to new environmental regulations.

Foreign trading relations have a significant impact on environmental protection. Western product criteria and environmental requirements may encourage industry to use, for example, EC standards even though they are not incorporated into the given regulatory system.

There is now an opportunity to develop the market economy and environmental protection in harmony; this has not existed before.

Difficulties   There is a tendency to connect stricter environmental regulations with a later stage of economic development – when 'we can afford it'.

A market economy is not an absolute self-controlling mechanism in the interests of environmental protection. The effect of a market economy is very ambiguous and may partly favour environmental protection interests (for example in the shutdown of polluting industries or the development of market incentives), but can also be damaging to the environment (for example, increased emissions may accompany growing production or the incapability of former state industries to clean up polluted sites).

The necessary economic incentives for environmental protection, as well as an understanding of the role of economic management in environmental protection, are lacking in most of the CEE countries' economies. To this we must also add new plans for privatization, joint ventures, concession licences and compensation for past nationalizations, all representing primary facets of the economic programme, but all without reference to environmental impacts.

The involvement of foreign money is directly connected to the new phenomena listed above, especially privatization. In order to attract foreign money the economic management is willing to ease environmental criteria.

It is clear that the countries' own resources are not enough for both pollution prevention and remedy, so the setting of priorities is an essential requirement at this level also.

Finally, the most important prerequisite for the efficient use of market forces is a free market, but this is only slowly developing in the CEE countries.

c) Technological development

The possibilities and difficulties in the field of technology also have a significant impact on the current system of environmental protection. Most of the existing problems can be solved or at least alleviated, without using a wide range of sophisticated technological instruments, but in some situations an advanced stage of technological development is indeed essential.

Opportunities The development of foreign trade and the involvement of foreign capital and technology provide a better opportunity for the financing and use of cleaner technologies.

A great proportion of the present technological infrastructure must be modernized in order to make the economy competitive. This may also involve the use of cleaner technologies.

The relatively inefficient monitoring capacity is increasingly improved due to foreign assistance projects (such as PHARE).

Difficulties The present technological resources are insufficient to meet the requirements of environmental protection and will not be changed substantially in the near future.

Monitoring and information systems are less developed – a good example is the difficulty of Hungary's telecommunication system.

The training of specialized environmental experts is still developing. Training is still concentrated at post-graduate rather than the graduate level, so it is less for general environmental skills than for specific ones.

2 Basic legislatory options

The relevant legal measures can be classified according to the specificity of regulations. The first group is the general and comprehensive substantive and procedural law, containing all the instruments and measures giving rise to an enforcement activity, possibly used in respect of any element of the environment. The second group represents the special rules for the different environmental elements or at least specialization of the general substantive rules according to these elements.[2] The Hungarian Act No. II. of 1976 on the protection of human environment, for instance, lists six environmental elements: land, water, air, flora and fauna, landscape and human settlement areas.

Furthermore two important types of environmental legislation can be distinguished: *framework legislation*, determining only the fundamental rules and giving room for further legislation, and *detailed legislation*.

---

[2] In Hungary there are more than 250 different legal regulations that directly or indirectly refer to environmental protection interests, but all of them were adopted at different times and under different circumstances.

Framework legislation has some beneficial qualities, such as flexibility in respect of future changes, the fact that it is easier to adopt gives more room for the adaptation to the specific elements, and it allows for the development of constructive practices. Consequently it may be too vague, largely dependent upon government interests for implementation, can easily be interpreted in a detrimental way, and can even be neglected.

By contrast, *detailed legislation* reflects a concrete legislative determination, gives clear rules for enforcement and also for controlling the enforcement, provides more stability for third parties, and is not so dependent upon the willingness of public administration to implement it. On the other hand it is not always sufficiently flexible, is more difficult to adapt, harder to harmonize with the requirements of different situations and possibly prevents the administration from developing constructive ideas.

Experience suggests that a comprehensive environmental law is necessary.[3]

The CEE countries today prefer framework legislation to more detailed legislation, particularly due to the relative lack of time for adoption. This is reflected in Bulgaria's 1991 environmental Act, the 1992 Act of the Czech and Slovak Federal Republic that has been adopted in both the new republics, Estonia's Act of 1990 and Latvia's 1991 Act. On the other hand, several other CEE countries were unable to approve their new laws: thus the 1976 framework law is still in force in Hungary, the 1980 Act on the protection of environment is still valid in Poland, as is the 1973 Act in Romania.

In Hungary the first parliamentary term of the transition ended in May 1994 without the adoption of the new and comprehensive general environmental act. The draft environmental law was ready at the beginning of 1994. Also a draft national environmental protection and nature conservation policy paper was presented at the end of March 1994, waiting for parliamentary consent. Due to the lack of time neither of the two drafts has yet been adopted.

---

[3] In the past several years we can present examples of this kind of legal evolution: the Environmental Protection Act 1990 (1990 c.43.) of Great Britain, the Act No.V of 1991, the Act to Protect the Environment in Malta; the general environmental protection Act of Bulgaria from October 1992; the framework Act of the – at that time – Czech and Slovak Federal Republic in December 1991; the new Dutch environmental Act of March 1993; but we may also mention the German general *Umweltgesetzbuch* draft, the drafting of which begun in 1989 and is still going on. The Hungarian government has also approved a general environmental draft law in December 1993. There are also some trends towards a comprehensive international covenant or draft on environmental law, such as the draft of the IUCN 'Covenant on environmental conservation and sustainable use of natural resources' from April 1991; or the drafting of a model Act on the protection of the environment done by experts gathered under the initiative of the Council of Europe first in October 1992.

3 The constitutional right to environmental protection

The best reflection of a basic philosophy how to regulate environmental protection[4] is the adoption of the constitutional right to environmental protection (but of course only if we take human rights issues seriously).[5] Although the Hungarian 1976 Act did grant to every citizen the right to live in an environment worthy of man,[6] this right has not been interpreted in practice by a court.

The Hungarian Constitution was amended in 1989 with the assumption that constitutional rights in the future would serve as the basis of legal action. This constitution regulated the right to environmental protection in two relatively different ways. Article 18 grants a separate right: 'The Hungarian Republic recognizes and enforces the right to a healthy environment for everyone.' Article 70/D treats this right as a tool for ensuring the highest possible level of physical and mental health. In addition to protecting the man made and natural environment this right is ensured by organizing an occupational health system, public health institutions and medical care.

The first of the above-mentioned two Articles is a direct adoption of a right to environmental protection, not only for the citizens but for everyone. This Article clearly expresses that the state is responsible for ensuring the implementation of this right. However, the obligation of the state does not mean that the state is the only responsible organ to protect the environment; it means instead that the state must create such a legal environment where there is no, or hardly any other, way to undertake any kind of activity in other than the environmental-friendly way.

In its decision No. 28/1994.(V.20.) the Constitutional Court interpreted this constitutional right to environmental protection. In the case in question there was an appeal against the constitutionality of the Act II. of 1992, Article 15, para. 1. This paragraph originally did not allow nature conservation areas to be reprivatized from the property of co-operatives. A year later the amendments of this paragraph opened up the possibility to place such areas in private ownership. These rules were considered unconstitutional by the Court because they might lead to the curtailment of nature conservation areas and to the degradation of natural values. The Court also stated that the private property of nature conservation areas in it-

---

[4] We may distinguish at least three basic regulatory philosophies concerning environmental regulation. The main purpose of regulation differs due to these different philosophies. The most general and common philosophy up until now focuses regulation on the present state of mankind and takes man as the main subject to protect. The second philosophy is to focus on future generations also, thus requiring greater efforts from the present generation, because they are the only guardians of the environment. The third and broadest philosophy is the concept of biodiversity.

[5] See further Chapter 2 by K-H. Ladeur in this volume.

[6] Act No.II of 1976, Art. 2 (2).

self was legal, but a set of obligations and limitations on the use of this property was missing. Thus the decision asked the parliament to adopt a law until 30 November 1994. According to the Court, the constitution requires that the level of protection of the environment should not be lowered or challenged, save only where the implementation of other constitutional values or basic rights is at issue. This means a balance of interests at the same level. This upgrading of environmental protection is the real value of the case, which will certainly have a lasting significance for legislation.

The decision referred also to a former one, the decision No. 996/G/1990. This was the first finding in connection with the right to environmental protection. The decision states that the right to a healthy environment constitutes an obligation for the state to establish and maintain specific legal and organizational institutions to protect this right, as they are the necessary conditions for its implementation. The level of the protection is not at the discretion of the state since this protection provides the foundations of human life, and harm to the environment is usually irreparable. While the state is free to choose the means and methods of protection, it has no freedom in allowing, in the effect, any kind of degradation or even the risk of such degradation.

4   Administrative law

a)   Licensing and environmental impact assessment

The basic preventive measure in environmental protection is the permit. Granting permits is a possible method of prevention but, in Hungary, environmental requirements are only an auxiliary element to the main permit procedure. The environmental administration may only give consent in respect of a more basic construction or operating permit. In the case of building permits there are 11 different authorities involved, the basic permit being given by the local government which is also generally responsible for the safeguarding of environmental protection interests. In the permit procedure for the use of public lands four authorities give agreement in every case and 14 others in special cases where environmental considerations arise, and then only with regard to nature conservation.

In these permit procedures environmental interests are represented by a number of different administrative organs responsible for media and entities such as soil, water, public health, landscape in general and so on. As a result the environmental interests are less likely to be formed into an integrated decision. In the case of a building permit the public health authorities examine the air pollution situation, the water authorities examine the water management situation, the agricultural administration observes the soil and general animal protection part, the industrial government surveys the energy part and the environmental specialized bodies check nature conservation, the handling of hazardous waste and noise abatement. No wonder complex environmental interests can easily be pushed into the background, as in most cases this environmental consent is merely a collateral agreement to the operating permit, and its impact on the plant operation is greatly connected with the personal enthusiasm of the public servant in question.

As a new element in permitting the environmental impact assessment (EIA) finally appeared also in Hungary by decree No. 86/1993 (VI.4.) Korm.r. There are two forms of the assessment: a preliminary assessment, and a detailed one. The annex to the decree determines which are those most important projects, where detailed assessment is required, otherwise the decision on the kind of assessment is made by the environmental inspectorate.

The most important change the decree brings about is the introduction of a genuine environmental permit. In the case of those activities that require an ETA, such a special permit must be obtained from the environmental inspectorate. This environmental permit has become a precondition for all the other permits, such as of a further building permit. Thus, the environmental permit does not replace any other permits, but precedes them.

The EIA obligation covers the environmental impacts of the investment necessary for carrying on some activity, the activity itself, by operations that are directly connected to the main activity (in particular, transport, waste and waste water treatment), the termination of the activity and the consequences of possible accidents or defects.

The preliminary assessment should contain: the purpose of the investment and its possible siting and technical alternatives; possible material and energy emissions; use of the environment, the possible impact on the environment; and the changes in landscape and ecological conditions, and the list of questions that are to be answered in a detailed assessment.

The content of the detailed assessment is roughly similar to the one prescribed by the EC Directive 85/337.[7]

The inspectorate may issue a permit or forbid the operation after the preliminary study. The third alternative is to require a detailed study. In the case of detailed study an open hearing is mandatory.

It is worth mentioning that a kind of environmental impact assessment procedure has appeared in most of the CEE countries in the last few years. In Bulgaria the 1991 general environmental Act introduced the EIA obligation; in the Czech and also the Slovak Republics the 1992 federal environmental Act adopted the same kind of process; in Poland the major rules were provided for by a ministerial decree in 1990; and ministerial regulations from 1990 provide for some EIA obligations in the process of issuing permits in Romania.

---

[7] See, in relation to this, Chapter 5 by C. Lambrechts in this volume.

b)   Administrative sanctions and financial incentives

The most frequently used administrative sanction in Hungary is the environmental protection fine. The present Act formulates the general rule, stating that all persons who pursue activities contrary to statutory provisions and official orders providing for environmental protection or fail to meet the obligations prescribed, may be (and sometimes must be) obliged to pay a fine for environmental protection according to the extent and hazard of such environmental pollution, harm or damage. The fine is considered as a measure to protect the general interests of the environment. If a polluter pays a fine, he still may be required to pay compensation for damages or may be subject to criminal penalties and so on. These fines are media specific.[8]

Although the regulation of environmental protection fines is rather heterogeneous, some common elements of the different fines can be listed: the fine is always imposed on the polluter by one of those authorities responsible for environmental protection; the fines represent a kind of strict liability, requiring no fault or negligence (except in the case of the land protection fine); the fine is always based upon a measurable quantity – either a standard or quantity of polluting materials or the size of the affected land or nature conservation area; fines can be individualized by using different modifying factors according to the circumstances of harm or pollution; in most of the cases there is a progressivity if the same activity is repeated; the funds are accumulated in environmental protection funds.

A different kind of administrative sanction is the administrative levy against a violator for a petty offence. A petty offence is a smaller violation used to penalize the negligent or intentional wrongdoing of private persons.

The present development of a market economy favours the use of economic incentives more than in the recent past. The best method of achieving compliance among the market players should be to use market-friendly measures which direct the potential polluter towards meeting environmental requirements.[9] The first, and until now the only, attempt towards economic incentives was to introduce a product fee on the price of petrol in the spring of 1992.

c)   Media-specific regulation

In 1976 the Hungarian parliament enacted the Act on the Protection of the Human Environment. Unfortunately, the Act was more for show than a serious attempt at environmental regulation. It establishes rules for protecting land, water, air, flora

---

[8]   Today fines exist in the following seven categories: land protection, water pollution, sewage pollution, air pollution, nature conservation, hazardous waste, and noise or vibration.

[9]   See further Chapter 13 on financial incentives by G. Bándi in this volume.

and fauna, landscapes and human settlements (including residential, recreational and business areas). Despite the Act, the different areas of environmental protection have developed separately with no real harmonization, thus illustrating the lack of integrated pollution control.

Land use planning and soil conservation   The Act on Land Use and Landownership of 1987 distinguishes four categories of land according to its use:

1   arable land;
2   developed lands;
3   special purpose land (such as military use or nature conservation);
4   land unsuitable for use.

The purpose of the Land Act is to protect soil quality and safeguard arable land for agricultural purposes.

Those who use arable lands are obligated, under the Land Act, to ensure the perpetual use of the land for agricultural purposes. If they use the land for purposes other than agriculture, they must ensure that this other use does not destroy the land's agricultural potential. Special land agencies organized under the Ministry of Agriculture are charged with enforcing these rules.

Under the Land Act, a permit is required for all land withdrawals. There are two kinds of permits: one for withdrawals of less than five years, and the other for withdrawals of more than five years. The permit process examines all the circumstances related to the proposed withdrawal, including the necessity of the withdrawal. Certain other requirements also must be met (for instance, less valuable lands must be withdrawn prior to more valuable lands). The Land Act creates two types of charges for land withdrawal: quantitative and qualitative. Quantitative charges are assessed on the basis of the quality of the land upon receipt of a permit to withdraw land from its current use. The landowner pays the charge into a special fund for the protection of arable land. A person withdrawing high quality land must pay a larger qualitative charge than a person withdrawing lower quality land. Those who wish to cultivate previously uncultivated land as a direct exchange for land withdrawn do not have to pay the charge. The qualitative charges are collected for negligent reduction in the quality of the land.

Generally, the regulations to protect soil conditions are ineffective. Because fines are assessed based on land classification rather than on the degree of pollution, fines do not reflect the seriousness of soil degradation.

Water pollution[10]   State ownership of waters (except artificial bodies of water) provides the basis for water management. The state thus acts as both the environmental protection authority and the owner. The agency delegated the responsibility for the management of water is the National Water Management Agency within the Ministry of Transport, Telecommunication and Water Management. It consists of a central body and twelve regional authorities. The environmental protection administration also has water quality and quantity responsibilities. The self-governments are responsible for sewage treatment and drinking water supplies.

Any activity affecting water requires a permit, except for such small scale activities as collecting rainwater for household use. Most permits are granted by the regional water authorities. In some cases the self-governments, where they have licensing rights, will grant permits. The permit system is the starting point for water protection. Water management plans designate the water uses for a region. The national water management plan ranks water uses, classifying them as residential, industrial and agricultural based on the country's overall water needs. These classifications may have both different quantity and quality requirements. A different permit is required to allocate the amount of water to be used. In addition, users must pay fees for different quantitative and qualitative water uses (this includes citizens, who must pay for household use). All charges are paid to a Water Management Fund.

Water quality is protected by means of water pollution standards and fines, as well as through sewage system pollution standards and fines. Fines are based on the general requirement not to contaminate waters, and to treat polluted waste water with pollution control equipment. They are imposed if pollution exceeds a fixed standard for any pollutant listed. These standards are different for each of the six water quality regions[11] and can also be increased or reduced for individual activities, depending upon water quality interests. This individual standard can be withdrawn or modified.

Fines can also be assessed according to the circumstances of the offence, such as the extent of the pollution and the method by which the pollutant entered the water. Penalties are assessed by the regional water authorities. Fines can be modified if the polluter agrees to clean up the water or on the basis of certain other factors (not including an inability to pay). Where a violation has been continuous, the regional water authority can increase the fine over time. Water quality is

---

[10]   Water Management is regulated under Act. No. IV. of 1964, implemented by several decrees.

[11]   The six water quality regions are (1) superior water quality region, including Lake Balaton and Csepel Island; (2) drinking water sources and recreational areas, such as Lake Velence; (3) industrial zones; (4) irrigation sources; (5) the Danube and Tisza River areas which do not belong to regions (1)–(4); and (6) all other regions.

measured by the water authority at the site of the waste water discharge at least twice a year. Polluters may request additional monitoring to demonstrate compliance and, in some cases, may be allowed to monitor discharges themselves.

Permits are also required for sewage discharge and are based on the same water quality standards. Sewage regulation is also subject to regional water quality standards and the individualization of standards and fines.

Air pollution control   The air pollution protection system dates back to 1973 and is far less well developed than the water protection system. The air pollution regulation was amended in 1986 and its final provisions came into force in 1989. Its main problems are the lack of monitoring capacity and the contradictory distribution of authority. The basis for air pollution protection is emission thresholds, which divide the country into three types of air quality zones. The air regulation includes general air protection requirements, mostly for stationary sources of pollution which allow the inspectorate to limit or stop activities if necessary. It also regulates air pollution through product licensing.

Sudden and dangerous pollution may require exceptional measures to be taken, including prohibition of the use of automobiles or ordering the use of different energy supply systems. Municipal and county self-governments are required to develop a special action plan for implementing emergency measures.

Two kinds of emission thresholds exist: territorial thresholds and technological thresholds. Territorial thresholds are based upon ambient air quality, and are divided into three kinds of stationary pollution sources: point sources, such as a chimney; building sources; and surface sources. Technological thresholds are set based upon available technology and the quantity of the final product. Both thresholds are general thresholds. As with water thresholds, the inspectorates have authority to tailor air thresholds to individual needs.

As with other areas of Hungarian environmental law, the actual implementation of the air pollution laws has been punitive rather than preventive. Three types of fines exist. The first is based upon emission thresholds for the different types of sources. Polluters are responsible for monitoring their activities. Point and building stationary sources must report emissions annually, while surface sources must do so upon the request of the authority. The amount of the fine is determined by the degree to which pollution exceeded the standard and the danger of the pollutant. The second fine is for violations of specific obligations, such as the burning of waste without a permit determined by a fixed sum per kilogram. The third type of fine is for emission of noxious gases. These fines are mandatory in theory, but in practice, the regulations are not enforced.

Penalties become progressively greater as the violation continues. If a polluter violates a standard for five years, the fine will be more than double the original fine. The added penalty can be eliminated if the polluter has taken steps to avoid further pollution. Fines are assessed every three months.

Solid and hazardous waste management   Three types of waste can be distinguished: industrial, household and hazardous waste. This distinction is based on regulative, not technical criteria. All three are governed by different organizational structures. Industrial waste is treated very straightforwardly in Hungary: if it is considered hazardous, then it is regulated; otherwise, industrial waste can be disposed of as household waste. Household waste is divided into two categories: liquid and solid. Both are governed by thresholds based on public health and hygiene considerations, both thresholds are ineffective: The regulations are intended to impose obligations on households, but no mechanism to selectively collect these wastes has been established. The collection of household waste is the responsibility of the self-governments, but the manner of collection and handling is not regulated. When household wastes contain hazardous substances, they technically should be regulated by the rules for hazardous wastes. In practice, however, this does not occur.

Hazardous wastes include any materials or residue, from industry or other activities, which may have a direct or indirect, intermediate or immediate harmful effect on the health of humans and/or wildlife. Hazardous wastes are listed by law[12] and are classified into three grades based upon their danger. A new waste, previously unknown or the result of a new production process, is considered hazardous until there is evidence to the contrary.

Similar to the regulation of air pollution, producers of hazardous wastes are responsible for monitoring and registering their wastes. The producer of the waste also must submit records to the environmental protection authority. The regulations also cover the transport and temporary disposal of wastes. The three different types of waste must be collected separately and disposed of without polluting the environment. Solid wastes are not to be mixed with water, although the environmental protection authority may make exceptions. The environmental protection authority and the public health authorities have the discretion to issue licences for the disposal of wastes. There are strict regulations for operating a hazardous waste dump. Disposal sites for other types of waste are left virtually unregulated, although a licence is required from the building authority.

Another set of regulations dictates the measures necessary to avoid the harmful effects of waste. The environmental protection authority implements these measures which include licensing and monitoring hazardous waste treatment facilities, establishing collection methods, and enforcing restrictions on the operation of hazardous waste facilities, suspending operations if necessary. If the producer of

---

[12]   Government Decree 56/1981.(XI.18.) on Hazardous Waste, Art. 20.

the waste does not re-use or sell it, he/she has the duty to neutralize it. Incineration, and any other method of neutralizing, requires a licence from the environmental authorities and a review by the public health authority.

Violators of hazardous waste regulations pay a hazardous waste fine (for example, for improperly registering a hazardous waste or improperly monitoring the hazardous waste facility). Violators of collection and treatment regulations and transport and temporary disposal regulations must also pay this fine. The fine is based on the quantity and class of the hazardous waste and the degree of danger posed by the violation. The quantity of waste is measured on a scaled system, rather than by the amount actually illegally disposed. The severity of the violation is also given a scaled rank. Repeat violators will be given slightly higher penalties. Lack of enforcement of these regulations is a great problem and as a result, many illegal disposal sites are found throughout the country.

The importation of wastes into Hungary requires a special permit which is granted when the imported wastes can be re-used. If the importer seeks to merely dispose of the wastes, the permits will be denied. Those who breach these import rules are required to restore the environment or make the waste harmless. As in many areas of environmental protection, enforcement by customs officials is weak.

Regional planning   Human settlements are protected through regional planning which sets priorities and restrictions for building and construction. The Ministry of Environmental Protection and Regional Policy is responsible for protecting human settlements. The problem with regional planning in Hungary is that it is tailored for a centralized administration and does not involve the local governments. Planning and regional development is regulated by very general requirements. Conflicts arise because the government is responsible for developing regional plans, whereas settlement plans are developed by local governments. The territory of a settlement can be used only according to the plans. However, the plans are outdated, and many settlements do not have them.

Land use within a settlement requires a permit from the local government's building authority. Building and construction activities must meet a number of environmental criteria, such as those outlined in the National Building Statutes of 1986. The issue of a building permit does not require an environmental impact assessment. Sanctions for failing to follow building and construction regulations can be severe, and they may include the destruction of the building.

Nature conservation   The Act on the Protection of the Human Environment divides nature conservation into two parts: the protection of flora and fauna and the protection of landscape. Nature conservation means generally that the responsible agency declares a region or a species of animals or plants to be protected. The declaration is an administrative decision and may be national or local. Any person may petition the appropriate agency to protect a species or natural object, but most cases originate within an agency under a plan for protection.

The current nature conservation rules, found in Law Decree No. 4 of 1982, cover only those parts of nature which must be protected because of their scientific, cultural or other common interest. Primary responsibility for protecting these resources rests with the National Bureau for Nature Conservation at the national level, and with eight nature conservation or national park directorates at the regional level. Some tasks are delegated to the local municipality.

There are four categories of nature conservation areas, distinguished by territorial importance. These are national parks; landscape protection districts; nature reserves; and natural monuments. The first three areas could qualify as biosphere reserves under international requirements. The level of protection accorded a nature conservation area depends on its classification. An area is chosen for general protection because of its special animals, plants or landscape; it maintains a different status than specially protected species. Species protection is always undertaken on a nation-wide basis, and prohibitions associated with this protection apply to Hungarians and foreigners alike.

Where an activity directly endangers a protected object or species, the activity can be ordered to be suspended for 30 days to three months. Infringement of nature conservation regulations is punishable by a fine that is based upon the gravity of the violation. Where the injury is to a protected nature conservation area, the fine is determined on the basis of the type of protected area that is involved. In the case of protected species, a nominal fine or a fine based on the theoretical value of that individual species is assessed. The protection authority is bound by an upper limit; there is no progressive increase in fines for repeated violations.

The concept of biodiversity is not known in the current Hungarian legislation, but it appears in a new nature conservation draft, together with the concepts of habitat protection, ecological corridors, vulnerable natural areas and so on.

General landscape   Other than the general obligations outlined in the General Act on the Protection of the Human Environment, there are no actual rules to protect the landscape. The laws of mining and regional planning offer some additional guidance, but areas not specially protected go unregulated.

Hunting and fishing   The state possesses exclusive ownership of all fish and wildlife in Hungary. The state licenses the right to fish and hunt to those who pay a fee. The state or the licensee, as exclusive owner of fish and wildlife, also has the duty to maintain and to develop the stock of fish and game. A conflict of duties is perceived because the Ministry of Agriculture is responsible both for the protection and the use of fish and game.

Forestry and mining The National Forestry Inspectorate of the Ministry of Agriculture is responsible for forestry management and protection. The regulations on forest use are geared towards effective utilization of the forests rather than towards their protection. Forests are treated in the same way as any other commodity. Many forest regulations are similar to land use regulations, particularly when the forests are used for purposes other than wood production. Some rules have attempted to harmonize agricultural and forestry interests. The forestry management rules do designate situations where a forest, or at a minimum trees, must be planted in areas of common interest, such as around villages and towns.

In Hungary, mining is largely monopolized by the state, but according the new Act on Mining[13] there are much wider possibilities for permits or concessions. The state issues full permits and provides concession licences. Landowners may apply for mining permits also for their own needs, but only for stone, sand, pebbles, and clay. Mining regulations contain some restrictions on taking land out of cultivation, but they do not prohibit miners from polluting the soil. Upon abandoning a mine, a mining company must recultivate the land. In the new Mining Act there are much greater environmental restrictions than ever before. Even the general rules contain provisions for environmental protection.

Pesticides Pesticides are considered dangerous materials under Hungarian law and are regulated under plant protection regulations. They must be licensed before they can be used. No special rules exist for licensing but public health and environmental issues have to be considered. There are three types of licences: testing licence, temporary licence, and final licence. A final licence cannot be granted unless a temporary licence has first been issued for a period of not less than three years. Most of the current licences in Hungary are temporary licences.

The use of pesticides is also governed by a few special regulations. Nature conservation areas and useful animals, such as the hedgehog and honey bee, are afforded special protection. For example, the use of pesticides dangerous to bees is prohibited in or around flower blossoms. Although, generally the farmer bears the cost of pest control, in cases where a region-wide threat is imminent and the agricultural producers do not have the financial means to sufficiently contain the threat, the state will assist with financial or other support.

5   Civil law

In the CEE countries, where most of the polluting activities were in state ownership, the opportunity to seek legal remedy in civil law was relatively low. This

---

13   Act XLVIII of 1993.

does not mean that these civil law options were not available, but in practice they were and, generally remain, uninvoked.

The following are the major options in the Hungarian Civil Code (Act IV of 1959) for safeguarding environmental protection interests:

- personal integrity rights;
- intellectual property rights;
- nuisance (neighbourhood rights);
- trespass (possession rights);
- private contractual relationships;
- compensation of damages.

Personal integrity rights represent a good means through which to pursue environmental protection interests because they protect the rights of personal life, health and physical integrity. However, they are rarely used to express the integrity of the private person against the state or the public administration. The consequences of the infringement of these personal integrity rights (as in the case with intellectual property rights, nuisance and trespasses) could be numerous, ranging from the simple statement that an activity is unlawful, to imposing conditions upon use, or even to stopping the unlawful activity until compensation is given. The court may even impose an extra levy on the wrongdoer if the other remedies, particularly compensation, do not fully redress the seriousness of the unlawful conduct.

Intellectual property rights can serve as preventive measures in two ways. A direct means is to include environmental requirements in thresholds for obtaining a licence for an invention. An invention may be granted a patent licence if it is new and progressive, implies a technological solution and may be reproduced. The precondition that an invention be progressive can include that the invention reduce (or at least not increase) pollution. The handbook on the use of intellectual property rights does in fact already contain such a suggestion.

The law on *nuisance* (or, in Hungarian terms, the regulations of neighbourhood rights and obligations) is an easy way to prove the infringement of environmental protection-based rights. Under Article 100 of Hungarian Civil Code, an owner must avoid those activities which needlessly disturb others (particularly neighbours) or endanger the exercise of the others rights. Nuisance is not restricted to the actions of immediate neighbours. There is uncertainty as to what conduct is needless, as neighbours must tolerate some level of disturbance.

Trespass (or, in Hungarian terms, the infringement of possession rights under Article 188 of the Civil Code) creates a theoretical right to the undisturbed possession of property. As with nuisance, here too the disturbance must be examined on a case-by-case basis and balanced against locally acceptable levels of disturbance.

All the above mentioned measures have a common characteristic that makes them especially useful in environmental protection. No negligence or intent is required on the part of the offender for any of these measures, which creates a kind of no-fault liability.

It is worth mentioning also that the courts deciding in civil law suits could develop a special practice of reviewing administrative decisions by using different civil law measures. The general judicial review of administrative decisions has been opened only since 1991. Until then the possibility of review was restricted to some 30 specific cases. Nevertheless, during this period the courts did try civil law cases, such as trespass, nuisance or tort, where the administrative decision proved to be a basis upon which the wrongdoing could be legitimated. In general, the courts did not accept an administrative decision as a defence but overruled it on a case-by-case basis. In one case the officially permitted opening hours of a restaurant were held to be a source of noise pollution. The Supreme Court did not expressly reject the permit given to the restaurant in theory, it was simply ignored by the court:

> ...any kind of industrial or commercial activity must be carried on without causing any harm to the rights of possession. If the opening hours are the sources of harm there is a possibility of ordering closure during the night hours.[14]

Contractual relationships may also embody environmental protection interests. This embodiment may weaken contractual obligations where there is a conflict of interests. For example in 1980 the Supreme Court stated that a contractor has the duty to follow environmental regulations even where responsibilities have been delegated to others.[15]

Finally we come to *compensation for damages* under the Civil Code . There are two ways to compensate the victim – under Article 339, which is a simple tort liability provision, or under Article 345, which is the strict liability standard. If the compensation of damages is connected with endangering the environment, it is subject to the strict liability provision of the Code pursuant to the rules relating to especially dangerous activities. The judicial practice of the latter has been far from being satisfactory, and case law has been limited to more simple individual cases primarily because of a lack of willingness to litigate. Preventive measures under Article 341 of the Civil Code must also be mentioned. This gives courts authori-

---

[14]   Case Pf.IV.21.023/1984.
[15]   Statement No. 25 (1980) of the College of Economic Cases of the Supreme Court.

zation to order preliminary obligatory steps (for example, to stop or limit the damaging activity) to prevent damage arising.

Most of the other CEE countries follow the same civil law pattern. For example, in Bulgaria Article 50 of the Law on Ownership of 1951 covers nuisance, Article 109 of the same Act covers trespass, and the Law on Obligations and Contracts of 1950 deals with fault-based liability – in Article 45 – and also with strict liability – in Article 50. The regulations of Article 29 of the Environmental Protection Law of 1991 also proceed in the same way when creating a new cause of action for environmental torts. Any person who intentionally or negligently harms another with pollution must pay compensation, and injured persons may ask for an injunction to halt the activity.

6   Criminal law

Criminal law can hardly be included as an instrument of deterrence in Hungary's environmental law, as there is no real practice of this kind. Criminal law can only be used as a last resort (*ultima ratio*) to protect environmental interests and has no concrete preventive element. An additional difficulty in using criminal law for environmental protection is the fact that, in Hungary, criminal responsibility cannot be imposed on legal entities (for example, corporations). Only natural persons may be liable under criminal regulations, or those who are acting on behalf of the legal entities.

The general environmental protection Act included a criminal provision for environmental violations and in 1978 the new Criminal Code (Act IV. of 1978) enacted two special offences: damaging the environment, and damaging nature. The distinction between these two crimes, which both involve a version of felony and misdemeanour, is based on whether nature conservation areas are affected. In addition, some general crimes such as bodily harm or even murder may be used in connection with environmental interests. In the small number of practical cases occurring in Hungary, the offence of endangering life in pursuance of professional regulations has proved to be the most popular one due to the fact that it is easier to find proof under this law. Of course this crime does not really reflect special environmental interests.

7   The institutional structure of environmental protection

a)   The organization of public administration

When evaluating the present organizational system of environmental protection, the most important questions to ask are whether this organization serves the interests of necessary integrated pollution control and whether the structure follows the basic requirement of separating the economic use of a natural resource from the protection of the same resource. One of the basic problems of the Hungarian environmental protection system was that this separation of interests could not be achieved as, even at the broadest level of government, the state administration and the state-owned economy existed hand-in-hand. The other major problem has always been the lack of harmonization and cooperation between different bodies having a role in environmental protection, in many cases due to lack of clear-cut division of responsibilities.

Parliamentary level Although it comes directly under public administration I should mention the parliamentary Environmental Committee which filters those issues to be considered by the parliament. Legislative drafts are always discussed in the Committee first.

Ministerial level In 1990 the Ministry of Environmental Protection and Regional Policy was established – the third version of the central environmental administration within three years. The ministry carries the greatest responsibility for environmental protection. In addition to its responsibilities are included regional planning, construction, the management of public and historic monuments and the supervision of meteorology services. Its environmental duties include air and water pollution, nature conservation, general landscape protection, noise abatement, waste management, radiation and forest protection. For its environmental responsibilities two centralized administrations have been established under the ministry, both acting on behalf of the ministry in public administration cases: the Chief Inspectorate of Environmental Protection, with 12 regional offices; and the National Office for Nature Conservation with eight regional offices, partly based on the existing national parks, partly on other nature conservation matters.

The second most important government institution for environmental protection is the Ministry of Transport, Telecommunications and Water Management. This ministry is responsible for water management and use, but not for the protection of water quantity and quality which is the responsibility of the Ministry of Environmental Protection and Regional Policy. The Ministry of Transport, Telecommunications and Water Management has a National Office of Water Management and 12 regional offices. These regional offices issue water permits and also supervise a great number of direct investments and water uses of their own.

Other ministries also have a great number of environmental responsibilities:

- The Ministry of Public Welfare and its Public Health Service is active in the field of any kind of pollution affecting public health.

- The Ministry of Land Cultivation with its centralized system of land offices governs soil protection, forestry management through the forestry service and fishing and hunting issues.
- The Ministry of Interior protects human settlements in general.
- The Ministry of Industry is responsible for mineral resources and energy.
- The National Atomic Energy Agency is the exclusive authority for the use and safety of nuclear power.

A number of conclusions are drawn from the above short overview. First, environmental administration is not integrated, and in a number of cases the user of the environment and the one responsible for its protection is the same body. Second, the establishment of national central administrative authorities has to a certain extent led to the duplication of their activities. There are several cases wherein parallel authorities complicate the situation and, on many issues, there is a dearth of authority – or at least no single organization that accepts overall responsibility. Third, although the government is responsible for harmonizing environmental interests, this has not been realized because of economic development pressures. The lack of cooperation and harmonization has been recognized and the present draft environmental laws propose to set up consultative bodies for this reason.

Local and regional level   On the local and regional level, the greatest power lies with in the regional offices of the different ministries. The local governments have much less power. Although they are not excluded from taking over a greater sphere of duties, their actual duties are determined by their narrow financial resources. Local government officials – the mayor and the manager – also have a number of administrative (including environmental) responsibilities, given to them by the central administrative bodies. This means that, in many cases, they do not act as local government officials, but as representatives of the central administration. The division of powers between the central administrative bodies and the local governments still remain a major discussion point.

The broad survey of the spheres of authority leads to the conclusion that local governments today play only a small direct role in environmental administration, although they may influence the local or smaller regional environment through the practice of their building and human settlement development authorities. The central administrative body of environmental protection has assigned the greater part of individual administrative affairs to the executive organs, and it has achieved this primarily within its own system of decentralized organizations. The creation of decentralized enforcement organizations may well have been the reason for the present interest of certain local governments in the issue.

It should also be noted that currently only local governments have the ability in practice, to directly influence the siting of a new polluting investment since they have authority over building and, currently, physical planning. They have this authority without limitation. The environmental inspectorates are nothing more than specialized agencies which give their consent to a basic permit.

If we accept the present system of local government as the basis of further decentralization, then it will probably be more difficult to enforce environmental rights and duties. This is due to the fact that the present system is based on municipality level local governments, and there is a current lack of medium-level local government. Under these circumstances, only a fraction of the administrative authority of the decentralized bodies could be delegated to local governments in the future. In light of local government financial problems, and consequent conflicts of interest, the greater part of these powers should be retained for the time being. In any event, it is arguable that a uniform nationwide practice is indispensable in affairs of this kind. The performance of these administrative tasks requires special expertise that is independent of local governments.

Regional policy, although it falls under the auspices of the environmental ministry, is absolutely disregarded. No one has taken responsibility for regional policy issues, and regional development plans have not been adopted, even though these regional plans should serve as the basis for local planning. The only 'legal rule' is an order of the Ministry of Interior, which has no legal consequence for organizations other than those subordinated to this Ministry. This is also true for the national land use development plans, which also serve as the sources of regional and local plans.

A final and important issue is the necessary coordination of local government actions. A system of regional level local governments or at least regional level institutionalized local government cooperation is essential. While, generally speaking, environmental authority and decision-making capacity is weakened by the decentralization of these functions to smaller villages or towns – this being justifiable in order to provide a decentralized and democratic division of power – the regional level of local government could assume a coordinatory function. This might include:

- finding ways of making local governments more interested in environmental protection;
- helping to promote cooperation between regional organs and local governments and between local governments themselves;
- promoting cooperation of local governments over environmental interests with the help of proper legislation;
- performing regulatory and decision-making functions in certain fields of reserved competence.

Public prosecuters' offices Among the other public bodies, public prosecutors offices are worth mentioning. They have general legal supervisory powers over the administration and partly over the economy and they are also responsible for criminal prosecution. Although the potential of public prosecutors' offices is great, in practice they have played only a minor role in environmental protection, and much less than is desirable. The primary reason for this is their lack of experience in environmental matters.

The judicial system   With new improved powers of judicial review over administrative decisions, the judicial system will soon have a much more direct input in environmental law enforcement. In addition, there is a growing interest on the part of litigants, mainly citizens, even to the extent of using the civil law. In the courts, political and economic pressures have less input.

b)   Public participation

A great potential ally for serious environmental regulatory and enforcement policies could be the public itself and those organizations (NGOs) which have environmental protection as their main purpose. Political history demonstrates an objection to public participation, under the rationale of socialist harmony of interests, represented by the state. As a follow-up to the prior section, an important precondition to public participation is public access to information.

The Hungarian parliament adopted Act LXIII of 1992 on the protection of personal data and the access to public interest data. The latter part of the Act entered into force in December 1992. The Act is the first general legal regulation requiring a modest level of publicity for data collected by the state and local government administration. There are two ways to inform the public: first, to actively publish the data, second, to make the data available for the public. The data must be of public interest and must not be categorized as official or business secrets. A public administrative body must disclose the information within 15 days of a request. There may be a fee for disclosure of data but this must not exceed the justifiable costs to the body. In any case where the disclosure of information is refused, an interested party may ask for a judicial review. The principal problem with this new Act is that, in the absence of a judicial interpretation of it, the field of publicly available data has not yet been clarified.

In respect of rule-making procedures, the former socialist requirement of open discussion of legislative drafts has been dismissed as being a formality which allowed the state to avoid real democratic legislation. According to parliament's current position, in a state governed by the rule of law there is no formal need for public comment procedures. Out of the previous concern for public participation only the right to call for a referendum prevailed.

The Constitutional Court procedure allows citizens to request the constitutional review of legal rules without requiring direct involvement of the citizen in the case. The Court's standing requirements probably belong to the broadest in the world, covering virtually all cases of post-regulatory supervision and, to a great extent, pre-regulatory control. Citizens may challenge the constitutionality of a regulation serving as the basis for a judicial or administrative decision affecting their constitutional rights. The Court may invalidate the regulation, but not the individual decision.

In administrative decision-making processes, such as permitting or direct orders there is no explicit rule for public participation. Under the general rules of administrative procedure, only 'interested parties' can become involved. The term 'interested party' is interpreted in a way that limits involvement to those 'whose rights or lawful interests are being affected'. The interpretation of this provision is presently limited to the narrowest possible sense, covering only direct and material interests.[16] In this respect the EIA provisions open up public participation somewhat.

In administrative and judicial procedures possible participation by NGOs requires a type of standing not recognized in Hungary. At present there is no legal right to bring a class action. The EIA process is the only one to cover public participation directly, including NGO rights, but these rules are still in a drafting stage. In civil litigation, a serious drawback, in addition to procedural rules (such as the failure to give standing to the NGOs), is the requirement that costs must be paid in advance. There is no statutory exception from this general rule based on the priority of environmental interest.

8 Basic methodological challenges the CEE countries face today

The most important part of developing enforceable environmental regulations in CEE countries is to determine which method to follow in the future. In this respect there is a tendency to copy some Western – EU or US – example that does not necessarily work in a different political, cultural and legal environment. A recent US publication on exporting environmental protection is worth mentioning in this context.

> Conditions that have provided fertile ground for environmental protection in the United States include cultural attitudes shaped by affluence, established free market institutions, heavily developed communication and other infrastructures, private industry sectors that seek profits from managing pollution and waste disposal, and industries that have learned to incorporate environmental

---

16 For a comparative view see Chapter 7 on public participation by C. Lambrechts in this volume.

considerations into their businesses. Such advantages are rare in Central and Eastern Europe and are largely absent in the former Soviet Union.[17]

From the different possible challenges faced by CEE countries in environmental law, we mention here only the following problems:

- command and control versus market-based approach;
- standard setting or technology requirements;
- double thresholds;
- public participation.

a)   Command and control versus market-based approach

The reconstruction of economic policy and the structure of economy may follow the same lines of economic growth as the West in the past 20–30 years, but the CEE countries may also have a better alternative – namely to enter into a new stage of economic development and use the more modern instruments only. In environmental policy – as it is strongly connected with economic growth – these two main options would mean either to focus rather on command and control mechanisms or to use market forces more intensively. Of course, historic examples could prove that the experiences encountered in the different stages of development are essential for the effectiveness of the consequent steps; thus the command and control instruments could also be understood as learning processes. On the other hand, many environmental problems can only be resolved by use of the original command and control techniques – the requirement of a permit prior to the introduction of a new business or product cannot be avoided. The best alternative for these countries is to strengthen command and control mechanisms while simultaneously implementing a wide range of economic incentives – from tax incentives to subsidies or environmental labelling.

b)   Standard-setting versus technology-based methods

A different methodological question is how to define the permissible and acceptable level of pollution. One option is to somehow put a quantitative ceiling on the immissions and/or emissions, thereby setting a standard. The other method is to restrict the pollution by applying some qualitative regulations to the polluting activity thereby regulating the technology.

---

[17]   Ruth G. Bell, Exporting Environmental Protection, *Environmental Law Reporter*, December 1993, p. 10701.

Situated between legislation and the public administration regulation, standard setting presents a challenge of translating environmental requirements into a numeric form in order to make enforcement programmes easier. The efficiency of the thresholds always strictly rely upon the main purpose of standard setting and the monitoring capacity of enforcement administration.

We can distinguish environmental quality objectives or ambient standards that fix the limit of immissions using a kind of ecological toleration concept, and discharge or emission standards that impose a fixed limit on the emission of pollutants and may be derived from the ambient standards or (as is more often the case) from the state of the art.[18]

The technology-based methods regulate the process, or the path to the discharge of pollution in a way to limit, or prevent, the pollution. These methods – sometimes also termed 'technology standards' – require that the polluters use a particular type of technology to control and/or monitor emissions. The most well known option is the best-available technology (BAT) option used also in the European Union. Sometimes the BAT requirement is qualified as BATNEEC – best-available technology not entailing excessive costs. This means that the relatively excessive extra costs are used as a limit to unrealistic requirements.

It goes without saying that the technology requirements sometimes are too vague for regulating the emissions. Also in most cases, these requirements need explanation and interpretation at lower administrative levels. Taking into consideration attempts in developing and CEE countries to attach not only an 'excessive' or 'unreasonable' qualification to the technology and also their current economic difficulties (which can serve as a good method of escape from strict regulations) there is no doubt that technology requirements alone are not satisfactory and not always reliable. Therefore, the two different methods should be used in combination.

c) Double standards for old and new investors?

In Hungary, the Civil Code generally states that the new owner is responsible for past damages and past liabilities, if there is no other agreement. The parties may agree that at least part of the liability for past damages stays with the former owner. This is the situation in a great number of privatization agreements, where the State Property Agency agrees with the investors – mostly with foreign investors – that the new owner receives an indemnification for future liability problems. Unfortunately these agreements are not generally preceded by a detailed environmental audit. If there is no specific agreement, the new owner may hardly escape from liability.

---

[18] See further Chapter 8 on standard-setting by G. Winter in this volume.

In a more general perspective there are several options to handle environmental protection needs in cases of new (and, in particular, foreign) investment:

- to impose comparatively less strict environmental requirements in order to attract new (and in paricular foreign) money;
- to use similar requirements for existing and new facilities, which amounts to a generally lower level of standards;
- to use higher level standards for new facilities and a graduated compliance schedule for existing ones;
- to use high standards immediately – which entails the risk of numerous bankruptcies.

In my view the third alternative – also to be supported by banking policy – should be adopted. Clear decision-making in this question is necessary to provide a firm basis for business planning.

Unfortunately current privatization contracts in Hungary contain no reference to either future environmental conditions or future changes in environmental management strategies. In recent years there have been only a couple of cases involving some particles of environmental considerations. The State Privatization Agency does not feel itself responsible for environmental requirements principally because the great desire for revenue from privatization agreements overrides considerations about the possible deleterious effects of these contracts. The situation is similar in most CEE countries.

d)   Public participation

When discussing public participation, mention should be made of the potential of public participation to achieve:

- just decision-making, as just decisions require a careful balance of interests and a careful evaluation of a given situation;
- acceptance of state decisions by the public;
- information from the public. Factual information is most important in local issues, where the local people sometimes have more knowledge on the particular situation than, for example, the regional environmental inspectorate;
- assistance in control and enforcement by providing relevant information.

It is also useful to highlight the conditions of public participation, because most of the CEE countries do not have an existing structure for public participation.

- Access to information must be regulated with all those aspects mentioned in the relevant points above, such as determining the terms of business secrets, and providing legal remedies.
- General and detailed rules of the obligation to involve the public in legal regulation and decision-making must be framed.
- An obligation to answer to public suggestions or questions must be established.
- Basic regulations can, and should, be interpreted in a way that gives general standing for the interested public in administrative procedures but, due to the possibility of wilful misinterpretation, it is essential nonetheless to clearly determine or to concretize standing requirements in administrative law.

23 Adaptation to EC Environmental Rules: Options for Central and Eastern European States

Ludwig Krämer

Table of Contents

There is a principle in the law and policy of the European Union, applicable to new acceding states, which provides that the existing legal rules must be taken over by the acceding state. A renegotiation, in particular of secondary Community law (Directives, Regulations), is not accepted. This does not, of course, exclude the possibility that the acceding state may negotiate a transitional period to provide time to adapt its legislation and practice to existing Community legislation. For Central and Eastern European States a description of adaptation provisions which were agreed in previous accession or enlargement discussions, might be of interest.

I   ACCESSION OF NEW MEMBER STATES IN THE PAST

When the UK, Denmark and Ireland joined the European Community in 1973, there were no specific Community environmental provisions. Thus, the Accession Treaty did not contain any transition provisions for environmental standards.

Neither did the Accession Treaty with Greece of 1979 provide any specific transition rule for environmental protection requirements.[1] As a result, all Community environmental provisions which existed by that time, became fully applicable on the day of Greece's accession. However, Directive 80/68 on the protection of groundwater granted Greece a four-year period to transpose that Directive into national law, whereas all other Member States were obliged to transpose that Directive within two years.[2]

The Accession Treaty with Spain and Portugal of 1985 stated that all environmental provisions were applicable to these two states from the day of their accession (1 January 1986), unless the annexes to the Treaty provided for specific exemptions.[3] No such exemption was given to Spain, specifically because Spain had not asked for it. Portugal asked for, and obtained, the right to apply five Directives on water and waste from 1989 on only; it was entitled to apply Directive 76/160 only from 1993 onwards.[4]

II   THE GERMAN UNIFICATION

When Germany was unified, transition provisions for the new Länder became necessary. Since no 'accession' to the Community took place, no Treaty was concluded. Rather, the necessary transition provisions were introduced in Community law by way of Directives which were adopted at the end of 1990. Each EC environmental Directive was discussed with the German authorities. On the basis of these discussions, the Commission made proposed specific transition periods for the different Directives, which the Council adopted, sometimes with some changes to the proposal.[5]

The discussion of these transition periods was particularly difficult, because the German authorities themselves did not exactly know the state of the environment in the new *Länder* and were therefore unable to indicate, with precision, what transition period would be necessary.

---

[1]   Treaty on the accession of Greece, ECOJ 1989, no. L 291, p. 71.
[2]   Directive 80/68, ECOJ 1980, no. L 20, p. 43, Art. 21.
[3]   Treaty on the accession of Spain and Portugal, ECOJ 1984, no. L 302, p. 9.
[4]   Ibid., p. 397.
[5]   Directives 90/656, ECOJ 1990, no. L 353, p. 59; 90/660, ECOJ 1990, no. L 353, p. 79.

The solution which the Council finally reached may be summarized as follows:

1   The transition period ended on 31 December 1995 for all Directives. This meant that even where longer transition periods might prove to be necessary for specific Directives, this would require an amendment of the Directive in question by the Council, upon proposal by the Commission and in cooperation or co-decision with the European Parliament.

2   Germany had to formulate and transmit to the Commission clean-up programmes in respect of practically all the Directives for which the transition period ended in 1995. These programmes were to allow the Commission and the other Member States, which were informed of them, to examine whether sufficient progress was being made.

3   For a number of Directives, the transition period ended in 1992 or 1994; for such Directives, plans or detailed information were to be transmitted to the Commission.

4   The Commission was given the ability to prolong the transition period for some Directives, on German request and after consultation with the Member States, until the end of 1995.[6]

5   New industrial installations did not receive any transitional period. Indeed it was considered that it would not be reasonable to allow installations to be built which did not comply with the general Community requirement of best available techniques (BAT). For the same reason, no transition period was granted for Directive 85/337 on the environment impact assessment of public and private projects; it was thought that it would be reasonable to start examining the impact of new projects on the Eastern German environment without delay.

It is scarcely likely that the solution accepted by the German *Länder* will serve as a model for Central and Eastern European countries. Indeed, the fundamental difference is that the German authorities did not know, at the time of negotiation with the EC, the exact state of the environment, or the measures necessary to clean up polluted areas and to adapt polluting installations and so on. Normally, a sovereign state cannot legitimately argue that it does not know precisely what is going on on its territory.

---

6   The Commission has amended Directive 90/656, since it turned out that Germany was unable to comply with the requirements of Directive 76/64 on the discharge of certain dangerous substances into the water, and its daughter Directives within the time-span provided by Directive 90/656 (end of 1992).

III   THE EUROPEAN ECONOMIC AREA AND THE ENLARGEMENT OF 1994–95

The efforts of Austria, Switzerland, Sweden, Norway and Finland to join the European Union were dealt with in a politically difficult time. In order to ensure a smooth transition the Agreement on the European Economic Area (EEA) was concluded at the end of 1993 with Austria, Finland, Iceland, Liechtenstein, Norway, Sweden and Switzerland[7] which provided, as regards the environment, that the Community provisions should also apply in the above-mentioned countries.[8]

A specific problem occurred, however, in that these countries considered their environmental provisions to be at least partly more protective than Community provisions. Where Community provisions were based on Article 130s of the EC Treaty, the solution leapt out from Article 130t, which allowed EC-Member States, and thus also EEA countries to maintain or introduce more stringent environmental protections. This was not the case as regards Article 100a of the Treaty, since this provision does not allow, in the view of the EC Commission, a deviation from Community-wide environmental standards.

The following solutions were found:

1   In principle, EEA countries took over the provisions of Community environmental Directives without amendment and without transition periods. Iceland obtained, for 13 Directives, transition periods till 1 January 1995 – about one year. For the majority of waste Directives, EEA countries obtained transition periods until the same date.[9]

2   Community legislation on chemicals was to be applied from 1995 onwards; however, outstanding problems were to be discussed and resolved in 1994.[10]

3   As regards the prohibition of chemicals, EEA countries were allowed to continue to apply their national, more restrictive, provisions for eight groups of chemicals. This situation was to be re-examined in 1995.[11]

The environmental provisions in the accession Treaties with Austria, Finland, Norway and Sweden closely follow the EEA Agreement.[12] As regards more stringent environmental provisions in the acceding countries which would be, under

---

[7]   Switzerland has since, following a national referendum, decided not to join the European Economic Area.

[8]   Agreement on the European Economic Area, ECOJ 1994, no. L 1, p. 3.

[9]   Ibid., p. 494.

[10]   Ibid., p. 307.

[11]   Ibid., p. 309.

[12]   The Accession Treaty for Austria, Finland, Norway and Sweden was signed at the end of June 1994.

Community provisions, based on Article 100a of the EC Treaty, the Accession Treaties provide that the acceding countries may continue to apply their more stringent provisions for a period of four years. During that time, the Community will reconsider its own provisions and examine whether it would be appropriate to make them as stringent as those of the acceding countries.

IV   IMPLEMENTATION AND ENFORCEMENT

Under Community law, Member States are obliged to adapt their national legislation and their practice to the requirements of the Community provisions. However, the implementation gap between the legal requirements and the state of the environment, which is the biggest legal problem in environmental law, also exists within the Community. Of course, the environmental requirements of Community law are not entirely complied with in all Member States, neither in the original Member States nor in those states which subsequently joined the EC, nor in the new and in the old German *Länder*.[13] For instance, drinking water does not comply everywhere with the requirements of Directive 80/778;[14] most Member States or regions still do not have waste management programmes;[15] the eleventh Commission report on the quality of bathing water mentions that in 1993, some 20 per cent of all bathing waters which come under Directive 76/160 continue to fall short of compliance,[16] and so on. It is one thing to transpose Community environmental provisions into national legislation, and another thing to ensure that the national, regional or local environment actually complies with the legal requirements.

The EC does not have inspectors to examine compliance with environmental provisions in Member States nor does it have either an environmental police or any means of sanctions to ensure or enforce compliance. The Commission which must, under Article 155 of the EC Treaty, ensure that environmental provisions are complied with,[17] therefore tries to increase public awareness for cases of non-

---

[13] See, in particular, Commission, *Report on the Application of Community Law in the Member States*, 8th report (1990), ECOJ 1991, no. C. 338, p. 1 (p. 204); 9th report (1991), ECOJ 1992, no. C 250, p. 1 (p. 150); 10th report (1992), ECOJ 1993, no. C 233, p. 1 (p. 40); 11th report (1993), ECOJ 1994, no. C 154, p. 1 (p. 42).

[14] Directive 80/778, ECOJ 1980, no. L. 229, p. 11.

[15] Such programmes are mandatory since 1977, see Directive 75/440, ECOJ 1975, no. L 194, p. 47.

[16] Commission, *Eleventh Report on the Quality of Bathing Water*, 1993.

[17] Art. 155, EC Treaty:

compliance on the one hand, and to initiate infringement procedures under Article 169 of the EC Treaty[18] in cases of a breach of EC law on the other hand. Both efforts do not only aim at obtaining formal compliance of national legal rules with EC legal rules, but also effective compliance with these provisions. Indeed, the continued discussions between the Commission and national public authorities on compliance, as well as ongoing attempts to have any breach of EC environmental requirements, via individual complainants, environmental organizations, journalists, local authorities and other groups, discussed in the public sphere, contributes, even in those Member States where the protection of the environment is not a top policy priority, to the creation of pressure to improve compliance. No government of any Member State is prepared to admit that it is not making serious efforts to comply with EC environmental requirements. And there is no marked difference in those Member States in which most or all of their environmental legislation derives from rules and provisions which had been adopted by the EC before their accession.

The formal procedures under Article 169 of the EC Treaty also help to raise awareness and ensure compliance. Formal letters, reasoned opinions and, in the last resort, applications to the Court of Justice do not leave national administrations unaffected, and on occasion even inform these administrations for the first time of the existence of the problem. For example, environmental awareness in Mediterranean countries, which do not really have a long tradition of showing concern for the environment, has increased over recent years – perhaps due in part to the enforcement activity of EC institutions.

Paying lip service to environmental requirements may also create problems when money is distributed via the different Community funds. The basic Regulations of the structural fund as well as of the cohesion fund each provide that measures

...financed by the structural funds or receiving assistance from the EIB or from any other financial instrument shall be in keeping with the provisions of the

---

In order to ensure the proper functioning and development of the common market, the Commission shall: – ensure that the provisions of this treaty and the measures taken by the institutions pursuant thereto are applied.. .

[18]   Art. 169 EC Treaty:

If the Commission considers that a Member-State has failed to fulfil an obligation under this Treaty, it shall deliver a reasoned opinion on the matter after giving the State concerned the opportunity to submit its observations.

If the State concerned does not comply with the opinion within the period laid down by the Commission, the latter may bring the matter before the Court of Justice.

Treaties, with the instruments pursuant thereto and with Community policies, including those concerning.. environmental protection.[19]

And although this requirement is not fulfilled in all cases, difficulties in cases of non-compliance seem sufficiently great to encourage administrations to work towards compliance of a project with EC environmental requirements.

V OPTIONS FOR THE ADAPTATION OF ENVIRONMENTAL LEGIS-LATION AND PRACTICE

The association agreements, which the EC concludes at present with various Central or Eastern European states, only contain general references to the environment.[20] They provide that there should be joint cooperative efforts to protect the environment. However, it is entirely left to Central or Eastern European states to ask for financial and/or technical assistance for specific environmental projects. And, for various reasons, which need not, and cannot be, discussed here, the number and importance of environmental projects for which such support is asked for is rather limited, other projects having priority.

The following options are available to Central and Eastern European countries to obtain specific rules as regards environmental requirements:

1   transition periods in the Accession Treaty;
2   application of Article 130s EC Treaty;
3   derogations within a specific Directive;
4   use of the structural funds and the cohesion fund to ensure compliance and improved environmental protection;
5   participation in EC law-making.

1   Transition periods in the Accession Treaty

This kind of provision has been used on several occasions in the past. The European Union is likely to ask for short transitions and is likely to argue on each specific Directive. Furthermore, it should be noted that any Accession Treaty is negotiated as a whole. The more acceding countries ask for derogations in their favour, the more they will have to accept related transition periods – for instance,

---

[19]   Regulation on the Community structural funds No. 2052/88, ECOJ 1988, No. L 185, p. 9 Art. 7.
[20]   Cf. Chapter 20 by G. Goldenman in this volume (in particular section V).

on the full access to the common market or the unrestricted exchange of agricultural products and so on. On this observation, concrete examples cannot be given, since causal links between the two aspects of the negotiation package do not exist. It should, however, be realized, that it will never be easy to obtain full and instant access to the advantages of the European Union if where the *'acquis communautaire'*, which includes environmental protection, is not taken over with the same speed.

2   Application of Article 130s(5) of the EC Treaty

This provision reads:

> Without prejudice to the principle that the polluter should pay, if a measure based on the provisions of paragraph 1 involves costs deemed disproportionate for the public authorities of a Member-State, the Council shall, in the act adopting that measure, lay down appropriate provisions in the form of
> – temporary derogations and/or
> – financial support from the Cohesion Fund ... .

This provision has not yet been applied. It refers to majority decisions by the Council under Article 130r(1), thus not on town and country planning, land use or management of water resources.[21] In the past, only a few environmental Directives contained specific transitional rules for specific Member States, principally Directive 75/716 on the sulphur content of petrol[22] – which includes longer delays for Ireland – and Directive 88/609 on air emissions from large combustion plants[23] where Spain was allowed to continue to use polluting technologies for a while.

Financial assistance from the EU for a Member State has, until now, only been envisaged in Directive 92/43 on the protection of fauna and flora and their habitats.[24] However, this Directive does not mention individual Member States. It was inserted in the Directive because southern Member States had insisted that EC funds be made available to them if they were to accept the provision for increased habitat protection in their countries.

After a transitory period between 1993 and 1994, the cohesion fund was definitely established in May 1994. Its pupose is to contribute to environmental and transport projects in those Member States where the per capita GNP is less than 90

---

21   See Art. 130s(2), EC Treaty.
22   Directive 75/716, ECOJ 1975, no. L 307, p. 22.
23   Directive 88/609, ECOJ 1988, no. L 336, p. 1.
24   Directive 92/43, ECOJ 1992, no. L 206, p. 7.

per cent of the Union average.[25] The fund is to be reassessed in 1999; nevertheless whatever form it then takes, it is likely that an acceding CEE state will be among the beneficiaries, since the 90 per cent principle is likely to be maintained. Although the 'general' access to the fund and the access under Article 130s(5) are theoretically independent from each other, in reality it is more than likely that the sums under each heading will, in one way or the other, be taken together. Therefore, an acceding state will have to decide whether or not it will rely on Article 130s(5), where its request will be scrutinized by all other Member States, since it is the Council which eventually allocates the money.

3 Derogations within a specific Directive

This possibility has already been discussed, in the context of Article 130s(5), in Section V.2 above. However, I am of the opinion that such a possibility is not restricted to the circumstances described in Article 130s(5), but that also, in cases where a Directive is adopted under Articles 100a, 75/84 or 43, there is a possibility for the Community legislator to provide for a transitory derogation for a specific Member State.

It is difficult to predict whether or not the accession of new Member States to the European Union, the discussion on subsidiarity and the general evolution of environmental policy will lead to a variable-speed European Union – where EC legislation provides for a common denominator but where some Member States get, via Article 130t of the EC Treaty or by an ad hoc provision in secondary law, the right to adopt more stringent protective measures and where other Member States get an explicit authorization to maintain or adopt less stringent protective provisions than the common denominator. Current EC Directives and proposals for Directives appear to demonstrate this tendency.

- The derogation which Spain had obtained under Directive 88/609 to authorize, until 1999, new large combustion plants which do not comply with the Directive's requirements has already been mentioned. The same Directive authorizes Member States to license large combustion plants with sub-EU-standard technology, where indigenous solid fuel or lignite is burned.
- The proposal for a Directive on the ecological quality of surface water[26] starts from the idea that there are five different groups of ecological qual-

---

[25] Regulation 1164/94, ECOJ 1994, no. L 130 p 1. This fund was preceded, before March 1993, by a 'cohesion financial instrument'; see Regulation 792/93, ECOJ 1993, no. L 79, p. 74.
[26] ECOJ 1994, no. C 222, p. 6.

ity.[27] The last two groups especially – where it is difficult to improve the water quality, and where unfavourable natural conditions make improvement in quality difficult – allow Member States to take measures only in order to avoid deterioration. Since Member States themselves decide to which waters these quality categories apply, they are capable of determining both the speed and intensity of the quality improvement of surface waters.

- Similar observations apply to the proposal for a Directive on air quality.[28] Here again, different areas are to be determined by Member States – good air quality, bad air quality, areas with improving air quality. However, an area with bad air quality is defined as an area where specific threshold values are exceeded and where measures need to be taken in order to ensure that threshold values are not exceeded during a specific period. Thus a Member State may avoid having to designate areas with bad air quality, simply by deciding that no measures need be taken in order to improve the air quality.

If there is really such a development, Central and Eastern European countries will find an easier situation, since they could keep environmental protection provisions to the Community minimum. However, there is the long-term consideration that the acceding State might all too easily place itself – or indeed be placed by others – amongst those states with a low environmental profile. This is a political choice for the acceding state. Indeed, all experience of EC environmental legislation shows that it is not possible to preserve, protect and improve the quality of the environment against, or in the absence, of the will of a Member State. Where a state is prepared to let its environment deteriorate – perhaps in the hope of securing a better economic competitive position –, the European Union cannot really compel it to do otherwise. The long-term economic disadvantages of such a low-profile approach to the environment do, however, seem obvious, particularly in Central and Eastern Europe.

4   Use of the structural funds and the cohesion fund to ensure compliance and improved environmental protection

Currently, there exist the following principal EU funds.

---

[27] Waters of high ecological quality, of good ecological quality, of ecological quality, waters where it is difficult to improve the ecological quality and waters where unfavourable natural conditions make the improvement of the ecological quality very difficult.

[28] ECOJ 1994, no. C 216, p 4.

a) Structural funds

The legal basis for these funds is Article 103b of the EC Treaty which indicates that the structural funds shall support the achievement of the objectives of Article 130a.[29] The structural funds consist of the following:

- The *European Regional Development Fund* which 'is intended to help to redress the main regional imbalances in the Community through participation in the development and structural adjustment of regions whose development is lagging behind and in the conversion of declining industrial regions'.[30]
- The *Agricultural Guidance and Guarantee Fund*, which is set up to enable the common organizations of agricultural markets to attain their objectives.[31]
- The *European Social Fund* which is established 'to improve employment opportunities for workers in the internal market and to contribute thereby to raising the standard of living'.[32]

Together, by virtue of Regulation 2081/93,[33] the structural funds have the following objectives:

1. promoting the development and structural adjustment of regions whose development is lagging behind;
2. converting the regions, frontier regions or parts of regions (including employment areas and urban communities) seriously affected by industrial decline;
3. combating long-term unemployment and facilitating the integration into working life of young people and of persons exposed to exclusion from the labour market;
4. facilitating the adaptation of workers of either sex to industrial changes and to changes in production systems;
5. promoting rural development by:

---

[29] Art. 130a EC Treaty:
   In order to promote its overall harmonious development, the Community shall develop and pursue its actions leading to the strengthening of its economic and social cohesion.
   In particular, the Community shall aim at reducing disparities between the levels of development of the various regions and the backwardness of the least-favoured regions, including rural areas.
[30] Art. 130c, EC Treaty.
[31] Art. 40(2), EC Treaty.
[32] Art. 123, EC Treaty.
[33] Regulation 2081/93, ECOJ 1993, no. L 193, p. 5, Art. 1.

(a) speeding up the adjustment of agricultural structures in the framework of the reform of the common agricultural policy;

(b) facilitating the development and structural adjustment of rural areas.

The sums which are earmarked for the structural funds (including a financial instrument for fishery guidance) are[34] 141,471 million ECU at 1992 prices, out of which 96,346 million ECU are destined for regions which may be categorized under objective no.1 above. The sums are divided on an annual basis, per objective and per eligible region.

Member States draw up, at the appropriate geographical level, plans for expenditure which indicate the particulars allocated to each fund. On the basis of these plans, the Commission, in agreement with each Member State, sets up Community support frameworks which specify priorities, financial plans and so on. Within this framework, the different projects are financed.

As can be seen from Articles 130a and 130b of the EC Treaty, the structural funds are targeted towards the promotion of economic cohesion and development within the EU. They are thus open to Central or Eastern European countries only after their accession.

b)   The cohesion fund

The cohesion fund aims 'to provide financial contribution to projects in the fields of environment and trans-European networks in the area of transport infrastructure'.[35] Until 1999 it is reserved to Greece, Spain, Ireland and Portugal. For the period 1993–99 it is endowed with 15,150 million ECU. An indicative division of funds provides that Spain shall receive between 52–58 per cent, Greece between 16–20 per cent, Portugal between 16–20 per cent and Ireland between 7–10 per cent of the total sum.

The projects, which are co-financed, are selected by the Commission, in agreement with the Member State in question. An appropriate balance must be ensured between environmental and transport projects.

Since the cohesion fund contributes to the improvement of economic and social cohesion among Member States, it is not open to Central and Eastern European countries, prior to their accession to the EC.

To what extent the sums which are made available to Member States under these two funds are used to improve the environmental infrastructure (water treatment works, waste disposal installations and so on) or alternatively, and more traditionally, to improve the economic infrastructure (motorways, railways, industrial

---

[34] Regulation 2081/93 (note 33), annex II.
[35] Art. 130d(2), EC Treay.

installations and so on) depends primarily on the decision of the Member State in question.

5 Participation in EC law-making

Sometimes it is suggested that states should be given some access to EC environmental decision-making procedures prior to their accession, to enable participation in the definition and formulation of environmental policy and individual measures. Attending committees, working groups and the like might help Central and Eastern European countries to gradually adjust their own legislative framework and their political orientation to the EC requirements; equally it would allow the EC to gradually integrate Central and Eastern European needs, priorities and requirements into its environmental planning of policies, programmes and individual measures.

All experience shows that this option is not valid. EC institutions and Member States are very reluctant to have non-EC countries participate in internal discussions. Indeed, this has never really happened in the past. Even acceding countries are only admitted to Council and committee deliberations in the very final stage of their accession, long after the signing of the Accession Treaty. And there is no significant difference in opinion between the Commission and Member States as regards the possibility of these types of discussion. The reason for this is probably that there is a certain solidarity among Member States, which jointly bear the disadvantages of having to expose their problems and difficulties and accept open discussions on internal matters and the sacrifices this involves. Rightly or wrongly, this shared interest is perceived not to exist with regard to a non-Member State, which perhaps would probably merely profit from participating in the discussion without really sharing the burden.

Furthermore, it would be difficult for the EC to refuse this kind of privileged participation to OECD countries such as the USA or Switzerland, or to accession applicants such as Turkey, and to ACP countries with an association status were it to grant such a favour to Central and Eastern European countries.

This option is thus not a real one and should not be seriously considered.

VI CONCLUSION

Experience shows that the adoption of the text of EC environmental legislation by a new acceding country is not the real problem. Rather, EC environmental law increasingly requires administrative procedures to be set up, clean-up and monitoring plans to be elaborated and progressively put into practice and authorization procedures, monitoring, surveillance and control mechanisms to be instituted. In other words, what is needed at the national level is a continuous, consistent and coherent environmental policy which aims at reducing the quantities of pollutants that are put into the environment, which tries to improve technologies continuously, and protects, preserves and improves the quality of the environment. Particularly in Eastern Europe, the difference between national legal requirements and environmental reality has been, until 1989, frightening: to reduce this difference will have to be the first priority of any environmental policy.

The second priority will have to be to get individuals and organizations interested in the protection of their environment. Environmental pollution, administrative inertia, and a failure to respect legal requirements must no longer be seen as an act of God which individuals and their groups have to endure. Rather, encouraging active, interested and participating citizens to defend their environment, form groups and discuss environmental issues with the administration, in the media and in other forums, is of paramount importance for the promotion and the defence of the general interest in the environment.

An ECU can only be spent once. When a Central or Eastern European state joins the European Union, there will be money made available to the state, from structural funds, the cohesion fund, the European Investment Bank and so on. It will primarily be the decision of the new Member State whether that money will be used for environmental rather than for economic projects. The conclusion of this chapter is thus that the priority to be attached to the protection of the environment and to the implementation and enforcement of the different standards to ensure this protection is the ultimate responsibilty of each Member State.

Index